LAS VEGAS GUIDE

BE A TRAVELER ~ NOT A TOURIST!

PRAISE FOR OPEN ROAD'S
LAS VEGAS GUIDE

"Very helpful in providing information such as what foods the various buffets around town offer, the types of entertainment and gaming found at each of the hotel/casinos, and points of interest that exist off the Strip.

Thorough explanations and tips on casino gambling ... especially useful to those who are in Vegas for a short time and need to pick their spots." – **Books of the Southwest**

"I want to commend you ... by purchasing your guide, I was able to save over $300 on food and beverages, and came home $900 richer." – **W. Pratt, South Carolina**

ABOUT THE AUTHORS

Larry Ludmer is a professional travel writer who makes his home in Las Vegas. He is also the author of Open Road guides to Arizona, New Mexico, Colorado, Utah and Washington State.

Avery Cardoza is the best-selling author of many how-to-win gaming books and advanced strategies, and is recognized as one of the top gambling authorities in the world. He is also head of Cardoza Publishing, the world's foremost publisher of gambling books, and Cardoza Entertainment, designer of pioneering gambling software. A Las Vegas resident, he has spent many years conducting extensive research into the mathematical, emotional, and psychological aspects of winning.

BE A TRAVELER, NOT A TOURIST - WITH OPEN ROAD TRAVEL GUIDES!

Open Road Publishing has guide books to exciting, fun destinations on four continents. As veteran travelers, our goal is to bring you the best travel guides available anywhere!

No small task, but here's what we offer:

• All Open Road travel guides are written by authors with a distinct, opinionated point of view – not some sterile committee or team of writers. Our authors are experts in the areas covered and are polished writers.

• Our guides are geared to people who want to make their own travel choices. We'll show you how to discover the real destination – not just see some place from a tour bus window.

• We're strong on the basics, but we also provide terrific choices for those looking to get off the beaten path and experience the country or city – not just see it or pass through it.

• We give you the best, but we also tell you about the worst and what to avoid. Nobody should waste their time and money on their hard-earned vacation because of bad or inadequate travel advice.

• Our guides assume nothing. We tell you everything you need to know to have the trip of a lifetime – presented in a fun, literate, no-nonsense style.

• And, above all, we welcome your input, ideas, and suggestions to help us put out the best travel guides possible.

LAS VEGAS GUIDE

BE A TRAVELER - NOT A TOURIST!

Larry Ludmer & Avery Cardoza

OPEN ROAD PUBLISHING

OPEN ROAD PUBLISHING

We offer travel guides to American and foreign locales. Our books tell it like it is, often with an opinionated edge, and our experienced authors always give you all the information you need to have the trip of a lifetime. Write for your free catalog of all our titles, including our golf and restaurant guides.

Catalog Department, Open Road Publishing
P.O. Box 284, Cold Spring Harbor, NY 11724

E-mail:
Jopenroad@aol.com

This book is once again dedicated to the Shuffler, the Doubler, and Grandma Kranmar.

6th Revised Edition

Copyright©2001 by Larry Ludmer & Avery Cardoza
- All Rights Reserved -

ISBN 1-892975-51-3
Library of Congress Control No. 00-136195

Front cover photo by FPG International. Bottom back cover photo courtesy of Las Vegas News Bureau. Top back cover photo by Nathaniel Stein. Maps by James Ramage.

TABLE OF CONTENTS

13. NIGHTLIFE & ENTERTAINMENT   247

14. SHOPPING   269

15. SPORTS & RECREATION   278

SIDEBARS & ILLUSTRATIONS

SIDEBARS & ILLUSTRATIONS

1. INTRODUCTION

Las Vegas is America's most exciting city, with more than 35 million visitors each year having the time of their lives! We'll show you all that this great town has to offer. If you follow our advice, and we have plenty of it, you'll be sure that you, too, will tell your friends that you had the time of *your* life.

Of course Las Vegas is built around gambling, but the city that never sleeps is much more. With the proliferation of gaming in so many other places, Vegas has gone way beyond just being the Mecca of gambling. It is a complete year-round destination resort that has something for everyone. For families with children there's good clean fun to be found in its theme parks and video arcades. Grown-ups, if they wish, can also discover Sin City, from the mild topless production shows at the big casinos to more risqué forms of entertainment. A trip to Vegas can also be a shopping extravaganza or a culinary adventure, a raft trip on Lake Mead, hiking in the beautiful Valley of Fire or a visit to the "Eighth Wonder of the World" – monumental Hoover Dam.

We'll show you unexplored Vegas; where to go Country and Western dancing; how to rediscover Elvis and Liberace; and where to find delicious bargain priced shrimp cocktails. You'll find out where to go to enjoy some of the country's finest golfing, tennis, boating and swimming, and if it's solitude and nature you want, where to go to explore your soul in the vast magnitude of the desert.

For people who never sleep or love to gamble, Vegas is paradise. While other travel guides may tell you how to play, we'll show you how to maximize your chances. Armed with gaming expert Avery Cardoza's inside tips, you'll learn everything you need to know to walk into the casino with confidence.

It all adds up to excitement and thrills. We'll show you all the possibilities to help make your trip to Las Vegas one of the best you've ever taken!

2. OVERVIEW

Few cities in the world have the kind of heart-charging excitement and limitless possibilities that Las Vegas has, and the Entertainment Capital does it without breaking a sweat. We'll give you a quick preview here of all that Vegas has in store so you can see how to plan your vacation and get the maximum enjoyment from it. Las Vegas is the true city of light – it has been documented via satellite images that Las Vegas is brighter from out in space than is Paris. But don't feel bad if you've seen Paris – you can enjoy it again here, Las Vegas style. A respected Wall Street gaming analyst once put it best when he commented that you go to Atlantic City (or any number of other gaming destinations) to gamble, but that you "go to Las Vegas to have fun."

GAMBLING

You can gamble day or night, 24 hours – the casinos never close. With about 40 casinos on the Strip alone and more than 165 in total, the novice gambler or pro alike will find non-stop action and excitement in any one of them.

Sit down at any table and you've got action. In our gaming chapter we'll show you how to play and increase your chances of winning at blackjack, craps, poker, roulette, slots, video poker and keno. Nevada is the only place in the United States where you can legally bet on sporting events other than racing.

THE STRIP & ITS HOTELS

When it comes to hotels, Las Vegas usually works under the assumption that bigger is better. The city boasts nine of the ten largest hotels in the world and completely dominates the top 25. Overwhelming visitor counts have driven demand and prices much higher than in the past. Vegas used to be an easy place to find hotel bargains. Not so, anymore. While it is competitive with (and mostly less expensive than) other major resort areas or large cities, there are more and more upscale hotels with

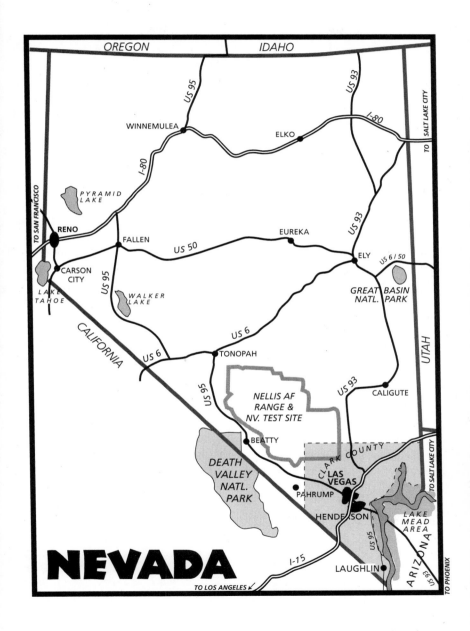

higher and higher prices. But, casinos still lure big players to their premises with free or discounted rooms, entertainment and food. Everyone else has to pay. There will be more said about "comps" later.

Synonymous with Las Vegas is the **Strip**. It is here that the true flavor and excitement of Las Vegas comes through, especially once the sun goes down. The Strip, of course, is where most of the largest and best known hotels are located. However, Strip hotels are much more than just places to stay and eat. Majestically lined up one after the other, they are more often than not major attractions in themselves that draw as many visitors as do the games of chance. From the world-class **Bellagio** and its Conservatory and works of art to the ultra-chic **Mirage** with its exploding volcano, lush tropical forest and Siberian tigers; to the working class **Excalibur** with its medieval castle theme featuring knights in shining armor; from the glory of ancient Rome at **Caesars Palace** and its magnificent Forum Shops to the splendors of ancient Egypt at the **Luxor**; from the dazzling skyline of **New York, New York** and its thrilling roller coaster to the plazas, canals and gondolas of **The Venetian**; or from the Eiffel Tower of **Paris** to the exotic wonders of mythical **Mandalay Bay** or the Desert Passage of **Aladdin** – the hotels of the Strip are a remarkable sight, a journey around the world or a trip back in time. They represent some of the most unusual and imaginative architectural designs to be found anywhere in the United States.

Great hotels aren't limited only to the Strip. For example, check out the colorful carnival called the Masquerade Village at **The Rio** or the *Sunset Stampede* at Sam's Town. The older downtown section, enlivened by the **Fremont Street Experience** has mostly less expensive hotels. Visitors can also save money by staying further afield from the Strip. There is no shortage of good hotels around town, some of which are themed just like those on their more famous neighbor.

It has been said that Las Vegas is the most egalitarian city in the world. Perhaps the greatest evidence of this is the fact that you can find a guy in a tee shirt and jeans rubbing elbows with a tuxedo clad high roller. It just goes to prove that there *is* something for everybody and whatever your taste or budget, you'll find it in Las Vegas!

FOOD

Not only is the gambling non-stop, so is the food. At any time, day or night, you can satiate your appetite. Try a juicy T-bone steak at three in the morning, or a three-egg omelet at midnight. It doesn't matter in Vegas. Bargain food prices, like hotel rates, have gone the way of the dinosaur although you can still eat lavishly for less than in most cities if you know where to look (and we'll tell you). The buffet, of course, is still the best way to eat the most for relatively small bucks.

But the most obvious and important recent trend in Las Vegas dining has been the debut of dozens of fine restaurants featuring a variety of cuisines prepared by some of the most renowned chefs in the world. Even a noted food critic from *The New York Times* had to admit (grudgingly, we surmise) that Las Vegas has taken its place alongside New York and Paris as one of the world's great dining cities. That would have been almost unthinkable ten years ago. The choices are almost endless and the prices range from low to more than a hundred dollars per person. So, *bon appetit!*

NIGHTLIFE & ENTERTAINMENT

What's a visit to Las Vegas without taking in a show or two? Extravagant shows and famous celebrities have been an important factor in making the desert oasis what it is today. The contemporary production show may take the form of a traditional Las Vegas style revue with beautiful feathery costumes and gorgeous, often topless, showgirls or it can be a high-tech extravaganza. The avant garde has also made its way from Broadway to the Strip. The big shows may be too pricey for some people and so the budget traveler may want to take in some less expensive lounge shows that feature up and coming entertainers. Comedy clubs, magicians, impersonators and even performers in drag are among the staple of the Las Vegas entertainment scene.

LADIES OF THE NIGHT

This may come as news to many, but prostitution is illegal in Clark County, of which Las Vegas is very much a part. But just over the county line, well, that's another story. Some of the famous "ranches" of Nevada call adjacent Nye and Lincoln counties their home. The town of Pahrump, located about 60 miles from Las Vegas, is one of the closer communities featuring this type of legal diversion. Within Las Vegas itself you can certainly find your pick of strip clubs and other adult entertainment. The Yellow Pages, street vendors handing out racy brochures to everyone who passes (including women) and newspaper boxes all along the Strip will let you know that there is no shortage of businesses providing "entertainers" for a price. Attempts to suppress distribution of those advertisements have been thwarted by civil libertarians as a violation of freedom of the press. Sure, that's exactly what the founding fathers had in mind!

While street prostitution has been heavily cracked down on in recent years (after all, Vegas does try to promote a family atmosphere to at least some extent), the many out-call entertainment services are a thinly veiled front that shows that the oldest profession is alive and well in Las Vegas.

For more participation-oriented visitors you'll find that Las Vegas has no shortage of classy nightclubs with dancing. These range from small local places to extravagant glitter domes in some of the biggest casino hotels. The music ranges from country western to heavy metal and everything in between.

And, for those whose tastes are more on the wild side, there is still plenty of sexy entertainment that earned Las Vegas its "Sin City" name. In short, once again, there's something for everyone.

EXCURSIONS & DAY TRIPS

There's a whole other world of sights and activities beyond the bright lights of Las Vegas and the Strip. Probably the most popular of these is a visit to **Hoover Dam** and the **Lake Mead National Recreation Area**. Less known to people outside of Las Vegas but equally wonderful in their own way are the colorful rock formations of **Red Rock Canyon National Conservation Area** and the **Valley of Fire State Park**. A short trip to nearby **Mount Charleston** brings summer visitors into a much cooler world – and skiing in the winter.

If you haven't had enough of the casinos you can take a two-hour trip to the Colorado River boomtown of **Laughlin**. Or stay closer and partake of the action in **Primm** on the California state line, just over a half-hour's drive from the Strip. UFO believers and those who think the government is keeping secrets from us will want to explore the **Extraterrestrial Highway** and the region near the infamous **Area 51**.

Longer excursions can take you to **Death Valley** and **Zion National Parks** and even the **Grand Canyon** although these, and others, are best done via overnight excursions. Regardless, the choices are almost endless.

SPORTS & RECREATION

On and off the Strip there's everything any prime vacation spot of comparable size can offer – miniature golf, city parks offering a full range of activities, fun and sun in the hotel swimming pool, even spectator sports.

Las Vegas has accepted the challenge from resorts around the world and favorably competes on any level and golf is certainly no exception. The area boasts almost three dozen golf courses and more are under construction or development. Included among them are some of the finest courses in the nation and many leading tournaments come to town every year to hold some of the sport's most prestigious events.

And since the weather is favorable year-round, you can also enjoy sports like tennis, swimming, hiking, boating and just about anything else that comes to mind – including bungee jumping or indoor skydiving.

When the weather turns a bit cold and snowy up in the mountains west of town, you've got excellent skiing and other snow-bound activities in Mt. Charleston's **Lee Canyon**. On a nice winter day you can swoosh down the slopes in the morning and water ski on Lake Mead in the afternoon. How's that for diversity!

SHOPPING

As in the case of dining, recent developments have put Las Vegas high up on the list of the foremost shopping destinations in America, if not the world. It used to be there were a few regional malls, plenty of souvenir shops and hotel gift shops. That has certainly changed.

The mundane shopping mall, no matter how big or pretty, is not good enough for the Strip! So, visitors will find a re-created street scene from the Roman Empire at Caesars Palace's **Forum Shops**, gondolas on the water at the Venetian's **Grand Canal Shoppes**, and several different Mediterranean scenes at the Aladdin's fabulous **Desert Passage**. These are more than just places to shop in the most upscale of retailers or to find that special piece in the many art galleries. They are attractions and destinations in and of themselves. Gawking is part of the experience. Live entertainment (and seemingly live as you'll read about later) is an on-going part of the shopping scene in these resort malls.

The bargain hunter will find several outlet malls not too far from the Strip and there are more than enough of the standard regional shopping centers for those seeking out that type of shopping experience. Whatever it is you're looking for and whatever price you're willing to pay, you're going to find it in Las Vegas' retail heaven.

THE BEST OF LAS VEGAS

With apologies to some other great places...

Best Buffet – *See the Best Buffet sidebar in Chapter 10*

Best Steakhouse – *Prime; Alan Albert's; The Steak House (Circus Circus)*

Best Gourmet Restaurant – *LeCirque; Aureole; Michael's; Andre's*

Best Italian Food – *Canaletto; Terrazza; Pasta Palace*

Best Seafood Restaurant – *Emeril's; Sacred Sea Room; Rosewood Grille*

Best Shrimp Cocktail – *Golden Gate Hotel (still only 99 cents!)*

Best Dancing/Nightclub – *Ra; Club Rio; Studio 54*

Best Traditional Revue– *Jubilee!*

Best Production Show – *Mystere; "O"*

Best Magic Show – *Siegfried & Roy; Lance Burton*

Best Excursion – *Red Rock Canyon*

Best Shopping – *Forum Shops; Grand Canal Shoppes; Desert Passage*

Best Thrill Ride – *Manhattan Express; Big Shot*

Best Motion Simulator – *Race for Atlantis; Search for the Obelisk*

Best Free Show – *Battle of Buccaneer Bay; Masquerade Village Sky Parade*

Best Exterior Hotel Architecture – *New York, New York; Venetian; Paris*

Best Interior Hotel Architecture – *Luxor; Venetian; Caesars Palace*

Best Casino Décor – *Bellagio; Mandalay Bay; Aladdin*

Best Place to Stay – *Bellagio; Caesars Palace; Venetian; Rio*

Best View of Las Vegas – *Voo Doo Cafe & Lounge*

Best Way to Pass the Time – *Walking the Strip at night*

Best Guidebook – *Las Vegas Guide, Open Road Publishing – what else?*

3. SUGGESTED ITINERARIES

In the old days many people came to Las Vegas for a couple of days. Some stayed as many as four but it was rare to see anything much longer than that, except for a few high rollers on an extended gambling junket. Because of the explosion of things to see and do in Las Vegas over the past years, the typical visitor is now spending more nights here than used to be the case. Of course, the Southern California weekender is still a popular mode of visitation but people coming from further away are, for the most part, making this a longer vacation. How long you should plan to stay in town depends on, in addition to your available time and budget, exactly what you want out of your visit. You can see the highlights in a few days but that won't allow for any extended amount of shopping, visiting some of the beautiful nearby natural attractions, or taking part in the many recreational opportunities, including one that somehow gets lost in the shuffle for many visitors – just plain relaxing.

The lists below will help you plan a trip which covers things to see, both major and minor. It doesn't specifically allow time for gaming, shopping or recreational pursuits. However, some of that can be done in the morning or evening hours after you've done your sightseeing. Going to shows is almost always an evening affair and if that is part of what you'd like to schedule, it should fit right in.

Keep in mind that different people operate at varying speeds. What takes one person an hour could occupy another individual for three times that long. These itineraries allow ample time for the average visitor to see a full day of sights, with a short lunch break. To make the most efficient use of your time try to arrange your activities by organizing sites you want to see that are located near one another. If you're going to be combining some of the area's scenic sights with hotel attractions then it makes sense to alternate days. That is, the Strip on one day, Hoover Dam and Lake Mead on the next, and then back to the Strip the following day.

If you have...

TWO DAYS
- Aladdin/Desert Passage
- Bellagio
- Caesars Palace/Forum Shops
- Luxor
- Mirage (see the volcano and do so *only* during the evening; detailed exploration of the hotel will be for a three day trip)
- New York, New York (see the exterior *only*; interior visit will be for a three day trip)
- Rio
- Treasure Island (Battle of Buccaneer Bay *only* and do so during the evening; remainder of the hotel will be for a four day trip)
- Venetian/Grand Canal Shoppes

THREE DAYS
Do all of the things above and add the following:
- Excalibur
- Fremont Street Experience (during the evening and also do a quick visit to Golden Nugget and Main Street Station)
- Mandalay Bay
- MGM Grand
- Paris

Remember to do the remainder of the Mirage and New York, New York.

FOUR DAYS
Everything in the three day visit plus:
- Hoover Dam and Lake Mead National Recreation Area (1/2-day excursion)
- Circus Circus
- Stratosphere

Remember to do the remainder of Treasure Island.

FIVE DAYS
Everything in the four day visit plus:
- Flamingo Las Vegas
- Imperial Palace Auto Collection
- Las Vegas Hilton/*Star Trek: The Experience*

- Liberace Museum
- Red Rock Canyon National Conservation Area

SIX DAYS

Everything in the five day visit plus:
- Hard Rock Hotel
- Harrah's
- Monte Carlo
- Orleans
- Tropicana
- Elvis-A-Rama

SEVEN DAYS

Everything in the six day visit plus:
- Henderson factory tours
- Primm

You'll also have time to add some of the other hotels you haven't seen or a few museums.

Even a week long visit to Las Vegas is longer than most people will actually stay so we won't bother to make any suggestions for trips beyond that length. If you are going to be staying longer in the area then just pick out additional attractions from later in this book. We would strongly suggest that trips of more than a week include an overnight or two-night excursion to some of the further afield natural attractions in neighboring states.

If you're here for a shorter period of time but plan to come back (something that statistics show the majority of Las Vegas visitors do), then you can pick up where you left off from the above itineraries. When working the Strip sights, and you plan to see all of the important hotels, you can avoid a lot of running around by grouping them by geographic location rather than just the day-by-day approach listed above. For instance, one day can be devoted to the Tropicana Avenue intersection, another to the Flamingo Road intersection, and so on.

4. A SHORT HISTORY

BEGINNINGS

Let's go back for a moment...way back to prehistoric times when the area that is now southern Nevada was a marshland teeming with wildlife and plants. It only slowly evolved into today's arid desert but the vicinity of Las Vegas was always to be an oasis because of the seepage of underground water. The region, isolated by the harshness of the Mojave Desert, was known only to the Native Americans until 1829, when a Spanish trader named **Antonio Armijo** got lost on his way to Los Angeles via the Spanish Trail. Fortunately, the party found water in a location about a hundred miles from present day Las Vegas. Following up on his discovery about a year or two later, **Rafael Rivera** discovered the site that the city now occupies and, because of the water, named it Las Vegas which is Spanish for *the Meadows*.

The first American to see the area was **Lt. John Fremont** during his 1844 expedition. Mormons from nearby Utah attempted to colonize the area starting in 1855 but abandoned the project only three years later due to harsh conditions and Native American opposition. Mormons still make up about eight percent of the Valley's population.

LT. JOHN FREMONT

*Southern Nevada was first mapped by the U.S. military. Army cartographer **John Fremont** was assigned the task, and after two trips he had produced maps of the entire region. On his first visit he camped around what is today Las Vegas Springs outside of town. His perseverance and outdoor skills were rewarded many years after his death by having streets and hotels named after him. Pretty cool being an explorer, huh?*

THE RAILROAD

As in so many other places in the wild west, it was the advent of the mighty Iron Horse that established Las Vegas and put it on the map, even if it was a pretty small dot! Chosen as a crossroads in the late 1800's due to a relatively plentiful water supply and, of course, strategic location, a railroad town soon sprung up when it finally came to town in 1904 in the form of the San Pedro, Los Angeles and Salt Lake Railroad (later to become the Union Pacific Railroad). Las Vegas was officially incorporated on May 15, 1905.

GAMBLING COMES TO TOWN

Gambling wasn't always legal in Nevada. In fact, a 1910 anti-gambling law made it illegal to play just about any game of chance, even in the privacy of one's own home. So, gambling went underground and flourished to some extent. The year 1931 was to become the seminal year in the history of Las Vegas. That year construction begun on Hoover Dam and Governor Fred Balzar signed a law legalizing gambling. Interestingly, the push for legalization came from a northern Nevada rancher named Phil Tobin who never even visited Las Vegas and had no personal interest in gambling. He realized, however, that it would be good for the state's economic well being.

A separate bill in 1931 also influenced events to come: it allowed a divorce to become legal and binding after just six weeks, the nation's first quickie divorce law. This came into immediate play when Hollywood movie moguls and screen stars began making the divorce pilgrimage, first to Reno, and then, with the completion of the Hoover Dam in 1935 (bringing in its wake new hotels and casinos), to Las Vegas.

Because of the dam construction and the mini-boom in the casino industry, Nevada (and particularly the Las Vegas area) weathered the Great Depression far better than most of the country did. The arrival of industry and Nellis Air Force Base during World War II was a further spur to the economy.

Gambling did not really take off in Vegas for quite a few years, largely because conservative Mormons controlled the politics and much of the business of the city. The dusty road that connected Vegas with Los Angeles was improved to a two-lane highway and the **El Rancho Vegas** became the first hotel/casino on what was to evolve into the Strip. That was in 1941. Other early casinos were the **Last Frontier**, the **Thunderbird** and the **Club Bingo**. These hotels were hits and showed other developers the tremendous potential of combing a casino with a hotel and showroom. Don't overlook the increasing availability of air conditioning as a factor in Las Vegas' growth after World War II.

With the opening of mobster Benjamin "Bugsy" Siegel's **Flamingo Hotel** in 1946, Las Vegas replaced Reno as the king of Nevada's gambling cities, a title it never relinquished. Bugsy's big, glitzy casino, the first of its kind in Vegas, was the first to attract high rollers. They now had a luxurious place where they could spend their money in style. There was now bait to attract the *whales,* casino parlance for the highest of the high rollers. Las Vegas had come of age.

The city prospered, but its reputation as a gangster hangout and center of prostitution grew too. The association in the public's eye of mobsters with Las Vegas held back the city's growth. In fact, it was during this period that Las Vegas was first referred to as **Sin City**.

HOWARD HUGHES

The decade of the '50's was important in the history of the city's growth. It saw the debut of the **Desert Inn** in 1950 and the **Sands** in 1952. Another major milestone occurred at the decade's end with the opening of the **Las Vegas Convention Center** in 1959. But the 1950's and 1960's were a time of especially colorful characters, people like **Nick the Greek**, one of the most famous gamblers in Vegas, the **Binion family**, owners of the famous Binion's Horseshoe Casino; and **Howard Hughes**, the iconoclastic and secretive billionaire who arrived on the scene in 1966 and, with his acquisition of the **Desert Inn**, lent Las Vegas the legitimacy it had long been seeking. Vegas was seen in a new light and began a remarkable period of growth that continues to this day.

Legend has it that Hughes moved to the DI and rented out all the rooms on the top floor and decided to stay. Since Hughes did not gamble, owner and Cleveland crime boss Moe Dalitz wanted him out so he could move some whales into his best suites. But Hughes enjoyed the creature comforts and was not interested in moving. So, the story goes, he bought the hotel for $13 million.

Hughes then went on a buying spree that ended with the controversial billionaire buying a good portion of Las Vegas, including six hotel/casinos, lots of land, the local airport, and practically everything else not nailed down to the desert floor. In effect, he bought out the mob. That, and the implementation of tougher standards for casino owners and management, scrupulously enforced by the **Nevada Gaming Commission** and the **Nevada Control Board**, effectively legitimized the business.

A LOOK AT THE STRIP...CIRCA 1970's

One of the things you will learn about Las Vegas as you continue through this book is that it never stays the same. Constantly reinventing itself to lure new visitors, the face of the Strip is completely different now than it was just a relatively short time ago. The full extent of the change can best be appreciated by taking our little tour of the Strip, as it was about 25 years ago.

The only hotels still around now from those days are the Tropicana, the original MGM Grand (but now called Bally's), Caesars Palace, Barbary Coast, Flamingo, the Frontier, Stardust, Circus Circus, the Riviera and the Sahara. But even in those cases, with few exceptions, they have changed and grown so much that most of them would be unrecognizable to the visitor from those days.

There were lots of empty spaces but the rest of the Strip had the Hacienda, the Dunes, Marina, old Aladdin, Castaways Motel, Holiday Inn Casino, the Sands, Desert Inn, Silver Slipper, and the Silver Bird plus a few other small casino joints. Everything except the Grand was a low-rise and the only real "sight" was Caesars. What a difference a quarter of a century makes!

THE AGE OF THE MEGA-RESORTS BEGINS

There were other great men to follow in Hughes footsteps and shape the city of Las Vegas. But Howard Hughes, Old Spruce Goose himself, the man who changed the face of Las Vegas, occupies the highest rung on the grandiose ladder of Las Vegas myth making. The 1960's saw the opening of **Caesars Palace** (1966) which, although not called that at the time, was in many ways the first of the mega-resorts that now line the Strip. Surprisingly, considering later developments, the arrival of Caesars didn't spark much of a building boom at the time. However, this period (which was also the end of the Hughes era) did usher in another epoch – the public corporation controlled casino/hotel industry that prevails today.

The mega-resort era was first pushed along by **Kirk Kekorian** who built the original MGM Grand Hotel. (That property is now Bally's while the current MGM Grand sits about a mile further south.) But it is **Steve Wynn**, former chairman of Mirage Resorts, who is the real father of today's Las Vegas scene. After using the money garnered by his sale of the Golden Nugget in Atlantic City to build the amazing **Mirage** in 1989, Wynn went on to build **Treasure Island** (1993) next door and he had two of the city's biggest successes. That, more than anything else, led other companies to invest more and more in Las Vegas. This early phase of resort building saw the construction of the **Excalibur** (1990) as well as the **Luxor** and **MGM Grand** (both in 1993).

CORPORATE VEGAS

As in many industries, consolidation has been the name of the game in casino/hotels, a trend that is likely to continue. Only Las Vegas properties are shown although the company may have others.

Boyd Gaming: California Hotel, Fremont Hotel, Main Street Station, Sam's Town and the Stardust. Boyd also operates several smaller casino-only facilities throughout Las Vegas and Henderson.

Coast Resorts: Barbary Coast, Gold Coast, the Orleans and Suncoast.

Harrah's Entertainment: Harrah's and The Rio.

Mandalay Resort Group: Circus Circus, Excalibur, Luxor and Mandalay Bay. The company also has a half-interest in Monte Carlo.

MGM Grand/Mirage: The recent merger of these two giants leaves this firm with Bellagio, Golden Nugget, Holiday Inn Boardwalk, MGM Grand, the Mirage, New York, New York and Treasure Island. They also have the other half of the Monte Carlo.

Park Place Entertainment: Bally's, Caesars Palace, Flamingo Las Vegas, Paris and the Las Vegas Hilton.

Station Casinos: Boulder Station, Fiesta, Palace Station, Santa Fe Station, Sunset Station and Texas Station. The company just acquired The Reserve and has several projects under construction in addition to some joint venture casino-only establishments throughout the area.

And, last but not least, billionaire financier Carl Icahn has acquired the Stratosphere, Arizona Charlie's and Arizona Charlie's East.

LAS VEGAS TODAY...

The demolishing of older resorts and their replacement with ever larger and more fantastic hotel/casinos continues almost without let-up. Once filled with numerous large open spaces, the Strip now has few parcels left to build on. With more than 125,000 hotel rooms, Las Vegas has more rooms to stay in than any other place in the world. It is a city that constantly keeps reinventing itself and which manages to always stay a step ahead of the competition.

The growth of gaming has spawned other development and industries as well. The current population of **Clark County** is now almost 1,500,000, with slightly less than a third living in Las Vegas proper (but the suburbs that have spread out from Vegas are for all intents and purposes part of the city). You may be interested to know that the Strip itself is not within the city limits of Las Vegas but in an unincorporated area of Clark County, most of which is called Paradise. Try that on your friends at trivia time. At the current rate of influx, some observers believe that the metropolitan area's population could surpass two million before the end of the new millennium's first decade.

Tourism is certainly alive and well. Figures for the latest year show that some 35 million visitors filled the casinos' and the state's coffers. A late 1990's building boom increased visitor counts by percentages that hadn't been seen in some time. Growth is expected to slow somewhat on a percentage basis. The typical visitor of today is younger than in the past and stays longer. He or she also spends a larger percentage of their money on non-gaming activities. Regardless, gambling is the driving economic force in Vegas with about $7 billion in gambling revenues being generated each year.

The current mayor of Las Vegas is **Oscar Goodman**, the man who earned a tidy sum by defending known mobsters when they were still a big part of the casino/hotel scene. He even had a small role in the movie *Casino* a few years back playing, of course, himself! During the campaign for election and for a short time after his victory some of Goodman's critics claimed that he would be bad for the city, image-wise. Sure. In reality we think most people actually felt his image would be a natural for Sin City. He was interviewed by newspapers all over the country and always managed to turn on the charm. As mayor he has taken a populist stance on many issues and seems to be doing quite well. Actually, the mayor of Las Vegas has a small role other than being the unofficial spokesperson. The mayor is only one member of the City Council and the entire council takes a secondary role to the Clark County Commissioners.

This amazing and exciting city has certainly come a long way from its sleepy origins as a railroad town. *The Meadows* no longer, Las Vegas has truly come into its own as a world class resort destination and a place to live and work.

•••AND TOMORROW

The growth of Las Vegas has been nothing short of remarkable on two fronts. First, what began as little more than Bugsy Siegel's casino is now one of the world's premier resort destinations. And, the dusty little town in the desert is, according to projections, to become a metropolitan area of more than two million people in the not-too-distant future. Yet, Las Vegas faces a number of challenges.

The first is the proliferation of gaming in other jurisdictions and over the internet. Vegas has met this challenge before and most experts agree that with all its attractions and amenities it will do so again, including rising above the challenge of expanded Indian gaming in neighboring California. Another challenge is the diversification of its economic base so as to avoid being almost completely dependence on tourism. Although great strides have been made in this area too, the city has a long way to go before it can said to be economically diverse.

Finally, the federal government's plan to store nuclear waste in Yucca Mountain poses another kind of threat. Almost a hundred miles away, Yucca is unlikely to have any negative health consequences for residents let alone visitors especially since the materials arriving at Yucca will arrive there mostly without passing through Las Vegas itself. However, nuclear waste is not good from a public relations standpoint. It may be a long time before Yucca becomes a reality, if ever. In the meantime it is a hot issue in this town and most people are willing to fight Washington to make sure it never happens. Time will tell.

THINKING OF MOVING TO VEGAS?

You certainly will have a lot of company if you're considering relocating to Las Vegas. Over the past few years an average of about 5,000 people moved into the Valley each month. Although this rate is now dropping somewhat the area remains the fastest growing in the nation, a status it is unlikely to relinquish for some time to come. Henderson, Las Vegas' neighbor to the immediate south claims the title of fastest growing city in America, but more about that in a later sidebar.

The attractions for new residents are many. The availability of jobs and the excitement of living in Action City are among the most obvious, but not exclusive. Although the overall cost of living is lower in many other places, many major items are cheap for Las Vegas residents. These include the absence of a state income tax, low real estate taxes and low utility costs. Even water is cheap, a big surprise to most people since Las Vegas is one of the driest areas in the country.

Savvy consumers can find inexpensive places to eat without trouble and plenty of entertainment at costs far less than in most cities. Las Vegas attracts young singles and families as well as a large number of senior citizens. It seems that the desert life is pleasing to a whole bunch of people, including one of your authors, who settled into Henderson in 1995.

5. PLANNING YOUR TRIP

WHEN TO VISIT

A lot of people who have the flexibility to come to Las Vegas at any time ask us when is the best time to visit. There are lots of factors that determine that and they often vary according to your own nature but two major considerations are the weather and crowds. Price, of course, is another important factor but it is somewhat related to the first two. Weather and crowds aren't quite as related as they used to be. The conventional wisdom once was that to avoid the crowds you came during the blazing hot summer since most people want to avoid the worst of the heat. While many visitors would prefer to be cooler, the fact is that the "slow dog days" of summer aren't slow at all. Oh, perhaps occupancy levels are down a bit as compared to other times, but the crowds will still be there. Not that big crowds are necessarily a disadvantage – that's because there is an even greater electricity in the air and a general carnival atmosphere when Vegas is jumping with its largest visitor counts.

Although Vegas is never lacking for lots of visitors, one of the slowest periods is the time from after Thanksgiving weekend to just before Christmas (except for one week when the rodeo is in town). Those who want to shun the hordes might find that a good time to come to town but it has a drawback if you plan to see a lot of shows. Many, especially the bigger production shows take a hiatus during the middle part of December. We do suggest, however, that you avoid coming to town during some of the largest conventions. Comdex in November is the best example.

Now to the weather. The Las Vegas Valley sits in the middle of the desert, actually the meeting point of three deserts: the **Mojave**, the **Sonoran**, and the **Great Basin**. As you might guess then, the temperature here can get pretty hot. The city is surrounded by mountains, the highest peak of which is **Mt. Charleston**, northwest of the city, at just under 12,000 feet. There is very little rainfall – about 4-1/4 inches per year – and an average of 294 days of sunshine including partially sunny days. It is dry, windy and hot much of the time.

July and August are the hottest months when the daily maximum temperatures almost always easily tops 100 degrees. Be prepared by dressing in fabrics that breathe and by wearing a hat and sunglasses. You can have rain showers at this time of the year but rainy days are almost unknown. The heat is mitigated to some extent by the low humidity. Even during the August "monsoon" season, when moisture from Arizona flows into the Valley, it is unusual for the humidity to rise beyond the 20's for any length of time. You will hear the locals complaining about the oppressive humidity when it gets to around 25 percent – they don't know what humidity is!

January and December are the coolest months; the average maximum is 60 degrees, but it can go below freezing so bring at least one warm jacket or sweater if you're planning to visit anytime during the winter. The spring and autumn months are the most comfortable, with the average temperatures in the 70's and 80's.

LAS VEGAS CLIMATE AT A GLANCE

	Average Maximum	Daily Average Minimum	Daily Precipitation
January	54 F	34 F	0.48"
February	59	35	0.22"
March	66	42	0.69"
April	81	54	0.21"
May	90	63	0.28"
June	102	72	0.12"
July	105	78	0.35"
August	104	75	0.49"
September	87	62	0.28"
October	80	54	0.20"
November	62	40	0.44"
December	60	36	0.36"

The worst thing about the Las Vegas weather isn't the heat and certainly not the lack of rain. It's the wind. The heating conditions and the surrounding mountains make for many windy days. Sustained winds of 25mph are not uncommon. On the other hand, the wind seems to take to extremes. It can be windy for a day or a week and then revert to calm or near calm conditions for days at a time. The change is, more often than not, quite abrupt. And don't expect the wind to cool you off in the summer. We like to refer to a windy 105-degree afternoon as the "blow dryer effect." The figures in the chart on the previous page are based on the National Weather Service's records dating back to the 1930's. It seems that, because of the paving over of the valley, the evenings do not usually cool off to their historic lows. How soon this will change the averages is anyone's guess. It does not seem to have had an effect on the highs which, like anywhere else, can often vary from above to below the norm from one week to the next.

WHAT TO PACK

The days when people came to Las Vegas dressed to kill are long since gone although you'll see just about every kind of dress, especially on a Saturday night. Don't be surprised to see a couple in jeans and tees sitting next to a well-dressed couple. It happens all the time. You can wear just about anything you want to in Las Vegas although some of the fancier restaurants have dress codes (we'll let you know in the Where to Eat chapter). Showrooms don't require fancy outfits either although they do frown on tank or halter tops, cut-off jeans and other similar non-attire.

We usually suggest packing light when going on vacation, however, if you're going to stay put in Las Vegas for several days and don't have to worry about constantly packing and unpacking, you might be more inclined to bring along a few more changes of outfits than is usual for touring.

In the summer make sure you have light colored clothes that breathe. Shorts and tees are quite the order of dress for the day but they aren't always the best choice. They seem to be a logical choice given the relentless heat and sunshine. But in reality, it makes more sense to cover up a little more skin and keep those rays off of you as much as possible. Sunscreen is advisable and sunglasses and a hat are a must. It's unlikely you'll need a jacket during the evening unless you chill quite easily. The wintertime is another matter. A light windbreaker is always a good idea and a little bit warmer outerwear will come in handy during the evening. We can't tell you how many times we've seen visitors walking around with bare arms and shorts in January, arms folded across their chests, and faces turning blue. They always have the same response: "It's the desert. I thought it was always hot!"

LAS VEGAS TOURISM INFORMATION

Prior to coming to Las Vegas you might want to contact the **Las Vegas Convention and Visitors Authority**, the largest "official" source of information on Glitter City. Their mailing address is *3150 Paradise Road,*

Las Vegas, NV 89109; Tel. 702/892-0711. They also have a room reservation service, *Tel. 800/332-5333.* Their website is *www.lasvegas24hours.com.* The Bureau folks can give you up-to-the-minute information on special events and show schedules for the time you will be in town. You might want to request a general information packet, or more specifically "Events & Attractions" and "Showguide." They contain schedules for two-month periods (for example, October-November).

Other useful places to call, depending upon your needs are:
- **Las Vegas Chamber of Commerce**, *711 E. Desert Inn Road; Tel. 702/735-1616*, who can fill you in on facts and figures about the area if you're considering relocation.
- **Nevada Commission on Tourism**, *Capitol Complex, Carson City, NV 89104; Tel. 800/638-2328*, if you want more detailed information about things to do outside the city limits or somewhere else in Nevada.
- **Las Vegas Events**, an events hotline of sort, *Tel. 702/731-2115;* find out by phone what's going on during your intended stay.

Finally, although there are many different websites with information on Las Vegas, most of them are rather topic specific and not suited to general planning. The exception is the comprehensive *www.lasvegas.com*, which has a multitude of information that will interest the cyber traveler and cyber planner. If you like to make your reservations on-line but aren't sure which hotel you wish to stay at then log on to Travelscape at *www.lvrs.com.* We've also included individual hotel websites in the hotel listings and websites for airlines and other services. Always remember, however, that many websites offer information that is of dubious value.

STAYING CONNECTED WHILE IN TOWN

Cyber lovers seem to have a need to stay wired regardless of where they are and what they're doing. Personally, we prefer to forget about the rest of the world as much as possible when we're traveling but for those of you who just can't resist the urge to log on and check your e-mail, here's some useful information.

While the Strip doesn't have anything that can be termed a true "cyber cafe," the Fashion Show Mall has a dozen high-speed terminals that can be used free of charge during regular mall hours. It has met with an enthusiastic response from users and, at latest report, mall management plans to continue offering the service. More and more hotels, especially the better ones, now offer in-room data lines if you're packing your own laptop.

Once you're in town you can still contact any of the above information sources. However, at that point it becomes easier to consult local newspapers or magazines for the latest scoop. See the appropriate section in the next chapter.

A LITTLE ADVANCE PLANNING

We usually recommend a fairly good amount of advance planning when it comes to having an itinerary. For Las Vegas, however, it isn't as important to do so as it is for a road vacation. You'll probably find that certain activities are more to your liking than others once you've been in town for a while. However, you should use this book to at least jot down the things that you feel will most appeal to you and at least have a daily framework for what you plan to do. Or, take the easy way and try one of our sample itineraries.

BOOKING YOUR VACATION

The first question to ask yourself is whether or not you need a travel agent. We usually prefer self-booking because it isn't at all difficult to read airline schedules, select and contact a hotel and make whatever other reservations are necessary, such as a car. However, many people feel uncomfortable about doing these things and prefer to let a travel professional do their work.

While most travel agents are familiar with Las Vegas (it is, after all, a frequent destination of many customers) you can't always assume that the agent knows that much more than you do. In fact, after reading this book you'll likely know more than he or she does. So, use an agent that has been recommended by others. Another good indication of reliability is to ascertain if the agent is a member of the American Society of Travel Agents (ASTA). Membership in that group or other industry organizations should be considered as a minimum requirement when selecting a travel agent.

Regardless of which travel agent you choose, their services should be free of charge to you. Some agents have begun instituting fees in recent years because airlines and other travel industry payers have been reducing commissions to agents. We don't doubt that it's becoming harder for agents to make a living but it shouldn't be at your expense when the majority still do it without charging the customer. This especially applies to booking a Las Vegas trip, which is an easy task for the agent.

Travel agents will generally recommend a package plan when going to Vegas. This includes airfare, hotel and sometimes a rental car. They also throw in various coupon books (see the Funbooks section in the next chapter for more on this topic) which are often of dubious value. You can often get a great deal using such packages but it isn't always the case. You should check out, either through the agent or on your own, what it would cost if you purchase each component separately. Not only may it be the same price or even lower, but it allows you to tailor it more specifically to your own needs. That can even be worth paying a little extra for.

Las Vegas is the kind of place where being on your own is best. There are few comprehensive guided tours and they aren't worth discussing. If you do not rent a car and wish to see some things outside of the city then you can purchase half or full day bus tours from numerous operators. These will be discussed later and can be arranged at just about any Strip hotel.

GETTING THE BEST AIRFARE

Even travel agents have trouble pinning down what the best airfare is on a given flight on a given day. It's like trying to hit a moving object. If you call one airline ten times and ask what it will cost to fly from New York to Las Vegas on the morning of July 10th and return on the afternoon of July 16th, you'll probably get several different answers. It wouldn't surprise us to hear that you got ten different responses! Unfortunately, such is the state of the airline fare game. The car rental companies and even hotels aren't much better. There are, however, some things to keep in mind when searching for the best air.

When you fly is important. Travel to Las Vegas will be cheaper during the mid-week than on weekends or shoulder days (Monday and Friday). The time of the year can also have a big effect. If you travel during the busiest times of the year the airfare will likely be higher. Night flights are considerably less expensive than daytime travel if you don't mind arriving on the "red-eye" special. Even then it might not be as cheap as you think. For example, if you arrive in Las Vegas at eleven in the evening you'll be paying for an extra night's hotel that you may not have had to if you had flown in the next morning. So be sure to check all the angles.

Advance confirmed reservations that are paid for prior to your flight are almost always the cheapest way to go. The restrictions on these low fares vary considerably. In general you must book and pay for your ticket at least seven to 30 days in advance. In most cases they require that you stay over a Saturday night. They are almost always non-refundable or require payment of a large penalty to either cancel or even make a change in the flight itinerary.

You can sometimes find big bargains by doing the opposite strategy – waiting for the last minute. If the airline has empty seats on the flight you select they're often willing to fill it up for a surprisingly low price. The problem with this is that you don't know if there will be an available seat at the time you want to go. Despite an increase in flights to Las Vegas over the past year or two, there is still a "shortage" of seats from many markets, especially the longer direct flights from the east coast. This is because Las Vegas is a leisure market and the airlines can't soak the customers the way they do on business flights. Vacation travelers are a lot smarter, dollar wise, than are their business counterparts. The bottom line is that if you have hotel and other reservations for a definite time, waiting for the last minute to get your air can be a dangerous game to play. Even if you do get a ticket at the last minute it can wind up being at a sky-high price.

Fares from one airline to another can sometimes be radically different, although most carriers flying the same route will usually wind up adjusting their fares to the competition. Whenever possible, try to go with a low-fare airline, several of which have extensive service into Las Vegas. One thing you should always be on the lookout for regardless of who you plan to fly with are promotional fares. Scan the newspapers or just call the airlines. It's always best to phrase your inquiry something like "what is the lowest available fare between Las Vegas and x on date y?"

Finally, we know that those accustomed to first class air are going to squirm in their seats at this but the cost of first class is simply not worth it – you're only going to be on the plane for a few hours. This isn't a weeklong cruise where you want to be pampered every minute. Go coach, bring along a good book (such as this) and enjoy the flight. Of course, if you have frequent flyer miles and can upgrade to first class, that's a different story.

FLYING TO LAS VEGAS

Las Vegas is served by more than 20 airlines. Here's a rundown on the major carriers including which cities they serve non-stop to Las Vegas.
• **AmericaWest**, *Tel. 800/247-5692; www.americawest.com.* Las Vegas is a major hub for this airline and flies non-stop to Atlanta, Baltimore, Boston, Chicago, Columbus, Dallas/Fort Worth, Denver, Detroit, El Paso, Ft. Lauderdale, Hartford, Houston, Indianapolis, Kansas City, Los Angeles (several greater Los Angeles area airports), Miami, Milwaukee, Minneapolis, New York/Newark, Oakland, Omaha, Orlando, Philadelphia, Phoenix, Portland, Reno, Sacramento, Salt Lake City, San Diego, San Francisco, San Jose, Seattle/Tacoma, Tampa, Tucson and Washington.
• **American Airlines**, *Tel. 800/433-7300; www.aa.com.* Non-stop service to Chicago, Dallas/Fort Worth, Los Angeles, Oklahoma City, Portland, Reno, San Diego, San Francisco, San Jose, Seattle/Tacoma and Tucson.
• **Continental Airlines**, *Tel. 800/525-0280; www.continental.com.* Non-stop service to Cleveland, Houston (their hub and transfer point to dozens of other localities) and New York/Newark.

- **Delta Airlines**, *Tel. 800/221-1212; www.delta-air.com*. Non-stop to Atlanta, Boston, Cincinnati, Dallas/Fort Worth, Los Angeles, New Orleans, New York, Orlando, Portland, Salt Lake City, Tampa and Tulsa. Good connections are available to their entire route system.
- **National Airlines**, *Tel. 800/757-5387; www.nationalairlines.com*. This Las Vegas based airline has grown quickly and has a good reputation for service and decent fares. Future route expansion is planned. Currently, they fly non-stop to Chicago, Dallas/Fort Worth, Los Angeles, Miami, New York, Philadelphia, San Francisco and Washington.
- **Northwest Airlines**, *Tel. 800/225-2525; www.nwa.com*. Non-stop service to Detroit, Los Angeles, Memphis, Minneapolis/St. Paul, Seattle/Tacoma, San Francisco and Tokyo.
- **Southwest Airlines**, *Tel. 800/435-9792; www.southwest.com*. The largest carrier in Las Vegas and a popular low cost one as well, they fly non-stop to Albuquerque, Amarillo, Austin, Baltimore/Washington, Birmingham, Boise, Buffalo, Chicago, Cleveland, Columbus, El Paso, Hartford, Houston, Indianapolis, Kansas City, Los Angeles (several greater Los Angeles area airports), Louisville, Lubbock, Midland/Odessa, Nashville, New Orleans, Oakland, Omaha, Orlando, Phoenix, Portland, Reno, Sacramento, St. Louis, Salt Lake City, San Antonio, San Diego, San Jose, Seattle/Tacoma, Spokane, Tampa, Tucson and Tulsa.
- **Sun Country Airlines**, *Tel. 800/752-1218; www.suncountry.com*. Non-stop service to Dallas, Detroit, Milwaukee and Minneapolis/St. Paul.
- **TWA**, *Tel. 800/221-2000; www.twa.com*. Non-stop service to their system hub in St. Louis.
- **United Airlines**, *Tel. 800/241-6522; www.ual.com*. Non-stop service to Chicago, Denver, Fresno, Los Angeles, Palm Springs, San Francisco and Washington with good connections to their entire flight system primarily through Chicago or Denver.
- **USAirways**, *Tel. 800/428-4322; www.usairways.com*. Non-stop service to Charlotte, Philadelphia and Pittsburgh.

Among some of the other airlines serving Las Vegas include **Alaska Airlines, Allegiant Air, Frontier Airlines, Hawaiian Airlines** and **SkyWest**. International visitors need to know that they can reach Las Vegas with direct non-stop service from Canada (**Air Canada** and **Canada 3000**), London (**Virgin Atlantic**) and Frankfurt (Lufthansa subsidiary **Condor**). At the present time these direct European flights are not available on a daily basis.

There are a few airlines offering air tours from Las Vegas to the Grand Canyon and other nearby scenic areas. These will be discussed in Chapter 16, *Excursions & Day Trips*.

6. BASIC INFORMATION

You'll encounter a variety of useful and interesting information in this chapter that will make you a more informed traveler. Major topics covered in their own chapter (hotels, dining, shopping, entertainment and sports and recreation) aren't included here.

ALCOHOLIC BEVERAGE & GAMING LAWS

The minimum drinking age is 21 years and, if you look underage, bartenders will not be bashful to request proper identification. The same restrictions apply to gambling. Parents should take note that Nevada gaming regulations prohibit children from loitering in the casino. You are not allowed to play if your child is present. Almost every casino is designed so that you have to pass through it in order to get anywhere. However, children can walk through the casino so long as they do not stop in an active gaming area. Casinos operate 24 hours a day, 365 days a year. Likewise, alcoholic beverages are always available. Many hotels, in addition to their numerous bars and free cocktail service for players, feature a liquor store on the premises.

BANKING, MONEY & CREDIT CARDS

After spending all of your money on shopping and shows (not to mention gambling), you may well need to replenish your cash stockpile. Most banks are open from 9am until 5pm on weekdays (with some later hours on Friday) and from 10am to 1pm on Saturday. Some are even open on Sunday.

Unfortunately, you won't find any banks on the Strip. So unless you're prepared to drive to a bank you'll have to rely on the ubiquitous automatic teller machines (ATM's) that are located in every casino in town. You can use your own ATM card if it's part of one of the large national networks such as *Plus* or *Cirrus*. If not, the casino ATM's are also cash machines for getting advances on your VISA, MasterCard or other major credit card. Watch out, though: a number of hotel ATM machines charge fees beyond the nominal charge you may find elsewhere. The fees on cash advances' for charge cards are, likewise, similarly exorbitant.

Credit cards are almost universally accepted in Las Vegas. All hotel and restaurant listings in this book will indicate which credit cards are accepted. In cases where four or less are valid the names of the cards will be shown. *'Most major credit cards accepted'* indicates five are valid (including American Express, Discover, MasterCard and VISA) while the acceptance of six or more cards will be indicated by *'Major credit cards accepted.'* The same cards valid for paying your hotel bill will always be accepted in that hotel for show tickets and all restaurants (except fast-food outlets). The acceptance of at least some credit cards at fee attractions will be indicated for those places charging $15 or more per person.

You should have no trouble using traveler's checks in casinos to buy chips. If you have good credit you may be able to take out a line of credit at most casinos, but call first and make sure that you can provide them with the necessary documentation (usually something like credit cards or a driver's license; some may require a bank statement).

CHILDREN

Besides making sure that you have something to occupy your little ones for your trip to Las Vegas, Chapter 17 will provide you with plenty of things to see and do that children will enjoy. Beyond this chapter, you might want to consider Open Road's *Las Vegas With Kids.*

DISABLED TRAVELERS

If you or someone you're traveling with is disabled, you might want to call ahead and find out what special services are available in your hotel. Although every major hotel has at least some disabled accessible rooms, overall facilities do vary. Las Vegas is better than many other cities in adapting its buildings and services for the disabled. The Las Vegas Convention & Visitors Authority has an **ADA (Americans with Disabilities Act) Coordinator's office** that can provide assistance, *Tel. 702/892-7525.*

You can also call or write to one of the following agencies for further information:

- **Nevada Association for the Handicapped**, *6200 W. Oakey Blvd., Las Vegas, NV 89102. Tel. 702/870-7050*
- **Southern Nevada Sightless Inc.**, *1001 N. Bruce Street, Las Vegas, NV 89101. Tel. 702/642-0100*

EMERGENCIES

No one likes to think about emergencies when the skies are blue and you're having a swell time but it's always good to know what to do in case trouble arises. Coordinated emergency services (police, ambulance and fire) throughout the Las Vegas area can be reached by dialing **911**. For urgent but non-emergency situations you can dial **311**. Like the 911 system, this will automatically route your call to the nearest law enforcement authorities. However, 311 service is not available from cell phones and, from pay phones, you must deposit the required local call fee. Alternatively, you can try **the Las Vegas Metro Police Department non-emergency number**, *Tel. 702/795-3111.* Metro handles policing duties for the entire Las Vegas area except for Henderson and North Las Vegas, which have their own police departments.

General care hospitals in the Las Vegas Valley are:
- **Desert Springs Hospital**, *2075 E. Flamingo Road. Tel. 702/733-8800*
- **Lake Mead Hospital**, *1409 E. Lake Mead Blvd., North Las Vegas. Tel. 702/ 649-7711*
- **Mountainview Hospital**, *3100 N. Tenaya Way. Tel. 702/255-5000*
- **St. Rose Dominican Hospital**: Rose de Lima Campus, *102 E. Lake Mead Drive, Henderson. Tel. 702/616-5000;* Siena Campus, *3001 St. Rose Parkway, Henderson. Tel. 702/616-5000*
- **Summerlin Hospital Medical Center**, *657 Town Center Drive. Tel. 702/ 233-7000*
- **Sunrise Hospital & Medical Center**, *3186 S. Maryland Parkway. Tel. 702/731-8000*
- **University Medical Center**, *1800 W. Charleston Blvd. Tel. 702/383-2000*
- **Valley Hospital Medical Center**, *620 Shadow Lane. Tel. 702/388-4000*

If you need a doctor or dentist rather than a hospital emergency room, call the **Clark County Medical Society**, *Tel. 702/739-9989,* or the **Clark County Dental Society**, *Tel. 702/255-7873* for a referral. In addition, there are literally dozens of walk-in "quick care" medical centers throughout the city. They can be found in the yellow pages. There is a walk-in medical practice at *3743 Las Vegas Blvd. South*, adjacent to the Polo Towers time share. The MGM Grand and Caesars Palace both have full service medical clinics for employees that are open to registered guests in need of medical attention.

There are many 24-hour pharmacies around, but the most convenient one for the majority of visitors will be **Walgreen's** which has two Strip locations. One is at *3765 Las Vegas Blvd. South (near Harmon Avenue)* and the other is at *3025 Las Vegas Blvd. South (Convention Center Drive).* In addition to prescriptions you can get other items such as sunscreen and aspirin for a lot less money here than at the hotel sundry shops.

FOREIGN VISITORS

Our friends from abroad, especially those from just over the northern frontier, love Las Vegas like few other American cities. For many, the allure of Vegas is not just the prospect of a quick buck; for better or worse, many foreigners perceive Las Vegas as the quintessential American city.

More visitors to Las Vegas arrive from Canada than from any other country, with over a million making the trip each year. Next in line are Great Britain, Germany, Japan, Mexico, France, Spain and Brazil.

If you need to change money you will get a better rate at most banks or foreign exchange shops than you will in the hotels and casinos. One exception is the **American Foreign Exchange**, *in the Las Vegas Hilton, Tel. 702/892-0100.*

It's a good idea to bring traveler's checks for the bulk of your cash, or even better, you can use most major credit cards at cash machines. You can exchange money at most hotels and banks, and of course at the airport.

The United States uses a 110-volt alternating current system, which can blow the socks off of electrical equipment not designed for it. Chances are you'll need a transformer for any electrical appliances you bring in, including electric razors. Also, we use a two-prong outlet with one prong slightly larger than the other. You can purchase cheap adapters in many places. Even our VCR standards are different so be careful about any tapes that you purchase. Pre-recorded videos of Las Vegas sold in many gift shops are often available in different international standards but this is not the case for blank tapes. So bring enough with you.

PASSPORTS & VISAS

If you are visiting the United States from abroad (other than Canada and Mexico) you will need a valid **passport** and, depending upon the country of origination, a **visa**. The American embassy in your home country or your own immigration authorities will know if there are any visa requirements. There are limits on what you may bring into the United States. These include $400 in duty-free gifts; one liter of alcohol (but the booze will count against your $400 total); and 200 cigarettes or 100 cigars. You'll have to report on a customs form if you are carrying in more than $10,000 in US currency.

The authorities are also touchy about bringing in agricultural produce and meat products, so if your plans call for importing some kind of foodstuff (or your pet plants), do yourself a favor and contact the **US Customs Service**, *1301 Constitution Ave. NW, Washington, DC 20229 Tel. 202/566-8195.*

FUN BOOKS & DISCOUNTS

"**Fun books**" are free coupon booklets given out in many hotels and casinos as well as other locations. You can probably pick one up in your hotel lobby or just ask one of the receptionists or employees. You can also usually find them in the complementary tourist magazines. Some hotels go so far as to have an employee in the street handing them out to passers-by. And, finally, if you're coming to Las Vegas on a package deal arranged through a travel agent, you're almost certainly going to get a fun book along with your other documents.

The coupons offer things like free drinks, gambling incentives such as three-for-two dollar plays at the tables, free pulls at slots, discounts on meals, and the like. The *Discover Nevada Bonus Book*, available from the Nevada Commission on Tourism also has lots of coupons. Keep in mind that although you do get something for nothing, it isn't a big deal by any means. They can save you a couple of bucks here and there and maybe a little more if you're not too choosy as to where you eat. That is, the better hotel buffets and restaurants are rarely, if ever, included in the coupon books.

Also be wary of "free trips" that are offered to you as part of many group travel arrangements. Often it's just a way of taking you to an off-Strip casino to gamble all day. If you like to gamble, fine, but otherwise you'll just be trapped at a place you don't really want to be until they take you back to your hotel or you pay for your own transportation. The Strip is also filled with representatives of various establishments who will constantly try to get you to take one of their deals. Our advice is: *don't bother*.

HEALTH

A weeklong stay in Las Vegas isn't much different from the stand-point of health precautions than staying in any other city in the United States. However, there are some potential pitfalls that, while not necessarily unique to Las Vegas, can be something that visitors will often fall victim to if they're not careful. **Sunburn** or **heat exhaustion** during the summer are definite threats. Drink plenty of fluids. Water is best but fruit juices also count toward your daily requirement. Take your sunbathing in the morning and in small doses. Use a good quality sunscreen. If you are going to be taking part in demanding forms of outdoor recreation during the hotter months, again, try to do it in the cooler morning hours. Wear protective clothing, including a hat. When in natural areas away from the city be sure to avoid contact with wild animals.

The American Southwest, including some rural areas near Las Vegas have had cases of **hantavirus**, a nasty flu-like illness that can be fatal. If you've been getting back to nature and show any flu symptoms it is imperative that you seek immediate medical attention. Also, this region of the country has seen the arrival of the Africanized honeybee, commonly known as "killer" bees. These are no more dangerous individually than an ordinary bee but they are more aggressive and attack in large numbers. If you should encounter a hive, assume it to be the Africanized version. Slowly back off.

The widespread availability of **alcohol** (including free drinks when you play) can be a temptation that some people will have trouble resisting. Pace yourself. Don't overdo it. It's likely that you'll wind up drinking a bit more in Las Vegas than at home but know your limitations or have a family member cut you off at the appropriate time. And remember that drinking alcoholic beverages does not count toward your water intake requirements. Alcohol can actually cause dehydration.

NEWSPAPERS, MAGAZINES & INFORMATION

The *Las Vegas Review Journal* (or RJ to the locals) is the city's largest newspaper and publishes every morning. If you happen to be in town on a Friday then it's a good idea to pick up a copy because the pull-out tabloid section titled "Neon" has a comprehensive listing of current entertainment and other useful information. The *Las Vegas Sun* is an afternoon newspaper that publishes weekdays and has a section in the weekend editions of the RJ. Its visitor information value is, however, sparse compared to the former. A number of other newspapers are published for residents but also have information that can be useful for visitors, especially those seeking alternative life-styles. Two publications in this category are *Las Vegas Weekly* and *City Life*. It is difficult to find these publications on the Strip. If you want them you will probably have to drive into areas where the locals reside and shop.

However, every hotel distributes one or more free magazines that feature information on current entertainment and happenings as well as general visitor information. The biggest is *What's On*. It is published every two weeks. This can be a valuable source of information but a word of caution is advised: having read this publication over the years we are of the opinion that articles and reviews contained in it definitely seem to favor the hotel/casinos and other businesses that advertise in it the most. *Las Vegas Style* (monthly) and *Las Vegas Today* (bi-weekly) both also offer some good information. *Showbiz Magazine* comes out every week and is almost as huge as *What's On*. It concentrates mostly on entertainment rather than on things to see and do and restaurants. More slender in content but still useful is the monthly *Where*.

When it comes time to get "in-person" information, there is no shortage of people who have set up shop, ostensibly to give advice, but actually to try to sell you something or steer you towards a particular place of business. General questions can usually be better answered by the staff at your hotel so try to avoid getting snagged at these "official" tourism sights. There are several kiosks that dispense computerized information and volunteers doing the same. They're more reliable but often not as knowledgeable as they should be. So, the other place to go for information is the **Las Vegas Convention & Visitors Bureau**. They have an office at the corner of Paradise Road and Convention Center Drive. It is located at the intersection's northwest corner just before you reach the entrance to the pedestrian bridge that crosses Paradise Road and connects with the Convention Center.

PLACES OF WORSHIP

This may be Sin City in the eyes of many, but people *do* live here and there are scores of houses of worship representing all major denominations. According to local lore Las Vegas has more churches and synagogues per capita than other city in America. There are even a few churches located on or very near to the Strip. Here are some of those that are closest to areas where most visitors will be staying should the urge hit you or you need some help in getting on a winning streak:

- **Guardian Angel Cathedral**, *336 Cathedral Way, between Desert Inn Road and Convention Center Drive; Tel. 702/735-5241)*. This Catholic church is just off the Strip. and draws many visitors, particularly for its Saturday afternoon mass.
- **St. Joan of Arc**, *315 S. Casino Center Blvd.; Tel. 702/382-9909*, a Catholic church located downtown.
- **First Baptist Church**, *300 S. 9th Street; Tel. 702/382-6177*. Not far from downtown casinos.
- **First Southern Baptist Church**, *700 E. St. Louis Ave.; Tel. 702/732-3100*, between the north end of the Strip and downtown.
- **Reformation Lutheran Church**, *580 E. St. Louis Ave.; Tel. 702/732-2052*, located as above.
- **First United Methodist**, *231 S. Third Street; Tel. 702/382-9939*. Downtown.
- **Temple Beth Shalom**, *1600 E. Oakey Blvd.; Tel. 702/384-5070*. Northeast of the Strip.
- **Shrine of the Most Holy Redeemer**, *55 E. Reno Avenue; Tel. 702/891-8600*. This Catholic church is located just off the Strip, a block south of Tropicana Avenue.

SAFETY TIPS

Any big city has crime and Las Vegas is no exception. Yet, considering the number of tourists that come through each year, the safety record for visitors is exceptional. The police (and hotel security forces which assist them) do a good job of protecting travelers. After all, it is the city's lifeblood. While some simple precautions are in order, Las Vegas is probably the only city in America where you can walk down the main street at one in the morning with a thousand dollars in your wallet and not get mugged! On the other hand, feeling too secure is never a good idea – anywhere, so familiarize yourself with this brief list of safety tips which cover crime and other matters.

- Avoid contact with panhandlers. Although most of them are harmless there have been some incidents in the past. If they come up to you just ignore them and keep walking. Panhandlers will be found on the Strip but even more so in the downtown area.
- Even though mostly everyone on the Strip and other popular areas is carrying a good deal of cash, don't attract attention to yourself by flaunting it. Keep money hidden until you have to spend it and don't wear expensive jewelry when wandering around outside.
- Stick to the Strip or the main part of Fremont Street late at night. There are some areas in Las Vegas you don't want to be in, especially at night.
- Lock your hotel room and use the deadbolt lock where provided. Do not let anyone in your room unless they have properly identified them-selves as a hotel employee. Even then, if you did not request service of some kind, verify their presence by calling the front desk.
- Use hotel safe deposit boxes for large amounts of cash and valuable jewelry when you aren't going to need them. Many hotels provide in-room safes.
- Acquaint yourself with the layout of the hotel. Identify the nearest fire exit and be sure everyone in your party, including children, knows what to do in case of a fire. (Fire precautions and escape routes are posted in each room – be sure to read them carefully.) Do not use elevators during a fire; always use the stairs.
- The busy and exciting surroundings can make it easy to get distracted as a pedestrian. Always exercise caution when crossing streets, especially the Strip and other major thoroughfares, which have multiple lanes and are quite wide. Wait for the signal that it is safe to cross. Use pedestrian bridges whenever they are available and *never* attempt to circumvent a bridge by crossing at street level where access to pedestrians has been blocked off. To do so is definitely asking for trouble.

• Although this is the desert and there is little rainfall, sudden downpours (especially summer thunderstorms) can result in flash flooding. This isn't a major problem along the Strip or downtown where any flooding is usually more of a nuisance than a danger, but it can be a life-and-death problem in outlying areas. Never cross a road that is flooded and stay away from all natural or man-made depressions and washes. You could quickly get swept away in a torrent from only a few minutes of heavy rain.

• The area surrounding Las Vegas used to be mining country and is filled with numerous abandoned mines. None of these are safe. People have been killed trying to explore these relics of the past, so *keep out!*

SENIOR CITIZENS

Discounts for senior citizens are often available for the asking. This includes airfare, hotels, restaurants, car rental, area attractions and even some shopping. So it pays to get some details from the right sources. Vegas is a great town for discounts so seniors can usually do pretty well for themselves here. Identification cards from such organizations like the **American Association of Retired Persons** (AARP) are often useful. These organizations sometimes even have special travel services for seniors.

Whether you're seeking general information or specific activities and events for seniors, a good source is the **Senior Citizens Center of Las Vegas and Clark County**, *450 E. Bonanza Road, four blocks from Casino Center Blvd, Tel. 702/229-6454.*

TAXES

The sales tax in Las Vegas is 7.25% and is added to the cost of all purchases with only a few exceptions. There is no sales tax on services. An additional 2% tax is levied on the cost of hotel rooms. But the worst tax that the state of Nevada soaks visitors for is the 17.25% (including the sales tax) on entertainment. This includes all shows and even restaurants, which offer a formal entertainment program. Well, someone has to help pay for the residents' services!

TELEPHONES

Nevada has two area codes but visitors to Las Vegas will generally only have to concern themselves with one. The **702** area code covers all of Clark County (which encompasses the entire Las Vegas area). Note that it may be necessary to use the 1-702 area code prefix for some of the outlying portions of Clark County. The "1" prefix is required before all other area codes and for all toll free calls (800, 877 and 888 area codes).

Public telephones are easy to find in all of the hotels. A local call costs 35 cents for the first three minutes.

When using a telephone from your hotel room be sure you understand the additional costs imposed by the hotel. This is usually clearly explained in printed material by the phone or in the guest's information booklet. If you have any questions be sure to call the front desk for clarification.

TIME OF DAY

Las Vegas is in the **Pacific Time Zone** (three hours earlier than the east coast) and it observes Daylight Savings Time. It's a good idea to wear a watch because it isn't easy to find a clock in any casino!

TIPPING

Las Vegas didn't invent the "folding favor" but tipping is a way of life in this city. So, more than ever the question that we must ask ourselves is: how much should I tip this guy or gal? Tipping varies from country to country so here a few rules for tipping Vegas-style. Of course, if you hit the million-dollar jackpot you'll probably feel like being more generous than the advice given here!

Gratuities are not built into the check at restaurants unless you have a party of more than a certain number, usually beginning at eight but sometimes less. For good restaurant service a 15% tip is the norm. You can be a big tipper by leaving 20% or more, which many people do if they feel the service is outstanding. Don't forget to tip your server at a buffet (the person who brings your drink and clears away the plates for the next round of eating). Many people think they don't have to, but it is customary to leave about one to two dollars a person for dinner. At the bar, leave a dollar for each round of drinks ordered. The same is true for the cocktail waitress in the casino who brings you your "free" drink. Valet parking attendants also need to be given a George or two.

For taxis, the standard tip is 10%; 10-15% for limousines. Give your bellhop a dollar or two for bringing your bags to your room but $3 or more if you have a number of heavy bags. A dollar per day is considered to be acceptable as a gratuity for your chambermaid. The gaming chapter has additional suggestions for tipping at the table.

In the old days you had to give an exorbitant tip to the maitre'd hotel in showrooms in order to get a good seat. Fortunately, almost every showroom has now gone to an assigned seating system so you don't have to tip the individual taking you to your seat. On the other hand, a dollar would be a nice gesture on your part. Those shows with cocktail service (as opposed to the self-service bars which are becoming more the norm) often include the gratuity in the price of the ticket. If not, a dollar per drink will be sufficient.

COMPS, LAS VEGAS STYLE

The bigger brother of fun books are **comps** *(literally, complimentary), which is gambling jargon for freebies. They are available to anyone who will be doing some serious gambling. Casinos will gladly supply you with comps for meals (including the better eating establishments), shows, rooms and even airfare. But it doesn't come easy or free; you've got to earn it by showing the casinos a sufficient level of action, or play.*

What about your acquaintance who constantly gets comped for the whole deal – airfare, room, shows and food? Jealous? Don't be. These comps are earned the hard way, and in all likelihood these gamblers drop so much money at the tables that the casinos are glad to comp them the whole shebang – again and again. Wouldn't you? A running joke in Las Vegas is the guy who finally sees the light and laments that his free breakfast cost him $389!

If you're looking to earn comps by gambling it will mean more than just gambling at your own pace. But if you're already a big player than comps are the way to go. The casinos will be more than happy to make you feel comfortable if you give them the chance at your gambling dollars.

How do you go about getting comps? It's simple – ask for them. The casino will let you know the deal. Or if you're already in the casino playing, don't be afraid to ask for some comps. A subtle suggestion to the pit boss such as "How's the food in the grill?" or "How's the show?" should get the message across. If your play is seen as adequate, hey, have a great meal – on the house.

Another type of comp is the **slot club***. See the sidebar on this in Chapter 11.*

7. ARRIVALS & DEPARTURES

GEOGRAPHIC ORIENTATION

Las Vegas sits in the southeastern tip of the state of Nevada. Clark County is bordered by three other states: California to the west, Utah to the northeast, and Arizona to the east and southeast. Situated in a beautiful valley about 2,100 feet above sea level, Las Vegas has low humidity – about 29 percent on average but usually lower in the summer – and ranges from hot to mild.

The highest mountains that rim the valley are to the west of the Strip. These are the **Spring Mountains**, with 11,918-foot high **Charleston Peak** being the tallest of the group. Several smaller ranges lie to the east with the dominant landmark being **Sunrise Mountain**. The southern border of the valley is the **Railroad Pass**. Just to the south of the pass is Boulder City, the **Lake Mead National Recreation Area** and **Hoover Dam**. The northern end of the valley doesn't have such a sharp beginning – it more or less fades away into other mountain rimmed desert valleys.

There aren't any significant rivers in the Valley – only a few **washes** that are usually dry except after torrential rains – and no natural lakes. There are a number of nice man-made lakes throughout the Valley.

BY AIR

The point of entry and exit for many of the 35 million visitors to Las Vegas is the large and modern **McCarran International Airport** (*general information: Tel. 702/261-4028; terminal paging: Tel. 702/261-5733*). McCarran is one of the busiest airports in the United States, remarkable for a city of Las Vegas' size.

More than 20 airlines serve Las Vegas and there are many additional charter lines. With the addition of the "D" gates in 1998, McCarran retains its leading position as one of the most modern, attractive and efficient airport facilities in the world. Moving walkways help you negotiate the long distances between the main terminal check-in and baggage areas and the gates. The "C" and "D" gates are reached from the main terminal via an automated rail system. The ride to the "D" gates is both elevated and underground.

When departing Las Vegas by air don't cut your time too short. Getting to your destination gate can be a long trip and with the crowds that often abound at peak periods you may find yourself having to run to catch your plane.

EASY-IN...EASY-OUT

Among the hassles of traveling anywhere are long lines to get registered in or check out of a hotel, and transporting your baggage. While these problems aren't unique to Las Vegas they can be aggravated to some degree in this town because of huge hotels and crowds. Even at quiet times there can be a horde of people trying to get into their rooms. This problem has traditionally been among the major complaints of travelers to Las Vegas.

*Many Las Vegas hotels have responded to the challenge of dealing with these long lines by coming up with a unique approach that begins as soon as you arrive at the airport. Several hotels now have **check-in services at McCarran Airport** so that when you get to the hotel you already have your key and can go directly to your room. Even your luggage will have been transported to the hotel without you having had to lug it around. Check-out has been made easier as well. Most hotels have electronic checkout that can be done via your room television, which is connected to the hotel's computer system. A few hotels have gone a step further and allow you to avoid lines at the airport by actually getting your boarding pass at the time you check out of the hotel! Now, that's a great idea. This is presently limited to only a few establishments, but the practice is likely to grow – ask your hotel when you book.*

***CAPS**, or **Chartered Airline Passenger Service**, takes airline passengers' baggage from hotels to the airport (and vice versa) for $6 each way. The hotels currently offering this service are the Aladdin, Bally's, Flamingo Las Vegas, Imperial Palace, Las Vegas Hilton, the Luxor, Mandalay Bay, Paris, the Riviera, and Sahara. Cooperating airlines are AmericaWest, Delta, Southwest, Sun Country and Virgin Atlantic. Again, both lists will probably be expanding soon since the service has proven to be quite popular.*

FROM THE AIRPORT TO THE CITY
Limos & Taxis

The city's bus service has two lines that go out to the airport but they aren't a convenient way to get to the Strip or most other areas with hotels.

McCarran is close in, however, just one mile from the southern part of the Strip and about five miles from downtown. You might want to consider taking one of the many **limousine services** located in front of the terminal (about $3.50 per person to the Strip and about $5 to downtown). The largest of these operators are **Ambassador Limo**, *Tel. 702/362-6200*, **Bell Transportation**, *Tel. 702/385-5466* and **LV Limo**, *Tel. 702/739-8414*. More expensive limos with upgraded services (like you need it for a ten minute ride!) is available from **Presidential**, *Tel. 702/731-5577* or **AKA Luxury Limo**, *Tel. 702/257-7433*.

The **Gray Line** airport shuttle, *Tel. 702/739-5700*, runs about the same price as a limo but isn't as much fun. You need to reserve the shuttle at least one day in advance. Other similar shuttle services are provided by **Star Trans**, *Tel. 702/646-4661* and **Bell Trans Shuttle**, *Tel. 702/739-7990*. Gray Line and other shuttle buses pick you up on the street across from the baggage claim area.

Taxis are also readily available at the terminal, but it'll cost you about twice as much as one of the limo or shuttle services. Among the larger taxi companies you'll see at the airport and around town are:
• **Ace Cab**, *Tel. 702/736-8383*
• **Checker Cab**, *Tel. 702/873-2000*
• **Desert Cab**, *Tel. 702/376-2687*
• **Western Cab**, *Tel. 702/382-7100*
• **Whittlesea Blue Cab**, *Tel. 702/384-6111*

You should definitely inquire with your hotel before you arrive to see if they offer free limo or van pickup from the airport. Such services used to be rare (except for high rollers) but they have become more common in recent years.

Car Rentals

If you want to rent a car, a number of car rental agencies have cars waiting for you just outside the airport and at selected hotels in the city.

It's always a good idea to call ahead and book a car, especially during peak periods such as weekends and major holidays. Car rental prices in Las Vegas are generally lower than in most places elsewhere in the country but do be sure to check on things such as free mileage if you plan to take any excursions out of town. Following are among the many car rental agencies you'll find in town, separated by national chains and local operators. The local phone number is either a central reservation point for all locations or is the office nearest the airport.

Note: **[A]**=airport location; **[S]**=Strip location; **[O]**=other location. An airport location doesn't always mean that the car will actually be within the confines of the airport. Sometimes it will be a short shuttle bus ride away but transportation is always provided at no extra charge.

National Chains
- **Alamo**, *Tel. 800/327-9633 or 702/263-8411.* A
- **Avis**, *Tel. 800/831-2847 or 702/261-5595.* A-S-O
- **Budget**, *Tel. 800/527-0700 or 702/736-1212.* A-S-O
- **Dollar**, *Tel. 800/800-4000 or 702/739-8408.* A-S
- **Enterprise**, *Tel. 800/736-8222 or 702/795-8842.* A-S-O
- **Hertz**, *Tel. 800/654-3131 or 702/736-4900.* A-S
- **National**, *Tel. 800/227-7368 or 702/261-5391.* A
- **Thrifty**, *Tel. 800/367-2277 or 702/896-7600.* A

Am EXP.
Emerald Club

Major Local or Regional Companies
- **Allstate**, *Tel. 800/634-6186 or 702/736-6147.* A-O
- **Practical Rent A Car**, *Tel. 800/233-1663 or 702/798-5253.* S
- **Resort**, *Tel. 800/289-5343 or 702/388-2142*
- **Savmor Rent A Car**, *Tel. 800/634-6779 or 702/736-1234.* A
- **US Rent A Car**, *Tel. 800/777-9377 or 702/798-6100.* A

BY BUS

Greyhound buses serve Las Vegas from all directions. It is the cheapest way to travel by far. *The main bus terminal is located downtown at 200 S. Main Street near Jackie Gaughan's Plaza Hotel; Tel. 702/384-8009 for the bus station, Tel. 800/231-2222 for reservations.* Greyhound has additional service to other parts of the Las Vegas area. They make stops at Station Casino locations around town. The schedules there aren't as extensive as at the main location but if you're staying off-Strip make inquiry at the time of booking.

BY CAR

If you're coming by car make sure that you have a full tank of gas, a spare tire and plenty of water because gas stations are few and far between on some stretches of the road and you wouldn't want to get caught short in the middle. Even if your car is in great shape, bring plenty of water as emergency protection against overheating. This is most important during the summer. Don't forget, it's a desert out there.

Driving long distances in the glaring sun can be hard on your eyes, so be sure to have a good pair of sunglasses. And we certainly hope your air conditioner is in proper working order. Summer temperatures will climb into the 100's just about every day and you might soon get to know what dough goes through to become bread.

Driving conditions are generally excellent but you should be aware that there could be occasional dust storms and winter snowstorms in the high mountain passes. In the event of a dust storm make sure your lights are on and drive cautiously. If visibility decreases to the point where you cannot see clearly then slowly pull off the road and wait for it to subside. You will also probably encounter at some point the almost inevitable road construction delay as well as heavy traffic. The latter, however, seems to be a bigger problem getting out of town after a busy weekend then when coming in.

Here are some numbers you might want to call for road conditions depending upon which way you're coming into town:

• **Nevada**, *Tel. 702/486-3116*
• **California**, *Tel. 213/628-7623 (southern) or 916/445-1534 (northern)*
• **Arizona**, *Tel. 520/779-2711*
• **Utah**, *Tel. 800/492-2400*

DRIVING DIRECTIONS

From **Los Angeles** take any major highway to I-10 heading east (the San Bernadino Freeway) past Ontario and then take I-15 north all the way into town. The trip is about 290 miles and should take about 4-1/2 hours without heavy traffic. The speed limit is 65mph up to the Nevada line where it goes up to 75mph for a short time until you get nearer to Las Vegas.

There is sometimes heavy fog near the Angeles Forest and, in the winter, passes in the high desert above 4,500 feet may get snowed in and require chains. Sometimes they may be closed altogether for short periods.

From other points in **Southern California** you'll still want to hook up with I-15 at the earliest opportunity and take it all the way into town as discussed above.

From **Northeastern Nevada** take US Highway 93 south until you hit I-15 and then go south on I-15. From **Utah** take I-15 south until you see the neon of Las Vegas. Cross-country travelers in the middle or northern part of the country can intersect with I-15 south from Interstate highways 70, 80 and 90.

From **Phoenix or Tucson** go north on US 93 past the Lake Mead National Recreation Area. This runs into I-515 and you can take either the Flamingo Road or Tropicana Avenue exits and proceed west to the Strip. I-515 continues directly into downtown if you're staying in that part of town. Strip hotels can alternatively be reached by using the Lake Mead Drive/I-215 exit of I-515 and taking I-215 west. It has exits at Las Vegas Boulevard and I-15.

From the **east** (and any time your route will take you past Flagstaff, Arizona, just south of the Grand Canyon), take I-40 to Kingman and the go north on US Highway 93 as indicated above.

BY TRAIN

There used to be regular Amtrak service into downtown Las Vegas – literally the heart of downtown as the station was located inside the Plaza Hotel. This service was discontinued a number of years ago. However, planning and reconstruction of track has begun to resume service from Los Angeles. When it does resume it will feature the high-speed Spanish *Talgo* trains. There is also talk of adding an additional station closer to the Strip.

But right now things are still up in the air – or maybe, off the track would be better. In the meantime, keep listening for that train whistle and periodically check with Amtrak if you would like to come to Vegas by train from Southern California. Amtrak does provide connecting bus service from Los Angeles at the present time.

8. GETTING AROUND TOWN

Las Vegas is an easy place to get around in without worrying about getting lost. Many of the big hotels on the Strip are within walking distance from each other, as are the casinos in the smaller downtown area, though you will need transportation between those two areas and to get to surrounding areas and excursion destinations.

BY FOOT

It's easy to walk the Strip or downtown. You won't need any transportation within these areas other than your feet unless your hotel is away from the Strip, you're feeling a bit lazy, or you've been withered by a hot desert sun that gets as high as 115 degrees in the summer. In such instances taxis or a city bus will nicely complement the pedestrian mode. Even when they're "next door" to one another, Las Vegas hotel properties are often so huge that it takes quite a bit of walking to get around. Wearing comfortable shoes is an absolute must.

Keep in mind that it is over four miles from one end of the Strip to the other so you either have to do it in small sections or rely on another means of transportation. Downtown is a couple of miles north of the northern end of the Strip and the main area is only about five blocks long.

We won't hesitate to repeat ourselves from earlier and remind you to always be alert for traffic when crossing the Strip. Drivers are just as preoccupied as pedestrians and this can lead to tragic consequences. Fortunately, this problem no longer exists at some of the Strip's busiest areas because a system of pedestrian bridges allows walkers to avoid traffic and cars to avoid the pedestrians. It also helps to ease traffic congestion a bit. The bridges, which are handicapped accessible, also offer great views of the Strip scene by day and night. Bridges connect all four corners of the Strip's intersection with Flamingo Road and Tropicana Avenue. There is also another bridge located just south of Spring Mountain Road and it connects the Treasure Island and Mirage vicinity with the Venetian. Other bridge possibilities are in the talking stage only so it means extra caution is in order when crossing at all other locations.

BY CAR

Despite the good results you can get sightseeing on foot, there is still nothing like the flexibility of a car. This convenience becomes a necessity if you're going to be venturing further afield and don't want to go the guided tour route. Las Vegas is an easy place to get around by car since the major streets are generally in a grid pattern and there are only a few important routes that you need to be familiar with. So let's start with a brief lay-of-the-land description.

Las Vegas Boulevard South is the main street of interest to visitors. That's the official designation of what is simply called "the Strip" – by both visitors and residents. It runs from north to south and is paralleled to the west by I-15. Another major arterial highway is I-515 (also US 93 and US 95) which runs from east to west just north of downtown (intersecting with I-15) and then it turns southeasterly and runs roughly parallel to the old Boulder Highway through Las Vegas and then on into Henderson and beyond. I-215 will eventually be a beltway system around much of the valley. For now it runs from just west of I-515 in Henderson to beyond I-15 and the Strip before turning north and ending at Summerlin Parkway. Part of the roadway is, at the present time, not a full highway but an interim frontage road.

The major east-west thoroughfares that cross the Strip are (from south to north): Tropicana Avenue, Flamingo Road, Sands Avenue (Spring Mountain Road from the Strip west), Sahara Avenue and Charleston Boulevard. Another important route is Desert Inn Road; however, in the area by the Strip it is a controlled access highway that goes underneath Las Vegas Boulevard without direct access to it.

It's now time for a dose of reality – dealing with traffic, especially on the Strip. Unfortunately, the Strip can be a horror to drive on at most times of the day and evening (after about ten in the morning at least through 11pm). It's often bumper to bumper and as things crawl along you'll see pedestrians whizzing past you. The best advice is to try to avoid driving on the Strip at all (except for what is, among visitors, almost an obligatory nighttime cruise to see Glitter City in action). There are a couple of ways to avoid the Strip or at least portions of it. On the west side of the Strip you can use **Industrial Road** to travel north-south roughly parallel to Las Vegas Boulevard and I-15. It is immediately behind the Strip hotels from Sahara Avenue south to the vicinity of Caesars Palace. Then it crosses over to the other side of I-15 but still provides access via all of the major intersecting streets. More help is on the way. **Frank Sinatra Drive** is scheduled to be completed by the end of 2001. This will run behind the hotels from Russell Road in the south to Flamingo Road in the north. On the east side the alternatives aren't as good since there aren't any parallel streets that run a long distance that are close to Las Vegas Boulevard. However, you can try using Koval Lane between Tropicana Avenue and Sands Avenue.

Traffic in places other than the Strip is commensurate with what you would expect in a big city. The good system of highways and broad streets keep it generally tolerable although the locals complain about it all the time. I-15 is crowded most of the time and road construction to add needed lanes doesn't help the situation. However, this project is nearing completion and there should be some relief in sight. Perhaps the most exasperating part of coping with driving in Las Vegas is not the traffic

GARAGE SECRETS

We have already alluded to how big the hotels are. The same goes for the garages and some places are easier to park in than others. It isn't always best to park where you'll be for a couple of hours – sometimes a nearby hotel will give you less headaches when it comes to getting in and out.

The newer hotels usually have a central or side ramp that accesses all levels of the garage so you don't have to get dizzy going round and round from one level to another. A few examples of these are Bellagio, Caesars, the Mirage, Treasure Island, and the Venetian. Some, such as the Luxor and Excalibur, have only two-level garages, so they're easy too. Avoid the MGM Grand garage if you can. It's big, confusing and has a naturally crowded design that is only partially helped by the addition of a new wing. If you're going to the Grand try parking at the Tropicana instead.

Almost all garages have direct access to the casino/hotel, often without going out into the street. To avoid waiting for elevators you should try to park on the garage level that has the bridge or other connection to the casino. Of course, these levels tend to fill up faster. If you're not going to park on the access level than the best alternative strategy is to head for a higher level which fills up slower and is, therefore, easier to find a space on. Likewise, more spaces are usually to be found further away from the casino end of the garage. Again, the time you spend walking will probably be less than trying to find a closer-in space. When parking at Mandalay Bay avoid the front elevators nearest to the casino unless you're parked right near them. They're almost always jammed, so it's better to use the elevator bank located in the center of the garage. Actually, along with the MGM, the Mandalay Bay garage is another one to avoid if you can.

itself but the long traffic signals at major intersections. With every-way turn lane lights it seems that you never get the green. Just be patient and your turn will eventually come. The flip side of this system is that a lot of cars can get through turns and you don't have to fight your way to make a left. Note that right hand turns are permitted on red unless specifically indicated otherwise. When away from the Strip be sure to monitor school zone speed limits carefully as the rules are strictly enforced.

At least parking is never a problem. All of the hotels have plenty of free parking (but in downtown you'll have to validate your parking in the casino). The Strip hotel garages are always behind the hotel itself but, due to the size of many resorts, it can be a little more than a short walk. All hotels have free valet parking which avoids the walking but, of course, it is customary to buy your car back from the valet parker for a buck or two. Moreover, even with the distance of some garages it will usually take longer for the valet to bring your car back than it does to walk to the garage. Studies show the average waiting time for valet service on pick-up is seven to ten minutes.

BY BUS & TROLLEY

Buses are an easy and fairly inexpensive away to get around. The Regional Transportation Commission of Clark County runs the **Citizens Area Transit** bus system that is called **CAT**; *Tel. 702/228-7433 for route information and schedules.* Trips on the Strip usually take longer than the scheduled time but the system is generally reliable.

The Strip has two routes. The main one is #301 and runs from the Vacation Village Hotel & Casino (at Sunset Road about two miles south of where most of the hotels begin) all the way to the Downtown Transportation Center (DTC). Service is frequent and runs 24 hours a day. The Strip Express bus (#302) covers the same route but has limited stops, so be sure to ask the driver before boarding if it will let you off where you are going. The fare is $2.00 and exact change is required. Discounts for frequent travelers are available at the DTC (Stewart and Casino Center Boulevard).

One other line that you may be able to make use of is the #402 Crosstown Express. This line has limited stops but connects many of the city's major shopping centers. CAT has almost 40 other routes that go to just about every part of the Las Vegas Valley. Other routes generally do not have service between the wee hours of 1:30am and 5:30am. The frequency varies by line from about 15 minutes to an hour. In recent years CAT has been increasing the frequency of service on many lines. The fare for all lines other than routes in the 300 series is $1.25 and free transfers between routes are available. Virtually all buses are handicapped accessible and they also have bike racks.

There are two "trolley" services to choose from, depending upon where you are. The privately owned and operated **Las Vegas Strip Trolley**, *Tel. 702/382-1404*, covers the Strip from the Stratosphere Hotel on the north side, all of the way down to Mandalay Bay at the southern end. The Trolley has the added convenience over the city buses of dropping you off at the doorway of most major hotels. This can save a fair amount of walking over CAT buses but it takes even longer as it can be a time consuming affair driving into and out of each hotel drop-off point. The charge is $1.50 (exact change required). The Strip Trolley begins at 9:30am and runs until 2am at approximately 15 minute intervals. The **Downtown Trolley**, *Tel. 702/229-6024*, is a bargain at 50 cents (and 25 cents for seniors) but it only covers (besides the small downtown core where you don't need wheels) an area that is off the visitor path. It's run by the city and operates until 10pm. Both trolleys are actually buses made to look like old-time trolley cars.

If you're not staying on the Strip and do not have a car, then be sure to make an inquiry as to shuttle services provided by the hotel you are staying at (or nearby ones). Many off-Strip properties, especially those not too far from the Strip, provide free transportation to and from the hotel. Some of the Strip hotels also have regular bus service to their non-Strip-affiliated hotels or otherwise. Two examples are the service between the Stardust (Strip) and Sam's Town (Boulder Highway); and between the MGM Grand (Strip) and Sunset Station (Henderson). The Rio also provides Strip transportation as does Coast Hotels, which has a bus connecting all of its properties to the Barbary Coast on the Strip.

BY TAXI & LIMOUSINE

Taxis are plentiful and easy to get either on the Strip or downtown. They're a bit tougher to get outside the main tourist areas. In fact, at other locations it is best to call for one. On the Strip they're lined up at every hotel waiting for fares. The current cost is $2.20 for the initial drop of the meter and then $1.60 for each mile thereafter, with nominal extra charges for more than three passengers. Then they also tack on 35 cents for each minute of waiting time. As in most cities, hold on to your hat – Las Vegas cabbies are justly famous for their aggressive approach to negotiating Strip traffic!

If taking a cab is not your bag, go for a limo. They're a fun way to travel in style, if you can afford it or simply want to splurge. The rates are reasonable compared to some cities – a range of $35 to $45 an hour to much more for some huge stretch limos, depending upon the amenities offered.

The standard limo offers a comfortable ride and a few amenities like stereo sound and a car phone. The stretch limos (which run about $60-$80

YOUR MAGIC LOCATOR GUIDE

To help arrange things more easily for you, all information on where to stay and eat, seeing the sights, nightlife and entertainment, as well as shopping, will be divided into five geographic sections in each of the chapters on the aforementioned topics. These are as follows:

The Strip: Las Vegas Boulevard South extending from Russell Road at the southern end to the intersection of Main Street (a little north of Sahara Avenue) in the north.

Off Strip: Areas adjacent to or very near the Strip. Establishments will either be on streets that cross Las Vegas Boulevard South or along Paradise Road between Tropicana Avenue and the Convention Center. It also covers Las Vegas Boulevard south of Russell Road.

Downtown: The old "casino center" area of Fremont Street and the surrounding blocks.

Around Las Vegas: Everything not included in the three above areas or in the following one. This area covers Summerlin as well as the so-called "Boulder Strip", which is Boulder Highway from its beginnings at Fremont Street all the way to the Henderson line.

Henderson: Anything within the city limits of Henderson, including Lake Las Vegas.

per hour) include bar service, cellular phone, color TV, stereo and other amenities. Sound too high for you? Well, what the heck – you're in Vegas. Treat yourself to one limo ride, have your picture taken, and make copies for all of your friends back home. The names and telephone numbers of the main taxi companies and limos are listed in Chapter 7, in the section on getting into town from the airport.

BY MONORAIL & TRAM

There are several short monorails and automated trams serving a number of Strip hotels. The oldest and still the longest is the one that connects the MGM to Bally's and Paris. The sleek Disneyland-style monorail runs from 9am until 1am. Another connects Monte Carlo with the Bellagio. The futuristic looking high-tech cars contrast sharply with the traditional interiors of these hotels. It runs 24 hours a day at approximately five minute intervals. Mandalay Resort Group operates a tram along its "Miracle Mile" with stops at the Excalibur, Luxor and Mandalay Bay. The station sequence can be a little confusing depending upon the direction you're traveling in so always read signs or ask questions. The line runs all day except between the wee hours of 2am and

4am. A third tram, and this one is very short, can take you between the Mirage and neighboring Treasure Island at all times except between 4am and 8am (closed only between 5am and 7am on Saturday and Sunday). All of the hotel transit systems are free of charge.

After years of talk (argument would be a better description), construction has finally begun on a more comprehensive Strip monorail system. It is a public-private project that, unlike hotel monorails, will be at a cost to the user. The problem is the word "Strip" because the location of the system won't make it particularly convenient for a lot of hotels. However, since it won't be in operation until 2004 we need not dwell on it for now. Government officials are also considering a future enhancement, which would extend the monorail to downtown and to the airport.

BY GUIDED TOUR

There are several companies offering guided tours that you might want to consider in lieu of renting a car. All offer city tours, trips to Hoover Dam and other locations within hailing distance of Las Vegas. Many offer longer excursion trips as well. For more information, see the section on excursions.

The more reliable tour operators for day trips ordinary and unusual are listed below. All arrange for pick-up at major hotels. If you're not staying at one of those then they'll tell you to meet them at their nearest pick-up point. Some will pick up at any hotel but may charge for this service.

• **Cactus Jack's Wild West Tour Co.**, *Tel. 702/731-2425*
• **Gray Line**, *Tel. 702/384-1234*
• **Guaranteed Tours**, *Tel. 702/369-1000*
• **Las Vegas Tour & Travel**, *Tel. 702/739-8975*
• **Sightseeing Tours Unlimited**, *Tel. 702/471-7155*

If you're interested in a more unusual type of tour that almost borders on "adventure," then consider **ATV Action Tours**, *Tel. 702/566-7400.* This firm specializes in highly personalized trips in sport utility vehicles for two to ten people. Besides the usual sights around Las Vegas, ATV Action will take you to the Extra-Terrestrial Highway, "Area 51," ghost towns, or just about any other place you might be interested in.

9. WHERE TO STAY

You're not going to read about pirate ship battles and volcanoes in this chapter. This is about hotels as places to stay, as in sleep (often a preciously limited item while in Las Vegas). Many of the hotels are, of course, important visitor attractions and, if they fall into this category, you will be referred to Chapter 12 for details. For those hotels that are not included under sightseeing, there will be a more complete general description of the property in this chapter.

Most of the major hotels have a "theme" whether it's in the lower price category such as Excalibur or the upscale Bellagio. The themes are almost as numerous as the hotels. Ancient civilizations or historical eras, famous cities, carnivals, and tropical motifs are among the most popular. The theme vogue has even spread off-Strip in recent years although not to the same extent. Downtown, on the other hand, remains essentially a place of hotels without a particular genre.

There was a time when Las Vegas hotel room prices were among the lowest in the country, even for the "top" hotels. Unfortunately, this is no longer the case as a result of several factors. Although gambling still is the biggest profit center for every hotel/casino, the new corporate structure of Vegas requires that each separate cost center (e.g., rooms, restaurants, entertainment) pulls its own weight financially. Cost increase number one. The emergence of world class hotels that *Conde Naste* would be proud of has had a large influence on prices because it makes it easier for even the lower end hotels to raise their rates. Cost increase number two. And, despite the availability of the nation's largest inventory of hotel rooms, demand has been fantastic and you know what that means, don't you? Cost increase number three! Yet, despite our complaints about the good old days of low hotel prices, Las Vegas still remains on a par or below the cost of most other major resorts and large cities. You just have to know how to find it and we'll try and help you along with that if you're a cost conscious visitor.

We've arranged the hotels by cost as shown in the table below. The rates shown and, hence, which category the hotel is listed in, are based on the so-called **rack rate**. However, in Las Vegas reality is nothing like what it seems to be at first glance. Since there is such a huge variation in the rack rate we've categorized each hotel by its average annual rack rate. The charges shown are based on double occupancy. Rates for suites will often be listed separately from those for "regular" rooms. In those instances where only one price range is shown it will be for standard through upgraded rooms. Suite prices have been omitted in these instances because there is, in our opinion, no reliable way to even come up with a meaningful estimate. Although each hotel professes to have a rack rate, in reality there is almost no such thing. The price for the same room in the same hotel can vary by an extraordinary amount depending upon when you stay there. Weekends and holidays are, of course, higher priced as are the busier months of the year. Special events like Super Bowl Sunday, the National Rodeos Final or major conventions also raise the price.

On the other hand, with all of the competition these days, the rates can also frequently be discounted from the rack rate. Travel agent-arranged packages often get good rates but you can get it on your own if you pick out the proper time. The harsh reality of the situation is that if reservations for a particular night should suddenly pick up, the rates will rise accordingly. With computers tracking occupancy and trends, the hotels can and do change on a moment's notice. Hotel management points out that prices can vary "widely." "Wildly" would be more appropriate. In short, the listed hotel prices are just a guide and may well bear little resemblance to the rate you actually get. (Return customers who have a track record of playing should make that known when reserving – the "casino" rate is usually an excellent price.)

When you have about 125,000 hotel rooms in one place, it obviously allows the buyer some space for maneuvering. Even so, things pretty well fill up at busy times and aren't ever really that slow. The overall occupancy rate is around 90 percent. That figure is the envy of the hotel industry which, on a nationwide basis, averages about a 70-75% occupancy rate. In addition, the Strip is higher than 90% – it's more like 95% filled because the total citywide figure is brought down by the large number of smaller hotels and motels that only average occupancy in the 60's or 70's. They are a good choice of last resort should the Strip be booked when you want to be in town.

Having said that, it should be apparent that advance room reservations are the way to go. If you are not booking through a travel agent you can make reservations with all of the major hotels through their own toll-free reservation number or, in most cases, via the internet. In addition, there are several general booking services for Las Vegas.

These are:
- **Accommodations Express**, *Tel. 800/211-3836 or 702/795-7666*
- **A to Z Reservation Service of Las Vegas** *Tel. 800/634-6727 or 702/736-2226*
- **Hotel Reservations Network**, *Tel. 800/964-6835; www.hoteldiscount.com.*
- **Las Vegas Convention & Visitors Bureau**, *Tel. 702/386-0770*
- **Las Vegas Reservations Systems**, *Tel. 800/233-5594 or 702/369-1919; www.lvrs.com*
- **Travelscape**, *Tel. 888/335-010; www.travelscape.com*

For those of you who like to stay in a national chain because you feel comfortable with their known facilities, they are well represented in the Las Vegas area. The lineup here includes most of the important chains except the luxury chains because those hotels will usually be in the detailed reviews later in this chapter. When a chain has multiple locations, those nearest the Strip are listed first.
- **Amerisuites**, *Tel. 800/833-1516*
  4520 Paradise Road, Tel. 702/369-3366
- **Best Western**, *Tel. 800/528-1234*
  Mardi Gras Inn, 3500 Paradise Road, Tel. 702/731-2020
  McCarran Inn, 4970 Paradise Road, Tel. 702/798-5530
  Parkview Inn, 905 Las Vegas Blvd. N., Tel. 702/385-1213
  Main Street Inn, 1000 N. Main Street, Tel. 702/382-3455
  Heritage Inn, 4975 S. Valley View Blvd., Tel. 702/798-7736
  Nellis Motor Inn, 5330 E. Craig Road (North Las Vegas), Tel. 702/643-6111
  Lake Mead Inn, 85 W. Lake Mead Drive (Henderson), Tel. 702/564-1712
- **Comfort Inn**, *Tel. 800/228-5150*
  211 E. Flamingo Road, Tel. 702/733-7800
  5075 Koval Lane, Tel. 702/736-3600
  910 E. Cheyenne Avenue, Tel. 702/399-1500
- **Courtyard by Marriott**, *Tel. 800/321-2211*
  3275 Paradise Road, Tel. 702/791-3600
  1901 N. Rainbow Blvd., Tel. 702/494-9819
  2600 N. Green Valley Parkway (Henderson), Tel. 702/434-4700

HOTEL ROOM RATE RANGES IN THIS BOOK

All rates are based on double occupancy and are exclusive of taxes:

Very Expensive	*More than $200*
Expensive	*$126-200*
Moderate	*$75-125*
Inexpensive	*Less than $75*

• **Days Inn**, *Tel. 800/329-7466*
  4155 Koval Lane, Tel. 702/731-2111
  5125 Swenson Street, Tel. 702/740-4040
  707 E. Fremont Street, Tel. 702/388-1400
• **Embassy Suites**, *Tel. 800/EMBASSY*
  3600 Paradise Road, Tel. 702/893-8000
  4315 Swenson Street, Tel. 702/795-2800
• **Fairfield Inn**, *800/228-2800*
  3850 Paradise Road, Tel. 702/791-0899
• **Hampton Inn**, *800/426-7866*
  4975 Industrial Road, Tel. 702/948-8100
  7100 Cascade Valley Court [Tenaya Way off of Cheyenne]), Tel. 702/360-5700
  421 Astaire Drive [off of Warm Springs Road & Marks], (Henderson), Tel. 702/992-9292
• **Hawthorne Inn & Suites**, *Tel. 800/527-1133*
  5051 Duke Ellington Way [Reno Ave. off of Koval Lane], Tel. 702/739-7000
  4975 S. Valley View Blvd., Tel. 702/798-7736
  910 S. Boulder Highway (Henderson), Tel. 702/568-7800
• **Holiday Inn**, *Tel. 800/HOLIDAY*
  Crowne Plaza, 4255 Paradise Road, Tel. 702/369-4400
  325 E. Flamingo Road, Tel. 702/732-9100
  8669 W. Sahara Avenue, Tel. 702/256-3766
  4050 Donovan Way [just off of I-15 at Craig Road], Tel. 702/649-3000
  441 Astaire Drive [off of Warm Springs Road & Marks], (Henderson), Tel. 702/990-2323
See regular listings for Holiday Inn Boardwalk and Fitzgerald's Holiday Inn.
• **Howard Johnson**, *Tel. 800/446-4656*
  1401 Las Vegas Blvd. South, Tel. 702/388-0301
  5100 Paradise Road, Tel. 702/798-2777
  3111 W. Tropicana Avenue, Tel. 702/798-1111
• **LaQuinta**, *Tel. 800/531-5900*
  3782 Las Vegas Blvd. South, Tel. 702/739-7457
  3970 Paradise Road, Tel. 702/796-9000
  7101 Cascade Valley Court [Tenaya Way off of Cheyenne], Tel. 702/360-1200
• **Motel 6**, *Tel. 800/331-3131*
  195 E. Tropicana Avenue, Tel. 702/798-0728
  5085 Industrial Road, Tel. 702/739-6747
  4125 Boulder Highway, Tel. 702/457-8051

• **Ramada Inn**, *Tel. 800/2-RAMADA*
  3227 Civic Center Drive (North Las Vegas), Tel. 702/399-3297
• **Residence Inn**, *Tel. 800/331-3131*
  3225 Paradise Road, Tel. 702/796-9300
  370 Hughes Center Drive, Tel. 702/650-0040
  2190 Olympic Avenue [Sunset Road & Green Valley Parkway] (Henderson), Tel. 702/434-2700
• **Rodeway Inn**, *Tel. 800/228-2000*
  167 E. Tropicana Avenue, Tel. 702/795-3311
• **Super 8**, *Tel. 800/800-8000*
  4250 Koval Lane, Tel. 702/794-0888
  4435 Las Vegas Blvd. North (North Las Vegas), Tel. 702/644-5666
  5288 Boulder Highway, Tel. 702/435-8888
• **Travelodge**, *Tel. 800/578-7878*
  3735 Las Vegas Blvd. South, Tel. 702/736-3443
  2830 Las Vegas Blvd. South, Tel. 702/735-4222
  1501 W. Sahara Avenue, Tel. 702/733-0001
  2028 E. Fremont Street, Tel. 702/384-7540

The variety of accommodations in Las Vegas runs the gamut from the most basic motel units to super-luxurious suites that are bigger than most people's houses. Just about the only type of accommodation you won't find in this town is the bed and breakfast inn. It seems that type of lodging doesn't fit in with the atmosphere and has never caught on. The only area B&B is located at Mt. Charleston, not exactly a convenient place to stay if you're going to be spending most of your time on the Strip.

All of the major hotels have extensive facilities for business meetings whether it be for a group of ten or ten thousand. Likewise, the hotels will

---

LOOK FOR RESTAURANT & LOUNGE DESCRIPTIONS IN OTHER CHAPTERS, TOO!

*At the end of each hotel listing there will be separate sections for **dining**, **entertainment** and **other facilities**. Many of these establishments can be found in the appropriate chapters that follow. For example, many restaurants listed in this chapter are also reviewed in the Where to Eat chapter. We'll also mention here that lounges with entertainment will be shown in the Entertainment listing, while drinking establishments without entertainment are referred to as bars and, if present, will be shown in the other facilities category. That last category mainly lists facilities normally associated with a hotel. It does not include what can be termed "attractions" – those are contained in the chapter on seeing the sights.*

be glad to make special rates and facilities for family gatherings and affairs. While this aspect of the hotels won't be discussed there will be, no doubt, some readers who might want to look into this aspect of the resort for their upcoming family or business events. If so, just ask at the front desk for the hotel's sales department and you'll be directed to the right place.

THE STRIP

Very Expensive

BELLAGIO, *3600 Las Vegas Blvd. South. Tel. 702/693-7111, Fax 702/792-7646. Toll free reservations 888/987-3456. Website: www.bellagioresort.com. 3,0005 Rooms. Rates: $159-499. Suites begin around $400. Major credit cards accepted. Located at the southwest corner of Flamingo Road. For Attractions, see Chapter 12.*

Given the elaborate and luxurious nature of Bellagio, you would expect nothing less in the way of accommodations. Bellagio won't disappoint in this regard as the guest rooms are among the loveliest in Las Vegas. The standard room measures a fairly generous 510 square feet and has attractive furnishings along with fine fabrics and wall coverings. The bathrooms have a separate tub and stall shower along with marble tile floors and elegant fixtures. The sleeping area contains a huge armoire that hides a complete entertainment system as well as an in-room safe. All rooms are grouped into one of four basic color patterns (as are all other classes of accommodations) which range from colorful to the more gentle to look at earth tones that are so popular in the southwest. Comfortable chairs and plenty of desk space are two nice features.

The Tower upgrade room (about $30 more) is a little bit fancier and has a whirlpool tub. Aside from these near-suite facilities are various classes of suites. The smallest suites, which are priced only a little above upgraded rooms, aren't out of the affordable price range for many people and are sumptuous homes away from home that feature his and her bathrooms and a TV that pops out of a piece of furniture so as not to block your view when it isn't in use. Many rooms have excellent views of the Strip, Bellagio's beautiful pool area, and the mountains. Getting back to the small suite, we especially like the double columns near the entrance that set off the foyer from the combined sitting/sleeping area. All units have an in-room safe and receive nightly turndown service.

More elaborate suites consist of multi-room units ranging from the one and two bedroom penthouse suites (minimum 1,500 square feet) all the way up to the luxurious private villas that are reserved for special guests of the hotel. Amenities depend upon the level of accommodations (things like slippers and terry cloth robes start at the small suite level), but fine quality toiletries and little conveniences like electronically controlled draperies are pretty well standard throughout all classes of accommodation.

Dining: Aqua (seafood), Cafe Bellagio (24 hour), Osteria del Circo (Italian), Jasmine (Chinese), LeCirque (French), Noodles (Asian), Olives (Mediterranean), Picasso (French/Spanish), Prime (steakhouse), Sam's American, and Shintaro (Japanese). Also, the Buffet and several locales for fast-food, snacks, espresso bar, ice cream and pastries. The Pool Cafe serves light fare.

Entertainment: The main showroom features "O". There are four elegant lounges: Allegro, Baccarat Bar, Fontana, and Petrossian. The latter features an elegant daily afternoon tea between two and five.

Other facilities: Casino, bars, fitness center and European style spa, swimming pools, beauty salon, gift/logo shop, shopping arcade, tennis courts, wedding chapel and game arcade. Arrangements for golf can be made.

FOUR SEASONS HOTEL *3960 Las Vegas Blvd. South. Tel. 702/632-5000, Fax 702/632-5222. Toll free reservations 877/632-5200. Website: www.fourseasons.com. 424 Rooms. Rates: $225-550. Major credit cards accepted. Located on the 35th through the 39th floors of the Mandalay Bay, just north of the intersection of Russell Road. The entrance and check-in area are separate from Mandalay Bay.*

The hotel within a hotel concept does have precedents elsewhere but it is the first such arrangement of its type in Las Vegas. The Four Seasons, however, is much more than just a few floors of another hotel. Besides the separate entry and registration area, it has elevators serving only the Four Season floors and numerous facilities that are located in their own public area away from those of Mandalay Bay. On the other hand, there is a direct connection between the two, so that Four Seasons guests have easy access to, for example, the casino at Mandalay Bay. Thus, Four Seasons' claim that it is a non-gaming hotel is really a technicality. But, the entry of Four Seasons onto the Strip was another important example of the increasing sophistication of the Las Vegas market.

Set on its own grounds that rival Mandalay Bay for exotic beauty if not in size, the Four Seasons brings with it a high level of service that is recognized world wide as a leader in the hotel industry. Nice little touches such as twice daily housekeeping (nightly turn-down service included), bottled water and a cold towel after you return from a morning jog, free use of poolside cabanas and much more, make this a luxurious place to stay. Afternoon tea service is offered daily in the Lobby Lounge.

The luxurious rooms and 86 suites (starting at over $500) offer striking views of the mountains and desert as well as of the Strip. The large and beautifully appointed rooms feature such amenities as in-room safe,

HOTEL/CASINOS

1. Aladdin
2 Alexis Park
3. Bally's
4. Barbary Coast
5. Bellagio
6. Bourbon Street
7. Caesars Palace
8. Circus Circus
9. Excalibur
10. Flamingo Las Vegas
11. Four Seasons
12. Gold Coast
13. Hard Rock
14. Harrah's
15. Holiday Inn Boardwalk
16. Imperial Palace
17. Klondike
18. Las Vegas Hilton
19. Luxor
20. Mandaly Bay
21. Marriott Suites
22. MGM Grand
23. Mirage
24. Monte Carlo
25. New Frontier
26. New York, New York
27. Orleans
28. Palace Station
29. Paris
30. Rio
31. Riviera
32. St. Tropez
33. Sahara
34. San Remo
35. Somerset House
36. Stardust
37. Stratosphere
38. Terrible's
39. Treasure Island
40. Tropicana
41. Vacation Village
42. Venetian
43. Westward Ho
44. Wild Wild West

POINTS OF INTEREST

A. Fashion Show Mall
B. Howard Hughes Center
C. Las Vegas Convention Center
D. Sands Expo & Convention Ctr.
E. Showcase
F. Thomas & Mack Center
G UNLV
H Wet 'N Wild

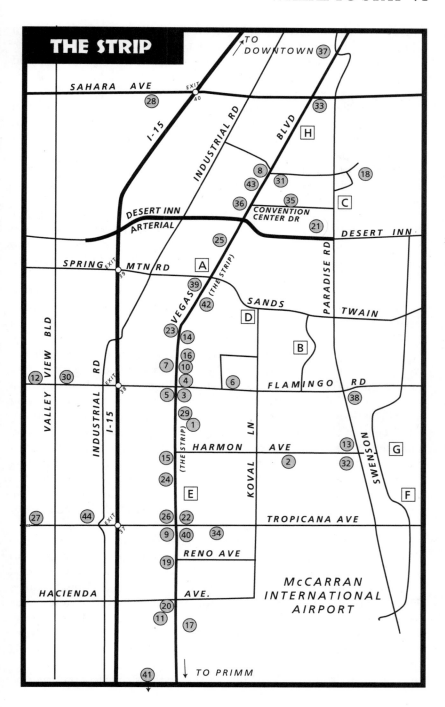

stocked refrigerator, iron/ironing board, non-allergenic foam or down pillows, hair dryer, terry cloth bathrobes, oversized towels and more. The huge bathrooms have a deep tub, separate glass enclosed shower and attractive marble vanities. The furnishings are highlighted by canopy draperies over the bed, a rich wood armoire, night tables and chairs.

Dining: Charlie Palmer Steak House and Verandah Cafe (24 hour). In addition, light snacks are available at the Club Bar, Lobby Lounge and at a poolside grill.

Entertainment: Lounge entertainment at the Club Bar.

Other facilities: Bar, swimming pool (in addition to access to Mandalay Bay's "beach" and wave pool), health and fitness center with complete spa facilities, and gift shop.

THE VENETIAN, *3355 Las Vegas Blvd. South. Tel. 702/414-1000, Fax 702/733-5404. Toll free reservations 877/8-VENICE. Website: www.venetian.com. 3,036 Rooms. Rates: $129-399. Major credit cards accepted. Located just south of the intersection of Sands Avenue (Spring Mountain Road). For Attractions, see Chapter 12.*

Advertised as an all-suite hotel, the Venetian meets opposition on that score from some people because the "standard" unit doesn't actually have separate rooms. However, we see no reason to quibble over labels given the high level of luxury and spaciousness at this elaborate resort.

Consisting of a generous 700 square feet (which is almost double the average hotel room size), the suite begins with a gracious marble foyer entrance area. The rooms have crown moldings and baseboards, and a wrought iron railing separating the bedroom area from a sunken living room. The bedroom features draped bed canopies, huge closet, armoire with Venetian floral designs and a safe. The living room has an entertainment center (each suite has two 27" TVs), mini-bar, fax machine/copier, three telephones and much more – all extremely tasteful and providing the comforts of home. A plush sofa converts into a queen-sized bed so that the entire family can save some money by staying in the same unit. The marble-floored bathrooms are equally impressive with their gold fixtures and generous use of marble accents.

The 4.5 acre outdoor pool area (with five separate swimming pools) is located on the third floor roof of the casino building. It is designed in the style of a Renaissance Venetian garden and contains lovely grounds.

Dining: Delmonico Steakhouse, Grand Lux Cafe (24 hour), Lutece (French), Pinot Brasserie (International), Royal Star (Chinese), Star Canyon (southwestern), and Piero Selvaggio's Valentino & Italian Grille. Restaurants located in the Grand Canal Shoppes are Canaletto (Italian), Postrio (California with Asian and Mediterranean influences), Taqueria Cañonita (Mexican), Tsunami Grill (Asian), Warner Brothers Soundstage 16 (American), and Zeffirino (Italian). There are also two food courts, one off the casino and the other in the shopping mall. Adjacent to Zeffirino is Tintoretto, an Italian bakery.

Entertainment: C2K is a multi-purpose theater/nightclub facility that houses, among other shows, *Melinda, the First Lady of Magic* and impersonator Andre Philippe Gagnon. La Siena Lounge. The *Artistie del Arte* roving entertainers perform in the Grand Canal Shoppes.

Other facilities: Casino, bars, swimming pools, gift/logo shop and shopping. The **Canyon Ranch SpaClub** is one of the world's premier operators of upscale health resorts and this 63,000-square foot health spa and fitness center may well be the most elaborate hotel based facility of its kind in Las Vegas. It features massage, skin care, body treatment rooms, movement therapy and every other imaginable way of improving yourself. It also has, besides its own healthy fare cafe, a beauty salon and medical center along with an indoor swimming pool for water aerobics and lap swimming.

Expensive

ALADDIN HOTEL & CASINO, *3667 Las Vegas Blvd. South. Tel. 702/785-5555, Fax 702/736-7107. Toll free reservations 877/485-2020. Website: www.aladdincasino.com. 2,567 Rooms. Rates: $99-169; suites from $199-5,000. Major credit cards accepted. Located just north of the intersection of Harmon Avenue. For Attractions, see Chapter 12.*

Remember the old Aladdin – one of the least expensive places to stay on the Strip? Well, forget that part because the fabulous new Aladdin is on a par with the most elegant hotels in town, including the prices. One thing that makes Aladdin different than other big Strip hotels is the layout and ease of getting from one place to another. That includes getting to your room. You can do so without having to go through the casino or other vast public areas. Even better, with two central elevator cores instead of the typical single core, no guest room on any floor is more than seven doors away from an elevator. For those who have visited Las Vegas and found themselves exhausted just getting to and from their room, this is definitely a welcome change and we hope it is a trend that future hotels incorporate into their designs. Maybe we've exaggerated the physical requirements of getting to a room just a little bit, but there is no doubt that this is an idea whose time has come. Not having to bring little children through the casino all the time will also be sure to please many parents.

About two thirds of the units are standard rooms while the rest of the accommodations are either upgraded parlor rooms or suites. The standard room isn't among the largest of the newer resorts but is still nicely sized at about 450 square feet. The decor is cheerful and the furnishings are comfortable and functional. We like the elaborate marble bathrooms that feature an oversized tub and a separate shower, not to mention the sink faucets that resemble Aladdin's lamp. Other amenities include internet connections and cordless telephones. There are also upgraded "parlor rooms" and suite accommodations that measure as large as 1,250 square feet.

Dining: Blue Note Cafe (American), Elements (steakhouse), London Club (International), P.F. Chang's China Bistro, and Tremezzo (Italian). Spice Market Buffet and Zanzibar Cafe (24 hour). The Desert Passage restaurants are Anasazi (Southwestern), Beluga Bar (seafood), Bice Ristorante (Italian), Commander's Palace (Cajun), Josef's (French), and Lombardi's (Italian/French). Expected to open just after our press time in the Spring of 2001 are three more dining establishments that will also feature entertainment. They will all turn into "after-hours" nightclubs of one sort or another. These will be Prana (a Eurasian supper club), Ibizia (Mediterranean) and Kass Bah. There are also several fast food establishments (including those in the Alakazam food court), Fat Anthony's (pizza and more) and an Italian deli called the Caffe Ferraro.

Entertainment: Blue Note Jazz Club, Theater for the Performing Arts, and multi-use showroom/nightclub. London Club and Sinbad's Lounge.

Other facilities: Casino, bars, swimming pool, logo/gift shop.

BALLY'S LAS VEGAS, *3645 Las Vegas Blvd. South. Tel. 702/739-4111, Fax 702/794-2413. Toll free reservations 800/634-3434. Website: www.ballyslv.com. 2,818 Rooms. Rates: $99-299; suites from $200. Major credit cards accepted. Located at the southeast corner of Flamingo Road. For Attractions, see Chapter 12.*

Consisting of two 26-story towers, Bally's has long been known for its large (450 square foot standard), commodious and brightly decorated rooms. Since this hotel doesn't have a theme around which to design its rooms, they opt for a simple "touch of class" – Bally's advertising slogan (that's even publicized on the side of one of the monorails that runs to the MGM). The standard rooms are among the better ones of any major hotel. Although Bally's is an older property they've kept the rooms in good shape and all are remodeled on a regular basis. Beyond the standard rooms are various suites with even more space (starting at 900 square feet and going all the way up to 2,000) and luxury. You may even want to opt for one of the Royal Penthouse Suites. They'll only set you back around $2,750 a night!

Dining: al Dente (Italian), Bally's Steakhouse/Sterling Brunch, Chang's (Chinese), Seasons (Continental), and Sidewalk Cafe (24 hours). Big Kitchen Buffet and a fast-food outlet in the casino. Along the shopping arcade are three more fast food places (Italian, Japanese and a deli).

Entertainment: The main showroom features the traditional revue titled *Jubilee!* Indigo Lounge.

Other facilities: Casino, bars, health club and spa, swimming pool, tennis, beauty salon, gift/logo shop, shopping, wedding chapel, and game arcade.

CAESARS PALACE, *3570 Las Vegas Blvd. South. Tel. 702/731-7110, Fax 702/731-7331. Toll free reservations 800/634-6001. Website: www.caesars.com. 2,400 Rooms. Rates: $89-500. Major credit cards accepted. Located at the northeast corner of Flamingo Road. For Attractions, see Chapter 12.*

Old by Las Vegas standards, you would never know it to look at this place. Renovations here seem to be a constant activity and sometimes they can also be characterized as reconstruction. The place just finished another big overhaul that, among other things, made the entire exterior more "Roman" in appearance in keeping with the architecture of one of the newer room towers. The guest rooms have always been and remain among the biggest and best in Las Vegas, regardless of what else they keep building. No wonder that Caesars retains its popularity amongst many return visitors and your authors. The best of the rooms (except for some of the luxury suites) are located in the newer Palace Tower.

Among the features found in many rooms throughout the hotel are mirrored walls and ceilings, round beds, and marble European style baths. Standard rooms in the Palace Tower are one of five different floor plans and average about 650 square feet. They have nine-foot ceilings, wood trimmed cabinets and wall treatments that were inspired by the lavish murals uncovered in Pompeii. The panoramic views from the Palace Tower easily surpass those in the other buildings. Also standard in the tower are whirlpool tubs, in-room safe, and mini-refrigerator.

Convenience amenities are quite numerous and include fine toiletries packaged in containers made to resemble ancient Ionic columns, iron/ironing board, and hair dryer. The closets even have automatic lights activated by sensors to detect when you open the door.

Not that you're likely to be one of the lucky ones staying at a Caesars suite, but just in case you're in the money or a guest of the casino, suites range from about 1,000 square feet to a humongous 11,750 square feet. Choices include Villa suites named for a city of the Roman Empire and contained within a lush Italian garden. There are also Fantasy Suites themed in Roman, Egyptian or Pompeiian decor and Penthouses in the Forum Tower. To say the least, the suites will dazzle even the most experienced connoisseur of fine travel.

Dining: Empress Court (Chinese), Hyakumi (Japanese), Neros (steakhouse), Terrazza (Italian), 808 (European/Pacific Rim). Palatium Buffet, Cafe Lago (24 hour), La Piazza Food Court, and deli. Within the Forum Shops are Bertolini's (Italian), Chinois (Asian), the Palm (American), Spago (International), and many fast, semi-fast and snack places including the Stage Deli and the Cheesecake Factory.

Entertainment: Periodic celebrity entertainment. Lounge entertainment at Cleopatra's Barge, and the La Piazza and Forum Lounges.

Other facilities: three casinos, bars, health spa and fitness center, swimming pools with outdoor whirlpool spa, tennis courts, beauty salon, gift/logo shop, two shopping areas, wedding chapel and game arcade.

MANDALAY BAY, *3950 Las Vegas Blvd. South. Tel. 702/632-7777, Fax 702/632-7100. Toll free reservations 877/632-7800. Website: www.mandalaybay.com. 3,266 Rooms. Rates: $99-269; suites from $250. Major credit cards accepted. Located between the intersections of Tropicana Avenue and Russell Road, immediately to the south of the Luxor. For Attractions, see Chapter 12.*

A distinguished and highly successful member of the new wave of Vegas mega-resorts, the vast 60-acre Mandalay Bay takes its tropical and mystical theme all the way up to each guest room. The standard room averages a nicely spacious 515 square feet and has been ornately appointed by an award-winning interior design team. Each room features, besides floor to ceiling windows for great views, a desk table with two chairs, his and her lighted closets, armoire with large screen TV, and iron/ironing board. Guests receive a robe and slippers. The oversized stone-floored bathrooms have separate tub and shower, twin vanities, telephone and hair dryer.

Mandalay Bay also has several hundred suites that range from just a little bit larger than the standard room, all the way up to a mansion sized 6,670 square feet. Wet bars and a spa type tub are the minimum additional amenities you'll find even in the smallest suite. Rooms on the 34th floor comprise the hotel's House of Blues club and have decor themes of Gothic, Moroccan or East Indian.

Dining: Aureole (American), Border Grill (Mexican), Trattoria del Lupo (Italian), Shanghai Lilly (Cantonese & Szechwan), China Grill, Red Square (Russian/International), Rumjungle (International), House of Blues (Creole/Cajun), Rock Lobster (American/seafood), and Raffle's Cafe (24 hour). Bay Side Buffet and several fast-food places and snack bars.

Entertainment: The Mandalay Bay Theater is now home to a new production show called *Storm. House of Blues* nightclub and entertainment complex; and the Special Events Center which holds 12,000 people and is used for concerts, sporting and other events. Island and Coral Reef Lounges.

Other facilities: Casino, bars, water recreation environment (including swimming pools, artificial beach with wave pool and river ride, and jogging track), health spa and exercise facility, gift/logo shop, shopping, and wedding chapel.

MGM GRAND HOTEL & CASINO, *3799 Las Vegas Blvd. South. Tel. 702/891-1111, Fax 702/891-1030. Toll free reservations 877/880-0880. Website: www.mgmgrand.com. 5,034 Rooms. Rates: $69-329. Major credit cards accepted. Located at the northeast corner of Tropicana Avenue. For Attractions, see Chapter 12.*

The overwhelming majority of the guest rooms (5,034 to be exact) are located in one of four separate 30-story high emerald green towers although, from the outside, the hotel appears as one huge building. Because of the size, some rooms seem like they're miles away from the casino and all the other action. While that's the case in quite a few of the larger Strip hotels, it's even more so at this Goliath. You can choose from one of nine different categories of guest accommodations ranging from standard to the most elaborate suites. The standard rooms are comfortably sized and furnished but nothing in particular to rave about. They do feature elegant black and white marble bathrooms and plenty of closet space.

There are several themes among this class of rooms, all geared to Hollywood in one way or another. Some are generic Hollywood while others take their theme from a particular motion picture such as *Gone With the Wind*. All of the usual amenities are present and we find the spacious closets and extra-thick towels to be nice conveniences.

There are hundreds of suites at the MGM varying a great deal in size and elegance. Starting with the Players Suites, which aren't that much bigger than the basic rooms, you can also choose from Spa, Vista, Lobby, Glamour, Patio, and Vista Parlor Suites, as well as one of 29 private villas in a separate wing called, appropriately enough, the Mansion. The largest suites range up to a staggering 6,000 square feet and some even come with their own elevator and private butler!

Dining: Hollywood Brown Derby (steakhouse), Mark Miller's Grill & Coyote Cafe (Southwestern), Dragon Court (Chinese), Emeril's (seafood), Gatsby's (Continental), Grand Wok (Oriental), Neyla (Mediterranean), Olio (Italian), Rainforest Cafe (American), Ricardo's (Mexican), Studio Cafe (24 hour), and Wolfgang Puck Cafe (American). Grand Buffet, Stage Deli (sandwiches), poolside Cabana Grille and food court.

Entertainment: The EFX Theater presents *EFX Alive!*, a high-tech production show. Celebrity performers appear in the Hollywood Theater and the Cabaret Theater while the biggest names in show business and sporting events take place in the Grand Garden Arena. There are also live performances on the stage of the Showbar Lounge in the Entertainment Dome. Studio 54 nightclub.

Other facilities: Casino, bars, complete spa complex with health and fitness center, swimming pools, beauty salon, gift/logo shop, shopping concourses, game arcade, youth activity center, and wedding chapel.

THE MIRAGE, *3400 Las Vegas Blvd. South. Tel. 702/791-7111, Fax 702/791-7446. Toll free reservations 800/374-9000. Website: www.themirage.com. 3,049 Rooms. Rates: $70-400; suites from $275-1,025. Major credit cards accepted. Located between Flamingo Road and Sands Avenue. For Attractions, see Chapter 12.*

Attention to detail is the hallmark of the finely appointed luxury rooms at the Mirage. Subtle colors like taupe, beige, and pink contrast with black accents. All of the carpeting, draperies, exquisite fabrics and wall coverings were custom designed for the Mirage and its tropical theme. Imported marble is generously used in entry ways and bathrooms. High quality art work graces each room. Few hotels feature "standard" rooms at this level of elegance. Upgraded accommodations feature double sinks, glass enclosed marble showers, whirlpool tubs and his and her closets. The hotel keeps its like-new appearance through one of the most ambitious programs of room remodeling in Las Vegas. It's almost a constant process at the Mirage.

Dining: California Pizza Kitchen, Caribe Cafe (24 hour), Kokomo's (steak and seafood), Mikado (Japanese), Moongate (Chinese), Onda (nouveau Sicilian), Renoir (French), and Samba (Brazilian). Buffet and snack bars.

Entertainment: The production show level magic of *Siegfried & Roy* and Las Vegas icon, celebrity impersonator *Danny Gans* each headline their own separate showrooms. Lounge entertainment at the Baccarat Bar (piano bar) and the lush Lagoon Saloon.

Other facilities: Casino, bars, health spa, swimming pool, golf (off-site), beauty salon, gift/logo shop, and shopping arcade.

NEW YORK, NEW YORK, *3790 Las Vegas Blvd. South. Tel. 702/740-6050, Fax 702/740-6989. Toll free reservations 888/696-9887. Website: www.nynyhotelcasino.com. 2,035 Rooms. Rates: $69-309. Major credit cards accepted. Located at the northwest corner of Tropicana Avenue. For Attractions, see Chapter 12.*

Many people who see New York, New York and don't stay there think that the towering skyscraper replicas are just a fancy facade. They're definitely more than that – they are the room towers, so you can tell people you stayed at the Chrysler Building or other famous New York City landmarks. The nicely decorated rooms and suites are accented in classic art deco style and are generally of a nice size, even if some don't appear to be so. That's because many rooms have a rather unusual shape or odd corners to conform with the unusual exterior shape of the hotel. If you don't mind not staying in a traditional four-corner room, then you shouldn't have any complaints with the accommodations.

Dining: America (24 hour), Chin Chin (Chinese), Gallagher's Steakhouse, Il Fornaio (Italian), ESPN-Zone (American), and Gonzalez y

Gonzalez (Mexican). In addition, the "Village Eateries" are the equivalent of a food court but are attractively arranged in an area that resembles the narrow streets of New York's lower east side. These places range from a kosher style deli to cafes to fast food. There's also a Nathan's Famous and other snack places in the Coney Island Pavilion on the arcade level.

Entertainment: The Michael Flatley inspired *Lord of the Dance* is presented in the Broadway Theater. Lounge entertainment at the Empire Bar and the Bar at Times Square.

Other facilities: Casino, bars, swimming pool, complete health spa and fitness center, beauty salon, gift/logo shop, shopping, and game arcade.

PARIS, *3655 Las Vegas Blvd. South. Tel. 702/946-7000, Fax 702/739-4609. Toll free reservations 877/796-2096. Website: www.paris-lv.com. 2,914 Rooms. Rates: $129-369; suites from $350-$1,219 and specialty suites up to $5,000. Major credit cards accepted. Located adjacent to Bally's just south of the intersection of Flamingo Road. For Attractions, see Chapter 12.*

The rooms in this delightfully themed hotel have an elegance and style that is above par for many Vegas hotels. They all feature beautiful custom designed furnishings, crown moldings, French fabrics and stately armoires. The spacious marble bathrooms boast separate tub and shower with European style fixtures, and an oversized vanity with make-up mirror. Amenities include hair dryer, iron/ironing board and in-room safe.

Dining: Eiffel Tower Restaurant (French), La Rotisserie des Artistes (French), Mon Ami Gabi (brasserie), Le Provencal (Continental), La Cafe Ile St. Louis (24 hour), La Chine (Chinese), Tres Jazz (Caribbean) and du Parc (seasonal poolside cafe). LeVillage Buffet, JJ's Boulangerie.

Entertainment: Le Theatre des Arts currently has celebrity entertainment. Lounge entertainment is available at Le Cabaret bar and the elegant Napoleon's. There's also music at Tres Jazz.

Other facilities: Casino, bars, complete European style spa and health club, swimming pool, tennis courts, beauty salon/barber shop, gift/logo shop, shopping concourse, and wedding chapel.

TREASURE ISLAND *3300 Las Vegas Blvd. South. Tel. 702/894-7111, Fax 702/894-7414. Toll free reservations 800/944-7444. Website: www.treasureisland.com. 2,900 Rooms. Rates: $70-270; suites from $150-1,000. Major credit cards accepted. Located at the southwest corner of Spring Mountain Road (Sands Avenue on the east side of the Strip). For Attractions, see Chapter 12.*

The "Adventure Resort" has always been one of our favorites since the day it opened. It was equally popular with families because of its being home to the pirate battle and the generally kid-friendly pirate theme throughout the hotel. Over the past several years the ownership has decided that Treasure Island needed to be made more "adult" friendly and the whole place has gone through some significant upgrading. Although the rooms may be at their best yet, we aren't as happy with the decor in public areas (but more about that when it comes time to see the sights).

The full name of this hotel is Treasure Island at the Mirage, which dates back to when management probably felt that it needed association with the neighboring Mirage to give it a touch of elegance. It doesn't need the Mirage for that anymore as the rooms, once definitely a notch below the Mirage, are now just as lovely. Soft earth tones, woodworking, traditional furnishings and fine European fabrics are now standard in every room and we like the canopy-effect headboards. Rooms on the upper stories have excellent views of either the Strip or the mountains. Treasure Island also offers a variety of suite accommodations.

Dining: Courtyard Grill (American); Buccaneer Bay Club (Continental), Francesco's (Italian), Terrace Cafe (24 hour), Madame Ching's (Chinese), and the Steak House. Buffet, deli and several snack bars.

Entertainment: Mystere has occupied the main showroom since the hotel opened. Hideaway Lounge.

Other facilities: Casino, bars, health spa and salon, swimming pool, beauty salon, gift/logo shop, shopping arcade, game arcade, and wedding chapel.

Moderate

BARBARY COAST HOTEL, *3595 Las Vegas Blvd. South. Tel. 702/737-7111, Fax 702/737-6304. Toll free reservations 888/227-2279. Website: www.barbarycoastcasino.com. 198 Rooms. Rates: $39-189; suites from $175-550. Major credit cards accepted. Located at the northeast corner of Flamingo Road.*

Named not for the North African pirates but rather the old San Francisco district noted for its bordellos and gambling houses before being destroyed in the 1906 earthquake, this smallest of the casino/hotels on the Strip has been a fixture for many years. And, given its location, why not? It is literally located in the middle of everything. Helping it survive against its bigger and certainly more spectacular neighbors is the friendly, old-time Vegas atmosphere. The decor in its public areas is reminiscent in style of Victorian-era San Francisco.

The guest rooms have been remodeled on several occasions and, besides containing most of the amenities you would expect from a more modern hotel, are now more attractive than in the past. Despite being more up to date there is still a definite hint of Victorian styling and even elegance, especially in the nicely textured wall coverings, original paintings on the walls, and the etched mirrors.

Dining: Drai's (American), Michael's Gourmet Restaurant (Continental), Victorian Room (24 hour Chinese/American). Fast food outlets.
Entertainment: None except for after-hours in Drai's.
Other facilities: Casino, bar, and gift shop.

FLAMINGO LAS VEGAS, *3555 Las Vegas Blvd. South. Tel. 702/733-3111, Fax 702/733-3528. Toll free reservations 800/733-2111. Website: www.flamingolv.com. 3,642 Rooms. Rates: $69-279. Major credit cards accepted. Located just north of the intersection of Flamingo Road. For Attractions, see Chapter 12.*

The extravagant but luxury tropical theme of this property is also reflected in the beautiful guest accommodations. Especially pleasing are the casual rattan furniture and the easy on the eyes soft color scheme. The rooms range in size from about average to somewhat larger and there are, of course, numerous suite options to choose from. Rooms on the upper floors have excellent Strip and mountain views but we also like those that face the hotel's 15 acres of expansive and well manicured grounds. Looking out your window on the latter will make you feel that you're more in Florida or Hawaii than in the middle of the desert. You'll also find all of the usual expected amenities of a first class hotel.

Dining: Alta Villa (Italian), Conrad's (steakhouse), Flamingo Room (American and Continental), Lindy's (24 hour), and Peking Market (Chinese). Paradise Garden Buffet and Bugsy's Deli. There's also a seasonal poolside grille.

Entertainment: The Flamingo Showroom hosts *Lasting Impressions* in addition to a Broadway play called *Men are from Mars, Women are from Venus*. There is also a daytime revue, *Bottoms Up*, in the same showroom. *Second City* is in Bugsy's Theater. Lounge entertainment is offered in the bar at the Race & Sports Book.

Other facilities: Casino, bars, complete health spa, swimming pool and aquatic park, beauty salon, gift/logo shop, shopping arcade, and wedding chapel.

HARRAH'S LAS VEGAS, *3475 Las Vegas Blvd. South. Tel. 702/369-5000, Fax 702/369-5008. Toll free reservations 800/634-6765. Website: www.harrahs.com. 2,700 Rooms. Rates: $69-259. Major credit cards accepted. Located between the intersections of Flamingo Road and Sands Avenue (Spring Mountain Road), opposite Caesars. For Attractions, see Chapter 12.*

The carnival theme so obvious in the public areas of this hotel doesn't extend to the guest rooms although they are quite colorful. With their white woods and bamboo, it is more tropical than carnival. However, they're quite nice and the rooms in the newer towers are fairly spacious. Who says that the rooms have to have the same theme as the casino anyway? Harrah's provides excellent accommodations and facilities at a reasonable price especially given the central location. Maybe it isn't quite in the "mega" class like some of its neighbors, but we doubt that many people would find any significant problems with staying here.

Dining: Asia (Oriental), Cafe Andreotti (Italian), Garden Cafe (24 hour), and the Range (steakhouse). Fresh Market Buffet, Winning Streaks Stadium Cafe (light American fare) and Club Cappuccino (pastries, etc.).

Entertainment: The main showroom features Clint Holmes and *Skintight.* The Improv comedy club. LaPlaya Lounge. Periodic entertainment is held outdoors beneath the Carnival Carousel.

Other facilities: Casino, bars, fitness center and spa, swimming pool, gift/logo shop, shopping, and game arcade.

HOLIDAY INN BOARDWALK, *3750 Las Vegas Blvd. South. Tel. 702/ 735-2400, Fax 702/730-3166. Toll free reservations 800/465-4329. Website: www.hiboardwalk.com. 653 Rooms. Rates: $49-129; suites from $250-350. Major credit cards accepted. Located just south of the intersection of Harmon Avenue.*

The Coney Island "fun house" exterior facade looks inviting for families but the interior public areas are without a theme and are only mildly attractive. This is a small hotel by Strip standards and some people like that idea. The rooms at the Boardwalk are typical of what you would find in most any Holiday Inn hotel. They're a decent size and nicely decorated with all the standard amenities (such as coffee maker, iron/ ironing board and hair dryer) but certainly nothing out of the ordinary. It is a reasonably priced place to stay given its location.

This hotel is owned by MGM/Mirage and is likely to be replaced by a new mega-resort at some time in the future. However, if you are looking for an affordable and decent place to stay in while being in the heart of the Strip, this can be a good choice for at least the next several years.

Dining: Cafe Boardwalk (Italian), deli (24 hour), Surf Buffet and an ice cream parlor.

Entertainment: The showroom has *The Dream King.* The Surf Club nightclub is a reasonable alternative to some of the Strip's more elaborate but much more expensive night spots.

Other facilities: Casino, bars, swimming pools, gift shop, shopping arcade, game arcade, fitness room, self-service laundry, and garden wedding gazebo.

IMPERIAL PALACE HOTEL & CASINO, *3535 Las Vegas Blvd. South. Tel. 702/731-3311, Fax 702/735-8578. Toll free reservations 800/634- 6441. Website: www.imperialpalace.com. 2,636 Rooms. Rates: $49-179; suites to $299. Major credit cards accepted. Located between the intersections of Flamingo Road and Sands Avenue (Spring Mountain Rad). For Attractions, see Chapter 12.*

Dating back to the 1960's and catering to middle America rather than the high rollers, the Imperial Palace maintains its popularity in the face of increasingly luxurious competition. It does so by continuing to offer reasonable rates in an ideal location right in the center of the Strip. The rooms aren't elegant but they're quite large and attractively decorated. However, they don't have a Far Eastern theme. The almost constantly busy casino is moderately themed but some public areas are showing their age and could use some sprucing up. Guest rooms are pleasant and feature light colors.

Dining: The Embers (steakhouse), Ming Terrace (Chinese), Rib House, Seahouse (seafood), and Tea House (American, also buffet). Imperial Buffet, Betty's Diner and several fast food outlets and snack bars.

Entertainment: Legends in Concerts occupies the main showroom. During the warmer months the Hawaiian Hot Luau is held by the pool area. Kabuki and Nomiya Lounges.

Other facilities: Casino, bars, health and fitness center, spa, swimming pool, gift/logo shop, shopping, game arcade, and wedding chapel.

LUXOR HOTEL & CASINO, *3900 Las Vegas Blvd. South. Tel. 702/ 262-4000, Fax 702/262-4454. Toll free reservations 800/288-1000. Website: www.luxor.com. 4,476 Rooms. Rates: $69-199; suites from $159. Major credit cards accepted. Located south of Tropicana Avenue at the intersection of Reno Avenue. For Attractions, see Chapter 12.*

Guest rooms are located either in the original 31-story high pyramid or in the more traditional step-pyramided East and West towers. The accommodations are first rate no matter which section you're in. All are nice sized rooms with an ancient Egyptian theme. The similarities, however, end there. Pyramid rooms (except for those on the fifth floor or lower) are reached by elevators that travel at a 39 degree tilt. They're called "inclinators" and you will feel yourself move slightly forward as they come to a halt.

The rooms, which have slanted windows that may make you think you're a bit tipsy, all surround the magnificent atrium. The open corridors afford fantastic views of the huge inner space, which is quite a sight unless you're prone to vertigo. The only shortcoming about staying in the pyramid is that the arrangement of the inclinators at each of the four corners can make for a long walk to some of the rooms. Of course, that's a problem in many Vegas hotels because of their size. East and West Tower rooms are more traditional from an architectural standpoint. The decor, however, is even a little nicer than in those rooms located in the pyramid.

Dining: Isis (Continental), Luxor Steak House, Papyrus (Asian), Pyramid Cafe (24 hour), Sacred Sea Room (seafood), and Hamada (Japanese). Pharaoh's Pheast buffet, Nile Deli, Salsa Fresh (Mexican) and a fast-food court.

Entertainment: The Luxor Theater, a beautiful showroom, is home to the *Blue Man Group* while *Midnight Fantasy* plays in Pharaoh's Theater on the Attractions Level. Lounge entertainment is available at *Neferterti's* while *Ra* is one of the hottest nightclubs in town.

Other facilities: Casino, bars, Oasis Spa (complete health club and swimming pool complex), gift/logo shop. shopping, and game arcade.

MONTE CARLO HOTEL & CASINO, *3770 Las Vegas Blvd. South. Tel. 702/730-7777, Fax 702/730-7250. Toll free reservations 800/311-8999. Website: www.monte-carlo.com. 3,014 Rooms. Rates: $59-299. Major credit cards accepted. Located between the intersections of Tropicana and Harmon Avenues. For Attractions, see Chapter 12.*

The pleasant and comfortable rooms at Monte Carlo belie the generally reasonable rates charged. The stated goal of this hotel has always been to provide luxury at affordable prices and they come very close to fulfilling that difficult promise. The decor is turn-of-the-century and is highlighted by fancy accents and rich looking bathrooms with plenty of marble, granite and brass. The lovely furnishings feature rich cherry woods. Although they're not among the biggest standard rooms in town, the size is more than comfortable. The hotel is a big place but has a smaller "feel" than many other hotels. Rooms are all arranged off of a Y-shaped tower, a common design technique in Las Vegas.

Dining: Andre's French Restaurant, Blackstone's Steakhouse, Cafe' (24 hour), Dragon Noodle Company (Oriental), Market City Caffe (Italian), and Monte Carlo Pub & Brewery. Buffet and fast-food court.

Entertainment: The main showroom hosts *Lance Burton: Master Magician*, which combines magic with some production show values. There is also entertainment in the Monte Carlo Pub & Brewery and at Houdini's Lounge.

Other facilities: Casino, bars, outdoor recreation facility with multiple pools and "river" ride, gift/logo shop, complete spa and fitness center, shopping arcade, hyper-market, game arcade, barber shop, beauty salon, tennis courts, and wedding chapel.

NEW FRONTIER, *3120 Las Vegas Blvd. South. Tel. 702/794-8200, Fax 702/794-8326. Toll free reservations 800/634-6966. Website: www.frontierlv.com. 986 Rooms. Rates: $49-179. Major credit cards accepted. Located between the intersection of Sands Avenue (Spring Mountain Road) and Convention Center Drive.*

There isn't all that much to be termed "new" in the New Frontier. They added the prefix when the hotel changed ownership several years ago after a lengthy labor dispute. In reality, it is one of the oldest still standing hotels on the Strip and certainly one of the least elaborate. That, plus it's relatively challenged location between the main portion of the Strip to the south and the older, budget Strip to its north, makes it a less than ideal place to stay. However, despite our negativism up to this point, it isn't a bad buy for the money. Rooms are divided between a pleasant atrium tower and low-rises that surround it. The more attractive rooms are in the tower, many of which are actually mini-suites with 600 square feet of space. Those in the surrounding buildings are typical motor inn design but have recently been redecorated in a pleasant enough manner. They also surround a pretty landscaped courtyard and pool area.

Dining: Gilley's Saloon & Barbecue, Margarita's Mexican Cantina, Phil's Angus Steakhouse. Orchard Buffet and New Frontier Deli (24 hour).

Entertainment: The showroom has "Legends of Comedy" and occasional other live entertainment.

Other facilities: Casino, bars, swimming pool, gift/logo shop and game arcade.

RIVIERA HOTEL & CASINO, *2901 Las Vegas Blvd. South. Tel. 702/734-5110, Fax 702/794-9451. Toll free reservations 800/634-6753. Website: www.theriviera.com. 2,109 Rooms. Rates: $39-259. Major credit cards accepted. Located north of Convention Center drive at the corner of Riviera Avenue. For Attractions, see Chapter 12.*

One of the most famous names in Las Vegas' long list of well known casino hotels, the Riviera maintains a large and popular following even after more than 40 years because of the reasonable rates and the value you get for your hard earned dollar. Many renovations have kept the rooms at a first class level. Among the common amenities are an in-room wet bar. The traditional but attractive decor is almost at a deluxe level, especially considering the price. Most of the units are contained in one of three towers ranging from 11 to 24 stories in height. Some low-rise units near the pool area, although mildly attractive, are not of the same quality as in the hotel towers. All of the guest towers and wings are named after a famous city on the Riviera. The hotel is also well known for its extensive entertainment schedule.

Dining: Kady's (24 hour), Kristofer's Steak House, and Ristorante Italianio. World's Fare Buffet and Mardi Gras Food Court.

Entertainment: Splash III (Splash Theater), *La Cage* (La Cage Theater), *Crazy Girls Fantasy Revue* (Mardi Gras Plaza), and Riviera Comedy Club. LeBistro Lounge. Also, celebrity entertainment at various times.

Other facilities: Casino, bars, swimming pool, health spa, beauty salon, barber shop, gift/logo shop, shopping arcade, game arcade, and wedding chapel.

STARDUST RESORT & CASINO, *3000 Las Vegas Blvd. South. Tel. 702/732-6111, Fax 702/732-6296. Toll free reservations 800/634-6757. Website: www.stardustlv.com. 2,335 Rooms. Rates: $50-250; $150-300 for suites. Major credit cards accepted. Located opposite the intersection of Convention Center Drive.*

The Stardust goes way back in Strip history. The large casino with its colorful facade is a throwback to the old days when casinos were a hundred percent glitz. If you like that sort of thing or if you just want to see how a Strip casino appeared in days gone by, it's worth taking a brief look at the Stardust. We don't mean to imply that the casino and other public areas haven't been kept up to date. They have – the hotel lobby area, for instance, is extremely attractive – but it's just that the whole feel of the Stardust is quite "retro."

Most of the Stardust's rooms are in the modern and sleek East and West towers that rise above the Strip and which is especially striking at night. The accommodations in the towers are excellent and features generous use of attractive wicker and other colorful furnishings in a modern and cheerful decor. The West tower has many upgraded accommodations including 725-square foot suites with wet bar that are fairly luxurious. In addition to the tower, the Stardust has a number of old motel style buildings in the rear of the property. Although they're less costly (cheap would be a better term), we don't recommend them. They're more than showing their age both inside and out and it doesn't seem that management is inclined to do much about their budget rooms.

Dining: Tony Roma's (ribs/steak), Island Paradise Cafe (24 hour), Tres Lobos (Mexican), Sushi King (Japanese), and William B's (steak/American/Continental). Coco Palms Buffet and snack bar.

Entertainment: Wayne Newton appears in the showroom. Other celebrities occupy the same venue about 12 weeks out of the year.

Other facilities: Casino, bars, swimming pool, gift/logo shop, shopping, game arcade, barber shop and beauty salon.

STRATOSPHERE HOTEL & CASINO, *2000 Las Vegas Blvd. South. Tel. 702/380-7777, Fax 702/383-4755. Toll free reservations 800/998-6937. Website: www.stratlv.com. 2,442 Rooms. Rates: $39-300. Major credit cards accepted. Located two blocks north of Sahara Avenue at the intersection of Main Street. For Attractions, see Chapter 12.*

The Stratosphere has very comfortable and nicely decorated rooms in a modern style that are a decent size and little more. They're a good value, however, as long as you don't mind being a little further away from the most popular parts of the Strip. In fact, except when the weather is cool enough for walking, a car is helpful if you're staying here. The hotel portion of the Stratosphere consists of an original tower of 1,440 rooms and a 1,002 room additional tower that was scheduled to open in August of 2001.

Either of the 24-story high hotel sections is simply dwarfed by the central observation tower and its thrill rides. So, if you're expecting a great view from your room, forget it. In fact, the surrounding area is definitely unattractive and you're best off not even looking out of the window! On the other hand, the rooms are definitely worth looking at and have a good number of amenities.

Dining: Fellini's Tower of Pasta (Italian), Montana's Steakhouse, Top of the World (Continental), Ferraro's (Italian) and Roxie's Diner. Stratosphere Buffet and several fast food outlets in the shopping center. A new 24-hour cafe will open upon completion of the new tower.

Entertainment: American Superstars and *Viva Las Vegas* both occupy the Broadway Theater. Lounge entertainment is in the Images Cabaret.

Other facilities: Casino, bars, swimming pool, gift/logo shop, game arcade and major shopping mall. Upon completion of the new section it will also have a complete poolside recreation area and spa.

TROPICANA RESORT & CASINO, *3801 Las Vegas Blvd. South. Tel. 702/739-2222, Fax 702/739-2469. Toll free reservations 888/826-TROP. Website: www.tropicanalv.com. 1,910 Rooms. Rates: $49-189; suites to $399. Major credit cards accepted. Located at the southeast corner of Tropicana Avenue. For Attractions, see Chapter 12.*

Another of the older properties in town, you have to distinguish between rooms in one of the two newer high rise towers versus the original low-rise motor inn style facilities. The former are quite good while the latter are more modest as to both size and decor. The two towers are the Paradise Tower (nearer to the casino) and the Island Tower. The latter is a little newer but the former has been recently remodeled. The rooms in the Paradise Tower are less "tropical" in motif but are richer looking. Island Tower rooms are better than average and feature a colorful tropical decor. Many units in both towers have outstanding views. The three-story garden units are colorful but more basic. Some have balconies. When it comes to the public areas, although there has been a considerable amount of refurbishing, some sections have a worn and rather tired looking appearance. That also applies to the entire low-rise accommodations section. If you can get a Tower location in the middle of the hotel's price range, then it's a good value. Its location at one of the two busiest Strip intersections makes it worth seeking out if you don't want to pay top dollar.

Dining: Calypso's (24 hour), Golden Dynasty (Chinese), Mizuno's Japanese Steakhouse, Pietro's (Continental), and Savannah Steakhouse. Island Buffet and deli.

Entertainment: The Tiffany Showroom is home to the famous *Folies Bergere*. In the daytime it is used for the *Illusionary Magic of Rick Thomas*. Comedy Stop. Celebrations and Tropics Lounges.

Other facilities: Casino, bars, outdoor recreation environment with swimming pools, indoor swimming pool, spa and fitness center, gift/logo shop, shopping, game arcade, and wedding chapel.

Inexpensive

CIRCUS CIRCUS, *2880 Las Vegas Blvd. South. Tel. 702/734-0410, Fax 702/734-5897. Toll free reservations 800/634-3450. Website: www.circuscircus-lasvegas.com. 3,893 Rooms. Rates: $29-129; suites from $99-259. Major credit cards accepted. Located between Convention Center Drive and Sahara Avenue at the intersection of Circus Circus Drive. For Attractions, see Chapter 12.*

Given the prices at Circus Circus you can't really expect too much. Then again, you can be pleasantly surprised with what you get for your money. Large and cheerfully decorated rooms have always been the order of the day at Circus Circus. With their latest expansion they also redid all of the older rooms and they are better than ever. While certainly not in the luxury category, you'll have all the comforts and amenities you need. The newer the tower section you stay in, the better the rooms. They also have a limited number of motel style units available in a section of the hotel called the Manor. They're a notch or two in quality below those of the main hotel but are definitely not bad for the price.

Dining: Blue Iguana (Mexican), Pink Pony Cafe (24 hour), Stivali (Italian), and the Steak House. Circus Circus Buffet and many fast food outlets, including those located on the Midway and in the theme park.

Entertainment: Free circus acts in the Midway.

Other facilities: Casino, bars, swimming pool, gift/logo shop, shopping, wedding chapel and game arcade.

EXCALIBUR HOTEL & CASINO, *3850 Las Vegas Blvd. South. Tel. 702/597-7777, Fax 702/597-7009. Toll free reservations 800/937-7777. Website: www.excalibur-casino.com. 4,032 Rooms. Rates: $55-200; suites from $149-375. Major credit cards accepted. Located at the southwest corner of Tropicana Avenue. For Attractions, see Chapter 12.*

Considering that this is one of the biggest Strip hotels, the accommodations aren't nearly among the best by any means. However, they're more than adequate for catching a few z's and, at the prices the Excalibur charges, what else can you expect? Our biggest complaint is the rather plain plastered walls, which are supposed to represent a "castle brick" motif, are too much like you'll find in a simple roadside motel. On the other hand, the wrought iron fixtures, dark wood furniture and some thoughtful colors do offer at least some semblance of the medieval look. You won't see the pastels or southwestern earth tones that are so ubiquitous throughout Las Vegas.

Dining: The Steakhouse at Camelot, Regale (Italian), Sherwood Forest Cafe (24 hour), and Sir Gallahad's Pub & Prime Rib House. Roundtable Buffet and several fast-food outlets and snack bars in the Village Food Court.

Entertainment: Tournament of Kings dinner show; Court Jester's Stage, Minstrel's Lounge, *Catch A Rising Star* comedy club.

Other facilities: Casino, bars, swimming pool, gift/logo shop, shopping arcade, game arcade, beauty salon, and wedding chapel.

KLONDIKE HOTEL & CASINO, *5191 Las Vegas Blvd. South. Tel. 702/739-9351, Fax 702/795-8710. Toll free reservations 888/272-8794. 150 Rooms. Rates: $29-129. Most major credit cards accepted. Located immediately to the south of the southern end of the Strip near Russell Road.*

One of the cheapest places on the Strip (some people might consider it to be a block or two south of the Strip), the small Klondike would be your basic roadside motel in any other locality. But, since this is Vegas, they've added a casino. The rooms are clean and comfortable but are on the small side with just the most ordinary of amenities. Since you're likely to spend very little time in your Klondike room, those shortcomings may be of little consequence to you if you want to travel on a budget. While this place is obviously below the quality level of every other hotel we've included on the Strip, it *is* better than the whole batch of small private motels that can still be found in a few places along the Strip.

Dining: 24 hour coffee shop/restaurant.

Entertainment: None regularly scheduled.

Facilities: Casino, bar, gift shop, and swimming pool.

SAHARA HOTEL & CASINO, *2535 Las Vegas Blvd. South. Tel. 702/ 737-2111, Fax 702/791-2027. Toll free reservations 888/696-2121. 1,750 Rooms. Rates: $48-145. Major credit cards accepted. Located at the southeast corner of Sahara Avenue. For Attractions, see Chapter 12.*

This venerable hotel dates from almost the origin of the Strip. It has recently undergone a thorough renovation as management tries to keep up with the ever increasing quantity and quality of the competition. The exterior has been nicely refurbished and we especially like the entrance area at night. The casino and most of the public areas have also received a facelift and are attractive or slightly better. When it comes to accommodations, however, the Sahara is still a few notches below the better hotels. On the other hand, you can get a reasonably nice, comfortable room with a fresh, airy appearance for a bargain rate. Room sizes vary from on the small side to about average.

Dining: Caravan Coffee Shop (24 hour), Paco's Hideaway (Mexican), NASCAR Cafe (American), and Sahara Steakhouse. Sahara Buffet and fast food outlets.

Entertainment: The Rat Pack is Back in the Congo Room and magician Steve Wyrick in the Sahara Theater. The Casbah Lounge also has live entertainment.

Other facilities: Casino, bars, swimming pool, gift/logo shop, shopping, and game arcade.

FAREWELL TO THE DESERT INN

*Las Vegas hotel owners rarely seem to look back, which might explain why the preservation of historic casino properties get so little attention. It was, therefore, no surprise when the long-standing **Desert Inn**, a Las Vegas landmark, was closed in August 2000 with the announcement that it would be demolished to make way for the future of Vegas hotels. But, because of the important role it played throughout the years, a little "DI" history is in order.*

The Desert Inn was built by Wilbur Clark, who was no stranger to mob connections and influences. Upon its opening in 1950 it became the fifth hotel to take its place on what would become the world famous Strip. From its earliest days the DI had a flair and elegance about it that would not be duplicated until the recent construction of the new breed of upscale hotels. It attracted the biggest names as guests and as entertainers, including Frank Sinatra. The property grew (the site at the time of its demise covered 220 acres) and prospered. Eccentric Howard Hughes moved into the top floor of the hotel but he became an unwelcome guest and management asked him to leave. He didn't want to. So, in 1966 he bought the hotel.

As the heart of the Strip headed further south beginning in the late 1970's, the DI's fortunes already began to change. It retained its elegance throughout but had trouble attracting enough traffic to be able to compete with the increasingly larger mega-resorts. Ownership changed hands several times and included ITT-Sheraton among others. When Steve Wynn acquired it in 2000 and shut it down, it marked the end of a distinguished 50 years of service for the Desert Inn. Many people will miss it for years to come.

WESTWARD HO, *2900 Las Vegas Blvd. South. Tel. 702/731-2900, Fax 702/731-6154. Toll free reservations 800/634-6803. Website: www.westwardho.com. 777 Rooms. Rates: $37-47. Major credit cards accepted. Located between the intersections of Convention Center and Circus Circus Drives.*

This is one of the world's largest motels. It isn't fancy or all that attractive – just basic four wall accommodations. In fact, we list it not because we have any real liking for it, but simply because that given it's location right on the Strip, it is a real bargain. So, for travelers on the tightest of budgets who simply want to catch a few winks between gambling, seeing the sights and other activities, Westward Ho fits the bill. Unlike most big Vegas properties where you have to walk what seems like a mile to get to your car, all of the rooms at Westward Ho have parking right outside your door. On the other hand, the maze-like layout of the motel buildings can be a bit on the confusing side.

Outside on the Strip you'll usually see a sizable line waiting for a chance to get a free pull on what must be the world's biggest slot machine – not the machine itself, but the display. You see, the results of your "pull" will show up king size on the hotel's big electronic marquee. We've never won anything of great value but lots of people get free show tickets or other trinkets.

Dining: Ca-Fae (24 hour coffee shop and buffet combination) and deli.

Entertainment: Casino Lounge. Various seasonally based shows in the Crown Room.

Other facilities: Casino, bar, seven swimming pools (each with Jacuzzi).

OFF-STRIP

Very Expensive

MARRIOTT SUITES, *325 Convention Center Drive. Tel. 702/650-2000, Fax 702/650-9466. Toll free reservations 800/244-3364. Website: www.marriott.com. 287 Rooms. Rates: $169-329. Major credit cards accepted. Located a few blocks east of the Strip and one block west of Paradise Road and the Las Vegas Convention Center.*

Although the price seems unusually high at first glance, it's not all that bad when you consider that you get a spacious suite with separate bedroom and sitting area, not to mention the respected Marriott name. However, you can get similar style accommodations for considerably less, so this place is best for those who desire excellent non-casino hotels or who are turned off by huge hotels. The decor is modern and seems to be preferred by a business clientele. Amenities include refrigerator and coffee maker in every unit. The 17-story high tower is an attractive mix of modern architecture with hints of art deco.

Dining: Allie Restaurant (American).

Entertainment: None

Other facilities: Bar, swimming pool, gift shop, and small exercise room.

Expensive

ALEXIS PARK RESORT, *375 E. Harmon Avenue. Tel. 702/796-3300, Fax 702/796-4334. Toll free reservations 800/223-0888. Website: www.alexispark.com. 500 Rooms. Rates $99-189 for "standard" suite; $149-339 for larger suites. Most major credit cards accepted. Located east of the Strip between Koval Lane and Paradise Road.*

One of the nicest hotels in town, the Alexis Park Resort features luxurious suites and mini-suites, each with a wet bar. Some have fireplaces. The Mediterranean style hotel also boasts nearly 20 acres of beautiful gardens, mini-waterfalls, a gorgeous pool area, and general opulence oozing out of every pore. As with the previous listing, it appeals to those who prefer a hotel without a casino.

Dining: Pegasus (Continental) and coffee shop.

Entertainment: None.

Other facilities: Bar, health spa and salon, swimming pools, putting green, tennis courts and wedding chapel.

HARD ROCK HOTEL & CASINO, *4455 Paradise Road. Tel. 702/693-5000, Fax 702/693-5010. Toll free reservations: 800/473-7625. Website: www.hardrockhotel.com. 670 Rooms. Rates: $75-300. Major credit cards accepted. Located at the intersection of Harmon Avenue, a little east of the Strip. For Attractions, see Chapter 12.*

The surprisingly upscale rooms don't really have a musical theme despite such touches as curtains with musical instrument patterns and four channels of audio programs. This is not to say, however, that the rooms are bad in any way. In fact, they are quite nice and are comparable with the better Strip properties. French doors add a touch of elegance to the interesting furnishings, which include iron lamps with parchment shades and beds with leather headboards. Generous use of bold colors greatly enhances the room appearance. The typical Hard Rock guest is definitely younger than the average visitor to Las Vegas but it certainly is not a property that is geared towards children. It's rock sophistication, right down to their Beach Club with it's swim-up gaming facilities (one of only two in Las Vegas)

Dining: The famous Hard Rock Cafe (American) is located outside of the hotel on the corner of Paradise and Harmon. Inside are Mortoni's (Italian), Mr. Lucky's (24 hour), Nobu (Japanese), A.J.'s Steakhouse, and the Pink Taco (Mexican). The Counter is another 24 hour facility, this one offering sandwiches and lighter fare. There's also a poolside bar and grill.

Entertainment: The showroom, "The Joint," is home to major rock concerts. Baby's Nightclub is one of the city's hot spots.

Other facilities: Casino, bar, "beach" environment with swimming pools; RockSpa also has a complete fitness center and salon; gift/logo shop and game arcade.

LAS VEGAS HILTON, *3000 Paradise Road. Tel. 702/732-5111, Fax 702/732-5805. Toll free reservations 800/732-7117. Website: www.lv-hilton.com. 3,174 Rooms. Rates: $99-349. Major credit cards accepted. Located immediately to the north of the Las Vegas Convention Center. For Attractions, see Chapter 12.*

The guest rooms are large, comfortable, no-nonsense facilities that meet the high expectations of those used to staying at the Hilton chain. We must mention, however, that it is difficult to predict the future when it comes to this hotel. Owner Park Place Entertainment had wanted to sell the property and already had a deal that fell through because the buyer couldn't get the necessary funds. Now the word is that they're going to keep it but that could be because they don't have another prospective buyer. The bottom line is that, although the Hilton has always been a classy establishment, we don't know what all of this uncertainty means in terms of facilities and services. Park Place had, for instance, already "transferred" their higher rollers to Caesars and other properties.

But let's return to the current situation. Rooms on the upper floors that face the Strip have spectacular views. There are a wide variety of guest room accommodations at the Hilton, ranging from standard rooms all the way up to three-bedroom suites. There are even a few suites with more than 10,000 square feet that have a parlor area that can accommodate 60 people, in case you want to have a few friends over for a drink. So, let's get back to a more realistic level, the standard rooms. These are comfortable, offering either traditional or modern style furnishings will all of the amenities you would expect from a first class hotel. On the other hand, we wouldn't characterize them as gorgeous or elaborate.

Dining: Andiamo (Italian), Benihana Village/Robata (Japanese), Garden of the Dragon (Chinese), Hilton Steakhouse, Margarita Grille (Mexican), and Quark's Bar & Grille (American). Buffet, Paradise Cafe (24 hour), snack bar, deli and several fast food outlets.

Entertainment: Live entertainment in the NightClub. The NightClub is also an after-hours place. Celebrity entertainment in the Hilton Theater.

Other facilities: Casino, bars, complete health spa and fitness center, swimming pool, golf (off-site), beauty salon, gift/logo shop, shopping arcade, and game arcade.

RIO SUITE HOTEL & CASINO, *3700 W. Flamingo Road. Tel. 702/ 252-7777, Fax 702/252-8909. Toll free reservations 800/752-9746. Website: www.playrio.com. 2,563 Rooms. Rates: $90-320 for the "standard" category of suites. Major credit cards accepted. Located west of the Strip between I-15 (Flamingo Road exit) and Valley View Boulevard. It can also be reached via Rio Drive off of Industrial Road. For Attractions, see Chapter 12.*

The "suites" of the Rio (except for luxury units that are really multi-room affairs and the even more elaborate "villas" that are priced out of the reach of the average person), are actually one oversized room with separate sitting and sleeping areas. That comes as a disappointment to some because of the name of the hotel, but the accommodations are beautiful and spacious, the minimum size being about 600 square feet. All have floor to ceiling windows and rooms on higher floors of the newest tower that face the Strip have absolutely fantastic views, especially at night. The mountain facing rooms aren't hard on the eyes either. The Rio's accommodations feature lots of nice little amenities, including an in-room safe to store all the loot you win at the tables.

The room prices at the Rio aren't bad considering what you get. It has received high honors from numerous travel industry sources (Zagat and the American Academy of Hospitality Services among others) and is considered one of the best resorts in the world. However, although we love almost everything about this hotel – accommodations, dining, attractions or whatever else – there is little doubt that they have been taking advantage of their popularity with both visitors and locals alike when it comes to prices. Almost everything except the rooms are overpriced compared to Vegas in general. We're almost attempted to call it gouging. But, you will have to judge for yourself.

Dining: All American Steakhouse, Antonio's Italian Ristorante (Italian), Bamboleo (Mexican), Buzio's (seafood), Fiore (American), Fortune's (Chinese), Mama Marie's Cucina (Italian), Mask (Oriental), Napa (French/Continental), Sao Paulo Cafe (24 hour), and Voo Doo Cafe (Cajun and Creole). Carnival World Buffet, Village Seafood Buffet, Toscano's Deli & Market, Star Deli & Bakery (New York kosher style deli) and several fast food outlets.

Entertainment: Scintas in the Copacabana showroom, *de la Guarda* in the theater of the same name, and celebrity entertainment in the Samba Theater. Club Rio nightclub, Rio Bamba Cabaret, Voo Doo, and Ipanema Bar Lounges.

Other facilities: Casino, bars, complete health club and spa, outdoor recreational environment with sand "beach" and swimming pools, golf (off-site), gift/logo shop, shopping, and game arcade.

ST. TROPEZ SUITES, *455 E. Harmon Avenue. Tel. 702/369-5400, Fax 702/369-1150. Toll free reservations 800/666-5400. 149 Rooms. Rates: $115-125, including Continental breakfast. Most major credit cards accepted. Located east of the Strip between Koval Lane and Paradise Road.*

A very attractive all-suite facility that is set around a pretty garden area, the two story buildings of St. Tropez are motel style in exterior appearance but the accommodations are much better than that. They are tastefully furnished in a southwestern motif and are well appointed. Along with the free breakfast, guests at this non-casino hotel are treated to evening refreshments.

Dining: Hippo & the Wild Bunch (American) is located adjacent to the hotel and several others are within walking distance.

Entertainment: None.

Other facilities: Swimming pool and fitness center.

Moderate

ORLEANS HOTEL & CASINO, *4500 W. Tropicana Avenue. Tel. 702/ 365-7111, Fax 702/365-7499. Toll free reservations 800/675-3267. Website: www.orleanscasino.com. 800 Rooms. Rates: $49-169. Most major credit cards accepted. Located west of the Strip at the intersection of Arville Street.*

Although this isn't the kind of hotel/casino that tourists come to marvel at, it is so attractive that we were severely tempted to include a section on it in the chapter on sightseeing. It is worth taking a look at if you have some extra time. The colorful exterior facade resembles the architecture of the French Quarter and contains figures of people in costume appropriate to the hotel's New Orleans Mardi Gras theme. The decor of the public areas is beautiful (we are especially impressed with the casino, which is one of the nicest in Vegas). The atmosphere is definitely party-city although not quite to the extent that the Rio achieves. Inside the main entrance are three bigger than life alligators standing upright and playing musical instruments. They're led by none other than Al E. Gator himself. Surrounding the main gaming area is more French Quarter style architecture with its famous wrought iron fences and populated by more life size figures of Orleans people from musicians to ladies of the night. Colorful gigantic masks are suspended from the high ceiling.

When it comes to accommodations the Orleans won't disappoint either. The rooms, located in a single high rise tower, are oversized and cheerfully decorated in the same New Orleans theme. They're very comfortable and attractively priced. It's a good place to stay if you're looking to save some money compared to most Strip properties. However, it is best to have your own set of wheels if you stay here, even though the hotel does offer free shuttle service to the Strip.

Dining: Canal Street Grille (American), Courtyard Cafe (24 hour), Don Miguel's (Mexican), La Louisiane (Cajun), Big Al's Oyster Bar, and Bones Rib Joint. French Market Buffet and several fast food outlets and snack bars.

Entertainment: Celebrity entertainment is offered in the showroom. Bourbon Street Cabaret lounge.

Other facilities: Casino, bars, swimming pool, bowling alley, gift/logo shop, game arcade, child care center, multi-screen cinema, fitness center, liquor store, beauty salon and barber shop, and wedding chapel.

The Orleans has just embarked on an expansion program that will add more than 600 rooms, two restaurants, an Irish pub with entertainment and an arena along with additional casino space and a much needed parking garage. Completion is expected sometime in 2002.

PALACE STATION HOTEL & CASINO, *2411 W. Sahara Avenue, Tel. 702/367-2411, Fax 702/367-2478. Toll free reservations 800/643-3101. Website: www.stationcasinos.com. 1,028 Rooms. Rates: $39-179. Major credit cards accepted. Located west of the Strip immediately adjacent to the Sahara Avenue exit of I-15.*

There has finally been some major needed redecorating at Palace Station, the oldest of all the very popular Station Casinos. The most obvious recent improvement is in the casino, which now has a much nicer decor with a Victorian theme. The accommodations are still of the standard hotel fare – nice rooms but nothing special – that is common in the lower priced Vegas hotels. Just missing out being walking distance from the Strip, it's generally a few bucks cheaper than hotels with a Strip address, which makes it a popular choice amongst the thrifty set.

Dining: The Broiler (American), Guadalajara (Mexican), Iron Horse Cafe (24 hour), and Pasta Palace (Italian). Gourmet Buffet, deli and fast food outlets.

Entertainment: Sound Trax nightclub and Palace Saloon lounge.

Facilities: Casino, bars, swimming pool, gift/logo shop, game arcade and child care center.

SAN REMO HOTEL, *115 E. Tropicana avenue. Tel. 702/739-9000, Fax 702/736-1120. Toll free reservations 800/522-7366. Website: www.sanremolasvegas.com. 711 Rooms. Rates: $59-200. Most major credit cards accepted. Located immediately to the east of the Strip and the Tropicana Hotel.*

This hotel is so close to the Strip that it could almost have been included with the listings for Strip hotels. It is definitely walking distance. The attractive and comfortable guest rooms are located either in the original motor inn section or a newer tower section. Try to get a room in the latter since they are somewhat more spacious and well appointed although none can be characterized as excellent.

Dining: Paparazzi Grille (steak and seafood), Pasta Remo (Italian), Saizen (Japanese) and Ristorante dei Fiori (24 hour combination coffee shop/buffet). There's also Luigi's deli.

Entertainment: Showgirls of Magic in the showroom. The Bonne Chance Lounge has occasional live entertainment..

Other facilities: Casino, bar, swimming pool, gift shop, game arcade and a poolside wedding arbor.

Inexpensive

BOURBON STREET HOTEL & CASINO, *120 E. Flamingo Road. Tel. 702/737-7200, Fax 702/794-9155. Toll free reservations 800/634-6956. 166 Rooms. Rates: $49-99. Most major credit cards accepted. Located immediately east of the Strip at Audrie Lane.*

Like the San Remo, this hotel is within easy shoe-leather reach of the Strip so it is quite convenient for those on a budget. The price is right given the location and the accommodations are decent. They consist of rooms with king or double beds or some upgraded executive and full suites with Jacuzzi. The public areas are small and are hardly worth a glance.

Dining: French Market Restaurant & Bar (24 hour).

Entertainment: Bourbon Street Comedy Theater.

Other facilities: Casino (no live gaming), bar.

GOLD COAST HOTEL & CASINO, *4000 W. Flamingo Road. Tel. 702/367-7111, Fax 702/367-8575. Toll free reservations 800/402-6278. Website: www.goldcoastcasino.com. 750 Rooms. Rates: $29-139; suites from $175-225. Major credit cards accepted. Located about a mile west of the Strip at Valley View Blvd., across the street from the Rio.*

The spacious and tastefully decorated rooms at the Gold Coast feature a pleasant and mostly southwestern style decor (despite the hotel's name). They are quite comfortable, especially considering the price. There are also a small number of suites featuring more luxurious decor, wet bar and refrigerator. It's just a little too far from the Strip to walk to, but the location is still quite good. They provide free shuttle service to the Strip. The public areas of the hotel aren't very elaborate but it is mildly attractive nonetheless. Like its more famous neighbor, the Rio, and other Coast Hotels, it is popular both with visitors and area residents.

Dining: Cortez Room (steakhouse), Mediterranean Room (Italian/seafood), and Monterey Room (24 hour American/Chinese). The Buffet and fast food outlets.

Entertainment: The showroom has a tribute to lady country-western singers called "Honky Tonk Angels". There's also a nightclub and the Gold Coast Dance Hall in addition to two lounges with entertainment.

Other facilities: Casino, bars, swimming pool, barber shop, beauty salon, bowling alley, gift shop, game arcade, and cinema. The child care center is unique in all of Las Vegas because it is the only one that is free of charge to hotel guests.

SOMERSET HOUSE MOTEL, *294 Convention Center Drive. Tel. 702/735-4411, Fax 702/369-2388. Toll free reservations 888/336-4280. Website: www.somerset-house.com. 104 Rooms. Rates: $40-50. American Express, Diners Club, MasterCard and VISA accepted. Located between the Strip and the Convention Center (Paradise Road).*

This is a standard motor inn facility with three stories that is well located for those seeking an inexpensive alternative to the Strip. About a third of the units are mini-suites. Most units have either a full kitchen or kitchenette. All have coffee makers. The rooms are a good size and the decor is decent.

Dining: A full service restaurant for lunch and dinner and a 24 hour coffee shop.

Entertainment: None.

Other facilities: Swimming pool. The Somerset is adjacent to a small shopping center.

TERRIBLE'S CASINO HOTEL, *4100 Paradise Road. Tel. 702/733-7000, Fax 702/691-2423. Toll free reservations 800/640-9777. Website: www.terribleherbst.com. 350 Rooms. Rates: $59-89. Major credit cards accepted. Located at the intersection of Paradise and Flamingo Roads, a little east of the Strip.*

What a terrible name! It's enough to scare away the guests. Well, not really, especially when the place comes with a recommendation from us or many locals who are familiar with the Terrible brand name (gas stations and convenience stores, bowling alleys and several small casinos) that means good value and service to lots of folks. Just for your information, "Terrible" is the company's logo character, a gun-slinging black silhouette known as the "best bad guy in the west." The site of this property was once occupied by the old Continental Hotel. The new owners completely gutted the interior and so, except for some structural steel, one could say that this became an entirely new hotel when it opened at the end of 2000. The accommodations are typical motor-inn as regards both style and quality.

Dining: Bougainvillea Cafe & Rotiserie (24 hour). Terrible's Buffet and deli.

Entertainment: Lounge.

Other facilities: Casino, bar, swimming pool. 46.01

VACATION VILLAGE HOTEL & CASINO, *6711 Las Vegas Blvd. South. Tel. 702/891-1700, Fax 702/896-4353. Toll free reservations 800/658-5000. Website: www.vacation-village.com. 313 Rooms. Rates: $39-69. Most major credit cards accepted. Located about a mile south of the beginning of the Strip at the intersection of Sunset Road.*

Slightly better than basic accommodations that feature a mildly attractive southwestern decor and plenty of light, Vacation Village is a good choice if your hotel budget is very limited. The rooms are comfortable and pleasant and the southwest feel is ever so slightly enhanced by the faux saguaro cactus in each room. At press time the hotel was planning on affiliating with the Holiday Inn chain. Although not walking distance from the Strip for most people (especially during the hotter months) you don't necessarily need a car to stay here. That's because the Strip bus begins its route right outside the hotel's entrance.

Dining: Denny's (24 hour), Sloppy Joe's (American) and Roberto's Taco Shop. Top Hat Buffet. CONF#54 LN

Entertainment: Koo Koo's Lounge.

Other facilities: Casino, bar, swimming pool, wedding chapel, pool hall and game arcade.

WILD WILD WEST GAMBLING HALL & HOTEL, *3300 W. Tropicana Avenue. Tel. 702/740-0000, Fax 702/736-7106. Toll free reservations 800/777-1514. 300 Rooms. Rates: $39-59. Most major credit cards accepted. Located west of the Strip at Industrial Road and near the Tropicana Avenue exit of I-15.*

Popular with the California budget set for many years as the old King 8 Hotel, the property is now under the ownership of Station Casinos. They've spruced it up a bit and rumor has it that more improvements will be coming. For now, although it has an old west theme you certainly won't mistake it for a Strip property (or even another Station Casino Hotel for that matter). Accommodations are basic but clean and comfortable and the location is quite convenient. Still, having a car helps because the walk to the Strip isn't that short.

Dining: Gambler's Grill (American).

Entertainment: None regularly scheduled.

Other facilities: Casino, bar, gift shop, swimming pool and spa.

MAXIM...OR MINIM?

Maxim's was for many years a popular place to stay off but near the Strip for budget-conscious visitors. However, the past few years have not been kind to this property. The absentee owners didn't seem to care and on-site management was skimming off the top. Financial difficulties led it into receivership and the casino closed. The hotel was entirely closed for a short time but has since reopened. Because of the lack of commitment to the property and its poor financial status, we can't recommend it as a place to stay. However, we mention it here because many past visitors will be wondering when they don't see it listed. So now you know the sad story.

DOWNTOWN

Again, the "attractions" aspect of all hotels in the downtown corridor are contained in the general downtown section in Chapter 12.

Expensive

GOLDEN NUGGET HOTEL, *129 E. Fremont Street. Tel. 702/385-7511, Fax 702/386-8362. Toll free reservations 800/634-3454. Website: www.goldennugget.com. 1,907 Rooms. Rates $59-199. Major credit cards accepted. Located in the Casino Center area between First Street and Casino Center Blvd.*

The most luxurious hotel in downtown Las Vegas, the Golden Nugget features a beautiful casino and other public areas highlighted by generous use of crystal chandeliers, Grecian marble and a general feel and look of European elegance. The guest rooms are equally inviting. Located in one of three towers, they are oversized (except for a few in the oldest section of the hotel) and all are attractively furnished. It seems that remodeling is a constant and the latest look is one of warm tones of beige and brown. Amenities include custom bath products, hair dryers, iron/ironing board, in-room safe, and lighted make-up mirrors.

Dining: California Pizza Kitchen, Carson Street Cafe (24 hour), Lillie Langtry's (Chinese), and Stefano's (Italian). Buffet.

Entertainment: The showroom hosts comedian David Brenner while The Lounge in the race and sports book has nightly live music.

Other facilities: Casino, bars (including the International Beer Bar with more than 40 varieties from around the world), swimming pool, beauty salon, gift/logo shop, and shopping. There is also an elegant salon and spa offering massage and eucalyptus steam room

Moderate

FITZGERALD'S CASINO HOTEL, *301 E. Fremont Street. Tel. 702/ 388-2400, Fax 702/388-2230. Toll free reservations 800/274-5825. Website: www.fitzgeralds.com. 650 Rooms. Rates: $45-150. Major credit cards accepted. Located in the Casino Center area between 3rd and 4th Streets.*

Affiliated with the Holiday Inn group, Fitzgerald's offers modern and comfortable rooms with pleasant furnishings. It is the tallest of the downtown hotels and rooms on the upper floors have excellent views. In-room amenities include a safe and iron/ironing board. The atmosphere at the casino and in the public areas is festive.

Dining: Limericks Steak House, Shamrock Cafe (24 hour), and Molly's (combination buffet and cafe).

Entertainment: Casino stage lounge.

Other facilities: Casino, bars, swimming pool, gift shop and fast-food outlet.

MAIN STREET STATION, *200 N. Main Street. Tel. 702/387-1896, Fax 702/386-4466. Toll free reservations 800/713-8933. Website: www.mainstreetcasino.com. 406 Rooms. Rates: $50-175. Major credit cards accepted. Located in the Casino Center area at the intersection of Stewart Avenue, two blocks north of Fremont Street.*

Victorian themed throughout, this is the most interesting of all the downtown establishments. Main Street definitely has the best rooms downtown after the Golden Nugget. They feature marble tile foyers with marble trim and bright and cheerful rooms that have a Victorian garden decor. There are in room safes and the plantation style window shutters are charming. Considering that the prices are lower, it may well represent the best combination of value and quality to be found in the downtown

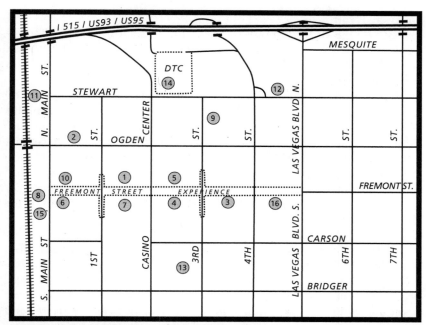

DOWNTOWN LAS VEGAS

1" = approx. 420 '

HOTELS/CASINOS

1. Binion's Horseshoe
2. California
3. Fitzgeralds
4. Four Queens
5. Fremont
6. Golden Gate
7. Golden Nugget
8. Jackie Gaughan's Plaza
9. Lady Luck
10. Las Vegas Club
11. Main Street Station

OTHER

12. City Hall
13. County Court House - Marriage License Bureau
14. Downtown Transp. Ctr.
15. Greyhound Bus Sta.
16. Public Parking Garage

Casino Center. The public areas are filled with interesting and often beautiful antiques. The Victorian decor accentuates the hotel's extensive antique collection quite well and gives it a warm and inviting feeling. We should point out that despite the "Station" in the name, this hotel is not affiliated with the Station Casinos group. It simply reflects its location along the railroad route and the former adjacent train station.

Dining: Pullman Grille (steakhouse), Triple-7 Brew Pub, and coffee shop. Garden Court Buffet.

Entertainment: Live music in the Brew Pub.

Other facilities: Casino, bar, and gift shop.

Inexpensive

BINION'S HORSESHOE HOTEL, *128 Fremont Street. Tel. 702/382-1600, Fax 702/382-5750. Toll free reservations 800/237-6537. 380 Rooms. Rates: $30-60. Major credit cards accepted. Located in the Casino Center area between First Street and Casino Center Blvd.*

This is a combination of two hotels. Of the overall room total only 80 are the original Binion's while the remainder were added when Binion's took over the old Mint Hotel. Although the former Mint rooms are definitely larger and more modern in decor, we still prefer the charm that comes with the Victorian decor of the older units. Especially attractive are the iron beds and rich wallpaper. Binion's has a popular following and always seems to be jammed. It helps give the place an exciting feel.

Dining: Binion's Ranch Steak House, Gee Joon (Chinese), and coffee shop (24 hour). Snack bars and deli.

Entertainment: None.

Other facilities: Casino, bars, roof-top swimming pool, and gift shop.

CALIFORNIA HOTEL & CASINO, *12 Ogden Avenue. Tel. 702/385-1222, Fax 702/386-4463. Toll free reservations 800/634-6255. Website: www.thecal.com. 650 Rooms. Rates: $40-110. Major credit cards accepted. Located in the Casino Center area between Main and 1st Streets, one block north of Fremont.*

Why a place called the California has a Pacific Island theme (as in Hawaii or Polynesia), we can't say for sure but the fact that many people who stay here are on package deals from Hawaii is a possibility. Although the California has been around quite a while, the decor is cheerful and gives the place a warm feel. The same can be said for the comfortable and adequate rooms, which also have the spirit of Aloha. The hotel is connected to the nearby Main Street Station via an enclosed bridgeway. The access to the bridge on the California side has a small number of shops.

Dining: Pasta Pirate Restaurant (Italian), Redwood Bar & Grille (American), and Market Street Cafe (24 hour). Snack bar.

Entertainment: None.

Other facilities: Casino, bar, gift/logo shop, shopping, and game arcade.

FREMONT HOTEL, *200 E. Fremont Street. Tel. 702/385-3232, Fax 702/386-4463. Toll free reservations 800/634-6182. Website: www.fremontcasino.com. 452 Rooms. Rates: $40-85. Major credit cards accepted. Located in the Casino Center area between Casino Center Blvd. and 3rd Street.*

The Fremont is similar to many other downtown hotels – older and more basic accommodations, although all of the rooms have been remodeled and are mildly attractive and comfortable. Some of the bigger rooms represent a high quality level at a great price. Likewise, the public areas and casino also follow the general downtown mold: darker, more crowded (because they're smaller), and on the plain and old fashioned side. This and most other downtown casinos are considerably more smoke-filled than on the Strip.

Dining: Lanai Cafe (24 hour), Second Street Grille (American/ Oriental), and Tony Roma's (ribs and steak). Paradise Buffet. Lanai Express fast food.

Entertainment: None.

Other facilities: Casino, bars, and gift shop.

FOUR QUEEN'S HOTEL & CASINO, *202 E. Fremont Street. Tel. 702/385-4011, Fax 702/387-5123. Toll free reservations 800/634-6045. Website: www.fourqueens.com. 700 Rooms. Rates: $29-149. Major credit cards accepted. Located in the Casino Center area between Casino Center Blvd. and 3rd Street.*

Another hotel with Victorian decor in the guest rooms, the twin towers of the Four Queens house comfortable rooms that are decently sized and attractively furnished. Their best feature is the four-poster bed. Upgraded suite accommodations have in-room Jacuzzis.

Dining: Hugo's Cellar (Continental), Magnolia's (American/International), French Quarter (Continental), coffee shop (24 hour). Fast food outlets.

Entertainment: None.

Other facilities: Casino, bars, and gift shop.

JACKIE GAUGHAN'S PLAZA HOTEL, *1 Main Street. Tel. 702/386-2110, Fax 702/382-8281. Toll free reservations 800/634-6575. Website: www.jackiegaughan.com. 1,037 Rooms. Rates; $40-90. Major credit cards accepted. Located in the Casino Center area at the foot of Fremont Street.*

The good part about the accommodations at the Plaza (aside from the almost ridiculously low price) are that they are oversized. Unfortunately, despite the fact that the rooms in this venerable establishment have finally received some overdue remodeling, the furnishings are still rather drab and simple. On the other hand, they are comfortable. The distant views from the upper floors are alright but if you face the railroad tracks don't even bother looking out your window. The Plaza is one of the few hotels that still has the old penny slots.

Dining: Center Stage Restaurant (American/Italian) and Plaza Diner (24 hour with a 1950's theme). Chop-Chop Chinese Buffet and several snack bars and fast food eateries in a food court.

Entertainment: The showroom features the adult oriented show called *Naked Angels.* Omaha Lounge.

Other facilities: Casino, bar, swimming pool, tennis, gift/logo shop, and wedding chapel.

LADY LUCK CASINO HOTEL, *206 N. 3rd Street. Tel. 702/477-3000, Fax 702/384-2832. Toll free reservations 800/523-9582. Website: www.ladylucklv.com. 791 Rooms. Rates: $45-125. Major credit cards accepted. Located in the Casino Center area, one block north of Fremont Street between 3rd and 4th Streets.*

The brightly colored and spacious rooms in the modern 25-story high tower are comfortably furnished and all boast refrigerators. There are also some poolside garden units. "Junior suites" have Jacuzzi tubs. Considering the prices charged, this is an excellent value. The rooms, however, are more attractive than the public areas that are, at best, mediocre.

Dining: Burgundy Room (Continental), Marco Polo (Italian), and Winner's Cafe (24 hour). The Express Buffet is a snack bar.

Entertainment: The showroom has a daytime celebrity impersonation show (*Stars of the Strip*). There is also entertainment in the evening. Lounge.

Other facilities: Casino, bars, swimming pool, and gift shop.

LAS VEGAS CLUB, *18 E. Fremont Street. Tel. 702/385-1664, Fax 702/ 387-6071. Toll free reservations 800/634-6532. 410 Rooms. Rates: $34-50. Major credit cards accepted. Located in the Casino Center area at the west end of Fremont Street, corner of Main Street.*

One of the older hotels in an area of older establishments, the Las Vegas Club consists of a small original building with small rooms and a newer tower with somewhat bigger accommodations. None are anything to write home about but you will get clean and comfortable facilities for a very low price. The hotel has a sports theme, especially in the newer wing where a part of the casino is made to look something like the inside of a stadium. Well, sort of – they didn't spend as much money as a Strip hotel would have so it isn't nearly as realistic. Their main claim to fame is a collection of sports (mainly baseball) memorabilia.

Dining: Great Moments Room (Continental), The Upper Deck (24 hour), and the Dugout (American).

Entertainment: None.

Other facilities: Casino and bars.

AROUND LAS VEGAS

Very Expensive

THE REGENT LAS VEGAS, *221 N. Rampart Boulevard. Tel. 702/869-7777, Fax 702/869-7771. Toll free reservations 877/869-8777. Website: www.regentlasvegas.com. 541 Rooms. Rates: $195-525; suites from $500. Major credit cards accepted. Located in the Summerlin area of northwest Las Vegas. Take US 95 north from downtown into Summerlin Parkway. Hotel located just south of the Rampart exit.*

Part of the sprawling master-planned community of Summerlin, the Regent is the first American venture of a Swiss-owned company. It opened in the second half of 1999 and was the first off-Strip resort built to cater primarily to the *Conde Naste* crowd. It attempts to lure travelers who usually go to Palm Springs or Scottsdale rather than by competing with Strip properties. The hotel consists of two approximately equal sized mid-rise guest buildings called *The Palms* and the *Spa Tower* that are linked together by a low rise structure that houses many of the hotel's restaurants and other public facilities. Spanish revival architecture is the overall theme of the buildings although there are two distinctive interior styles for the guest wings. The lobbies and other public areas boasts a simple elegance and tranquility although the round domed casino is quite eye catching. There are 11 acres of lovely grounds and gardens with more than 800 palm trees and several waterfalls. The property is within a five minute drive of no fewer than five different golf courses. The Paseo de Vida is where you will find a small but pretty shopping arcade in addition to some of the hotel's upscale restaurants.

Standard guest rooms measure a spacious 560 square feet and feature walk-in closet, bar, separate sitting area with sofa, and writing desk. Marble bathrooms boast double vanities, whirlpool tub and separate shower. Some units feature French doors. Approximately 80 suites range from just a tad better than the basic rooms to extravagant facilities with more than 2,000 square feet of space. One super suite measures three times larger than that.

Dining: Ceres (seafood), Parian (American), Hamada of Japan, J. C. Wooloughan Irish Pub, Oxo (steakhouse), and Spiedini (Italian). Upstairs Market Buffet and the Waterside Cafe (seasonal, by the pool).

Entertainment: Live music in the Irish Pub and Addison's Lounge in the casino.

Facilities: Casino, bar, putting green, swimming pool, gift/logo shop, and shopping arcade. Golf arrangements can be made by the concierge. The *Aquate Sulis* is a full service luxury health spa that bears the original Roman name of the public bath that would later become the English town of Bath. Massage, facials, aroma therapy, body wraps, scrubs, yoga and thalassotherapy are among the many treatments offered. The spa has its own salon and boutique.

Moderate

BOULDER STATION HOTEL & CASINO, *4111 Boulder Highway. Tel. 702/432-7777, Fax 702/432-7730. Toll free reservations 800/683-7777. Website: www.stationcasinos.com. 268 Rooms. Rates: $59-109. Major credit cards accepted. Located just to the south of the Boulder Highway exit of I-515, between Desert Inn Road and Sahara Avenue.*

Colorful decor and modern furnishings highlight these nice sized and comfortable rooms at a great price. It isn't that far from the action of the

Strip as long as you have transportation. The casino is quite attractive, especially the live gaming area with its high ceiling and stained glass that depicts famous old trains. We also like the polished wooden floors in some areas of the casino, a contrast with almost all casinos, which usually have carpeting throughout the gaming area. The place has a lively atmosphere and is popular with the locals for its many fine restaurants. Many of these are the same name and style as those at the nearer to the Strip Palace Station but we generally like the overall appearance and atmosphere here better.

Dining: The Broiler (American), Guadalajara (Mexican), Iron Horse Cafe (24 hour), and Pasta Palace (Italian). Feast Buffet and several fast-food outlets and snack bars.

Entertainment: The Railhead has celebrity entertainment and also serves as a nightclub.

Other facilities: Casino, bar, swimming pool, gift/logo shop, game arcade, child care center, and multi-screen cinema.

DOUBLETREE CLUB HOTEL, *7250 Pollock Drive. Tel. 702/948-4000, Fax 702/948-4100. Toll free reservations 888/444-CLUB. Website: www.clubhotels.com. 190 Rooms. Rates: $89-119. Major credit cards accepted. Located immediately to the west of the Warm Springs Road exit of I-215. Alternatively, take Las Vegas Blvd. south to Warm Springs and then east.*

This hotel is actually designed for the business traveler (their Club Room has many business services including a CopyMax self-service business center), but the prices are comparable to other high quality non-casino hotels, so there's no reason you can't use if for a Vegas vacation. It's conveniently located to the airport as well as the Strip as long as you have a car. Each spacious room features a work desk, coffee maker, iron/ironing board, and hair dryer, among other conveniences and amenities. And, since this is a Doubletree family member, you can get those delicious chocolate chip cookies upon check-in.

Dining: Au Bon Pain Bakery Cafe (breakfast, snacks and light meals). Applebee's Neighborhood Bar & Grille is immediately adjacent to the hotel.

Entertainment: None.

Other facilities: Swimming pool and fully equipped exercise room.

SAM'S TOWN, *5111 Boulder Highway. Tel. 702/456-7777, Fax 702/454-8014. Toll free reservations 800/634-6371. Website: www.samstownlv.com. 650 Rooms. Rates: $45-150; suites from $125-300. Major credit cards accepted. Located where Harmon Avenue and Nellis Boulevard intersect Boulder Highway. For Attractions, see Chapter 12.*

The rooms at Sam's Town have a definite western flair when it comes to decor, although it is a modern western style rather than cowboy old west. They're spacious, comfortable and very attractive. Many units overlook the beautiful 25,000 square foot atrium lobby that goes by the name of Mystic Falls Park and we prefer the view from them over those that face the street. The latter sometimes have good distant mountain or Strip views but those on the lower floors only look out on the generally unattractive Boulder Strip. There are also a good selection of suites of varying luxury.

Dining: Billy Bob's Steak House & Saloon, Mary's Diner (American), Papamio's (Italian), Fresh Harvest Cafe (24 hour), Willy & Jose's Cantina (Mexican). Firelight Buffet, deli, fast food court and ice cream parlor.

Entertainment: The multi-use *Sam's Town Live* is a venue for celebrity entertainment as well as being a nightclub. Lounge entertainment in Roxy's Saloon.

Other Facilities: Casino, bars, swimming pool, bowling alley, gift/logo shop, shopping, game arcade, 18-screen cinema with stadium style seating, and "A Place for Kids" child care center .

SANTA FE STATION HOTEL & CASINO, *4949 N. Rancho Drive. Tel. 702/658-4900, Fax 702/658-4919. Toll free reservations: 800/872-6823. Website: www.stationcasinos.com. 200 Rooms. Rates: $49-99. Most major credit cards accepted. Located at the intersection of US 95 and just north of Lone Mountain Road.*

The southwestern furnishings and decor in the bright and cheerful rooms of the Santa Fe make it a delightful place to stay if you don't mind being a little bit further away from the main centers of action in Las Vegas. To some people, of course, the relative peace and quiet is a big plus. On the other hand, we don't think too many people come to Vegas for a rest cure. The mountain view from some rooms are pretty decent. All of the public areas at the Santa Fe have a genuine southwestern flavor and an air of elegance. Now that it has been acquired by Station Casinos they have, of course, added a few railroad items – such as a wall mural showing the famous Santa Fe locomotive engines. Considering the prices and everything else, we think this hotel is an excellent value.

Dining: Taos Steakhouse, Santa Fe Cafe (24 hour), Capri Ristorante (Italian). Food court.

Entertainment: Lounge with live entertainment.

Other Facilities: Casino, bars, swimming pool, bowling alley, and ice skating rink. Gift shop.

TEXAS STATION HOTEL & GAMBLING HALL, *2101 Texas Star Lane, N. Las Vegas. Tel. 702/631-1000, Fax 702/631-8120. Toll free reservations 800/654-8888. Website: www.stationcasinos.com. 200 Rooms. Rates: $59-129. Most major credit cards accepted. Located at the intersection of Rancho Road and Lake Mead Blvd.*

Although the number of rooms is quite small by Las Vegas standards, especially considering the big casino at Texas, they more than make up for the lack of quantity with their high quality. The rooms are big and comfortable, featuring wrought iron fixtures and genuine oak wood furniture. The rich and warm brocade upholstery adds a final nice touch.

The public areas have a few pretty features as well. A beautiful statue of a white stallion is located in the center of one of the casino bars. Most of the hotel's restaurants are attractively situated along a "river" walkway to one side of the casino.

Dining: Guadalajara (Mexican), San Lorenzo (Italian), Austin Steakhouse, and Yellow Rose Cafe (24 hour). Feast Around the World Buffet and large food court.

Entertainment: Lounge entertainment at the wildly Texan themed Armadillo Lounge.

Other facilities: Casino, bars, swimming pool, gift/logo shop, shopping, game arcade, "Kid's Quest" child care center, bowling alley and multi-screen cinema.

Inexpensive

ARIZONA CHARLIE'S, *740 S. Decatur Blvd. Tel. 702/258-5200, Fax 702/258-5192. Toll free reservations 800/342-2695. Website: www.azcharlies.com. 257 Rooms. Rates: $48-69; suites from $105. Major credit cards accepted. Located a half mile south of the Decatur Blvd. exit of US 95 or west from the Strip via any major intersecting street west to Decatur and then north.*

You'll get clean and comfortable rooms that are attractively decorated and are almost a steal as long as you have a car to get to other places. (There isn't much of anything to see or do in the area where this hotel is located.) The public facilities aren't particularly attractive but are almost always crowded with local residents from the area who like to try their luck and are pleased with the value they find at Arizona Charlie's.

Dining: China Charlie's (Chinese), Yukon Grille (American/ steakhouse), and Sourdough Cafe (24 hour). Wild West Buffet and several outlets in a small food court.

Entertainment: The Naughty Ladies Saloon hosts a variety of musical programs. There is also entertainment on Monday night during NFL football games.

Other facilities: Casino, bars, swimming pool, gift/logo shop, and game arcade.

ARIZONA CHARLIE'S EAST, *4575 Boulder Highway. Tel. 702/951-9100, Fax 702/951-1046. Toll free reservations 800/362-4040. Website: www.azcharlies.com. 300 Rooms. Rates: $45-75. Major credit cards accepted. Located in the middle of the "Boulder Strip" between Flamingo and Desert Inn Roads. From the Strip, take Flamingo Road east.*

You know how in most cases you usually wind up liking the original better than the sequel? Well, that's not the case here because we find

Charlie's East to be a much nicer place than the one on Decatur. The casino and public areas are smaller but they're much brighter and attractive. There is very little in the way of the old west theme here because the property was originally intended to have a Mediterranean decor. However, it never opened as such because the original owner couldn't get a gaming license. Carl Icahn came along and snatched it up. He decided to keep the spanking new interior despite the fact that it doesn't go along with the name. We hope it stays this way because it is just fine exactly the way it is.

Guest accommodations are all suites but don't get all carried away. It is essentially an upgraded motel facility with clean and decent rooms at an attractive price. It's good for those who want a little extra space as it is more in the style of accommodations found in some extended-stay facilities.

Dining: Yukon Grille (American/steakhouse) and Sourdough Cafe (24 hour). Wild West Buffet and a small food court.

Entertainment: The casino lounge has live music.

Other facilities: Casino, bar, gift shop, swimming pool and whirlpool.

CASTAWAY'S HOTEL & CASINO, *2800 E. Fremont Street. Tel. 702/ 385-9123, Fax 702/385-9123. Toll free reservations: 800/826-2800. Website: www.castaways-lv.com. 468 Rooms. Rates: $34-59. Major credit cards accepted. Located where Fremont Street becomes Boulder Highway (Corner of Charleston Blvd.).*

Over the years hotel names in Las Vegas are getting to be kind of confusing. This is NOT the old Castaways that was on the Strip where the Mirage now stands. However, it IS the same hotel that opened in 1954 under the name Showboat. At press time the new owners had only begun to rework the public areas from the showboat theme to one that is more tropical. As a result, we can't really tell you how things are going to work out. However, at the time of the changeover the rooms in the tower section were clean and comfortable. Although standard fare, you will definitely get your money's worth. We wouldn't expect that to change. The older motel section behind the main tower is older and below par. We would avoid them. The new owners plan to eventually knock them down and replace it with a convention center and other facilities but that is probably a few years off. Public areas are cheerful and attractive despite a variety of different themes from various eras of the hotel's long history. If you like bingo then it is worth mentioning that the hotel's Bingo Gardens is one of the largest and most attractive facilities of its kind in Las Vegas.

Dining: Blue Marlin (Mexican/Spanish seafood) and Prime Cut (steakhouse). Las Brisas Buffet and Pelican Rock Coffee Shop (24 hour). There are also several fast food outlets.

Entertainment: The attractive Castaways Cabaret (formerly the Mardi Gras Room) hosts a variety of entertainment programs and the outer bar area also has live entertainment.

Other facilities: Casino, bars, swimming pool, bowling alley, arcade, and gift/logo shop.

FIESTA HOTEL & CASINO, *2400 N. Rancho Drive, N. Las Vegas. Tel. 702/631-7000, Fax 702/631-7070. Toll free reservations 800/731-7333. Website: www.fiestacasinohotel.com. 100 Rooms. Rates: $49-99. Most major credit cards accepted. Located at the intersection of Lake Mead Blvd., across the street from Texas Station.*

The Fiesta has been acquired by Station Casinos although the company plans on keeping the Fiesta brand separate from those properties with a Station name. With budget priced average to slightly better accommodations in a motor-inn type facility, this is another hotel that's located on the fringe and requires transportation. Recent expansion and renovation of the public areas have turned the Fiesta from a small locals place into a very attractive and not so small casino. It has a lively atmosphere.

Dining: Blue Agave (seafood), Garduno's (Mexican), Old San Francisco Steak House, Mr. G's (24 hour), and Roxy's Pipe Organ Pizzeria. Festival Buffet, deli and many fast food outlets.

Entertainment: The Roxy Theater has live entertainment as does the Cabo Lounge.

Other Facilities: Casino, bars, game arcade, gift shop, and swimming pool.

NEVADA PALACE HOTEL & CASINO, *5255 Boulder Highway. Tel. 702/458-8810, Fax 702/458-3361. Toll free reservations 800/634-6283. 220 Rooms. Rates: $29-49. Most major credit cards accepted. Located on the "Boulder Strip" between Tropicana and Harmon Avenues.*

This is far from a palace as the motel style accommodations are quite basic. It's not high on our recommended list as a place to stay but will do in a pinch when rooms are hard to come by. It's also acceptable if you're on a really tight hotel budget. You will need a car to stay here.

Dining: La Pasta Bella Steak & Seafood (also buffet option), Herman's deli, and Boulder Cafe (24 hour).

Entertainment: None regularly scheduled.

Other facilities: Casino and bar.

SILVERTON HOTEL, *3333 Blue Diamond Road. Tel. 702/263-7777, Fax 702/896-5635. Toll free reservations 866/544-4455. 304 Rooms. Rates: $39-109. Most major credit cards accepted. Located about a half-mile west of Las Vegas Blvd. at Industrial Road and the Blue Diamond Road exit of I-15.*

Although it has been a number of years since this hotel was renamed Silverton, it will always be "Boomtown" to us. That's mainly because the old west mining town appearance of the exterior was better reflected in the original name. Well, enough longing for the old days. Silverton is a friendly little place where the budget minded traveler will find decent accommodations for the price. It is motor inn style and that is appropriate because you will need a car to stay here. (You can be on the Strip in about five minutes but walking isn't an option and the shuttle service isn't always convenient.)

Dining: Fireside Cafe (24 hour), All American Buffet and deli.

Entertainment: Rattlesnake Ricky's Lounge. They sometimes have outdoor concerts by the pool.

Other facilities: Casino, bar, swimming pool, gift/logo shop, and arcade..

SUNCOAST HOTEL & CASINO, *9090 Alta Drive. Tel. 702/636-7111, Fax 702/636-7124. Toll free reservations 877/677-7111. Website: www.suncoastcasino.com. 216 Rooms. Rates: $56-89. Major credit cards accepted. Located in Summerlin at the intersection of Rampart Blvd., adjacent to the Regent Las Vegas. Take US 95 north from downtown to Summerlin Parkway and then south at the Rampart Blvd. exit.*

This new hotel (it opened in September, 2000) is a delightful place. Although not a big hotel (an expansion to about 400 rooms is already planned), the casino and other public areas are surprisingly spacious and the attractive Mediterranean theme is very pleasing. The atmosphere can even be said to have a feel of elegance. All of the rooms in this ten-story hotel are a generous 550-square foot and are well decorated in a modern style. Floor to ceiling windows in every unit allow excellent views of the surrounding areas which encompass beautifully manicured golf courses and the nearby foothills and mountains. The top floor is occupied entirely by larger suites. Although the Suncoast may be a few dollars more than most of the other inexpensive hotels in this geographic section, the quality is also higher and it represents an excellent value.

Dining: Primo's (steakhouse), Via Veneto (Italian), Senor Miguel's (Mexican), the Oyster Bar, and Cafe Siena (24 hour). St. Tropez Buffet, fast food outlet, ice cream parlor, and Seattle's Best Coffee.

Entertainment: The showroom is home to celebrity entertainment.

Other facilities: Casino, bars, gift/logo shop, liquor store, barber shop and beauty salon, exercise room, bowling alley, and 16-screen cinema.

HENDERSON

Very Expensive

HYATT REGENCY LAKE LAS VEGAS, *67 MonteLago Boulevard. Tel. 702/457-1234, Fax 702/558-5111. Toll free reservations 800/554-9288. Website: www.hyatt.com. 496 Rooms. Rates: $160-325; "casitas" from $299. Major credit cards accepted. Located about seven miles east of the Lake Mead*

Drive exit of I-515 and then left at the entrance of the Lake Las Vegas Resort and right on MonteLago, following signs.

For years Hyatt lovers have been asking when was Hyatt going to come to Vegas? Well, they're about 17 miles away from the Strip but those who are seeking a luxurious full service resort environment reminiscent of the best of Scottsdale will definitely find that here. Because of its location we haven't included this hotel in the chapter with attractions but if you are in the neighborhood it is definitely worth seeing even if you aren't going to be staying here.

Situated on 21 acres fronting the beautiful 320 acre man-made Lake Las Vegas, the surrounding colors of the mountains and a distant view of the Strip are nothing short of spectacular. So are the elaborate grounds, which have gardens, several elaborate pool areas and even a white-sand beach. But the most beautiful feature of all is the hotel's tiered lobby which enters at the street and goes down three levels to the patio which, in turn, drops a couple of more levels down to the lake shore. Besides providing a wonderful lake panorama, the lobby itself is a sight for the eyes with its fountains, tiles and unusual lighting fixtures. It is generally a Moroccan/North African theme and is done with typical Hyatt flair and style.

Accommodations, although spacious and furnished nicely with lovely colors, are generally a tad below the level of what you would expect from the public areas. Standard in-room features include hair dryer, coffee maker, iron and ironing board, refrigerator and safe. There are also suites with a separate parlor area and several two to four bedroom "casitas" (little houses) with private entrances. The latter are truly worthy of the best that can be found in Scottsdale or Palm Springs.

Finally, although the hotel does have a casino, this isn't anything like a Vegas casino in many ways. It is quite small since this is not considered to be a gaming establishment per se. The casino is simply for the convenience of guests. Nonetheless, it is an attractive little place and even has windows so you can take in the beautiful surrounding scenery while you play. Imagine that on the Strip!

Dining: Japengo (Pacific Rim) and Cafe Tajine (Moroccan inspired Continental). Also, snacks and light meals at Marrakesh Express and in season at the Sandsabar & Grill outdoor cafe.

Entertainment: A Moroccan trio plays in the Arabesque Lounge.

Other facilities: Casino, bar, swimming pool with full water recreation area and sand beach, adjacent golf course, sailing, fishing, Spa Moulay with treatment rooms, sauna and full service fitness center, and Camp Hyatt children's program.

Moderate

SUNSET STATION HOTEL & CASINO, *1301 W. Sunset Road. Tel. 702/547-7777, Fax 702/547-7606. Toll free reservations 888/786-7389. Website: www.stationcasinos.com. 456 Rooms. Rates: $49-159. Major credit cards accepted. Located two blocks west of the Sunset Road exit of I-515. For Attractions, see Chapter 12.*

This hotel is one of the few "locals" hotels that is glamorous enough to be compared with its bigger Strip competition. The beautiful decor isn't limited to the public areas. All of the oversized guest rooms are comfortably furnished and decorated in pleasing light shades with a hint of southwest or Mediterranean colors and style. There are also more luxurious petite and king suites available at higher rates.

Dining: Capri Ristorante (Italian), Costa del Sol (seafood; separate Oyster Bar), Guadalajara (Mexican), Sonoma Cellar (steakhouse), Sunset Brewing Company (micro-brewery/American/pizza), and Sunset Cafe (24 hour). Feast Around the World Buffet and several fast-food eateries.

Entertainment: The Club Madrid is a showroom for celebrity entertainment and also serves as a nightclub. They also have an outdoor amphitheater where concerts are held (except in summer).

Other facilities: Casino, bars, swimming pool, gift/logo shop, game arcade, child care center, and multi-screen cinema.

Inexpensive

THE RESERVE HOTEL & CASINO, *777 W. Lake Mead Drive. Tel. 702/558-7000, Fax 702/558-7008. Website: www.stationcasinos.com (will change upon impending ownership transfer). 224 Rooms. Rates: $39-119; suites from $89-219.. Major credit cards accepted. Located at the Lake Mead Drive exit of I-515. For Attractions, see Chapter 12.*

The safari theme that enlivens the public areas is continued all the way to the attractive and spacious guest rooms. Don't worry about all the jungle decor – it's safe to turn the lights out at night. One possible disadvantage of this hotel (if you don't have a car) is its location – not only is it a considerable distance from the Strip, but it isn't in the part of Henderson where you're surrounded by many restaurants and shopping opportunities as was the case with Sunset Station.

As we went to press Station Casinos had finally completed acquisition of the property. Rumor has it that they intend to expand it and also do a redesign to fit the company's Fiesta brand. If that happens, good-bye to the safari theme. However, as the latter is not likely to happen for at least a couple of years you can go by what we've said about the Reserve as it is now.

Dining: Congo Jack's Cafe (24 hour), Serengeti Spaghetti Company (Italian), Tusk's Wood-fire Grille (steakhouse), and Taco Zulu Mexican Grille. Grand Safari Buffet and Pasta Mombasa Cafe (lighter fare).

Entertainment: Wasimbas Lounge.

Other facilities: Casino, bars, swimming pool, Jacuzzi, sand volleyball court, gift/logo shop, and arcade.

TIME SHARES & EXTENDED STAY ACCOMMODATIONS

If you like to visit Las Vegas every year or even several times a year (and many people do), you might want to consider a time share unit. Most are apartment style facilities and you have a guaranteed place to stay at a definite time. Costs run from modest to extremely expensive (almost as much as buying a small vacation home) depending upon how big and how luxurious the facilities are. Here's a rundown on some popular Las Vegas time shares:

CARRIAGE HOUSE, *105 E. Harmon Avenue. Tel. 702/798-1020 or 800/221-2301.*

Located a few blocks from the Strip near the MGM Grand. Also has some hotel units.

FAIRFIELD COMMUNITIES' LAS VEGAS RESORT, *265 E. Harmon Avenue.*

Located just a few blocks from the Strip and near the Hard Rock, this will be one of the largest and most elaborate facilities of its type when it opens during the summer of 2001. They have a sales office in Harrah's if you want more information.

HILTON GRAND VACATIONS CLUB, *Tel. 800/799-4482.*

HGVC must be successful because they have recently expanded into their second location. The first is the **HGVC Flamingo**, *at the Flamingo Hotel, Tel. 702/697-2900.* Occupying a luxurious art-deco style building behind the gardens of the Flamingo, this is a beautiful facility in every way and has the added advantage that guests can make use of all the facilities of the Flamingo Hotel. **HGVC Las Vegas Hilton**, *455 Karen Avenue, Tel. 702/946-9210* has been operating about two years. It consists of studio units and one or two bedroom villas.

POLO TOWERS, *3745 Las Vegas Blvd. South. Tel. 702/261-1000 or 800/935-2233.* A nice property located in the middle of the action. The Polo Towers also has some regular hotel units.

RAMADA VACATION SUITES, *100 Winnick Avenue. Tel. 702/731-6100.*

More for the budget time share buyer, this slightly off-Strip property isn't in the same level of luxury as the preceding places by a long stretch.

Now, if you come to Las Vegas less often but spend a longer period of time (over a week), you'll probably find it is more economical to put your baggage down in an extended stay hotel. There are many places of this type throughout the Las Vegas area but you have to be careful since many of them are of dubious quality and sometimes attract less than the best element. However, a few that are satisfactory are **Budget Suites of America** (seven locations), **Extended Stay America** (three locations), and **Residence Inn**. The latter is a Marriott subsidiary and is the highest in terms of quality of all the extended stay places and their addresses can be found in the listing of national chain properties.

ANOTHER WAY TO AN EXTENDED STAY - LUXURY CONDOS

Our millionaire readers will be interested in this news. All others will just have to read it and weep. A new trend in Las Vegas is the building of luxury high-rise condominiums. While these can certainly be the primary residence of the owner, a large number of owners bought with the intention of making this a second home because they like to visit Vegas so much. The foremost example of this new breed of living is **Turnberry Place***, a three-building complex in its own private park setting along Paradise Road near the Convention Center and only blocks from the Strip. Units begin at around $400,000 and go up to in excess of $2 million. If that isn't upscale enough for you then you can buy a unit at the* **Park Towers** *where prices begin at $750,000 and rise all the way to $5 million. Of course, at both properties you get concierge service with that so it's worth the price! Then again, with hotel prices rising so much it may be the way to go. We wish!*

Turnberry Development also owns Strip property formerly occupied by the El Rancho. They haven't decided if they're going to build a hotel/casino on the land or another condo. If it is the latter, it won't be the first condo on the Strip. The **Jockey Club***, adjacent to Bellagio, was once a hotel but was converted into condominiums. They aren't nearly as luxurious or expensive as Turnberry Place. There are also plans to build a condo adjacent to the Aladdin, just off the Strip.*

CAMPING & RV SITES

Las Vegas is one of the few big cities where you can hook up your RV right in the middle of town. While there aren't that many RV campsites on the Strip, there are plenty within a ten or fifteen minute drive. All of the places below have full RV facilities.

Several are located on the property of major hotels. If you can pitch your tent there, it will be so noted.

- **American Campgrounds**, *3440 N. Las Vegas Blvd., N. Las Vegas. Tel. 702/ 643-1222.* Tent sites.
- **Arizona Charlie's East**, *4575 Boulder Highway. Tel. 702/951-5911 or 800/ 970-7280*
- **Boulder Lakes RV Resort**, *6201 Boulder Highway. Tel. 702/435-1157*
- **Castaways Hotel RV Park**, *2800 Fremont Street. Tel. 702/385-9164*
- **Circusland RV Park**, *2880 S. Las Vegas Blvd., part of Circus Circus Hotel. Tel. 702/794-3757 or 800/444-2472*
- **Covered Wagon RV Park**, *6635 Boulder Highway. Tel. 702/454-7090*
- **KOA Campground**, *4315 Boulder Highway. Tel. 702/451-5527.* Tent sites.
- **Oasis Las Vegas RV Resort**, *2711 Windmill Lane. Tel. 702/260-2020*
- **Road Runner RV Park**, *4711 Boulder Highway. Tel. 702/456-4711*
- **Sam's Town Hotel RV Park**, *5225 Boulder Highway. Tel. 702/454-8055*
- **Silverton Hotel RV Resort**, *3333 Blue Diamond Road. Tel. 702/263-7777 or 800/588-7711*

10. WHERE TO EAT

As was briefly mentioned at the outset of this book, up until recently gourmet folks looked down upon Las Vegas as a sort of culinary wasteland. All that has changed in practically the blink of an eye as scores of outstanding restaurants have opened up all over the city, but especially in the better Strip hotels. The casino moguls have attracted some of the nation's premier chefs to work here and the result is a selection of first class restaurants that rival New York or San Francisco. And the dining Renaissance shows no signs of a slowdown as new places continue to open on a regular basis.

The non-gourmet won't have any problems in finding a place to eat either. The sheer number and variety of restaurants makes choosing which ones to recommend to you a daunting yet enjoyable task. Whether you dine at a major hotel, in one of the many independent restaurants along the Strip, or elsewhere around town, you're sure to find something to your taste and budget.

Major hotels generally have anywhere from four to ten restaurants but some of the newer and bigger hotels can even have as many as 15 eateries. In this chapter we'll separate the eating places into two main sections: restaurants and buffets. A common feature of the hotel is the coffee shop. These 24 hour restaurants serve family style meals that are quite good at reasonable prices. To use the term "coffee shop" would often be demeaning to their quality. So, while we'll sometimes use the term "cafe" (which is what the hotels usually call them to make them sound even nicer), we'll also throw in "coffee shop" once in a while to simply distinguish them from other restaurants. Except for one very special cafe we won't include them in the regular reviews but do see the sidebar later in this chapter for information on some of the better ones. Overall, you won't go wrong by dining in most of them.

RESTAURANT PRICE CATEGORIES

Prices are for entree and are exclusive of beverage, tax and gratuity. The price ranges shown here apply only to restaurants and not buffets:
Very Expensive: *More than $40*
Expensive: *$26-40*
Moderate: *$12-25*
Inexpensive: *Under $12*

Reviewing all of the good restaurants in a city like Las Vegas isn't possible unless you have a 500-page book just on that topic. There are literally hundreds of places that can be said to have something going for them. Here we'll take a closer look at more than 130 different restaurants of all types that we think are worthy of your business. Although the emphasis will be on the higher priced categories, we've included everything from coffee shops to the fanciest gourmet restaurant. Not included in that extensive listing are about 40 buffets that are described in further detail in a separate section of this chapter. Also check out Chapter 13, *Nightlife & Entertainment*, for a few fine eateries that emphasize entertainment along with the food.

THE STRIP

Very Expensive

ANASAZI, *Aladdin (in the Desert Passage). Tel. 702/836-0989. Major credit cards accepted. Lunch and dinner served daily. Reservations are suggested.*

The famous Santa Fe restaurant has joined the list of gourmet restaurants that have opened a Las Vegas branch. The dramatic entrance area is designed to resemble a *kiva*, the ceremonial chamber of the ancient Anasazi. The remainder of the interior is more modern in style but is unmistakably southwestern and Native American in its decor. It consists of the "courtyard" which is the main dining room and several other smaller rooms. There's an exhibition style kitchen. Anasazi features the delicate textures of New Mexican cuisine.

This isn't Tex-Mex or southwestern, but the cooking has elements of both. Most cooking is done in a large wood-burning oven. Some good choices from the menu include either the wild boar tamale or foie gras nacho eggplant for starters and, for the main course, either one of three duck dishes, roast lobster served with crispy crab cakes or the delicious cinnamon chili-rubbed beef. During the time when the main dining room is closed between lunch and dinner you can order from a limited menu at the bar.

AUREOLE, *Mandalay Bay. Tel. 702/632-7401. Major credit cards accepted. Dinner served nightly. Reservations are suggested.*

Chef Charlie Palmer of New York has opened shop in Las Vegas. The much honored Palmer has received numerous awards, including the best restaurant in the Big Apple. In the short span of less than two years Aureole has impressed the toughest cuisine critics from around the world and Aureole has taken its place among the "must" restaurants for the true gourmet. Seasonal American and Italian dishes are prepared by long-term Palmer disciples Joe and Megan Romano. Only the freshest ingredients are used. The simple but somehow still luxurious interior is highlighted by the unique four story high wine tower. The stewards don harnesses and are hoisted up the tower to retrieve bottles from the "Cellar in the Sky." The wine list, of course, is top notch with a couple of vintages reaching the astronomical $40,000 a bottle. Wow – that's a quick way to blow your dining budget! The service at Aureole is impeccable, as should be in the case of a fine restaurant, but sometimes doesn't happen in restaurants as large as this one is (383 seats).

COMMANDER'S PALACE, *Aladdin (in the Dessert Passage). Tel. 702/ 892-8272. Major credit cards accepted. Lunch and dinner served daily. Reservations are suggested.*

The Brennan family's New Orleans restaurant is justly world famous and, if you have ever eaten there, you won't be disappointed with their Las Vegas edition. The menu is quite similar, featuring New Orleans and Creole favorites, but they have done a little refining to include some southwestern elements by adding some locally available fresh ingredients. There are two members of the Brennan's who will serve as on-site management so you know they'll be true to the long standing traditions of Commander's Palace. Their marvelous Bananas Foster for dessert is, of course, going to be a menu staple here as well.

DELMONICO STEAKHOUSE, *The Venetian (on Restaurant Row). Tel. 702/733-5000. Major credit cards accepted. Dinner served nightly. Reservations are required. Dress code.*

Emeril Lagasse is one of America's best known chefs and, from the way he has been opening up restaurants, one of the most successful as well. He now brings his outstanding New Orleans Creole style steakhouse to the Strip and our response is completely positive. The succulent beef is prepared to perfection and served with flair in outstanding surroundings. Here, you can sit back and relax in leather booths with exquisite detail and savor what is definitely among the top steak places in town, and with all the great steakhouses in Las Vegas, that's saying a lot. They also have an excellent wine list.

EIFFEL TOWER RESTAURANT, *Paris. Tel. 702/948-6937. Major credit cards accepted. Dinner served nightly.*

Situated on the 11th floor of the Eiffel Tower replica, this unusual and elegant restaurant provides stunning views and beautiful surroundings. Given the location, and the prices, we wish we could say that this was one of the best restaurants in Las Vegas as far as food and service are concerned. Although we don't have a lot of complaints, the Eiffel Tower doesn't merit any special note in either of those more important categories. The menu is mostly traditional French although the kitchen staff has done some Americanization. That's probably alright for the masses but those paying a premium price in a restaurant of this type would, no doubt, prefer authentic French. The restaurant has a piano bar for entertainment.

GATSBY'S, *MGM Grand. Tel. 702/891-7777. Major credit cards accepted. Dinner served nightly except Sunday. Reservations are suggested.*

The most gourmet dining experience among several that are available at the MGM, Gatsby's is an elegant room where the California style French cuisine is superb. Intimate surroundings and professional, highly personalized service make for an enjoyable evening. In addition to the excellent selection of beef and fish entrees, Gatsby's has a number of vegetarian dishes. Some of the specialties of the house include ostrich, pate de foie gras, and Dover rack of lamb. The wine list is one of the longest in Las Vegas. Three separate wine cellars, one each for white, red, and champagnes, has more than 600 wines representing the entire world. Guests can see the wine cellar display inside the restaurant.

ISIS, *Luxor. Tel. 702/262-4773. Major credit cards accepted. Dinner served nightly. Reservations are suggested. Dress code.*

One of the most beautiful dining rooms in the city, it's almost worth a trip here just to experience the surroundings. There are the requisite (for the Luxor) Egyptian artifacts but the most beautiful feature is the colonnaded walkway surrounded by magnificent statues and generous amounts of glass embossed with the wings of Isis. Oh, yes, we might also mention that Isis has been declared by a number of "experts" to be one of the best restaurants in the nation. And Isis was actually here a couple of years before Las Vegas' dining Renaissance began in earnest. The food is delicious and imaginative Continental cuisine, served either in the traditional manner or with some twists conjured up by the acclaimed culinary staff. This is one of the restaurants worth spending extra on.

LE CIRQUE, *Bellagio. Tel. 702/693-8150. Major credit cards accepted. Dinner served nightly. Reservations are required. Dress code.*

Right off let's tell you that this isn't the restaurant for those on a limited budget. Seating only 80 guests, Le Cirque will set you back about $100 for a five course meal and a full seven courses runs more than $125, although you can get just the main course for around $45. Another New York City spinoff (which seems to be among the big trends in Las Vegas fine dining), it features excellent Continental cuisine. The appetizers are especially appealing, such as the foie gras saute or ravioli de truffe blanche. The intimate dining room allows the expert staff to offer careful and personalized service. Le Cirque has an outstanding wine list that includes more than 400 selections form all over the world. A knowledgeable sommelier will help you select just the right one.

LE PROVENCAL, *Paris. Tel. 702/967-7999. Major credit cards accepted. Lunch and dinner served daily.*

The informal and almost quaint dining room makes this a nice place to dine. The menu has both Italian and French entrees to choose from and all are well prepared and served by a competent staff. There's an open kitchen. We don't, however, see the justification for the prices because Le Provencal doesn't break any culinary ground. Prices are lower for lunch and if you don't mind a somewhat more limited menu then it makes a nice place for an afternoon meal. But then you'll have to cut back on your dinner budget. Maybe a coffee shop or buffet would be in order. Anyhow, their pizza with garlic, chicken breast and mushrooms is outstanding.

LUTECE, *The Venetian. Tel. 702/414-2220. Major credit cards accepted. Dinner served nightly. Reservations are suggested. Dress code.*

Perhaps this outstanding French restaurant would be more at home a couple of miles down the Strip at Paris because *Lutece* is the original Celtic name of Paris. But, then again, the Venetian abounds with great restaurants and this is only one of many you'll encounter here. Celebrity chef Ebehard Muller has taken the best of his New York restaurant of the same name and left the Las Vegas branch under the talented guidance of chef Robert Kirchoff.

The restaurant is both elegant and simple with its modernistic style. One wall is curved and provides a graceful atmosphere. The location overlooks the Strip facing the outside plaza of the Venetian. That adds to the ambiance, especially if you choose to dine al fresco on the terrace. The menu begins with delectable appetizers including caviar and foie gras. Entrees are equally wonderful and include pheasant and meat dishes although fresh fish and seafood are in most prominence. From the latter group we suggest the roasted lobster that has been shelled and bathed in cognac butter. Lutece has an extensive wine list and helpful sommelier to go along with the rest of the attentive staff.

MARK MILLER'S GRILLE ROOM & COYOTE CAFE, *MGM Grand (Studio Walk). Tel. 702/891-7349. Major credit cards accepted. Lunch and dinner served nightly.*

Located on the busy promenade, this two-room restaurant is the popular and usually quite crowded Las Vegas branch of the nationally famous eatery of the same name that originated in Santa Fe, New Mexico. Acclaimed chef Mark Miller serves modern southwestern style cuisine in a casually elegant and extremely attractive atmosphere in the Grille Room. While it is an excellent dining experience we do think it is on the overpriced side because good southwestern cuisine can usually be found at far less taxing prices (except for the aforementioned Anasazi). However, if you have a few extra bucks from your gambling winnings, you won't go wrong investing them here. The more moderately priced Coyote Cafe is out "street front" facing the Studio Walk. Even here prices tend to go into the Expensive category.

PICASSO, *Bellagio (on the lower level of the Via Bellagio). Tel. 702/693-7223. Major credit cards accepted. Dinner served nightly except Wednesday. Reservations are suggested. Dress code.*

One of what is a seemingly unending list of great restaurants at Bellagio, the Picasso features an interesting cuisine that combines French with a Spanish influence. The result is superb. You'll find such wonderful dishes as poached oysters, shrimp and scallops, grilled lamb noisettes or roasted veal chop, to name just a few. Pastry chef Patrick Coston does an outstanding job with the desserts. Original works by Picasso, of course, adorn the walls of this beautiful restaurant. When Steve Wynn was heading up Mirage Resorts, he liked to frequent Picasso. We're sure that he still drops in for a bite.

PRIME, *Bellagio (on the lower level of the Via Bellagio). Tel. 702/693-7223. Major credit cards accepted. Dinner served nightly. Reservations are suggested. Dress code.*

Bellagio's elegant steakhouse includes, in addition to first cut beef, a nice selection of seafood and chops. However, every course is wonderful. Appetizers include dishes such as crab mango salad and garlic soup with frogs legs. The sumptuous desserts make for a perfect ending to an outstanding meal, all exquisitely served by a knowledgeable and professional staff. The gorgeous room features exquisite draperies and although it's fairly big, it has the feel of a private dining salon.

RENOIR BY ALESSANDRO STRATTA, *The Mirage. Tel. 702/791-7111. Major credit cards are accepted. Dinner served nightly except Monday. Reservations are suggested.*

One of Las Vegas' finest French restaurants (although the menu shows definite American influences), Renoir's exquisite cuisine is a personal statement of its well known master chef. This award winning restaurant will impress you from the moment you walk in and are surrounded by beautiful works of art, complemented by the carefully selected color scheme. The food is simply wonderful but we were most impressed by the little extras – the tasty tidbits between courses and the great selection of breads including first rate bread sticks flavored with

LAS VEGAS - GOURMET CITY

A few years ago any connoisseur of fine food wood have had a big laugh if he or she saw the words Las Vegas and gourmet together. We've already alluded to how fine dining has come to the desert big time, but here are a few other things to consider.

The names of the top chefs in America are well represented, either in person or in restaurants that they own. Among this prestigious roster are **Wolfgang Puck** *(who currently has four different restaurants in Las Vegas),* **Emeril Lagasse** *(two restaurants),* **Charlie Palmer** *(two restaurants),* **Vincent Scotto** *and* **Todd English***. Gourmet devotees will obviously recognize some other names as they read through the restaurant listings.*

The other important measure of just how far this gourmet culinary trend has come is how often it is mentioned by noted publications. Major magazines and newspapers have all covered the story but perhaps the most telling statement was one that was recently carried in one of the most respected of fine dining publications. It unequivocally stated that the best 25 restaurants in Las Vegas are on a par with the best 25 restaurants of any city in the world. So, enjoy. That is, if you can afford it!

aged cheese and wrapped in prosciutto. The service is impeccable but will be considered too formal and stuffy for many diners. Then again, that's probably to be expected in a place where dinner is going to be in triple digits for one person.

SEASONS, *Bally's. Tel. 702/967-7999. Major credit cards are accepted. Dinner served Tuesday through Saturday. Reservations are suggested. Dress code.*

The name of the restaurant reflects their policy of changing the menu with the seasons of the year. No matter what time of the year you visit, however, you will encounter wonderful beef and seafood dishes as well as more unusual selections from around the world. The emphasis is on Continental cuisine. They have a large selection of fine wines including one of the biggest choices of champagne in Las Vegas. The decor also changes according to the season and features generous amounts of colorful fresh flowers.

ZEFFIRINO, *The Venetian (in the Grand Canal Shoppes). Tel. 702/414-3500. Most major credit cards accepted. Lunch served Monday through Friday; dinner served nightly. Sunday brunch. (Breakfast served during major conventions at the hotel.) Reservations are suggested.*

Long time Genoan chef extraordinaire Vincent Scotto has come to Las Vegas to personally supervise the culinary artistry at Zeffirino. Mr. Scotto has earned a reputation that has enabled him to cook for such luminaries as the Pope and Frank Sinatra, among many others. The specialties of the house are Italian seafood entrees prepared in wood fired ovens. Many of the ingredients are imported from Italy. The surroundings are elegant and the extensive wine list (more than 130 different selections) is superb. The service usually befits the decor and the notable status of the chef, but we have had reports of long waits (even with reservations) on weekend nights. It has quickly taken its place among the top restaurants in Las Vegas. You'll be able to find several entrees that are only in the Expensive price category.

Expensive

ALAN ALBERTS, *3763 Las Vegas Blvd. South. Tel. 702/740-4421. Major credit cards accepted. Dinner served nightly. Reservations are suggested.*

Not one of the city's oldest restaurants but certainly one of the most respected, Alan Albert's has a well deserved reputation for fine dining. You'll be treated to delectable vintage steaks and superb prime rib. The attractive dining room contains interesting Las Vegas memorabilia. The service is first rate but friendly, much more like you would find in a simple local restaurant. They also serve excellent seafood, especially the fresh lobster.

ANDRE'S FRENCH RESTAURANT, *Monte Carlo. Tel. 702/798-7151. Major credit cards accepted. Dinner served nightly.*

See the listing in the Downtown section for details.

BICE RISTORANTE, *Aladdin (in the Dessert Passage). Tel. 702/732-4210. Most major credit cards accepted. Lunch and dinner served daily.*

No, it doesn't rhyme with dice – it's pronounced "bee-chay" because it's Italian. However, there are definite world-wide influences ranging from Asian to South American, which is fitting, because Bice has about 25 locations around the world (including three others in the United States). The attractive decor is based on what you would have encountered in a fine restaurant in Cairo during the 1950's. Highlights are the wooden floor and large ceiling fans. The extensive menu has numerous pasta and risotto dishes as well as lobster and other fresh fish and seafood along with many meat and steak dishes. All are well prepared with the best ingredients and graciously served by a pleasant wait staff. The dessert menu is somewhat limited but they elevate tiramisu to a new art form.

CONRAD'S, *Flamingo Las Vegas. Tel. 702/733-3111. Major credit cards accepted. Dinner served nightly except Tuesday and Wednesday.*

A beautiful room with rich, warm woods and plenty of brass trim give Conrad's the atmosphere of a private ranch club. The menu includes a good variety of gourmet steaks, chops and seafood that are all well prepared to your specifications and graciously served. Sophisticated elegance all the way.

DRAGON COURT, *MGM Grand (Studio Walk). Tel. 702/891-7380. Major credit cards accepted. Dinner served nightly. Reservations are suggested.*

Not your run of the mill Chinese restaurant, Dragon Court features a beautiful and romantically intimate atmosphere along with first class service and excellent traditional Mandarin and Cantonese cuisine. The menu selection is quite large and features beef, seafood, poultry, and vegetarian selections. The fan-tailed crispy fried shrimp is a great appetizer. We also like the pupu platter and the honey glazed barbecued pork.

DRAI'S, *Barbary Coast. Tel. 702/737-0555. Major credit cards accepted. Dinner served Wednesday through Saturday. Reservations are suggested.*

The third restaurant owned by a Hollywood producer and his first in Las Vegas, Drai's is a sophisticated restaurant that features American cuisine influenced by both Italian and southern French cooking styles. Try the glazed Chilean sea bass or the leg of lamb that has been roasted for seven hours. Don't forget dessert – our favorite is the incredible Hot Chocolate Souffle! The restaurant features a fine selection of wines and champagnes. Drai's is a haven for the late night gourmet and even offers a special menu with entertainment that lasts from 8pm until six in the morning. There is no entertainment on Wednesday.

EMERIL'S NEW ORLEANS FISH HOUSE, *MGM Grand (Studio Walk). Tel. 702/891-7374. Major credit cards accepted. Lunch and dinner served daily. Reservations are suggested.*

A great place for the seafood lover. Lobster and fresh fish are featured along with Emeril's unbeatable barbecued shrimp. Most dishes are served Creole or Cajun style. For lunch or a more casual diner, we suggest having your meal in their adjoining seafood bar. To top off a wonderful meal, try one of Emeril's freshly baked pies, like the banana cream, which is almost as famous as celebrity chef and author Emeril Legasse.

EMPRESS COURT, *Caesars Palace. Tel. 702/731-7731. Major credit cards accepted. Dinner served Thursday through Monday. Reservations are suggested. Dress code.*

A beautiful Asian restaurant with the typical glamorous surroundings you almost always expect at Caesars Palace. Featuring delicious Chinese cuisine prepared by a chef imported directly from Hong Kong, you'll enjoy such wonderful dishes as shark-fin soup and abalone. The specialty teas are excellent. The elegance doesn't stop at the decor – the chinaware is equally impressive. The service is top-notch.

HYAKUMI, *Caesars Palace. Tel. 702/731-7731. Major credit cards accepted. Dinner served Tuesday through Saturday. Reservations are suggested.*

For elegance in Japanese dining, Hyakumi has few peers in Las Vegas or anywhere else. Authenticity is important at Hyakumi (which translates into English as something like one hundred tastes), so there's *teppan yaki* style dining in a beautiful garden like atmosphere. The chefs expertly prepare sushi and sashimi as well as a good selection of other Japanese dishes. The choice of Japanese spirits, including sake, is also one of the best. In addition to the a la carte selections, you can opt for one of three prix-fixe *teppan yaki* four course feasts which run into the Very Expensive category.

JASMINE, *Bellagio. Tel. 702/693-7223. Major credit cards accepted. Dinner served nightly. Reservations are suggested.*

Perhaps the most upscale Chinese restaurant in town, Jasmine's gourmet chefs prepare the most delicious traditional Cantonese, Szechuan and Hunan style dishes. A typical meal might include the outstanding dim sum lobster dumplings for openers, followed by shark's fin and chicken served with sauteed sea cucumbers. There are also a few really unusual dishes, including Thai sashimi. While there is a decent selection of meats and poultry, the menu emphasizes a variety of fish and seafood dishes. Several entrees run into the Very Expensive category.

LA ROTISSERIE DES ARTISTES, *Paris. Tel. 702/967-7999. Major credit cards accepted. Dinner served nightly.*

This is one of the more unusual looking restaurants in Las Vegas and is quite attractive. The two-story art deco dining room gives patrons a choice: look out on the casino from the second floor or watch the chefs prepare your dinner on the first level. The wait staff wears traditional Parisian garb – aprons and bow-ties. Slow-roasted meats and game dishes are the stars of the menu (try the excellent pheasant) but there is also a good selection of fresh fish and seafood. The dessert cart makes it almost impossible to resist finishing your meal with some really fattening cakes and pastries.

THE LOBSTER HOUSE, *3763 Las Vegas Blvd. South. Tel. 702/740-4431. Major credit cards accepted. Dinner served nightly.*

This restaurant hasn't been around as long as the more famous Rosewood Grille, but in the few years it has been open it has given the other place a good run for the money. Featured menu highlights are delicious fresh Maine lobster, Alaskan King Crab and a nightly selection of fresh seafood dishes. The chef is from Hawaii and he adds a little South Seas flair to several dishes. Some excellent steak entrees are available as well.

MICHAEL'S GOURMET RESTAURANT, *Barbary Coast. Tel. 702/737-7111. Major credit cards accepted. Dinner served nightly. Two seatings (between 6:00 and 6:30pm or between 9:00 and 9:30pm). Reservations are required.*

The Barbary Coast certainly isn't one of the Strip's more elaborate or larger hotels but it does have its fair share of fine dining. You already have encountered Drai's, but Michael's is quite the antithesis. Ranking with the best restaurants, this Las Vegas tradition is a traditional but beautifully decorated Victorian style room that is best known for its brilliant stained glass domed ceiling. The fine service will also be appreciated by guests but the true star of the evening is their famous Continental cuisine. Simply put, it is absolutely delicious. Featured dishes are dover sole, rack of lamb, scampi and Chateaubriand for two. Two outstanding choices for dessert are the Cherries Jubilee or Bananas Foster. The place and the slow pace is tranquil, something not always the case in Las Vegas. Even though it is expensive, you could easily spend more in other places and wind up getting a lot less for your hard earned bucks.

MIKADO, *The Mirage. Tel. 702/791-7223, Major credit cards accepted. Dinner served nightly.*

The dining room is one of the most beautiful in town (and the best decor for Oriental cuisine) but despite the authentic Japanese style, the dining experience doesn't leave you with the same feeling. The food is quite good and compares favorably with most of the better Japanese restaurants. It's also one of the most expensive Japanese eateries in Las Vegas.

NEYLA, *MGM Grand (Studio Walk). Tel. 702/736-2100. Major credit cards accepted. Dinner served nightly.*

For great food, atmosphere and fun, you would do well to choose this Mediterranean grill. The dining room features beautiful arched ceiling and lots of greenery to offset some areas of overly plain modernism. While the large menu has selections of an international nature, the heart and soul of Neyla is their Middle Eastern, and particularly Lebanese, cuisine. Among the latter are such delights as hommus, stuffed grape leaves, felafel and many types of kebobs. Can't decide – then go for the Mezza, a traditional sampling of Lebanese delights that can satisfy anyone's appetite. The chef is Middle Eastern trained. The wines are highlighted by vintages from Lebanon's productive Bekaa Valley. After dessert try a *tryan hookah* – the traditional Turkish water pipe. Neyla also features live entertainment during dinner in the form of a beautiful belly dancer who just loves to get the gentlemen involved in the act.

OLIVES, *Bellagio (on the Via Bellagio shopping concourse). Tel. 702/693-7223. Major credit cards accepted. Lunch and dinner served daily.*

Famous Boston chef Todd English first ventured into Las Vegas with Olives. Under the excellent direction of executive chef Victor LaPlaca, this delightful Mediterranean style restaurant still retains a hint of its Boston roots: you can have cod cakes and lobster remoulade served with Boston baked beans! The delicious and unique salads are definitely worth trying. The lunch menu includes a number of American favorites (especially the side orders) but the a la carte pricing makes it too expensive for anything but dinner unless you've been very fortunate at the gaming tables.

ONDA, *The Mirage. Tel. 702/791-7223. Major credit cards accepted. Dinner is served nightly. Reservations are suggested.*

Onda is a fine Italian restaurant in just about every sense but we still retain fonder memories for the more casual elegance of its predecessor, the *Ristorante Riva*. However, its been over two years since the change to a more formal experience was made and it obviously isn't going back to the old way. The menu features traditional Northern Italian cuisine with professional service and a good list of wines.

OSTERIA DEL CIRCO, *Bellagio. Tel. 702/693-8150. Major credit cards accepted. Lunch and dinner served daily. Reservations are suggested.*

Alright, we know what you're probably saying – another Bellagio restaurant. We promise, this is the last. But, on the other hand, there's no debating the top quality of this hotel's restaurants. In this case you'll find outstanding Tuscan cuisine in a beautiful setting that, like most of the fine restaurants at Bellagio, overlooks the lake. The lobster, calamari and other delights from the sea are the best items on the menu and they're all served with a unique variety of vegetables. The service is excellent.

THE PALM, *Caesars Palace (in the Forum Shops). Tel. 702/732-7256. American Express, Diners Club, MasterCard and VISA accepted. Lunch and dinner served daily.*

The modest entrance of the Palm leads into an attractive and mostly traditional styled restaurant with caricatures of famous people adorning the walls. Maybe that's one of the reasons why many celebrities are known to frequent this restaurant. This excellent steakhouse is celebrated for its wonderfully prepared food and the large, even huge, portions. Notable in that category are lobsters weighing in at between four and five pounds. They're not only bigger but, according to many experts, more tasty than their smaller relatives.

P.F. CHANG'S CHINA BISTRO, *Aladdin. Tel. 702/836-0955. Most major credit cards accepted. Lunch and dinner served daily.*

There are more than 50 P.F. Chang's located throughout the country (including two others in Las Vegas) and while we usually tend to exclude such chains from our recommendations because so many people are already familiar with them, we'll make an exception here. That's because of the absolutely marvelous physical aspects of this restaurant. First, it is dramatically built right into the spectacular facade of the Aladdin, overlooking the Strip, the hotel's waterfall and "rock" walls. The restaurant itself has two stories and has both indoor and outdoor seating for its 360 guests. As has become so popular, the kitchen is exhibition style. Oh, yes – the food. Like all Chang's, it is delicately seasoned and is largely based on combinations of the traditional Chinese concept of *fan* and *t'sai*. The former consists of rice, noodle or dumpling dishes while the latter has meat, seafood and vegetables.

PINOT BRASSERIE, *The Venetian (on Restaurant Row). Tel. 702/733-5000. Major credit cards accepted. Breakfast, lunch and dinner served daily. Reservations are suggested.*

California French style cuisine featuring grilled steaks, poultry, seafood and wild game as well as pasta, along with an extensive selection of European and American wines are on tap at Pinot. The beautiful dining room features many items imported from France in order to duplicate the feel of an authentic French brasserie. There's an exhibition style kitchen (part of which can be seen by passers-by on Restaurant Row) with a large rotisserie. There's also an oyster bar.

POSTRIO, *The Venetian (in the Grand Canal Shoppes). Tel. 702/733-5000. Major credit cards accepted. Dinner served nightly. Reservations are suggested.*

Wolfgang Puck's Venetian entry features more California cuisine, this time with the influences of both Asia and the Mediterranean thrown in for great taste. The large menu changes daily and includes everything from gourmet pizzas to grilled quail, *foie gras terrine*, lamb chops and duck. This casual bistro has colorful decor with bright reds catching your eye from outside. The attractive bar area has a wood-burning pizza oven. The restaurant also has an exhibition style kitchen. Service at Postrio is excellent. You can sit in the beautiful interior portion of the dining room or "outside" right on St. Marks Square. Well, it really seems like you're dining outside! Some moderately priced entrees are available.

THE RANGE, *Harrah's. Tel. 702/369-5084. Major credit cards accepted. Dinner served nightly. Reservations are suggested.*

Advertising claims to the contrary, Harrah's isn't known as *the* hotel for fine dining. But, when it comes to the Range, you could easily pay a lot more at plenty of other restaurants in Las Vegas and not have nearly as excellent a dining experience as you can get at this outstanding eatery. The decor and atmosphere are both geared toward creating a feel of casual elegance as you gaze out onto the Strip through the large windows. The steak, seafood and chicken dishes are all expertly prepared and the portions are generous. You must, however, save some room for their wonderful desserts. The service is first rate and live music adds to the pleasing atmosphere. The Range's wine list is impressive.

RED SQUARE, *Mandalay Bay. Tel. 702/632-7777. Major credit cards accepted. Dinner served nightly. Reservations are suggested.*

After a successful debut in Miami's ritzy South Beach, Red Square headed west to Vegas for its next venture. It features the same elaborate Russian style decor that was such a hit in Florida. The dinner selections are a combination of traditional Russian cuisine along with Continental, Italian and American specialties. All in all, there's something for everyone on the menu. Red Square also boasts an elaborate frozen ice bar that includes more than a hundred different types of frozen vodkas and "Russian inspired" martini's. Fortunately, they don't serve Molotov cocktails. And in case you want them to keep a special bottle of vodka just for you – they'll be more than happy to oblige. You see, Red Square has private vodka lockers that celebrities seem to go for. It's hard to miss Red Square because a larger than life statue of a headless Vladimir Lenin stands outside the entrance. We want to let you know that the rumor of Red Square's and other Mandalay Bay restaurant chefs meeting the same fate if guests complain about their dinners is definitely untrue.

ROSEWOOD GRILLE, *3339 Las Vegas Blvd. South. Tel. 702/792-5965. Major credit cards accepted. Dinner served nightly. Reservations are suggested.*

Although nothing to look at from the outside, this is perhaps Las Vegas' most famous non-hotel seafood restaurant and it is worthy of its reputation. Winner of more awards than you can count, the Rosewood Grille's European trained chef prepares jumbo steamed Maine lobster and wonderful scampi dishes among other delights of the sea. You also can't go wrong with their smaller selection of nicely done beef dishes. The restaurant also boasts an excellent wine list (they've won Wine Spectator Awards for many years running) and an attentive staff that is happy to answer any of your dining questions.

SAMBA, *The Mirage. Tel. 702/791-7223. Major credit cards accepted. Dinner served nightly. Reservations are suggested.*

Shades of the Rio! This final member of a group of upscale restaurants at the Mirage forgoes the more formal and sometimes stuffy environment and service for a colorful and fun atmosphere. It is our favorite dining spot while at the Mirage. Located just off the casino, the South American style decor is a dazzling display of color and music that helps to foster the good time atmosphere. Yet, the food is first class all the way. Delicious steaks and fresh seafood are the entrees of choice, all done up the Brazilian "Rodizio" way, which means great rotisserie taste and an almost perfect amount of seasoning. The service is friendly and efficient. There's a decent wine list although it isn't nearly as extensive as you will find in most of the more formal high end restaurants.

SMITH & WOLLENSKY, *3767 Las Vegas Blvd. South. Tel. 702/862-4100. Most major credit cards accepted. Lunch and dinner served daily.*

Smith & Wollensky originated on New York's Second Avenue back in 1977 and has since opened restaurants in several other cities. Joining the Strip's flock of restaurants in 1998, this S&W has already taken its place amongst the better places to eat in Las Vegas. This one looks almost exactly like the original New York eatery, from the exterior's painted over tenement building look, to the old time interior with its wooden floors. The menu features superb steaks and prime rib along with a decent selection of seafood. The appetizers are superb. However, everything here is completely a la carte, so there's a good chance that your main course will likely run you into the Very Expensive category.

STAR CANYON, *The Venetian (on Restaurant Row). Tel. 702/733-5000. Major credit cards accepted. Dinner served nightly. Reservations are suggested.*

This is "New Texas" cuisine at its best. No, this isn't your ordinary Tex-Mex joint. Star Canyon is a sophisticated restaurant in many ways, although the decor has some light cowboy touches to go with the elegant ranch look. The menu, too, is a complex combination of styles – southwestern with a bit of French culinary ideas thrown in, as well as other influences. Among the items that are absolutely delicious are the pinto bean-wild mushroom ragout, the red chile onion rings, chile relleno cooked with smoked chicken, and grilled sirloin with sweet potato enchiladas. A real treat for the taste buds – all we can say is, wow!

TERRAZZA, *Caesars Palace. Tel. 702/731-7731. Major credit cards accepted. Dinner is served nightly.*

This is a large (220 seats) and exquisitely designed restaurant that has a level of elegance that is almost enough to be considered decadent and, therefore, well suited to be a subject of Caesars' empire! You can dine al fresco facing the beautiful Garden of the Gods pool area or inside an octagon shaped glass enclosed pavilion. Either way the surroundings are spectacular. You can observe the preparation of Terrazza's northern Italian cuisine in their exhibition style kitchen. The food is on a par with the surroundings – sophisticated and wonderful. We love their rack of lamb but if you're looking for some non-meat items then try the rigatoni alla bocsaiola or the risotto. There's a good wine list and a helpful and knowledgeable staff. The adjacent lounge has entertainment on some evenings.

TOP OF THE WORLD, *Stratosphere. Tel. 702/380-7711. Major credit cards accepted. Lunch and dinner served nightly. Reservations are suggested.*

You can't have a tall tower anywhere without having the obligatory revolving gourmet restaurant. We don't mean this as a knock in the subject case because the view from the 833-foot level is extraordinary. The menu features steaks, fresh fish, and seafood, including lobster. As the restaurant rotates completely in one hour, you will have more than enough time to take in the entire 360-degree panorama during the course of your dinner. The service is good and the food is certainly better than average, but the prices are justified only if you really must have that view while you eat.

TRATTORIA DEL LUPO RESTAURANT, *Mandalay Bay. Tel. 702/ 740-5522. Major credit cards accepted. Lunch and dinner served daily.*

The famous husband and wife team of Wolfgang Puck and Barbara Lazarof have found success at several restaurants in Las Vegas. This is one of their latest ventures and it's a great Italian eatery. The authentic trattoria atmosphere is fun and casual as patrons watch from a piazza like setting as pasta and baking chores are handled by the outstanding kitchen staff. They even have a wood burning rotisserie and pizza oven for that real Italian taste. The cuisine features dishes from all parts of Italy – – northern, southern and regional, so no matter what your taste in Italian is, you'll find it here. The center of this most attractive restaurant features a beautiful bar that contains the restaurant's wine room. And the wine selection is outstanding.

TREMEZZO, *Aladdin. Tel. 702/785-9013. Major credit cards accepted. Lunch is served on weekdays; dinner served nightly. Sunday brunch.*

Located on the mezzanine level adjacent to the Roc Bar and also overlooking the Strip, Tremezzo offers excellent northern Italian cuisine in a spacious dining room with decor that is nothing less than stunning. There is a good selection of pasta but the menu is heavily weighted towards veal and fresh fish. Fine wines are in abundance. You can dine outside on the patio and take advantage of Tremezzo's great location. The service is excellent without being stuffy and the whole experience is one of casual elegance.

A STERLING BRUNCH

*One of the more venerable dining traditions in Las Vegas for those who love fine food and service is to head on over to Bally's on Sunday's between 9:30am and 2:30pm for their famous **Sterling Brunch**. The setting for this magnificent affair is Bally's Steakhouse – which at other times is just one among many of a seemingly endless list of excellent steakhouses to be found throughout Las Vegas. However, the Sterling Brunch is something very special. Feast on sturgeon, caviar, shushi and an endless variety of wonderfully prepared dishes, many of which just aren't found on most Sunday brunch menus. Drink champagne and be served by tuxedo clad waiters in beautiful surroundings. And, it will only set you back $53.*

Moderate

AL DENTE, *Bally's. Tel. 702/967-4656. Major credit cards accepted. Dinner served Saturday through Wednesday.*

Yes, you can get "gourmet" pizza here, but Al Dente is mainly for those looking for great Italian food, both traditional and unusual. The antipasto and pasta dishes are especially appetizing. The pasta is always right – "al dente." Ditto for the glorious desserts which could easily have come right out of a Rome cafe.

ALTA VILLA, *Flamingo Las Vegas. Tel. 702/733-3333. Major credit cards accepted. Dinner served Tuesday through Saturday.*

What could be better than another excellent Italian restaurant! This is a casual but very attractive place for good food. From the moment you enter the restaurant with it's lovely fountain, you're in for an enjoyable time. The interior is designed to resemble an old Italian villa and there is plenty of nicely done stonework to give it a feel of authenticity. They have a nice selection of traditional Italian dishes at a reasonable price. The wine list is more than adequate.

ASIA, *Harrah's. Tel. 702/369-5084. Major credit cards accepted. Dinner served nightly. Reservations are suggested.*

As the name implies, this restaurant highlights food from throughout the Far East, although fine Chinese cuisine is predominant. The food is just about as good as at any Oriental restaurant in town so we consider this to be a better than average value for fine dining. The decor is absolutely stunning, featuring elegant Oriental themes in a colorful yet refined manner. The service is also well above average.

BORDER GRILL, *Mandalay Bay. Tel. 702/632-7403. Most major credit cards accepted. Lunch and dinner served daily.*

Right at the outset let's tell you the biggest complaint we have with the Border Grill – it's location near the entrance to the Shark Reef is a long hike from the rest of the hotel. But if you like to walk or just want to work up an appetite, then it's location isn't a problem at all. Border Grill has a lively and almost fiesta-like atmosphere. It's cheerful and colorful although perhaps a bit too much on the modern side to fully convey the feel of a true Mexican restaurant. The two-level restaurant has a main dining room, cantina and taqueria. The latter, located upstairs, has a limited menu served counter style. The main dining room is divided into smaller rooms and you also have the option of dining out on the patio. This California import, the original home of the "spicy hot tamales" serves well prepared and authentic Mexican cuisine that tends toward the hot side.

CAFE LAGO, *Caesars Palace. Tel. 702/771-7731. Major credit cards accepted. Breakfast, lunch and dinner served daily.*

Everything about this elegant restaurant belies its status as Caesars' 24-hour cafe. While it does cost a few dollars more than most of the other hotel cafes, it is definitely worth it. We regard this new entry onto the dining scene (September, 2000) as highly as many of the restaurants operated by those famous chefs. This place is sure to raise the bar for facilities of its type. So, what's so special? Let's start with the decor. The beautiful dining area is almost a semi-circle surrounding a brick wall of arches. The outer edge overlooks Caesars' gorgeous pool area. A wall of water cascades behind blue glass. Combined with a lovely color scheme and other decorative items it is a joy to look at. The menu has a diverse selection of attractively prepared and tasty dishes. You also have the option of selecting your meal from a buffet. During the evening the Cafe offers live music.

CANALETTO, *The Venetian (in the Grand Canal Shoppes). Tel. 702/ 733-5000. Major credit cards accepted. Lunch and dinner served daily.*

Bravo! Here's an Italian restaurant that can satisfy the most demanding gourmet as well as the person looking for beautiful surroundings, all at an affordable price. Difficult to do, but Canaletto has surely succeeded. This two-story restaurant is the only dining establishment in the Venetian that has a truly Venetian theme itself. You can dine "outside" on the patio of St. Marks Square just a few feet from the Grand Canal, or in the main dining room with its navy blue striped booths, polished hardwood floors and 16-foot high ceilings. The upstairs consists of several small private dining rooms styled like a Venetian *palazzo*. The exhibition style kitchen is a sight to behold. The service is exceptional. Both the food and wine concentrate on the cuisine of the Veneto region but there are also a good number of Northern Italian staples such as risotto, gnocchi and polenta. This is one of the few good restaurants anywhere where we can say you get more than what you paid for.

COURTYARD GRILLE, *Treasure Island. Tel. 702/791-7111, Major credit cards accepted. Lunch and dinner served daily.*

Formerly the Black Spot Grille (the recent name change coincides with, in our opinion, management's unwise de-emphasis of the pirate theme), this "outdoor" style cafe in the indoors is still an attractive casual eatery with good food. Overlooking both the casino and the shopping promenade at Treasure Island, the menu staples are burgers, several types of pasta dishes and excellent salads. We also recommend their wood-fired pizza and calzones. The atmosphere is very friendly. Several entrees are in the Inexpensive category.

DIVE!, *3200 Las Vegas Blvd. South, outside the Fashion Show Mall. Tel. 702/369-3483. Most major credit cards accepted. Lunch and dinner served daily.*

This place isn't a "dive" but it does serve mainly standard fare such as burgers and chicken along with pizza and pasta. Although some items are in the Inexpensive category, we can say that just about everything is overpriced. In return, however, you get a rather unique atmosphere (unless you happen to be from Los Angeles where the original *Dive!* is located). The place, both inside and outside, is designed to resemble a submarine. *Dive!* logo merchandise is on sale in the gift shop.

THE EMBERS, *Imperial Palace. Tel. 702/794-3261. American Express, Discover, MasterCard and VISA accepted. Dinner served Wednesday through Saturday. Reservations are suggested.*

It's hard not to highly recommend The Embers because it is a real bargain when you compare it to other fine steakhouses. The surroundings are quite elegant, like that of a private club, and the service is warm and attentive. The steak and prime rib, as well as lamb, veal and a smaller selection of seafood entrees, are among the tops in town. You will be hard pressed to find a better steakhouse at any price. This is truly the style restaurant for the rich at prices the middle class will appreciate.

GILLEY'S SALOON, DANCE HALL & BAR-B-QUE, *New Frontier Hotel. Tel. 702/794-8200. Major credit cards accepted. Dinner served nightly; lunch only on Saturday and Sunday.*

With a name like that could you possibly go wrong if you're looking for a fun meal? We think not. The latest branch of the now famous Texas honky-tonk, Gilley's combines good fun with good food – "real" food such as ribs, Texas style steaks and the like. The value is excellent; you'll even find quite a few entrees in the Inexpensive category. Entertainment takes many forms at Gilley's, including live performers on a huge stage, dancing and line dancing, and the mechanical bull. We suggest you try the latter *before* you eat!

HARLEY DAVIDSON CAFE, *3725 Las Vegas Blvd. South. Tel. 702/740-4555. Major credit cards accepted. Lunch and dinner served daily.*

Although the popularity of "theme" restaurants seems to have peaked in many places throughout the country, they still do very well in Las Vegas where the genre has taken on a life of its own. The H-D is no exception and features many popular American dishes like burgers, steak, ribs and such. The food is alright but certainly nothing special and the value is average at best. However, lots of people like to have an "experience" when they eat out and this place is that. The front of an oversized motorcycle protrudes from over the entrance and several Harley-Davidson cycles are on display. There's all sorts of celebrity memorabilia and the back wall of the restaurant is a giant American flag constructed of metal chains painted red, white and blue. It's unique American pop art. That isn't available for sale in their retail shop but just about everything else is.

HOUSE OF BLUES, *Mandalay Bay. Tel. 702/632-7777. Major credit cards accepted. Lunch and dinner served nightly.*

This huge restaurant has art and memorabilia from entertainers of the Deep South along with original Bas-relief portraits. Some of it looks like a church; other portions are decorated with bottle caps from beer! It's highly eclectic to say the least (and maybe even eccentric), but it is lots of fun. The House of Blues is part of a larger entertainment complex of the same name within Mandalay Bay. In keeping with the theme, the menu features southern inspired regional cuisine. The catfish, barbecued ribs and "Blues" burgers are all good but we think you're better off spicing things up a bit with such delights as jambalaya, gumbo and ettoufee. If you're into Gospel music, then you should definitely go for the live entertainment at their Gospel Brunch.

LOMBARDI'S, *Aladdin (in the Desert Passage). Tel. 702/731-1755. American Express, Discover, MasterCard and VISA accepted. Lunch and dinner served daily.*

Beautifully situated at the broad plaza-like "Lost City" area of Desert Passage, Lombardi's has an attractive main dining room and an even better "patio" seating area. It is actually like three restaurants in one since you can choose from a menu that includes elements of an Italian trattoria, a French bistro, or a Moroccan cafe. Regardless of what you select from the menu, however, all of the food is well prepared and nicely served. Some entrees are in the Expensive category.

MON AMI GABI, *Paris. Tel. 702/944-4224. Major credit cards accepted. Lunch and dinner served daily.*

From the standpoint of atmosphere and style, Mon Ami Gabi is a delightful Parisian themed cafe with mostly authentic French food. However, many of the dishes (some of which get pretty close to the Expensive category) have been semi-Americanized. The food and the service are alright but definitely aren't anything to rave about. What prompted us to include it here is the cafe's location – right on the Strip at street level. With the Eiffel Tower in full view, one can't help but being reminded of dining in the real city of Paris. It's a fantastic place to people watch while you eat as well as to view the fountains of Bellagio right across the street. Of course, you might not want to do that in the middle of a blazing summer afternoon. We suggest it for cooler times for those seeking a more upscale lunch experience rather than dinner.

OLIO, *MGM Grand. Tel. 702/891-7775. Major credit cards accepted. Lunch and dinner served daily.*

This new Italian restaurant is highly unusual and lots of fun. The food is also quite good but there are lots of Italian eateries with good food so let's take a look at the fun side of Olio. The attractive architecture features curved ceiling and plenty of color. Among the desserts is a selection of 21 different flavors of authentic gelato (ice cream, for the unitiated). Its served from a "gelato wall" by pretty gelato girls dressed in silver outfits that look like they were from a 1950's B-grade science fiction movie! Then there's the antipasto table. The 60-foot long table can accommodate 40 diners and how much you pay depends upon how many items you select. And there is a wide selection. The same is true for the regular menu which has everything from lobster, shrimp, lamb, calamari and champagne seafood salad to ravioli and pizza (five different varieties of the latter). The multi-level dining room stays open until late into the evening for those who like to take their dinner after most people have gone to bed. It's always nice to find a new restaurant in one of the major hotels that won't break you.

Of course, if you want to spend more at Olio, you certainly can. There is a $100 per person tab for dinner in their private "Teatro" screening room where, on Sunday nights you can watch the *Sopranos* while being served a traditional five-course Italian dinner.

PAPYRUS, *Luxor. Tel. 702/262-4774. Major credit cards accepted. Dinner served Thursday through Monday. Reservations are suggested.*

Excellent although straight-forward Chinese food is the feature as this casual but extremely attractive restaurant. We like the large selection and the friendly and efficient service. It may not be the best Chinese restaurant in town, but if you're looking for one on the Strip that gives you high quality at an affordable price, then Papyrus is a wise choice.

RAINFOREST CAFE, *MGM Grand. Tel. 702/891-8580. Major credit cards accepted. Breakfast, lunch and dinner served daily.*

Thee are other Rainforest Cafes scattered about the country but none are quite as elaborate as the Las Vegas version. What else would you expect? For those of you who aren't familiar with RFC's, the imaginative setting and fun that goes along with it is, perhaps, more important than the food. You'll dine inside a veritable jungle, complete with thick vegetation, rushing waterfalls, animals large and small (some moving and making noises), colorful birds and, of course, periodic downpours accompanied by thunder and lightning. We especially like the chairs at the bar, which have colorful animal tails! There's also a fascinating gift shop with more animals (including a ferocious looking alligator), butterflies, tropical aquariums, and much, much more.

Oh, yes...the food. The Cafe boasts a big selection of popular dishes, especially American but with a smattering of just about anything. It isn't great but it is better than what you'll usually find in many of these theme restaurants. The prices are a bit on the high side considering what you get but someone has to pay for the great atmosphere.

ROCK LOBSTER, *Mandalay Bay. Tel. 702/632-7405. Major credit cards accepted. Lunch and dinner served daily.*

Another fun spot to eat in at Mandalay Bay. Although there are many lobster based dishes at this restaurant, it isn't really a seafood restaurant in the true sense. The diverse menu features a little of everything including burgers and pasta. It's just as good for a sandwich or light dinner as it is for a full course meal. Rock videos are continuously projected on the walls of this modern styled restaurant so the ambiance, if you can term it as such, is definitely not for everyone.

RUMJUNGLE, *Mandalay Bay. Tel. 702/632-7777. Major credit cards accepted. Dinner served nightly.*

We really do like the selection of restaurants at Mandalay Bay and *rumjungle* (no capitalization and one word, please) is no exception. Many of the restaurants at this hotel have attracted the attention of a younger crowd because of their unique style and fun atmosphere (remember Red Square, for instance?) – but none do it better than *rumjungle*. This is a whole lot more than just a restaurant; it's a dining and entertainment experience. It begins the moment you enter and encounter the dancing fire wall that alternately becomes a wall of water. Inside the rum and spirits rise over an illuminated bar and the open pit fire where the cooking is done is a backdrop for the "dueling congas" dance floor. It's just wild. So is the food, much of which is served by waiters carrying flaming skewers. The menu contains a good variety of chicken, meat and fish, all distinctively prepared in a most tasty manner. In addition to the normal bar drinks, *rumjungle* has an almost endless list of the most exotic beverages you could ever imagine. On the dance floor you can sway to a variety of different rhythms including Latin, Caribbean and African. For an evening to remember, *rumjungle* gets a definite thumbs up from us. Straddles the Expensive category.

SACRED SEA ROOM, *Luxor. Tel. 702/262-4772. Major credit cards accepted. Dinner served nightly.*

Awaiting you at the Sacred Sea Room is a beautiful dining establishment decorated with tile mosaics and hieroglyphic murals to keep in touch with the Luxor theme. Although the surroundings are elegant the atmosphere is much more casual. Sacred Sea serves a big variety of fresh and salt-water fish that includes favorites from America, Europe and the South Pacific. They also have a decent selection of non-fish entrees for the land lubbers in your group.

THE STEAK HOUSE, *Circus Circus. Tel. 702/794-3767. Major credit cards are accepted. Dinner served nightly. Sunday brunch. Reservations are suggested.*

This eatery is in the same class as the Embers – great steaks perfectly done and served in an inviting atmosphere at almost bargain prices. The Steak House is an award winning establishment in a hotel that is otherwise not particularly associated with fine dining. You'll see your dinner being grilled mesquite style in the restaurant's exhibition kitchen. The service is excellent. All of this makes this restaurant one of the most popular steakhouses in town.

STIVALI, *Circus Circus. Tel. 702/691-5820. Major credit cards accepted. Dinner served nightly.*

Part of Circus Circus' master plan to upgrade the dining facilities of what was previously a mostly undistinguished place for restaurants, Stivali is a beautiful Italian eatery that has a good selection of traditionally prepared entrees. Their fresh home made pastas and savory sauces are truly excellent and make just about any item from the menu a delicious treat. We especially recommend trying their stuffed portabella mushrooms.

TAQUERIA CAÑONITA, *The Venetian (in the Grand Canal Shoppes). Tel. 702/414-3773. Major credit cards accepted. Lunch and dinner served daily.*

One of only a few restaurants at the Venetian that won't dig deep into your pockets, Taqueria Cañonita is a delightful Mexican restaurant situated right on the Grand Canal. Do ask for a table close to the edge so you can watch the gondoliers as they sing their way past you. The large menu contains just about everyone's favorite Mexican dishes although some unusual items can also be found. The menu contains "platos chicos" and "platos grandes" which literally means small and large plates. While you obviously can have one small item and a bigger main course, a popular way of dining at Taqueria Cañonita is to simply have a larger number of the platos chicos. It makes for a great way to acquaint yourself with a variety of Mexican dishes all of which are delicious at Taqueria. There are about three dozen platos chicos to choose from. A very informal atmosphere prevails but the service is quite good.

WARNER BROTHERS STAGE 16 RESTAURANT, *The Venetian (outside the main entrance of the Grand Canal Shoppes). Tel. 702/733-5000. Major credit cards accepted. Lunch and dinner served daily.*

This is one of the most unusual of the themed restaurants in town. It certainly is a lot of fun if you're seeking non-stuffy dining. You'll eat on a "movie set" such as Casablanca, only to find that the set changes to another motion picture while you are dining. And so do the costumes of the staff, which always match the set you're on. The food is only a little above the standard fare American found in most other themed restaurants and, like those, is on the overpriced side. However, this place is so different that we still feel obligated to highly recommending it.

WILLIAM B's, *Stardust. Tel. 702/732-6111. Major credit cards accepted. Dinner served nightly. Reservations are suggested.*

Another great restaurant where you would expect the prices to be much higher (although a few items do edge into the Expensive category). William B's has been around for many years and has a pleasant and rather subdued turn-of-the-century atmosphere. It is casual but extremely attractive. The selection of entrees covers a wide range of American cuisine. Although it is best known for fine steaks and prime rib, diners can choose from a surprisingly large menu that includes veal, pork, poultry and fish. The desserts are wonderful. Service is excellent and features professional and knowledgeable waiters who perform their tasks without being stuffy.

Inexpensive

JJ's BOULANGERIE, *Paris. Tel. 702/946-4060. Major credit cards accepted. Lunch and dinner served daily.*

The aroma of fresh baked bread will lure you into JJ's as you stroll along Le Boulevard. It's a great appetite stimulant. In addition to a variety of delightful breads, this pleasant and casual place serves sandwiches, salads, pastries and several types of filled croissants. The bread from here is served at all of Paris' restaurants and it is delivered by bicycle twice daily. You may just see the friendly bread-maker in his traditional French outfit cycling through the hotel!

LA PIAZZA FOOD COURT, *Caesars Palace. Tel. 702/731-7731. Major credit cards accepted. Lunch and dinner served daily. A limited number of stations open for breakfast.*

This is not your ordinary food court with independent stores like the major national burger chains and similar eateries. Instead, you can choose from a wide selection of well prepared food (sandwiches as well as hot plates, salads, desserts and more) at individual stations that run the gamut from Oriental and from Mexican to Italian. Once you've made your selections and pass through the central check-out counter, you can take a seat in the large and comfortable dining area that overlooks the casino. There's even a full service bar. La Piazza is also the scene for live entertainment during the later evening hours.

TRES LOBOS, *Stardust. Tel. 702/732-6111. Major credit cards accepted. Dinner served Tuesday through Saturday.*

An extensive menu of good Mexican cuisine highlights this friendly and attractive restaurant. The fajitas and chimichangas are especially good. The adjacent Cantina is a nice, lively spot for drinks and chatter.

OFF-STRIP

Expensive

ANTONIO'S ITALIAN RISTORANTE, *Rio Hotel. Tel. 702/247-7923. Major credit cards accepted. Dinner served nightly.*

The traditional Italian fare in this attractive dining room with exhibition style kitchen is simply excellent. Antonio's has a humongous wine list with more than 300 available selections. Service is efficient and friendly and not overdone in keeping with the overall casual atmosphere. You can get away with a couple of entrees in the Moderate price category.

BUZIO'S, *Rio Hotel. Tel. 702/247-7923. Major credit cards accepted. Lunch and dinner served daily.*

This is a great place for the freshest and finest seafood dishes. The room is casual elegant – lots of wood and brass and overlooking a corner of Rio's beautiful pool area. The service is excellent and the extensive menu will present you with a real problem deciding what you want. Patrons can watch as their dinner is prepared in the open, exhibition style kitchen. Buzio's mussels and clam dishes are outstanding. Try them and we're sure you won't be disappointed. The oyster bar is a local favorite.

STRIP HOTEL COFFEE SHOPS - AN ALTERNATIVE TO EXPENSIVE DINING

Disappointed that so many of the restaurants are expensive? Don't fret. As we indicated earlier, the 24-hour hotel coffee shop is a good place for a tasty meal at a good price (entrees in both the Moderate and Inexpensive categories). You can get any meal at any time of the day, a real convenience in Las Vegas where normal hours are often thrown out the window. They're among the best choice for breakfast, too, as most other restaurants aren't open in the morning. Almost all have the word "cafe" in their names, an indication of the informal atmosphere that prevails. If you want a sit-down meal that isn't fancy but is well prepared, they're an excellent choice. That also applies if you have children since the little ones won't enjoy the fancy restaurants.

Here's a rundown on the coffee shops, oops – we mean cafes, that we consider to be among the best:

AMERICA RESTAURANT (New York, New York): Fun atmosphere and fine food. The selection is quite large and features American and international favorites along with some unusual items. The huge map of the United States that's suspended from the ceiling is an eye-catcher.

CAFE BELLAGIO (Bellagio): Adjoining the magnificent Conservatory, this is among the most elegant looking 24 hour restaurant of any Las Vegas hotel (and a bit higher priced, too). The food is excellent and the service is efficient. If you ever wondered what an upscale coffee shop is, this is it.

GRAND LUX CAFE (The Venetian): The Grand Lux may have the biggest menu in town with more than 200 items to choose from including tons of great desserts. The attractive room has hand painted ceilings, wall mosaics, limestone tables and marble flooring. Although, like the preceding entry, a little higher priced than most of the 24 hour restaurants, the Grand Lux has quickly become known for its large portions.

CAFE LAGO (Caesars Palace): This is the ultimate 24 hour cafe. See the detailed listing in the Moderate price listings.

RAFFLE'S CAFE (Mandalay Bay): Although this is a huge place you'll feel like you are in a smaller restaurant because it is divided into many different rooms. The beautiful decor is exotic-tropical and some areas overlook the pool. The menu has a good selection of entrees. Try their onion rings as an appetizer or side – they're great. Service at Raffle's is attentive.

Other good choices in this category are the Garden Cafe (Harrah's); Studio Cafe (MGM Grand), and Zanzibar Cafe (Aladdin).

HILTON STEAKHOUSE, *Las Vegas Hilton. Tel. 702/732-5755. Major credit cards accepted. Dinner served nightly. Reservations are suggested.*

This is one of the older steakhouses in Las Vegas and they've been doing it right for a long time. The beautiful decor is highlighted by rich dark wood booths surrounded by equally pleasing etched glass. The walls are adorned with works of art. The steaks are outstanding but the extensive menu also features a good variety of well prepared veal, lamb and fresh seafood in addition to poultry and pork. Careful, attentive service is another hallmark of this traditional restaurant.

MASK, *Rio Hotel. Tel. 702/247-7923. Major credit cards accepted. Dinner served nightly.*

An outstanding selection of Far Eastern delights awaits you at this unusual restaurant that combines casual atmosphere with elegant style. The food is well prepared and nicely presented by a thoughtful and efficient wait staff. Some of the featured menu items include a variety of sushi dishes and *teppan yaki* style dining. The decor is that of a rain forest.

MORTON'S OF CHICAGO, *400 Flamingo Road. Tel. 702/893-0703. Most major credit cards accepted. Lunch and dinner served daily.*

Morton's is an exclusive chain located in major cities and their chefs certainly know how to do steak and roast beef right – thick and juicy and cooked just the way you order them. They recently moved from their former location in the Fashion Show Mall on the Strip to just off-Strip at the entrance to the Hughes Corporate Center. That was probably a good idea because at these prices it helps to be on a corporate spending account. Anyhow, their new digs are larger while managing to improve on the elegance and atmosphere. Morton's service is also well respected in dining circles. It's worth the price if you really appreciate great beef.

NAPA, *Rio Hotel. Tel. 702/247-7961. Major credit cards accepted. Dinner served Wednesday through Sunday.*

Napa has an interesting menu spanning many types of Continental cuisine although gourmet French is most in evidence. The surroundings are plush and the service is excellent. Many entrees are not of the type that you will see on the menus of most fine restaurants. For example, we especially like the eggplant stuffed with grilled lamb. With more than 600 different wines to choose from, Napa has one of the most extensive lists in the city and a knowledgeable staff to help you select just the right vintage.

PAMPLEMOUSSE, *400 E. Sahara Avenue. Tel. 702/733-2066. Major credit cards accepted. Dinner served nightly. Reservations are suggested.*

This fine restaurant is located only a block off of the Strip behind the Sahara Hotel. You would hardly suspect it from the modest exterior but Pamplemousse boasts a delightful country French cottage atmosphere with an enclosed patio. Very popular with the locals looking for fine

French cuisine at affordable prices, Pamplemousse has also been selected as one of the best restaurants in the nation on several occasions by numerous sources. The menu features steak, seafood and veal but we especially like the duck. The service is attentive and the pace very relaxed – in fact, there are only four seatings each evening.

VOO DOO CAFE, *Rio Hotel. Tel. 702/247-7923. Major credit cards accepted. Dinner served nightly.*

You've already encountered several restaurants at the Rio and that's because we have to concur with the general view among both locals and savvy travelers that the Rio is exceptionally well endowed with great restaurants. The Voo Doo Cafe is one of the more unusual restaurants at the Rio. While there aren't that many Cajun/Creole restaurants in Las Vegas, this one is, without much doubt in our minds, the best among the few for a variety of reasons. First and foremost is the excellent food. The efficient and friendly service is another reason. And last, but certainly not the least, is the location. The attractive dining room sits atop the towering Rio with the best view of the Strip of any place in town – restaurant or otherwise. Even the Stratosphere's "Top of the World" doesn't match this one. The restaurant also has a separate lounge upstairs with live entertainment and an open deck with the same great view. Together, the two portions of the Voo Doo Cafe make for a most memorable evening.

A NEW RESTAURANT ROW

The area along Flamingo and Paradise Roads less than a mile east of the Strip has become a hot spot for fine dining if you like some of the better chain restaurants. Situated in the high rent district around the edge of the attractive and campus-like Hughes Corporate Center, the restaurant roster includes (in addition to the aforementioned **Morton's**) **McCormick & Schmicks** *(seafood),* **Cozymels** *(Mexican),* **Lawry's Prime Rib, Z'tejas Southwestern Grill, Ruth Chris Steak House, Gordon Biersch Brewpub** *and* **Del Frisco's,** *an upscale steakhouse. Nearby is another branch of* **P.F. Chang's China Bistro.** *All of these establishments feature attractive physical plants to go along with their nationally or almost nationally famous cuisine.*

Moderate

BATTISTA'S HOLE IN THE WALL, *4041 Audrie, off of Flamingo Road. Tel. 702/732-1424. American Express, Diner's Club, MasterCard and VISA accepted. Dinner served nightly. Reservations are suggested.*

Located across the street from the Flamingo Road side of Bally's, this place has become something of a Las Vegas institution. The same chef has been cooking excellent pasta, veal piccata, steak, and seafood since 1973. A casual and fun atmosphere prevails and it attracts locals, tourists, and quite a few famous celebrities. You can get anything from pizza to a full dinner, the latter served with an unlimited amount of an excellent house wine. They also make the best cappuccino in Nevada.

BENIHANA VILLAGE, *Las Vegas Hilton. Tel. 702/732-5755. Major credit cards accepted. Dinner served nightly. Reservations are suggested.*

Consisting of several different dining rooms around a garden-like setting, there are pools, plenty of statues, and sound effects such as chirping birds and a thunderstorm to enhance your dining pleasure. Don't forget they had all of that well before the Rainforest Cafe! Getting back to the main topic, the Japanese food is quite good and features authentic table side Hibachi preparation. The chefs at Benihana are well known for the "show" they put on. One of the nicest of the restaurants within the restaurant is *Robata*.

BOISON'S, *4503 Paradise Road. Tel. 702/732-9993. Most major credit cards accepted. Dinner served nightly. Reservations are suggested.*

This restaurant has been rewarded on several occasions by readers of the local newspaper and it is deserving. A warm and inviting dining room that is well suited to the enjoyment of finely prepared cuisine, Boison's features Continental and French specialties along with some excellent Italian entrees. They have a first rate wine list and the service is also of a high quality. Several entrees are in the Expensive category.

THE BROILER, *Boulder Station, Tel. 702/432-7777; and Palace Station, Tel. 702/367-2411. Major credit cards accepted. Dinner served nightly.*

Either location of this attractive restaurant features an excellent selection of fish and seafood entries as well as steak. This isn't a fancy place by any means but if you're looking for large portions of well prepared food at a reasonable price, the two Broilers are a solid choice. If there is any edge to one over the other it goes to the Boulder Station location because it has the outstanding Oyster Bar.

CANAL STREET GRILLE, *Orleans Hotel. Tel. 702/365-7111. Major credit cards accepted. Dinner served nightly. Reservations are suggested.*

This is primarily a steakhouse but the prime rib and other selections are also worthy of consideration. Everything is prepared exactly to your specifications and the true flavor comes through as the chef has chosen not to experiment with your dinner. The atmosphere is one of understated elegance. There is no glitz but comfortable surroundings that include a warm fireplace and luxurious booth seating.

FERRARO'S RESTAURANT, *5900 W. Flamingo Road. Tel. 702/364-5300. Most major credit cards accepted. Lunch and dinner served daily.*

Family owned and operated since 1985, Ferraro's is a good place for traditional Italian food. The specialties are fresh seafood and great osso buco. This establishment has won several awards, including one given out by the American Academy of Restaurants. For entertainment, Ferraro's features a piano bar. Their wine cellar has an excellent selection. There is also a branch of Ferraro's at the Stratosphere Hotel as well as in Henderson, but all of the locals will tell you that the original location is still the best.

FIORE, *Rio Hotel. Tel. 702/247-7923. Major credit cards accepted. Dinner served nightly.*

Another of the Rio's many attractive restaurants that continue a tradition of warm surroundings, efficient and friendly service, and, most of all – outstanding food. From the name Fiore you would expect Italian cuisine. While there is some of that in several regional specialties representing the northern coastal style of preparation, Fiore also has entrees from the south of France and a big selection of American style cuisine. The rack of lamb is always excellent. For something a little more out of the ordinary we suggest the pheasant ravioli. Delicious desserts and an extensive wine list are also notable features of Fiore. Several entrees go into the Expensive category.

LA LOUISIANE, *The Orleans. Tel. 702/365-7111. Major credit cards accepted. Dinner served nightly.*

For a real Cajun style treat, this is a reasonably priced alternative to some of the more expensive restaurants of its type. The atmosphere is attractive and very casual and the food is excellent. For appetizers choose from several dishes featuring clams and oysters (on the half shell) or crab or shrimp. Their gumbo soup is almost worth the trip all by itself. Entrees feature a variety of beef and pork dishes but the featured items are the more than half a dozen fish and seafood selections. All entrees include a visit to the bountiful salad bar. Do leave some room for desserts such as macadamia nut pie or sweet potato pecan pie.

QUARK'S BAR & RESTAURANT, *Las Vegas Hilton. Tel. 702/697-8725. Major credit cards accepted. Lunch and dinner served daily.*

If you follow Star Trek, you know that some of the food eaten by those alien species isn't always very appetizing to us "yu-mahns." Well, Quark's has a few of those outer space dishes but don't be alarmed – they're just slightly disguised American favorites like burgers and beef or chicken. The food at Quark's is alright but don't expect gourmet. What people do come here for is the quirky atmosphere and decor. They do have some wild specialty drinks, too. Your order will be taken on a tricorder and Klingons and Ferengi are available to recommend some of the intergalactic specialties of the house. And if you need an explanation of that, you probably won't enjoy dining at Quark's - so don't ask.

DOWNTOWN

Expensive

ANDRE'S FRENCH RESTAURANT, *401 S. 6th Street. Tel. 702/385-5016. Major credit cards accepted. Dinner served nightly.*

Andre's was *the* gourmet restaurant in Las Vegas before it became commonplace. Owner and chef Andre Rochat has been delighting guests at this restaurant since way back in 1980. It has consistently been an award winner including honors from the Wine Spectator every year since 1989. The decor and atmosphere is that of an elegant Provencal home. The main dining area is divided into three sections with the names of Lyon, Paris and Marseilles. There are also several special private rooms.

The classic French cuisine is superb and the menu selections are quite extensive for a restaurant of this type. There are choices of both cold and hot hors d'oeuvres with our favorite being the hot Napoleon of Polenta and wild mushrooms with goat cheese sauce and veal demi glace. Unfortunately, we don't have the room to go into the exquisite menu details but we also highly recommend the onion soup au gratin. Entrees include fish, poultry, veal, beef, lamb, venison and several vegetarian items, all imaginatively prepared with wonderful sauces. Then there's a delectable dessert cart or pre-order the Grand Marinier souffle.

We might add that although there is absolutely nothing wrong with Andre's other location in the Monte Carlo Hotel on the Strip, we like the original downtown location better even though we're unable to quite put our finger on a logical reason. Perhaps we're just traditionalists.

HUGO'S CELLAR, *Four Queens Hotel. Tel. 702/835-4011. Major credit cards accepted. Dinner served nightly.*

This is one of the most elegant restaurants to be found downtown, something of a surprise considering the generally non-elegant surroundings of the Four Queens. Things start out on the right track immediately upon entering when each female guest is presented with a fresh red rose. The atmosphere is right out of New Orleans. Prime rib and steak are excellent but Hugo's also serves a nice variety of fish and seafood. The cellar in the name comes from the fact that Hugo's has its own wine cellar with an extensive list to choose from. The service is wonderfully attentive without being overbearing.

SECOND STREET GRILL, *Fremont Hotel. Tel. 702/385-6277. Major credit cards accepted. Dinner served nightly.*

Long considered to be one of the better eating places in the downtown area, the Second Street Grill has received kudos from a number of sources ranging from surveyed locals all the way to the prestigious Zagat survey. It has great atmosphere with its superbly comfortable seating and rich wood trim. The cuisine is American with strong influences from around the Pacific Rim. There is a good selection of veal, beef, seafood and poultry.

Moderate

BINION'S RANCH STEAK HOUSE, *Binion's Horseshoe Hotel. Tel. 702/382-1600. Major credit cards accepted. Dinner served nightly.*

Very good steak and prime rib at affordable prices along with good service and a nice atmosphere. Need we say more? Alright, we will – the restaurant is located on the 24th floor of the hotel and affords a good view of Las Vegas.

BURGUNDY ROOM, *Lady Luck Hotel. Tel. 702/477-3000. American Express, MasterCard and VISA accepted. Dinner served nightly. Reservations are suggested.*

Gourmet dining and downtown don't often go together but, like Hugo's, there are several classy joints in the area and the Burgundy Room is one of them. In fact, in our opinion, this is the best of the downtown dining rooms in any of the Casino Center hotels, especially after you factor in price versus value considerations. The decor is reminiscent of 19th century Paris and contains many fine original works of art (this room had "class" before Vegas decided that was a good idea.) The menu features the usual selection of steaks and seafood along with a few other entrees, but they are all extremely well prepared and served very nicely.

CENTER STAGE, *Jackie Gaughan's Plaza Hotel. Tel. 702/386-2110. Major credit cards accepted. Breakfast, lunch and dinner served daily.*

Because this attractive dining room overlooks all of the glitter of Glitter Gulch through large windows, the Center Stage is a great place to be when the Fremont Street Experience is on. It's also a wise choice for those who want a nice restaurant at a reasonable price and don't want it to be too fancy. This one has been around forever and it still attracts a sizable crowd even with the increasing competition as time goes by. American cuisine is featured but there's also a large Italian influence. Friendly service is another long-standing tradition at the Center Stage.

LILLIE LANGTRY, *Golden Nugget Hotel. Tel. 702/385-7111. Major credit cards accepted. Dinner served nightly.*

Don't let the name fool you – this is a first rate Chinese restaurant. The atmosphere is that of San Francisco's Chinatown at the turn of the century and is quite attractive. Excellent service and food are the hallmarks of Lillie Langtry, which has a reputation as one of the better places in Las Vegas to go to when you're looking for Chinese cuisine.

RACE ROCK, *495 Fremont Street. Tel. 702/382-RACE. Major credit cards accepted. Lunch and dinner served daily.*

It's hard to miss this restaurant – the front end of an oversized monster truck juts out from the second floor of the building in which Race

Rock is located. That's an introduction to the car and truck racing theme that prevails throughout this casual and fun eatery. Racing lovers will probably be in heaven. The food isn't bad (a large selection of burgers, sandwiches, pizza, several pasta dishes, steak and ribs) although we are most fond of their humongous appetizers such as the Onion Explosion, hot chicken wings or nachos. Catchy names geared to the racing theme substitute for the usual regular course names, for example, "Start Your Engines" is the title given to the appetizers. Our main complaint with Race Rock is that the prices are too high for this kind of restaurant. The entrees generally run between $14 and $18 so a full course meal will run you well over $25 a person.

STEFANO'S, *Golden Nugget Hotel. Tel. 702/385-7111. Major credit cards accepted. Dinner served nightly. Reservations are suggested.*

If you're looking to have Italian food while downtown, then Stefano's is clearly the unequaled choice along Fremont Street. It has a traditional atmosphere and menu. The wine list is good and the service is just fine. It's very popular with downtown hotel guests and even draws from a larger circle of visitors and residents.

AROUND LAS VEGAS

Expensive

RANCH HOUSE, *6250 Rio Vista (US 95 to Ann Road). Tel. 702/645-1399. Most major credit cards accepted. Dinner served nightly.*

Dating all the way back to 1955 (which is almost ancient for a Las Vegas restaurant), this place has an out-of-the-way location, although not as much as in the past when this part of town was nearly open sagebrush country. It still has a secluded atmosphere where you'll find first rate service and award winning cuisine. The menu features steaks, chicken and fresh seafood, all well prepared over an authentic mesquite grill and served in ample portions. If you're a good trooper and completely finish the humongous "Diamond Jim Brady" steak, then dessert is complements of the house. It's worth the trip.

SPIEDINI RISTORANTE, *The Regent Las Vegas. Tel. 702/869-8500. Major credit cards accepted. Dinner served nightly.*

Gustav Mauler is a renowned creator of culinary delights (one of only less than five dozen American chefs with the title Master Chef). He also runs the Oxo steakhouse at the Regent. This Milanese style Italian eatery is a delightful place to dine. The style of decor is one of modern elegance with high ceilings and unusual chandeliers. We especially like the plush booth seating as opposed to the tables. The large menu has, among its many specialty highlights, osso buco, scallopina al funghetto, costoletta alla Milanese and Fagottino di Melanzane (a mouth watering eggplant dish). There is also a big selection of pasta and risotto entrees. Spiedini features a highly professional wait staff and an excellent wine list.

Moderate

BILLY BOB'S STEAK HOUSE & SALOON, *Sam's Town Hotel. Tel. 702/454-8031. Major credit cards accepted. Dinner served nightly. Reservations are suggested.*

A great place for those who like to have their thick, juicy steaks in a casual and fun atmosphere, Billy Bob's is situated along the beautiful Mystic Falls Park in the hotel's atrium. The restaurant is almost legendary for its 28-ounce rib-eye steak but just about everything on the menu is excellent. It's a large place with five different dining rooms. They even have an old fashioned piano player. Try one of the numerous great specialty drinks from the bar.

BLUE MARLIN, *Castaways Hotel. Tel. 702/385-9156. Major credit cards accepted. Lunch served Friday through Sunday; dinner nightly except Wednesday. Reservations are suggested on weekends.*

This is an attractive dining room that features the decor and atmosphere of southern Baja, Mexico. The cuisine is mostly Mexican but for dinner they have a small but excellent selection of fresh fish and seafood prepared Spanish style. If you've never had Iberian food then you're in for a special treat. The Blue Marlin also features 14 different types of salsas to accompany your food and a variety of tequillas. The service is friendly which also helps to make this a good choice for a delicious meal without having to spend a great deal of money.

CELEBRITY DELI, *4055 Maryland Parkway. Tel. 702/733-7827. American Express, MasterCard and VISA accepted. Breakfast, lunch and dinner served daily, except breakfast and lunch only on Sunday.*

This deli serves both sandwiches and hot dinner plates. The Jewish eatery is kosher style, which means that the meat is kosher but that they don't adhere to strict orthodox religious regulations that prohibit, for example, a restaurant from mixing meat and dairy dishes. While some of the hot specials are quite tasty, we prefer the overstuffed deli sandwiches such as corned beef, pastrami or combinations. Preceded by a cup of matzoh ball soup and accompanied by a huge order of thick French fries, it's a meal!

COUNTRY INN, *2425 E. Desert Inn Road, Tel. 702/731-5035; 1401 S. Rainbow Blvd., Tel. 702/254-0520; and 1990 W. Sunset Road (Henderson), Tel. 702/898-8123. Most major credit cards accepted. Breakfast, lunch and dinner served daily.*

The small local chain offers very attractive country style decor with lots of plants as well as kitchen and dining room trinkets on shelves and hanging from the walls, along with a nice central rotisserie where a turkey is always basking in golden glory. Dinner at Country Inn is a simple but tasty affair that features excellent turkey, pork or roast beef. Generous tossed salad and delicious home made rolls with honey accompany every meal. The apple pie for dessert is excellent. For solid family dining you can't possibly go wrong with any of the Country Inns – nothing fancy, just wholesome home style food. Some entrees are in the Inexpensive category.

HABIB'S PERSIAN CUISINE, *4750 W. Sahara Avenue. Tel. 702/870-0860. American Express, Discover, MasterCard and VISA accepted. Lunch and dinner served daily except Sunday.*

Habib's serves a nice selection of well prepared Middle Eastern dishes with an emphasis on lamb and vegetarian items. The multi-course fare includes many kebob items. Pleasant atmosphere and friendly service. Friday and Saturday nights are the best times to dine here because then you can be entertained by belly dancers. There are several other good Middle Eastern restaurants in Las Vegas including some on the Strip (Neyla) or closer to it (Marrakech on Paradise Road) but we don't think any of them beat Habib's when it comes to the overall combination of food and fun at a reasonable price.

MEDITERRANEAN CAFE, *4147 S. Maryland Parkway. Tel. 702/731-6030. Most major credit cards accepted. Dinner served nightly; market open daily.*

From Middle Eastern to its close cousin, Mediterranean cuisine. The Cafe has frequently been voted by locals as the best in the Mediterranean category and with good reason. The food is extremely well prepared and served in generous quantities. The selections cover the gamut from Greek to Middle Eastern with a smattering of Italian thrown in for good measure. The cafe claims that their food is addictive and it's not much of an overstatement. We do have two small complaints. The first concerns the atmosphere. Although the owners have attempted to give it a Mediterranean look with Greek murals and hanging plants and grapes, the strip-mall storefront location lacks any real warmth. So, you might not want to come here if you want to impress someone with the surroundings. The other negative is that everything is a la carte. Not that the prices are so high but the entree should include the Greek house salad that you have to pay three bucks for. The cafe also has an adjacent mini-market where many locals come to buy their favorite Mediterranean items. Beer and wine only.

MOUNT CHARLESTON RESTAURANT, *1300 Old Park Road (Kyle Canyon) at the Mount Charleston Lodge. Tel. 702/872-5408. Most major credit cards accepted. Breakfast, lunch and dinner served daily.*

In a wonderful natural setting about 45 minutes north of Las Vegas, the Mount Charleston Restaurant serves excellent beef but is probably best known for its fresh game dishes. While we don't necessarily advise you to take a trip all the way up here just for the restaurant, it will top off a nice day if you plan on taking in the scenery of the Mount Charleston area.

PAPAMIO'S ITALIAN KITCHEN, *Sam's Town Hotel. Tel. 702/454-8041. Major credit cards accepted. Dinner is served nightly; Sunday brunch.*

Overlooking the waterfall area of the Mystic Falls Park atrium, Papamio's is an attractive restaurant featuring an exhibition style kitchen. You can choose from a wide range of both traditional and contemporary Italian cuisine. The atmosphere is very casual and the service is both friendly and efficient. All of that makes it no surprise that the place is usually hopping.

PASTA PALACE, *Boulder Station Hotel. Tel. 702/432-7777. Major credit cards accepted. Dinner served nightly.*

While there's absolutely nothing wrong with Papamio's, the place to go for Italian on the Boulder Strip (or anywhere in town, for that matter) is right here at the Pasta Palace. Start off with an attractive dining room with true Mediterranean atmosphere, add excellent seafood, veal, and, of course, pasta dishes and then toss in attentive and friendly service at very reasonable prices – and what do you get? Fine Italian dining that is simply hard to beat at any price. The freshly baked Italian bread is mouth watering and is served in huge baskets. Likewise, the house wine (complimentary with some entrees) is excellent.

If we have one complaint it's that the dessert menu is somewhat limited (although tasty) and overpriced compared to the excellent value you get for the bountiful entrees. Then again, after all that food you may not have room for dessert. There's also a Pasta Palace at the Palace Station Hotel. Although it, too, is excellent we don't quite have the same high level of praise as we do for the Boulder Station location. Perhaps its because the surroundings are a little less attractive.

THE TILLERMAN, *2245 East Flamingo Road. Tel. 702/731-4036. Major credit cards accepted. Dinner served nightly.*

A family owned business that has established its reputation among residents over the past twenty-plus years, the Tillerman features a menu dominated by fresh seafood and fine aged beef. It has received recognition from the respected *Wine Spectator Magazine*. The pleasing dining room features tiled floors and lots of greenery to complement the traditional dark woods. The service is friendly and professional. Well worth the relatively short ride from the Strip.

Inexpensive

GARDUNO'S, *Fiesta Hotel & Casino, Tel. 702/631-7000. Major credit cards accepted. Lunch and dinner served daily.*

It seems that Mexican restaurants are especially likely to have a fun atmosphere and Garduno's fits that bill perfectly. Besides the main dining area, Garduno's has the Margarita Factory (over 300 different varieties) and the world's largest collection of tequila bottles. The latter numbers in excess of 2,000! The food is great and you can dine outside on the patio when the weather is comfortable. We're hard pressed to come to a conclusion as to whether we prefer Garduno's or the next Mexican restaurant. So read on.

GUADALAJARA, *Boulder Station Hotel, Tel. 702/432-7777; Palace Station Hotel, Tel. 702/367-2411; and Sunset Station (Henderson), Tel. 702/ 547-7777. Major credit cards accepted. Lunch and dinner served daily.*

Although some entrees do reach into the Moderate price category, this is definitely an excellent value. Authentic Mexican food is served in great quantities by a friendly and efficient wait staff in colorful outfits that go well with the delightfully colorful atmosphere. It sure is a great formula for success and all three locations are always busy. Good Margaritas and good times are in store for you at all of the Guadalajara restaurants. Until very recently the Mexican restaurant at Sunset Station was named Rosalita's and we thought it was a touch above the Guadalajara brand. Although they weren't that far apart from one another it remains to be seen whether the change there is for the better.

ROXY'S PIPE ORGAN PIZZERIA, *Fiesta Hotel & Casino, Tel. 702/ 631-7000. Most major credit cards accepted. Lunch and dinner served daily.*

Pizza and other Italian favorites are on the menu here but the main star is the original New York Roxy Theater organ which was transplanted here a few years ago. It has 29 pipes and musical interludes are presented nightly between 5pm and 10pm. Unfortunately, as we went to press the new owners of the Fiesta (Station Casinos) were planning on some changes which might mean that there won't be room for the organ. They have, however, "promised" that they will try to find a new home for the organ. So if you plan on going to Roxy's more for the organ than the pizza, then do check in advance as to the status.

HENDERSON

Expensive

CARVER'S, *2061 W. Sunset Road. Tel. 702/433-5801. Most major credit cards accepted. Dinner served nightly.*

Specializing in excellent steaks and chops, Carver's features a pleasant and dignified atmosphere with attentive and highly professional service. This is a traditional style restaurant with no gimmicks of any kind – which may well be just the type of place you might be looking for after several nights of sampling the far more unusual dining opportunities that Las Vegas has to offer.

SONOMA CELLAR STEAK HOUSE, *Sunset Station Hotel. Tel. 702/547-7777. Major credit cards accepted. Dinner served nightly.*

Because Station Casinos has built a good portion of its reputation and success among locals and visitors through high quality, moderately priced restaurants, Sonoma does represent a major departure from that concept. Not in quality, but in price and style. This upscale restaurant is designed around a wine cellar theme and even gives the impression of being underground. Consisting of two separate and beautifully appointed tapestry covered dining rooms, Sonoma emphasizes fresh ingredients, expert preparation and personalized service. As befits a restaurant with this name, there is a huge wine list featuring the products of Sonoma county.

Moderate

CONDUCTOR'S ROOM, *US Highways 93/95 at the Railroad Pass (in the Railroad Pass Hotel & Casino). Tel. 702/294-5000. Major credit cards accepted. Dinner served nightly.*

This attractive Victorian style dining room (burgundy colored wallpaper and dark colored booths) is located in a decidedly down-scale "locals" casino at the southeastern end of Henderson. It is definitely off the beaten path except if you're coming back from a day at Hoover Dam and the Lake Mead Recreation Area. In that instance, this makes an excellent place to stop off for dinner. The menu includes well prepared prime rib, several surf and turf entrees along with a selection of fresh fish and veal. There are daily specials. Several entrees are in the inexpensive category. The service is very good. Whether or not you order dessert, all meals end with a dramatic touch – chocolate covered cherries served in a bowl over smoking dry ice.

COSTA DEL SOL, *Sunset Station Hotel. Tel. 702/547-7777. Major credit cards accepted. Dinner served nightly in the main dining room; lunch and dinner daily at the Oyster Bar.*

A very attractive restaurant that serves excellent fresh fish and seafood, mostly in the Mediterranean style. The atmosphere is casual but especially so at their popular Oyster Bar. The whole place has the appearance of a rocky grotto. The service is friendly and efficient.

HOUSE OF JOY, *7380 S. Eastern Avenue. Tel. 702/896-4648. Most major credit cards accepted. Lunch and dinner served daily.*

It seems that most of the Chinese restaurants on the Strip and even around the rest of Vegas are of an upscale nature. So what do you do when you want a casual and unpretentious atmosphere to enjoy excellent traditional Chinese food? You come to the House of Joy which is, hands down, the best local Chinese restaurant around. You'll be served huge portions of delicious food from their vast menu of beef, chicken, seafood and vegetables. All types of Chinese cuisine are well represented. Most of it is on the mild side (our only disappointment) so if you like things hotter then be sure to ask for it. The service is quick and amazingly efficient, the surroundings more than pleasant enough, and the prices are just right (with quite a few entrees in the Inexpensive category). The hot and sour soup is superb.

RENATA'S, *4451 E. Sunset Road. Tel. 702/435-4000. Most major credit cards accepted. Dinner served Tuesday through Saturday.*

Consisting of a warm and inviting dining room as well as a more casual bistro, Renata's offers fine dining that features Continental dishes along with Chinese and a good selection of steaks and fresh seafood. The Bistro allows you to create your own dinner specialties from a list of available items. Both rooms are attractive and the service is quite good.

SOME MORE GOOD CHEAP EATS

Being a smart reader you've probably noticed that the majority of good restaurants listed here have been in the Expensive category or higher. Notwithstanding the more moderately priced 24-hour cafes, there are quite a few good places around town where you can get a meal for under $10 a person. Many are local or regional chains. The only problem is that most of them are not that close to the Strip, meaning that you have to have a car to reach them (or else your savings will go down the tubes on taxi fare). Here's a quick rundown on some of the better places that fall within this genre.

5 & Diner, 1825 E. Flamingo Road; 8820 S. Eastern Avenue; 6840 W. Sahara Avenue; 1900 N. Buffalo Drive; and 375 N. Stephanie Street, Henderson. A 1950's style theme with basic American favorites.

Blueberry Hill, 1550 E. Flamingo Road; 3790 E. Flamingo Road; 1723 E. Charleston Blvd.; 1280 S. Decatur Blvd.; 5000 E. Bonanza Road; and 2855 N. Green Valley Parkway, Henderson. Lot's of decent food at surprisingly low prices.

Sweet Tomatoes, 375 N. Stepahnie Street, Henderson; 2880 N. Rainbow. A bountiful buffet of vegetarian items.

BUFFETS

The Las Vegas buffet is in a class all by itself. It's almost an institution in this city. Every major Strip hotel (with the exception of New York, New York and the Venetian) has one, an indication of its acceptance and importance in even the luxury level hotels. Buffets used to be places for the budget conscious traveler to go to, or the person without very active taste buds. There was plenty of food at ridiculously low prices although the quality wasn't very good. In fact, many people felt that it wasn't much better than hospital or school cafeteria food. Not very appetizing sounding to say the least.

Although there are some buffets that still fit the old description, they're fewer and fewer as the years go by. The culinary renaissance that has hit Las Vegas restaurants in general also applies to the buffet. Food quality has increased immeasurably (although you still can't call most buffets "gourmet") and so is the availability of freshly prepared dishes. Chefs now routinely prepare orders to your specifications at 'cooking' or 'action' stations. Of course, the prices of the buffets has also increased but they're still usually a big bargain by comparison with most restaurants. For the price of an entree at a moderately priced restaurant, you can get all you can eat soup, salad, main course, vegetables, dessert and non-alcoholic beverage. How can you go wrong? We often wonder why visitors to Las Vegas sometimes stop into a fast-food place. For a couple of dollars more you can choose from a vast selection of much better food. Remember to leave a tip for the person who clears the table and brings your beverage.

The buffet is the ultimate paradise for gluttons but even if you don't have the humongous appetite, it's still an excellent choice. It's tempting to try a little of everything but people who are able to control themselves will walk out satisfied without feeling like they're going to explode. We suggest not filling yourself up on a lot of breads. Do have a salad since that's good for you and it will take up a little room so you don't overdo the heavier foods. Since many buffets are known for their outstanding desserts make sure you leave some room for the finale. People watching at buffets is entertaining and desserts are the best part of the show. You'll often see someone waling back to their table with one tiny piece of cake on their plate, accompanied by their partner juggling six plates with assorted cakes, pies and pastries.

Las Vegas has literally hundreds of regular restaurants, but as mentioned earlier, space limitations prevent including a full listing of them. On the other hand, there are a limited enough number of buffets to include *all* of the worthy choices. Therefore, while we have no doubt that you could find a good restaurant that wasn't included in the previous section, the omission of a buffet on this list is deliberate. If it isn't here, *don't* try it. In our opinion it fits the old time buffet description we mentioned at the outset. Those are the ones you'll most often see free coupons for. They aren't worth it even at that price!

Here's a money saving tip courtesy of your favorite travel authors. Most buffets have the same menu for lunch as they do for dinner. At most, they add a couple of things for dinner, maybe some shrimp or the like. Lunch is always several dollars cheaper. So, unless you have to have that extra item or two, use lunch as an early dinner and save yourself some money. This is especially true for the more expensive buffets. For a family of four the savings can be as much as $15. Not bad for the same food, huh?

Price categories for buffets differ from regular restaurants because the tab includes everything from appetizer and salad through dessert including unlimited refills on non-alcoholic beverages. Thus, a $15 buffet is considerably less expensive than an "equally" priced regular restaurant where that same $15 only gets you the main course and perhaps a soup or salad. The category that each buffet is in is based on the cost for dinner. Lunch ranges from $2 to $8 less. Many buffets have different prices from one evening to another because they have "specialty" nights where something extra, prime rib or seafood, for example, is featured. However, the range is usually only a few dollars. This is the main reason why you will see some listings with two price categories. The other reason is that some were almost exactly on the border line and, with the usual annual price increase, might just edge into the next category by the time you visit.

The price categories are:
· **Expensive** - Over $18
· **Moderate** - $11-18
· **Inexpensive** - $10 or less

The only additional costs are for a gratuity and alcoholic beverages. A few buffets have add-ons such as a lobster for several dollars extra but this is an exception to the rule. All buffets are open daily for breakfast, lunch and dinner unless specified otherwise. Brunch (generally Sunday but sometimes Saturday as well), will be indicated where available. Inquire about children's prices since quite a few do have lower prices for little appetites.

THE BEST BUFFETS IN TOWN

This is like trying to pick the winner of a beauty contest. The choices are so appealing that it isn't an easy task. So, after careful consideration (and taking price/value into account), here are the best places to pig out:

· **Main Street Station** (Garden Court Buffet)
· **The Bellagio Buffet**
· **The Orleans** (French Market Buffet)
· **The Rio** (Carnival World Buffet)
· **Paris** (Le Village Buffet)

Honorable mention goes to **Bally's** (Big Kitchen Buffet), *the* **Reserve** (Grand Safari Buffet), **Flamingo** (Paradise Garden Buffet), *and* **Sunset Station** (Feast Around the World Buffet).

THE STRIP

ALADDIN (Spice Market Buffet), *Expensive.*

One doesn't usually come across a buffet that can be described as "casually elegant" but the Spice Market Buffet does fit the bill rather nicely. There is a very good selection of well prepared foods from around the world, which also fits in nicely with the hotel's international theme. There are several live "action" stations where food is prepared to your order.

BALLY'S (Big Kitchen Buffet), *Moderate.*

One of the more elaborate buffet spreads in a city known for all-you-can-eat eating, the Big Kitchen offers a wide selection of nicely prepared dishes in an attractive setting upstairs from the casino. Shrimp is a specialty for which this buffet has become well known. While we don't have any complaints, there are buffets of equal quality that don't charge quite as much.

BELLAGIO (The Buffet), *Expensive. Brunch.*

Who says that upscale hotels can't have a buffet to entice the gourmet crowd? This buffet is a wonderful culinary experience. The selection is better than average as far as the number of dishes is concerned. What separates it from most competitors is the large number of items that are not part of most buffets, things like pheasant, venison, mussels and much more. There are many seafood dishes. Everything is freshly prepared and is of a high quality. Scrumptious desserts complete the picture. The surroundings are attractive but not overly fancy considering what the rest of Bellagio looks like.

CAESARS PALACE (Palatium Buffet), *Moderate to Expensive. Brunch.*

Large napkins, lots of glass and brass, and a general ritzy atmosphere is what the Palatium has to offer dining patrons. The food selection is a little disappointing although they do have some items not found at most of the lower priced buffets. Moreover, we don't find any special quality for your extra dollars. Dinner patrons can add on a lobster to the basic buffet entry fee.

CIRCUS CIRCUS (Circus Circus Buffet), *Inexpensive. Brunch.*

For a long time this was a popular place with the budget set and was known for a huge selection of food at unheard of prices. It didn't have much more but the school cafeteria quality and surroundings didn't seem to bother most patrons. We're glad that the facilities and food have been substantially upgraded (as were the prices but it is still cheap). The food is still a bit below the general quality of Las Vegas buffets but there is no denying that it represents excellent value.

EXCALIBUR (Roundtable Buffet), *Inexpensive.*

Almost everything that was said about the preceding entry also applies to this establishment (owned by the same company), including the more recent improvements. Even the menu's are virtually identical. As a result, unless you are really into budget eating, we wouldn't recommend eating dinner at both Circus Circus and Excalibur on the same trip. Our biggest complaint about the Roundtable: one continuous food line for most items that makes going back for seconds or other choices far less convenient than the "station" concept that most buffets have adapted.

FLAMINGO LAS VEGAS (Paradise Garden Buffet), *Moderate.*

The "room" (and it's huge) is the most elaborate of any buffet in town, consisting of three separate circular dining areas overlooking the Flamingo's beautiful waterfalls and grounds. Each has a big tree in the center. The spacious food serving areas are equally impressive as they feature fancy statues and multi-tiered niches filled with plants. The Paradise Garden has gone to an all seafood menu on more than one occasion in the past couple of years. But they don't seem to be that sure about it so you might want to make enquiry about the nature of the food before signing up. Regardless, however, the Flamingo has always offered higher than usual quality food, an outstanding salad bar and beautiful to look at as well as delicious desserts. We also like the little extras at this buffet such as the extra fork so that you don't have to eat every course with the same utensil and the friendly staff that is generally several notches more attentive than at many buffets.

HARRAH'S (Fresh Market Buffet), *Moderate. Brunch.*

Colorful decor and a festive atmosphere highlight the Fresh Market Buffet. There are people-sized pieces of fruit and vegetables all over the place (which may inspire the kids to eat their veggies). The selection is only slightly above the standard Strip buffet and the food quality just about matches that same level. We could recommend it more highly if it were a couple of bucks cheaper. After all, this is Harrah's, not Caesars Palace. On the other hand, it's a better buffet than at Caesars!

HOLIDAY INN BOARDWALK (Surf Buffet), *Inexpensive.*

No one would ever claim that this is one of the better buffets in Las Vegas but what was once a joke has been improved to the point that if you're looking for a really cheap place to eat, this could be for you. Pleasant surroundings and a decent selection of less than top quality food. This is just about the only buffet that's open after hours. They have a good "Steak & Eggs" buffet from 11pm through 6am.

LUXOR (Pharaoh's Pheast), *Moderate.*

Catchy name. Located on the hotel's lower level, this is one of the most unusual looking buffets in Las Vegas. It's designed to resemble an archaeological site and you're surrounded by ladders, partially unearthed ancient ruins, gold coins and much more. While this may not sound particularly inviting in print, take our word for it – it's attractive and fun. Unfortunately, things go a little downhill after that. The selection is barely average and the same can be said for the food. Overall, however, it isn't a bad buy if you're simply looking for a lot to eat at a low price.

MANDALAY BAY (Bay Side Buffet), *Expensive. Brunch.*

Like most of the newer mega-resort buffets, this one features "live action stations" and very good quality food. The attractive room accommodates 500 diners but it is sectioned off nicely and has a much cozier feel. If you sit by the windows that overlook Mandalay Bay's 11-acre tropical lagoon, the exotic atmosphere is even more inviting. Our only complaint is that the selection could be bigger. Overall, a good place to eat but, considering all the factors, not one of the better price values for a Las Vegas buffet.

MGM GRAND (Grand Buffet), *Moderate. Brunch.*

Long gone now is the Oz theme which has been replaced by a much fancier and adult oriented atmosphere. The food is quite decent but, like the previous listing, the selection isn't on a par with the better buffets.

THE MIRAGE (Mirage Buffet), *Moderate. Brunch.*

Colorful and pleasant surroundings are accompanied by a decent selection of very nicely prepared food. This is like many other buffets in that it meets or slightly exceeds the standards of the "average" buffet but doesn't have anything particular that distinguishes it. Therefore, the price (which edges close to the next category up) doesn't make it the best of values. Also, this is the Mirage. You would expect better. Our recommendation is that if you want to go to a buffet in a classy joint, you may be better off spending a few dollars more and going to Bellagio.

MONTE CARLO (Monte Carlo Buffet), *Moderate. Brunch.*

This is a very attractive buffet that features Casbah-like Moorish architecture and dining areas broken down into smaller sections for a feeling of greater privacy. Even the food service area is pretty. The food selection is generally good (although the salad bar could be better) and the quality is average to a little better. However, even though it isn't one of the cheapest buffets, when you consider the location and everything else, this is one of the better values on the Strip.

PARIS (Le Village Buffet), *Expensive. Brunch.*

This is the most unique buffet in Las Vegas and the only one themed to the hotel. That applies not only to the decor, which has attractive dining rooms that resemble either a quaint town square or a French country home, but the food. There is an excellent selection of superior quality (especially for a buffet) dishes representing the five culinary regions of France: Alsace, Britanny, Normandy, Burgundy and Provence. Even if you don't particularly care for French cooking you should find more than enough to your liking here. Although much of it is authentic French, a considerable number of entrees have been toned down enough so to be more acceptable to those who don't go for some of the heavier aspects of

French cooking. This is the place to go for those who are seeking an alternative to the often similar food selections at most buffets.

SAHARA (Sahara Buffet). *Inexpensive. Brunch.*

This is the lowest priced buffet of any of the large hotels and, despite some shortcomings, at the prices charged has to be considered an excellent value. The large room has a North African theme and is mildly attractive. There is a decent selection of adequately prepared food that doesn't break any culinary ground. But, then again, you couldn't expect that for what you pay. This is one of the relatively small number of buffets where drinks are self-service.

STARDUST (Coco Palms), *Inexpensive to Moderate.*

The tropical foliage and wrought iron make this a most attractive room. The selection of international dishes changes each day and there are five action cooking stations. This buffet features an unusually large number of items for the health conscious diner. A relatively good value.

STRATOSPHERE (Stratosphere Buffet), *Inexpensive to Moderate. Brunch.*

The dining room is a colorful affair with miniature hot-air balloons all over the place. You'll get good value here, too. The food is tasty and there is an excellent selection of salads and veggies. Where they do fall a little short is in the main-course area – a few more hot meat dishes would be an improvement. You get your own drinks at the Stratosphere Buffet.

With the expected summer 2001 completion of the new tower at Stratosphere, an additional buffet will be opening. However, as of press time we didn't have any definitive details so you can check it out and let *us* know.

TREASURE ISLAND (The Buffet), *Moderate. Brunch.*

There are two separate dining rooms each with their own (identical) food service area. It's one of the few places at TI that still has a pirate theme although who knows how long that will last. One slight drawback to this buffet is that there is a limited number of items to choose from and there is no room for action stations (the dining rooms are rather small too and when it gets crowded, which is often, you can feel a little cramped. However, we've never had any problem filling our plate to capacity and the quality of the food is excellent. We love the little deli sandwiches that they have. Although we've griped a bit we do like the TI buffet and can feel confident in recommending it to you.

TROPICANA (Island Buffet), *Moderate. Brunch.*

The tropical theme decor of the Island Buffet is quite colorful and blends in nicely with the surrounding areas of the hotel. It overlooks the pool area and attractive grounds. The food selection and quality are both only average and you won't find anything unusual on the menu. It would be a better value if it were priced a few dollars less.

OFF-STRIP

LAS VEGAS HILTON (The Buffet). *Moderate. Brunch.*

Another one with an imaginative name! Don't these places have guys getting paid lots of money to come up with something with a little more flair? Well, all is forgiven because this buffet has excellent food and a very good selection that combine with a pleasant atmosphere. In addition, the helpful staff is exceedingly friendly. Although this place won't make the top five, if you're in the neighborhood you certainly won't be making a bad choice if you opt to dine here.

THE ORLEANS (French Market Buffet), *Inexpensive to Moderate. Brunch.*

The hotel closed its original poor old buffet a couple of years ago and reopened it in a new location. The only thing that stayed the same is the name. This is, without a doubt, one of the best buffets in town. The dining room is attractive and spacious. The food service area is colorful and well laid out. But the best thing is the selection and quality. Few hotel buffets have a bigger selection then what you can find at one of their seven action stations. And everything is delicious, from the great onion rings to the numerous seafood items. The latter has to be considered unusual given the reasonable price. This is worth the short ride from the Strip.

PALACE STATION (Feast Gourmet Buffet), *Inexpensive to Moderate.*

Don't get carried away by the name. Although this is a decent buffet in every respect, it is little more than that. It's a couple of notches below the Feast Around the World buffets at some of Station Casino's other properties (Sunset and Texas) and it's a single notch below when it comes to the quality of the food and the surroundings. Maybe we're spoiled by the better Station buffets because through the years this has proven to be a very popular place.

THE RIO (Carnival World Buffet), *Moderate. Brunch.*

To its credit, this is the place that brought buffets out of the industrial food category and into an art form in its own right. Although the competition has caught up in many places you'll still find what is probably *the* biggest selection of food in Las Vegas. The food stations stretch for what seems to be an endless journey of delights. In addition to the many separate ethnic food areas, the Mongolian Grill is one of the most popular buffet spots in the city. Everything at the Rio is quite delicious. This is also a good buffet for children because one of the food stations has hot dogs and burgers and shakes, something you won't find in most buffets.

On the other hand, adults can have a thick and juicy steak cooked to order. The dessert selection is also outstanding and delicious. The only problem with the Carnival World is its popularity – there can be huge lines at times. The Rio has implemented a new system at those times to expedite the flow by telling you when you can come back and get in without having to wait on line. It seems to work.

THE RIO (Village Seafood Buffet), *Expensive. Lunch and dinner.*

The only buffet in Las Vegas that is devoted entirely to delicacies of the sea at all times. (The Flamingo, although said to be "all seafood" does have other items). This is a small room, especially when compared to the huge Carnival World, and the selection is naturally smaller. However, because of the narrow nature of the menu you are likely to find quite a few seafood items that you don't often encounter elsewhere. Crab, shrimp, and mussels, among others, are always available. The food quality is excellent as is almost expected from the Rio.

DOWNTOWN

FREMONT HOTEL (Paradise Buffet), *Moderate. Brunch.*

The second best downtown buffet. The setting is very attractive, from the colorful aquarium at the entrance, to the foliage filled dining room. Extravagant chandeliers and comfortable booths give this room the feel of a nightclub and help to enhance your enjoyment. The food selection is a bit beyond average and the quality is just fine. However, this is downtown and we don't think that you can call it a bargain.

GOLDEN NUGGET (The Buffet), *Inexpensive to Moderate. Brunch.*

Our personal opinion is that The Buffet isn't all that worthy of being included in this list, especially given the price, because of its small selection and undistinguished food. However, a lot of people do seem to give it favorable reviews. If you do go we suggest checking out their all day Sunday Brunch which features such delights as Eggs Benedict, blintzes and creamed herring.

MAIN STREET STATION (Garden Court Buffet), *Moderate. Brunch.*

This is the only downtown buffet that surpasses the one at the Fremont and it is definitely as good or better than any place in town. It has everything going for it. The beautiful, almost idyllic looking dining room features a high ceiling with intricate wood lattice-work, graceful palms and many interesting antiques. The humongous food selection is grouped by type of cuisine and includes Chinese, Mexican, Italian (they have great pizza), treasures form the sea, and several others. Also on tap are an excellent salad bar and desserts that will drive you out of your mind!

We have yet to try anything from the dessert bar that wasn't excellent. We haven't actually done a count but this is probably the biggest selection after the Carnival World. The food is among the best tasting of any Vegas buffet and every section is eye appealing. (Even their mashed sweet potatoes turns the ordinary into something special.)

AROUND LAS VEGAS

ARIZONA CHARLIE'S (Wild West Buffet), *Inexpensive.*

We were debating whether or not to include this place in our list of recommended buffets. We've given in to popular demand more than our own feelings here because, even though this is a good value, it doesn't have that much to offer. The surroundings are drab and the food selection is only so-so. It's success stems from the fact that a lot of locals looking for a bargain wind up there because there aren't any other good buffets located close by.

ARIZONA CHARLIE'S EAST (Wild West Buffet), *Inexpensive.*

As in the case of the casino appearance, the newer Arizona Charlie's is better. The dining room is pleasantly attractive and quite intimate. Although there's a western mural at the entrance the decor is decidedly floral. You'll find a friendly atmosphere along with what is definitely not a bad selection of food. There's certainly enough to fill your plate and still have you saying that there were other things you would have liked to sample. We think the food is better here than at the original Charlie's as well. An excellent value.

BOULDER STATION (Feast Gourmet Buffet), *Inexpensive to Moderate. Brunch.*

This is virtually identical to the buffet of the same name at Palace Station. See the listing for that location in the off-Strip section.

FIESTA HOTEL (Festival Buffet), *Moderate. Brunch.*

Let's tell you right up front that the Festival just missed making our best and honorable mention list. It gets good marks on all accounts. The selection is quite extensive and the quality is also quite good. We like the espresso bar that serves up specialty coffees and other beverages (at a slightly additional charge). We also like the festive Mexican "outdoor" cafe atmosphere and the colorful serving stations. You won't go wrong by venturing to the Fiesta when it comes time to buffet.

LAS BRISAS BUFFET (Castaways), *Inexpensive to Moderate.*

When the Castaways was the old Showboat we weren't thrilled with their Captain's Table Buffet. However, our first look at the revamped facility showed a lot more than just a name change. The decor was nicer, the food selection better and the quality a whole lot improved. While still not one of the best buffets, it now is more than good enough to be included with our list of recommendations. If you're on the Boulder Strip then give it a try.

REGENT LAS VEGAS (Upstairs Market), *Moderate to Expensive. Brunch.*

Bet you can figure out where in the Regent this buffet is located. The large circular room with its domed ceiling has an elegant look and both the food selection and quality are good. You will find some unusual items as you make your way around the serving area which is supposed to justify the prices. That, and the name of the hotel. We like it but have our doubts as to whether it is worth the price.

SAM'S TOWN (Firelight Buffet), *Moderate. Brunch*

This all-new facility adjoining the best views of Mystic Falls Park replaces the original "Great Buffet" which we never liked despite having to admit that it was extremely popular. This more upscale eatery features natural light through 25-foot high windows and thematic lighting that changes from one time of the day to another. For a buffet it is unusually attractive (actually one of the nicest) and features a combination of modern style along with Art Deco touches. It is divided into small dining areas for a high degree of privacy. The food is excellent although we would be happier if the selection (which is just average) would be bigger. The menu changes on a daily basis and there are several action cooking stations. The layout of the food service area is such that when the place gets crowded it is almost like one continuous food line rather than separate stations.

SILVERTON (All American Buffet), *Inexpensive to Moderate. Brunch.*

They can change the hotel's name all they want but their buffet still remains as a good choice. The atmosphere is about as informal as you can get – the food service area consists chiefly of chuck wagons and the several dining rooms also reflect a mostly western theme. It's quaint and attractive. The food is real good and the selection is better than average, especially considering the prices. Even their higher priced seafood and prime rib evenings are an excellent value. Leave some room for dessert, of course – you might want to build your own strawberry shortcake, a perennial favorite here. One word of caution – this buffet frequently has promotional evenings where the prices are outrageously low. However, the flip side is that the selection is limited on those evenings. You might want to verify that they aren't having one of their super specials when you want to visit unless, of course, the even lower price is more attractive to you then the regular selection of dishes.

SUNCOAST HOTEL (St. Tropez Buffet), *Inexpensive to Moderate.*

This hotel is owned by the same folks who brought you the buffet extravaganza at the Orleans. It's obvious from the moment you enter that they tried to pattern this after that success. Well, it doesn't reach that level. Not that the place isn't attractive or that the food isn't good or that there isn't enough to choose from. It scores adequately or better on all those fronts and we do like this place. However, in every way this is a *miniature* version of the French Market Buffet and so you just can't be quite as impressed. This is definitely an excellent value.

TEXAS STATION (Feast Around the World), *Inexpensive to Moderate. Brunch.*

First, a little explanation is in order concerning the Station Casinos buffets, all of which are excellent. They are divided into two levels, the Feast Around the World (here and Sunset Station), and their "regular" buffets at Boulder and Palace Stations. The latter two are lesser "models" of the Feast Around the World. The Texas Station feast features a number of action stations, each with a different type of cuisine. The selection and food quality are both excellent. As you'll see later, however, we do have a preference for the one at Sunset Station even though it isn't that different from the food standpoint.

HENDERSON

THE RESERVE (Grand Safari Buffet), *Moderate. Lunch and dinner. Brunch.*

This is one of the very best buffets in the Las Vegas Valley and it is unfortunate that it is a little out of the way for most visitors. (Try stopping here if you're on your way back from Hoover Dam.) It's also an excellent value. No wonder the locals never want to cook. Action stations include Italian, American, Chinese and a Mongolian Barbecue along with a separate station for seafood. Then again, you'll find several fresh fish and seafood dishes scattered around the other cuisines as well. The salad bar and dessert area are also notable for their extensive selection. The freshly baked cakes are delicious. Overall food quality is quite high.

SUNSET STATION (Feast Around the World), *Moderate. Brunch.*

Choose from Country Barbecue, Chinese, Italian, and several other separate food areas. You'll enjoy the food from whichever stations you select. The central dessert bar is a sight to be seen – the decor as well as the sinful collection of delicious delights. You can even make your own "root beer float." The entire buffet is very attractive and is highlighted by a zodiac themed ceiling in the central rotunda along with a statue of Atlas holding up the world. You'll probably feel like you're holding up something heavy after you finish your meal – namely, your full stomach.

What puts this place just a notch or two above its Texas Station counterpart is the decor. If possible, ask to be seated in the main center room because that is where the attractive nature of this place stands out. The separate dining rooms to either side of the main room aren't nearly as nice.

11. GAMBLING IN VEGAS!

CASINO BASICS

In this chapter we'll get you oriented to the casino gambling environment and show you the all-important techniques of money management. **Avery Cardoza**, the best-selling writer of more than a dozen gambling books and strategies and the foremost gambling publisher in the world, has prepared the following chapter with visitors to Las Vegas specifically in mind. No other living gambler/author has as much experience teaching the basics of the games, and as much experience winning!

Converting Traveler's Checks & Money Orders to Cash

The dealers accept only cash or chips at the table, so if you bring traveler's checks, money orders or the like, you must go to the area of the casino marked **Casino Cashier** to get these converted to cash. Be sure to bring proper identification to ensure a smooth transaction.

Casino Chips

Chip denominations run in $1, $5, $25, $100 and $500 units. If you're a big stakes player, you may even find $1,000, $2,500, $5,000 and $10,000 chips available!

The usual color scheme of chips is as follows: $1 chips are silver dollars, $5 chips will be red, $25 - green, and $100 - black. Chips of larger deniminations, such as $500 or $1,000, may be white, pink or other colors.

In casino parlance, $1 chips are generally referred to as *silver*, $5 chips as *nickels*, $25 chips as *quarters*, and $100 chips as *dollars*. Unless playing at a 25¢ minimum craps table, $1 chips are the minimum currency used.

Betting

Casinos prefer that the player uses chips for betting purposes, for the handling of money at the tables is cumbersome and slows the game. However, cash can be used to bet with, though all payoffs will be in chips.

House Limits

The house limits will be posted on placards located on each corner of the table. They will indicate the minimum bet required to play and also the maximum bet allowed.

Minimum bets range from $1 and $5 per bet, to a maximum of $500, $1000 or $2,000 a bet. Occasionally, 25¢ tables may be found as well, but don't count on it. If special arrangements are made, a player can bet as much as he can muster in certain casinos. The Horseshoe Casino in Las Vegas is known to book any bet no matter the size.

In 1981, a man walked into the Horseshoe and placed a bet for $777,777. He bet the *don't pass* in craps, and walked out two rolls later with one and a half million dollars in cash!

Converting Chips into Cash

Dealers do not convert your chips into cash. Once you've bought your chips at the table, that cash is dropped into a dropbox, and thereafter is unobtainable. When you are ready to convert your chips back to cash, take them to the cashier's cage where the transaction will be done.

Free Drinks and Cigarettes

Casinos offer their customers unlimited free drinking while gambling at the tables or slot machines. In addition to alcoholic beverages, a player can order milk, soft drinks, juices or any other beverages available. This is ordered through and served by a cocktail waitress.

Cigarettes and cigars are also complimentary and can be ordered from the same cocktail waitress.

Tipping

Tipping, or **toking**, as it is called in casino parlance, should be viewed as a gratuitous gesture by the player to the dealer or crew of dealers he feels has given him good service. Tipping is totally at the player's discretion, and in no way should be considered an obligation.

If you toke, toke only when you're winning, and only if the crew is friendly and helpful to you. Do not toke dealers that you don't like or ones that try to make you feel guilty about not tipping. Dealers that make playing an unpleasant experience for you deserve nothing.

MONEY MANAGEMENT

Your trip to Las Vegas can be a great one, but only if you don't lose your shirt at the tables. Don't be one of those gamblers who, as the saying used to go, drives into town in a $20,000 Cadillac and leaves in a $150,000 Greyhound bus.

To be a winner at gambling, you must exercise sound money management principles and keep your emotions under control. The temptation to ride a winning streak too hard in the hopes of a big killing, to bet wildly during a losing streak, or to try for a quick comeback, can spell doom. Wins can turn into losses, and moderate losses can turn into a nightmare.

Instead, one must plan ahead and prepare for the game. It's important to understand the nature of the gamble. In any gambling pursuit where luck plays a role, fluctuations in one's fortunes are common. It is the ability of the player to successfully deal with the ups and downs inherent in the gamble that separate the smart gamblers from the losers.

Here are the three important principles of money management:

1. Never gamble with money you cannot afford to lose either financially or emotionally.

Do not gamble with needed funds no matter how "sure" any bet seems. The possibility of losing is real, and if that loss will hurt, you're playing the fool.

2. Bankroll yourself properly.

Undercapitalization leaves a player vulnerable in two ways. First, a normal downward trend can wipe out a limited money supply (sometimes very quickly). Next, and more important, the bettor may feel pressured by the shortage of capital and play less powerfully than smart play dictates.

If the amount staked on a bet is above your head, you're playing in the wrong game. Play only at levels of betting you feel comfortable with.

3. Know when to quit – set stop-loss limits.

What often separates the winners from the losers is that the winners, when winning, leave the table a winner, and when losing, restrict their losses to affordable amounts. Smart gamblers never allow themselves to get destroyed at the gamble.

Minimizing losses is the key. You can't always win. If you're losing, keep the losses affordable - take a break. You only want to play with a clear head.

When you're winning big, put a good chunk of these winnings in a "don't touch" pile, and play with the rest. You never want to hand all your winnings back to the casino. Should a losing streak occur, you're out of there – a winner!!!

EYE IN THE SKY

Look above the playing area in any casino and you'll see dark, half-circle globes that look like light fixtures. What you're seeing is casino security in action, the ubiquitous "Eye in the Sky." The device is a one-way surveillance camera, used by security to ensure that no cheating occurs, either by players or dealers. Cameras are also located in other key spots in the casino, usually behind glass doors or walls. Considering that every conceivable kind of cheating has at one time or another been attempted in Las Vegas, the casinos have become pretty expert in spotting ne'er-do-wells.

But what you and I consider cheating sometimes differ from what the casino considers cheating. The biggest difference between the casinos and the players is over card counting in blackjack. Most players and experts argue that card counting is merely a way of regaining the edge the house has given itself in every hand. Gamblers argue that not counting is akin to a major league baseball player holding back on his slugging advantage, or not bagging a ball easily within reach. To the casino operators, card counting is cheating, pure and simple - so be careful if you're going to count!

A QUICK GUIDE TO CASINO ACTION

Every casino/hotel as well as just about every other casino in town will have a variety of slot machines and other electronic gaming options. You can apply the rule of thumb that the larger the casino, the more machines there will be and the greater the chance of finding more unusual machines. Table games are another matter. Some of the smallest casinos are essentially slot clubs and you'll find no table games or only a limited number (usually blackjack). Larger casinos (and that includes every major Strip property) will have plenty of live gaming options for you to choose from, including blackjack, craps, roulette and poker (against the house). Keno and Big Six are also staples.

Poker rooms are where you play against other individuals and not the casino. However, the house takes a percentage. These are less common and are listed in the accompanying table along with some betting options that aren't always found. We've listed over 30 of the largest casinos as well as some others that are popular with visitors. Besides baccarat, you can find mini-bacarrat. It's the same game except that the stakes are lower and is found in most hotel/casinos with table games.

GAMING AVAILABILITY BY HOTEL/CASINO

	Bacarrat	Bingo	Poker Room	Race/Sports Book
Bally's	X			X
Barbary Coast	X			X
Bellagio	X		X	X
Binion's	X	X	X	X
Caesars Palace	X			X
Circus Circus	X		X	X
Desert Inn	X			X
Excalibur	X		X	X
Fitzgerald's			X	
Flamingo Hilton	X		X	X
Four Queens		X		Sports only
Gold Coast	X	X		X
Golden Nugget	X			X
Hard Rock	X			X
Harrah's	X		X	X
Imperial Palace				X
Las Vegas Hilton	X			X
Luxor	X		X	X
Main Street Station				
Mandalay Bay	X		X	X
MGM Grand	X		X	X
Mirage	X		X	X
Monte Carlo	X		X	X
New York, New York	X			X
Orleans	X		X	X
Palace Station	X	X	X	X
Paris	X			X
Rio	X			X
Riviera	X	X	X	X
Sahara	X		X	X
Sam's Town	X	X	X	X
Stardust	X		X	X
Stratosphere	X		X	X
Treasure Island	X			X
Tropicana	X			Sports only
Venetian	X			X

NEVADA CRAPS LAYOUT

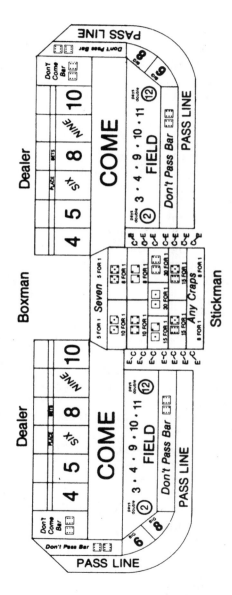

Any other number thrown on the come-out roll, the 4, 5, 6, 8, 9, and 10, becomes the **point**. Once a point is established, there are only two numbers that matter to pass or don't pass bettors - the 7 and the point. If the 7 is thrown before the point is thrown a second time, pass line bettors lose and don't pass bettors win. And if the point repeats before the 7, then the opposite is true; the pass line bettors win, and the don't pass bettors lose. All other throws are immaterial. For example, if the point is a 6, rolls of 12, 3, 8, and 10 are completely inconsequential. It's only the 7 or the point, the 6, that affects these wagers.

The **shoot**, as this progression of rolls is called, will continue until the point repeats, a winner for pass line bettors, or until a 7 is rolled, called **sevening-out**, a loser on the pass line but a winner for don't pass bettors. The very next roll will be a new come-out roll, and a new shoot will begin.

The shooter will continue to roll the dice until he either sevens out or voluntarily gives up the dice. And then, in a clockwise direction, each successive player gets a chance to be the shooter, or that player may decline and pass the privilege to the next player. There is no benefit (nor downside) to being a shooter. The only requirement a shooter has, other than throwing the dice, is to make either a pass or don't pass bet.

Winning pass and don't pass bets pay even-money. For every dollar wagered, a dollar is won.

The Bets
In addition to the pass and don't pass bets discussed above, the player has a wide choice of bets available. We'll look at these below.

Come and Don't Come Bets
Come and don't come bets work exactly like the pass and don't pass except that these bets can be made only *after* the come-out roll, when a point is already established. (Pass and don't pass bets can be made only on a *come-out roll*.)

The throw of a 7 or 11 on the first roll is an automatic winner for come bets while the throw of a 2, 3, or 12 is an automatic loser. Don't come bets work the opposite way; a 7 or 11 on the first throw is an automatic loser, and the 2 or 3 is a winner. The 12, or in some casinos the 2 instead, is a tie for don't come bettors, just like on the don't pass.

Any other throw, the 4, 5, 6, 8, 9, or 10 establishes a *come point*. Once that occurs, only the 7 and the point are consequential rolls for come and don't come bettors. Come bettors win when the point repeats before the 7 is thrown, and lose if the 7 occurs first, while don't come bettors win if the 7 is thrown before the point repeats.

For example, if the first throw after the placing of a come bet was a 5, throws of 11, 2, 9 and 8 have no effect on this bet. Should the next roll be a 7, the come bettor will now lose that point, while don't come bettors with established points will win. (Incidentally, the 7 will make losers on all *established* pass and come points, and winners on *established* don't pass and don't come points.) Newly placed come bets though, before a point is established, would be winners on that throw of a 7.

These bets are made by placing the wagers in the area marked *Come* or *Don't Come*, and pay even-money on winners.

Free-Odds Bets

Free-odds bets, so named because the casino enjoys no edge on them, are the best bets available to the player, and should be a part of every player's winning strategy. To make a free-odds bet, the player must first have placed a pass, don't pass, come or don't come wager, since the free-odds are made in conjunction with these bets.

Free-Odds: Pass Line

After a point is established (a 4, 5, 6, 8, 9, or 10), the pass line bettor is allowed to make an additional wager, called a **free odds** or **single odds** bet, that his point will repeat before a 7 is thrown. He may bet up to the amount wagered on his pass line bet and does so by placing the chips behind that wager. For example, if $10 is bet on the pass line, the player may bet $10 as the free-odds wager.

On points of 4 or 10, the casino will pay 2 to 1 on a free-odds win, on points of 5 or 9, it will pay 3 to 2 and on points of 6 or 8, it will pay 6 to 5. Notice that these are the exact odds of winning. For example, if the point is a 6, there are five ways to win (5 ways to roll a 6) and six ways to lose (six ways to roll a 7) - 6 to 5 odds. So if the player bet $10 on a free-odds point of 8, he would win $12 on that bet, getting paid the true odds of 6-5.

Free Odds: Don't Pass Line

Works the other way. Free-odds bettors wager that the 7 will be thrown before the point repeats. Since the odds favor the bettor once the point is established, there being more ways to roll a 7 than any other number, the don't pass free-odds bettor must **lay odds**, that is, put more money on the free-odds bet than he will win.

The allowable free-odds bet is determined by the *payoff*, not the original bet. The bettor is allowed to win only up to the amount bet on the don't pass line.

We'll assume a $10 don't pass bet, which means the player can win only up to $10 on the free odds bet. On points of 4 or 10, the player must lay $20 to win $10; on points 5 and 9, he must lay $15; and on points 6 and 8, he must lay $12 to win that $10.

To sum up, the player must give 1 to 2 odds on points of 4 and 10, 2 to 3 odds on points of 5 and 9, and 5 to 6 odds on points 6 and 8.

Don't pass free odds bets are made by placing the wager next to the don't pass wager in the don't pass box.

Free Odds: Come and Don't Come Bets

These bets work the same as the free odds on the pass (corresponds to the come bet) and don't pass line (corresponds to the don't come) except they can only be made *after* the come point is established.

The only other difference is that the free-odds bet is not in play on the come-out roll, though the come bet itself is. (The free odds on the don't come, pass and don't pass bets are always in play.)

You make these wagers by giving your chips to the dealer - they'll place the bets for you.

Double Odds

Some casinos offer double odds as an inducement to the bettor. These work just like the odds bets described above except that even more money can be bet on the free odds wager. In the case of double odds, double the money could be wagered on the bet.

Place Bets

These are bets that a particular point number, the 4, 5, 6, 8, 9 or 10, whichever is bet on, will be rolled before a 7 is thrown. The player can make as many place bets as he wants, and bet them at any time before a roll. Place bets of 4 or 10 are paid at 9 to 5, on 5 or 9 are paid at 7 to 5 and 6 or 8 are paid at 6 to 5. These bets are not in play on the come-out roll.

Big 6 and Big 8

These are bets that the 6 (Big 6) or 8 (Big 8) are rolled before the 7. Winning bets are paid off at even money.

Field Bet

This is a one roll bet that the next roll of the dice will be a number listed in the field box - a 2, 3, 4, 9, 10, 11 or 12. Rolls of 2 and 12 pay double, all others in the box pay even money. Rolls of 5, 6, 7 and 8 are losers. This bet can be made anytime. (In some casinos, the 2 or 12 may pay triple.)

One Roll Bets

These bets are about the worst you can find in a casino. They're found in the center of the layout and are made by giving the chips to the dealer.

The **Any 7** is a bet that the following roll will be a 7 and pays the winner 4 to 1; **Any Craps** is a bet that the following roll will be a 2, 3 or 12, pays 7 to 1; **2 or 12** is a bet that the next roll will be a 2 (or 12). You can bet either or both, pays 30 to 1. **3 or 11** is a bet that the 3 or the 11, whichever is chosen, will come up next. Pays 15-1.

The **Horn Bet** is a four-way bet that the next roll will be a 2, 3, 11 or 12. Pays off 15-1 on the 3 or 11 and 30-1 on the 2 or 12. The other three losing chips are deducted from the payoff.

Whenever the numbers 4, 6, 8 and 10 are rolled as doubles, the roll is said to be thrown **hardways**. Betting *hardways* is a wager that the doubled number chosen comes up before a 7 is thrown, or before the number is thrown *easy* (not as a double). Bets on hardways 6 or 8 pay 9 to 1, and on hardways 4 or 10, pay 7 to 1.

Right and Wrong Betting

Betting with the dice, pass line, and come betting, is called ***right betting***. Betting against the dice, making don't pass and don't come bets, is called ***wrong betting***.

Betting right or wrong are equally valid methods of winning, with equivalent odds.

Winning Strategy

To get the best chances of beating the casino, you must make only the bets that give the casino the least possible edge.

You can see from the chart that bets vary in house edge from the combined pass line: double odds wager where the house has but a 0.6% edge to the horn bet where the house edge can be as high as 16.67%!

To win at craps, make only pass and come bets backed up by free-odds wagers or don't pass and don't come bets, and back these wagers up with free-odds bets.

These bets reduce the house edge to the absolute minimum, a mere 0.8% in a single odds game or 0.6% in a double odds game if this strategy is followed.

By concentrating our bets this way, we're making only the best bets available at craps, and in fact, will place the majority of our bets on wagers the casino has absolutely no edge on whatsoever! This is the best way to give yourself every chance of beating the casino when the dice are hot and you've got bets riding on winners.

Try to keep two or three points going at one time by making pass and come bets if you're a right bettor, or don't pass and don't come bets if you're a wrong bettor and back all these bets with the full free odds available.

Money management is very important in craps, for money can be won or lost rapidly. However, try to catch that one good hot streak, and if you do, make sure you walk away a winner.

HOUSE EDGE IN CRAPS CHART

Bet	Payoff	House Edge
Pass or Come	1 to 1	1.41%
Don't Pass, Don't Come	1 to 1	1.40%
Free Odds Bets*	***	0.00%
Single Odds**	***	0.8%
Double Odds**	***	0.6%
Place 4 or 10	9 to 5	6.67%
Place 5 or 9	7 to 5	4.00%
Place 6 or 8	7 to 6	1.52%
Field	2 to 1 on 12	
	1 to 1 other #s	5.56%
Field	3 to 1 on 12	
	1 to 1 other #s	2.78%
Any Craps	7 to 1	11.11%
Any 7	4 to 1	16.67%
2 or 12	30 for 1	16.67%
	30 to 1	13.89%
3 or 11	15 for 1	16.67%
	15 to 1	11.11%
Hardways 4 or 10	8 for 1	11.11%
6 or 8	10 for 1	9.09%

*The free odds bet by itself
**The free odds bet combined with pass, don't pass, come and don't come wagers
***The payoffs on the free odds portion of the bets vary. See discussion under free odds for payoffs.

SLOTS

The allure of slot machine play has hooked millions of players looking to reap the rewards of a big jackpot!

There are basically two types of slot machines. The first type, the **Straight Slots**, pays winning combinations according to the schedule listed on the machine itself. These payoffs never vary.

The second type of machine is called **Progressive Slots.** These too have a standard set of payoffs listed on the machine, but in addition, and what sometimes makes for exciting play, it has a big jackpot which progressively gets larger and larger as each coin is put in. The jackpot total is posted above the machine and can accumulate to enormous sums of money!

SLOT CLUBS

There's hardly a hotel/casino in Las Vegas that doesn't have a slot club. You sign up at their casino club desk and get a card that looks like a credit card. Each time you play at slots or video poker you put the card in the machine and earn points for as long as you play. The points can be redeemed for free meals, gift items, room discounts and, increasingly, for cold cash. Different hotels have different ways of awarding points but the general rule is that you add up points quicker on the higher denomination machines. Some of the more upscale hotels only allow slot club card use on $1 machines, although that is still the exception to the rule.

Is this a great deal or what? Well, yes and no. A one-time visitor will have to play an incredible amount in order to earn enough points to get something. On the other hand, if you come to Vegas regularly (once a year to eighteen months is the typical use requirement to keep your point total active) and you like to gamble at the same place, then it makes sense to sign up for a card. There is no cost to join so you don't lose anything by having the card. Some hotels even give out little trinkets just for signing up. They also frequently award bonus points at the time you join.

The Basics

Slots are easy to play. Machines generally take anywhere from 1 to 5 coins. Insert the coins into the machine, pull the handle, and see what Lady Luck brings.

There are many types of slot machine configurations but all work according to the same principle - put the money in and pull! Some machines will pay just the middle horizontal line, while others pay on winning combinations from left to right, diagonally, and other combinations .

Often, the number of lines the machine will pay on depends on the amount deposited. One coin may pay the middle line, a second coin will pay the top line as well, a third coin - the bottom line, a fourth - the diagonal and a fifth - the other diagonal.

SLOTS CITY

Slots are huge money-makers for the casinos. On average, the typical Vegas slot machine pulls in more than $100,000 a year. Many casinos now offer a cushy slots area that allows you the pleasure of plunking $100 tokens into the one-armed bandits. And if that's too puny, several machines let you deposit $500 a throw!

With computer advances, many slot machines have gone electronic. You can now push a spin button instead of pulling the lever. And many of the machines are tied together either in citywide or statewide networks, so the jackpots keep growing and growing.

Operated by IGT (International Game Technology), five networks are now in operation. **Nevada Nickels Network** requires three nickels to win a statewide jackpot; **Quartermania** requires two quarters to win; **Fabulous Fifties** requires two half-dollar coins to win; **High Rollers** demands two $5 tokens to win big; and the most widespread of the networks, **Megabucks**, mandates a wager of three dollars to hit the huge enchilada. Megabucks jackpots start at $7 million. The record so far is a bewildering $36 million.

In case you were planning on winning one of the outsized slots jackpots, casinos pay off over time in regular payments. But several casinos now pay some jackpots on the spot: the Boyd Group, operator of the California, Sam's Town, Fremont, and Stardust, offers a 25¢ slots network paying out $250,000 jackpots immediately. And Mandalay Resort Group's eight casinos in the state pay out $500,000!

More winning rows do not necessarily equate to better odds of winning. The odds are built into the machine and no amount of lines played will change them. The most important factor is how loose or tight the machines are set by the casino. That is what determines the odds facing a slots player.

Winning Strategy

The most important concept in slots is to locate the machines with the loosest setting, or with progressive machines, to play only the machines with the highest jackpot.

Some casinos advertise slots with returns as high as 97% to the player, others, even as high as 99%! Obviously, the player stands a much better chance of winning at these places than others where a standard return of only 84% might be the norm. On some machines, players may not even get an 84% return.

In general, the poorer paying machines will be located in areas where the casino hopes to grab a few of the bettor's coins as he passes through an area or waits on a line.

Airport terminals, restaurants, show lines, bathrooms and the like tend to have smaller returns.

On the other hand, casinos that specialize in slots and serious slots areas within a casino will have better payoffs. These casinos view slots as an important income, and in order to keep regular slots customers, bettors must hear those jackpot bells ringing - after all, winning is contagious!

Some machines are set to pay better than others, and these slots will be mixed in with poorer paying ones, so it's always a good idea to look for the hot machine. Better yet, ask the change girls. They spend all day and night near the slots and know which machines tend to return the most money. When you hit a jackpot, don't give the money back – make sure you walk away a winner!

KENO

There are 80 numbered squares on a keno ticket which correspond exactly to the 80 numbered balls in the keno cage. A player may choose anywhere from one number to fifteen numbers to play and does so by marking an "x" on the keno ticket for each number or numbers he or she so chooses.

The Basics

Twenty balls will be drawn each game and will appear as lighted numbers on the keno screens. Winnings are determined by consulting the payoff chart each casino provides. If enough numbers are correctly **caught**, you have a winner, and the chart will show the payoff. The more numbers caught, the greater the winnings.

Bets are usually made in 70¢ or $1 multiples, though other standard bets may apply, and a player may bet as many multiples of this bet as he desires as long as the bet is within the casino limits.

Marking the Ticket

The amount being wagered on a game should be placed in the box marked *Mark Price Here* in the upper right hand corner of the ticket.

Leave out dollar or cents signs though. $1 would be indicated by simply writing 1- and 70¢ by .70. Of course, any amount up to the house limit can be wagered. Underneath this box is a column of white space. The number of spots selected for the game is put here. If six spots were selected on the ticket, mark the number 6, if fifteen numbers, mark 15.

This type of ticket, which is the most commonly bet, is called a **straight ticket**.

5 SPOT STRAIGHT TICKET

MARK PRICE HERE

1	2	3	4	X	6	7	8	9	10
11	X	13	14	15	16	17	18	19	20
21	22	23	24	25	26	27	X	29	30
31	32	33	34	35	36	37	38	39	40

KENO LIMIT $50,000.00 TO AGGREGATE PLAYERS EACH GAME

41	42	43	44	45	46	47	48	49	50
51	52	53	54	X	56	57	58	59	60
61	X	63	64	65	66	67	68	69	70
71	72	73	74	75	76	77	78	79	80

KENO RUNNERS ARE AVAILABLE FOR YOUR CONVENIENCE.
WE ARE NOT RESPONSIBLE IF TICKETS ARE TOO LATE FOR CURRENT GAME

Split Tickets

A player may also play as many combinations as he chooses. **Split tickets** allow a player to bet two or more combinations in one game. This is done by marking two sets (or more) of numbers from 1-15 on a ticket and separating them by either a line, or by circling the separate groups. Numbers may not be duplicated between the two sets.

On split tickets in which several games are being played in one, the keno ticket should be marked as follows. In addition to the x's indicating the numbers, and the lines or circles showing the groups, the ticket should clearly indicate the number of games being played.

For example, a split ticket playing two groups of six spots each would be marked 2/6 in the column of white space. The 2 shows that two combinations are being played, and the 6 shows that six numbers are being chosen per game. If $1 is bet per combination, we would put a 1- and circle it underneath the slashed numbers to show this, and in the *Mark Price Here* box, we would enter 2, to show $2 is being bet – $1 per combo.

Winning Strategy

Keno is a game that should not be played seriously, because the odds are prohibitively against the player. The house edge is typically 20% and higher - daunting odds if one wants to win in the long run.

One thing to look out for are casinos that offer better payoffs on the big win, so a little shopping might get you closer to a bigger payoff. For example, some casinos will pay $50,000 if you catch all the numbers while another pays just $25,000. Why not play for the $50,000?

Keno is a great game to test out your lucky numbers. Picking birth dates, anniversaries, license plate numbers, and the like offer a big pool of possibilities to see which ones will really pay off. If you know your lucky numbers, you may just give them a whirl and see if you can't walk away with a $50,000 bonanza!

POKER

Poker is played with a 52 card deck and can support anywhere from two to usually a maximum of eight or nine players. There are many variations of this great game, the most popular being seven card high stud, high-low stud, lowball, draw poker, seven card stud, hold'em, and of course, jacks or better and anything opens.

Let's go over the ranks of the hands in ascending order, from the lowest ranking to the highest. We'll employ the following commonly used symbols: ace = A, king = K, queen = Q, Jack = J, and all others by their numerical symbol, such as nine = 9 and so on.

RANKS OF POKER HANDS

One Pair - *Two cards of equal value, such as 7-7 or K-K.*

Two Pair - *Two sets of paired cards, such as 3-3 and 10-10.*

Three of a Kind - *Three cards of equal value, such as 9-9-9.*

Straight - *Five cards in numerical sequence, such as 3-4-5-6-7 or 10-J-Q-K-A.*

Flush - *Any five cards of the same suit, such as five hearts.*

Full House - *Three of a kind and a pair, such as 2-2-2-J-J.*

Four of a kind - *Four cards of equal value, such as K-K-K-K.*

Straight Flush - *A straight all in the same suit, such as 7-8-9-10-J, all in spades.*

Royal Flush - *10-J-Q-K-A, all in the same suit.*

Low Poker Rankings

In low poker, the ranking of hands are the opposite to that of high poker, with the lowest hand being the most powerful. The ace is considered the lowest and therefore the most powerful card, with the hand 5 4 3 2 A being the best low total possible.

Play of the Game

Many games use a **blind**, a mandatory bet that must be made by the first player to act in the opening round of play, regardless of cards. Some games require an **ante,** a uniform bet placed by all players into the pot before the cards are dealt.

Except for the times when a bet is mandatory, as is usually the case in the initial round of play, the first player to act in a betting round has three options: He can **bet** and does so by placing money in the pot, he can **check** or **pass**, make no bet at all and pass play on to the next player; or he can **fold** or **go out**, throw away his cards and forfeit play in the hand.

Once a bet is placed, a player no longer has the option of checking his turn. To remain an active player, he must either **call the bet**, place an amount of money into the pot equal to the bet; or he can **raise (call and raise)**, call the bet and make an additional bet. If a player doesn't want to call the bets and raises that have preceded him, then he must fold and go out of play. Each succeeding player, clockwise and in turn, is faced with the same options: calling, folding or raising.

When play swings around to the original bettor, he or she must call any previous raises to continue as an active player as must any subsequent players who have raises due, or he must fold. A player may raise again if the raise limit has not been reached.

The number of raises permitted vary with the game, but generally, casino games limit the raises to three or five total in any one round, except when only two players are left, when unlimited raising is allowed. A player may only raise another player's bet or raise, not his own bet.

Play continues until the last bet or raise is called by all active players, and no more bets or raises are due any player. The betting round is now completed and over.

Check and raise, a player's raising of a bet after already checking in a round, is usually allowed.

Betting Limits (Limit Poker)

Betting in poker is often two-tiered, such as $1-$2, $1-$3, $5-$10, $10-$20 and $30-$60. When the lower limit of betting is in effect, for example in a $5-$10 game, all bets and raises must be in $5 increments, and when the upper range is in effect, all bets and raises must be in $10 increments. We'll show when these are in effect for the individual games.

Table stakes is the rule in casino poker games, and states that a player's bet or call of a bet may not exceed the amount of money he has in front of him.

A *tapped-out* player can still receive cards until the showdown and play for the original pot, but can no longer take part in the betting, and has no part in the **side pot** in which all future monies in this hand are placed by the remaining players.

The **showdown** is the final act in a poker game, after all betting rounds are concluded, when remaining players reveal their hands to determine the winner of the pot. The player with the best hand at the showdown wins all the money in the pot, or in the unlikely event of a tie, then the pot is split evenly among the winners.

If only one player remains in the game at any time, there is no showdown and the remaining player automatically collects the pot.

The biggest differences between casino poker and private poker games is that the dealer in a casino game is not a player as he would be in a private game, and that the casino dealer receives a **rake**, a small cut of the action for his services.

Understanding the Rules of the Game

Though poker is basically the same game played anywhere, rules vary from game to game. Before playing, know the answers to the following questions:

1. What are the betting limits?
2. Is "check and raise" allowed?
3. Are antes and blinds used, and if so, how much?
4. What are the maximum number of raises allowed?
5. When playing a casino game, the additional question, "How much is the rake? should be asked.

Draw Poker Variations

All bets before the draw in draw poker games, high or low, are in the lower tier of the betting limits when a two-tiered structure such as $1-$2 or $5-$10 are being used, and in the upper limit after the draw is completed.

Draw Poker: Jacks or Better

Each player is dealt five cards face down, and their identity is known only to the player. There are two betting rounds. The first occurs before the **draw**, when players have an opportunity to exchange up to three unwanted cards for new ones, or up to four cards, if the remaining card is an ace. (Casinos allow players to exchange all five cards if desired.)

The draw occurs after the first betting round is completed with each remaining player, proceeding clockwise, drawing in turn. The second round of betting follows the draw, and once completed, the showdown occurs.

Draw Poker: Anything Opens

This variation is played exactly the same as in jacks or better except that any hand, regardless of the strength, may open the betting.

Lowball: Draw Poker

In this game, the lowest hand wins. The ace being the lowest value is the best card, and the hand 5 4 3 2 A, called a **wheel** or **bicycle**, is the best hand.

In lowball, the high card counts in determining the value of a hand: the lower the high card, the better the hand. When the high cards of competing hands are equivalent, the next highest cards are matched up, and the lowest value of these matched cards determines the winner. The hand 8 6 4 3 2 beats 8 7 3 2 A, because the former has a 6 as its high card versus a 7 in the latter (both hands have 8 so it's discounted).

When competing hands are the same, the hand is a tie and the pot is split. Straights and flushes are not relevant in lowball and do not count.

Players may draw as many cards as they want at the draw, exchanging all five cards if so desired.

There are two betting rounds, one before the draw and one after, and then there is the showdown, where the lowest hand collects the plot.

Seven Card Stud Poker Variations

In each variation, players form their best five card combination out of the seven dealt to produce their best hand. In seven card high stud, the highest ranking hand remaining wins the pot. In seven card low, the lowest hand wins.

In high-low stud, players vie for either the highest ranking or lowest ranking hand, with the best of each claiming half the pot.

In each variation, players receive three initial cards, two face down and one face up. This marks the beginning of the first betting round. The next three cards are dealt face up, one at a time, with a betting round accompanying each card. The last card, the seventh, comes **down and dirty**, and is the third and last closed card received by the players.

At the showdown, remaining players now hold three **hole cards** (hidden from the other players' view) and four open cards. These are their final cards. One more round of betting ensues and then the showdown occurs.

Hold 'Em

This is the game best associated with free-wheeling poker. Players receive two down cards and combine these with five face-up community cards that are pooled in the middle to form their best five card hand.

Altogether, hold 'em has four betting rounds, beginning with the initial deal where all players receive two face down hole cards. The player to the left of the dealer must make a mandatory opening bet in the opening round. Subsequent players must either call (or raise) to play, or they must fold.

Once the initial betting round is over, it is time for the **flop**. Three cards are turned face up in the center of the table and this is followed by the second round of betting.

Two more open cards, one at a time, will be dealt face up in the center of the table, with a round of betting following each. This is followed by the showdown, where the highest ranking hand wins, or, if all opponents have folded, then the last remaining player takes the pot.

BACCARAT

Baccarat is a game that combines the allure and glamour of European tradition with relatively low house odds, 1.17% betting Banker and 1.36% betting Player.

Baccarat can be played by anyone. There's no need to bet mini-fortunes or even to play at high stakes. It is a leisurely game, and there are only two decisions you need to make: how much you want to bet and which position, Player or Banker, you decide to wager.

If you're still intimidated by the big tables, the mini-baccarat tables, now found in most casinos alongside the blackjack tables, can be a good place to begin play and become accustomed to the game.

The low casino edge makes baccarat a perfect place to try your favorite betting system, and at the same time, it's a game you can play in style!

The Basics of Play

Baccarat is a simple game to play. The **dealer** or **croupier** directs all the action according to fixed rules.

Baccarat is played with six to eight decks of cards dealt out of a shoe. Bets must be placed before the cards are dealt and are made by placing the chips in the appropriate box, **Banker** or **Player**, located in front of the bettor on the layout.

No matter how many players are betting in a game, only two hands will be dealt; one for the Banker position and one for the Player position.

Cards numbered 2 to 9 are counted according to their face value: a 2 equals 2 points, a 7 equals 7 points. An Ace equals one point. The 10, Jack, Queen, and King have a value of 0 points and have no effect when adding up the points in a hand.

Points are counted by adding up the value of the cards. However, hands totaling 10 or more points have the first digit dropped so that no hand contains a total greater than 9 points. For example, two nines (18) is a hand of 8 points and a 7 5 (12) is a hand of 2 points.

The hand with the closest total to 9 is the winner, while the worst score is zero, called **baccarat**. A tie is a standoff or **push**, and neither hand wins.

There are two opposing sides, the **Player** and the **Banker**, and initially, after the betting is done, each side will receive two cards. Bettors may wager on either hand.

A dealt total of 8 or 9 points is called a **natural**, and no additional cards will be drawn. It is an automatic win unless the opposing hand has a higher natural (a 9 vs. an 8), or the hand is a tie.

On all other totals, the drawing of an additional card depends strictly on established rules of play and will be handled by the croupier. There is never more than one card drawn to a hand.

The Player's hand will be acted upon first, and then the Banker's hand.

Let's sum up the rules for drawing a third card and than we'll show the rules in chart form for both the Banker and Player positions.

Situation 1 – Either the Player or the Banker position has a natural 8 or 9. It is an automatic win for the hand with the natural. If both hands are naturals, the higher natural wins. (A natural 9 beats a natural 8.)

If the naturals are equal, the hand is a tie.

Situation 2 – If the Player position has a 0-5, Player must draw another card; if a 6-7, the Player must stand.

Situation 3 – If Player stands, than the Banker hand follows the same rules as the Player – it must draw on totals of 0-5 and stand on 6-7.

Situation 4 – If Player draws, Banker must draw or stand according to the value of the third card dealt as show below in the Banker Rules chart.

BANKER RULES

Banker Two Card Total	Banker Draws When Giving Player This Card	Banker Stands When Giving Player This Card
0 - 2	0-9	
3	0-7, 9	8
4	2-7	0-1, 8-9
5	4-7	0-3, 8-9
6	6-7	0-5, 8-9
7	Banker Always Stands	
8-9	A Natural – Player Can't Draw	

Note that unless the Player has a Natural, the Banker always draws with a total of 0-2.

PLAYER RULES

Two Card Total	Player's Action
0-5	Draw a Card
6 or 7	Stand
8 or 9	Natural. Banker cannot draw.

The winning hand in baccarat is paid at 1 to 1, **even money**, except in the case of the Banker's position where a 5% commission is charged on a winning hand. Commission is charged because of the inherent edge the Banker position has over the Player position.

With the commission, the Banker edge over the bettor is only 1.17%, quite low by casino standards. The house edge over the Player position is only slightly more, 1.36%.

During actual play, this commission is kept track of on the side by use of chips, and bets won in the Banker position are paid off at even money. This avoids the cumbersome 5% change-giving on every hand. The commission will be collected later; at the end of every shoe, and of course, before the player parts from the game.

Mini-Baccarat

This is the same game as regular baccarat except that it's played on a miniature blackjack-type table, and the bettors do not deal the cards.

ROULETTE

Roulette offers the player a multitude of possible bets, more than any other casino table game. All in all, there are over 150 possible combinations to bet. While roulette still gets some table action in Las Vegas, it is not nearly as popular as the *single zero* European game which offers the player much better odds than the American double zero game.

THE AMERICAN WHEEL

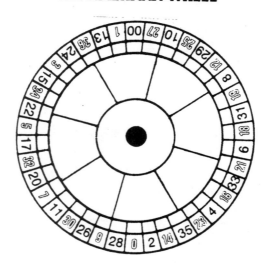

The Basics

Roulette is played with a circular wheel containing 36 numbers from 1 to 36 and a betting layout where players can place their wagers.

The Play of the Game

Play begins in roulette with the bettors placing their bets on the layout. The wheel is spun by the dealer who will also throw the ball in the opposite direction from which the wheel is spinning. When the ball is about to leave the track, the dealer will announce that bets are no longer permitted.

When the ball has stopped in a slot, the outcome is announced, and the dealer settles bets.

Let's now look at the bets available at roulette:

THE BETS

Single Number Bet - A single number bet can be made on any number on the layout including the 0 and 00. To do so, place your chip within the lines of the number chosen, being careful not to touch the lines. Otherwise you may have another bet altogether. Payoff is 35 to 1.

Split Bet - Place the chip on the line adjoining two numbers. If either number comes up, the payoff is 17 to 1.

Trio Bet - The chip is placed on the outside vertical line alongside any line of numbers. If any of the three numbers chosen are hit, the payoff is 11 to 1.

4-Number Bet - Also called a **square** or **corner** bet. Place the chip on the spot marking the intersection of four numbers. If any come in, it is an 8-1 payoff.

5-Number Bet - Place the chip at the intersection of the 0, 00 and 2 to cover those numbers plus the 1 and 3. If any of these five land, the payoff is 6-1. It is the only bet not giving the house an edge of 5.26%. It's worse - 7.89%!

6-Number Bet - Also called a **block** bet. Wagers are placed on the outside intersecting line that separates the two sets of three numbers chosen. The payoff is 5-1.

Columns Bet - A chip placed at the head of a column, on the far side from the zero or zeros, covers all 12 numbers in the column and has a winning payoff of 2-1. The 0 and 00 are not included in this bet.

Dozens Bet - A bet on 1-12, 13-24 or 25-36. They're called the first, second and third dozen respectively. The winning payoff as in the column bet is 2 to 1.

THE EVEN MONEY BETS

You can also bet:

- **Red-Black** - There are 18 black and eighteen red numbers. A player may bet either the red or the black and is paid off at 1 to 1 on a winning spin. Bets are placed on the black or white diamond.
- **High-Low** - Numbers 1-18 may be bet (low) or 19-36 (high). Bets are paid off at 1 to 1. Bets are placed in these particular boxes.
- **Odd-Even** - There are 18 even numbers and 18 odd numbers. Winning bets are paid at 1 to 1. Bets are placed in the odd or even box on the table.

THE ROULETTE LAYOUT

		0		00
1to18	1st 12	1	2	3
		4	5	6
EVEN		7	8	9
		10	11	12
◇	2nd 12	13	14	15
		16	17	18
◆		19	20	21
		22	23	24
ODD	3rd 12	25	26	27
		28	29	30
19to36		31	32	33
		34	35	36
		2-1	2-1	2-1

Winning Strategy

It must be stated clearly: the casino has the mathematical edge over the player in roulette. No betting strategy or playing system can overcome those odds. Except for the five number bet which is at 7.89%, all bets at roulette give the house a 5.26% advantage.

You can have fun at roulette and come home a winner if you catch a good streak. Money management is all-important - protect your losses and quit when ahead. Betting strategies can work - in the short run - and provide the player with a fun, working approach to winning. And really, that's what the game is all about.

ROULETTE PAYOFF CHART

Roulette Bets	#	Payoff
Single Number	1	35-1
Split Bet	2	17-1
Trio	3	11-1
4-Number (Corner)	4	8-1
5-Number	5	6-1
6-Number or Block	6	5-1
Columns Bet	12	2-1
Dozens Bet	12	2-1
Red or Black	18	1-1
High or Low	18	1-1
Odd or Even	18	1-1

 # column is the amount of numbers covered by the bet.

VIDEO POKER

This game is rapidly becoming the most popular machine game in the casinos. Decision-making and skill is involved, and proper play can make you a winner!

Video poker is basically played as draw poker. To play, anywhere from one to five coins are inserted into the machine. Press the button marked **DRAW/DEAL** (Sometimes the cards will be dealt automatically. In these cases there's no need to press the draw/deal button.)

The Draw/Deal Button

Five cards are dealt. Players may keep some or all the cards and do so by pressing the button marked hold underneath the corresponding card they wish to keep. **HELD** will appear on the screen underneath each card chosen.

The DRAW/DEAL button is now pressed and those cards not chosen to be held will be replaced with new ones. This set of cards is the final hand.

A player may keep all five original cards and does so by pushing the hold button under each card; or he or she may discard all five original cards if so desired. This is done by pressing the DRAW/DEAL button without having pressed any of the hold buttons.

If your hand is a winner, the machine will flash "WINNER" at the bottom of the screen. Winning hands are automatically paid according to the payoffs shown on the machine.

Deuces Wild and Jokers Wild

Besides the Jacks or Better machine discussed above, some video poker machines are played as **deuces wild** or **jokers wild**. Wild cards can be given any value or suit and the machine will interpret wild cards in the most advantageous way for the player.

For example, the hand 2 2 5 6 8 in deuces wild would be a straight: one 2 would be used as a 7 and the other as either a 9 or 4. The 2s could also be used as eights to give three of a kind, but since the straight is more valuable to the player the machine will see it as a straight.

Wild card machines have different payoff schedules than the jacks or better machines, and these payoffs will give credit only on a 3 of a kind hand or better.

Jacks or Better Payoffs

The following chart shows typical payoffs for video poker on a Jacks or Better machine. This machine is known as an **8-5 machine**, so named for the payoffs given on the full house and flush respectively.

PAYOFFS: JACKS OR BETTER: 8-5 MACHINE					
Coins Played	1	2	3	4	5
Jacks of Better	1	2	3	4	5
Two Pair	2	4	6	8	10
Three of a Kind	3	6	9	12	15
Straight	4	8	12	16	20
Flush	5	10	15	20	25
Full House	8	16	24	32	40
Four of a Kind	25	50	75	100	125
Straight Flush	50	100	150	200	250
Royal Flush	250	500	750	1000	4000

Progressives

Besides the straight machines discussed above, there are progressive machines, as in slots. All payoffs, like the straight machines, are fixed except in the case of a royal flush, where this grand-daddy pays the accumulated total posted above the machine on the electronic board.

This total slowly but constantly rises, and on a quarter machine in Las Vegas can rise into the thousands of dollars. Then the game gets more interesting!

WINNING HANDS IN VIDEO POKER

Jacks or Better - *Two cards of equal value. Jacks or better refers to a pairing of Jacks, Queens, Kings or Aces.*

Two Pair - *Two sets of paired cards, such as 3-3 and 10-10.*

Three of a Kind - *Three cards of equal value, such as 9-9-9.*

Straight - *Five cards in numerical sequence, such as 3-4-5-6-7 or 10-J-Q-K-A.*

Flush - *Any five cards of the same suit, such as five hearts.*

Full House - *Three of a kind and a pair, such as 2-2-2-J-J.*

Four of a kind - *Four cards of equal value, such as K-K-K-K.*

Straight Flush - *A straight all in the same suit, such as 7-8-9-10-J, all in spades.*

Royal Flush - *10-J-Q-K-A, all in the same suit.*

Winning Strategy

The big payoff in video poker on the jacks or better machines is the royal flush - a whopping 4,000 coins are paid for this score when five coins are played.

On progressive machines, if five coins are played, the total could be a great deal higher, possibly as high as $3,000 (12,000 coins) on a quarter machine.

Of course, the royal doesn't come often. With correct strategy, you'll hit one every 30,000+ hands on the average. This doesn't mean, however, that you won't hit one in your very first hour of play!

Meanwhile, you'll be collecting other winners such as straights, full houses and the like. With proper play, all in all, you can beat the video poker machines.

To collect the full payoff for a royal flush, proper play dictates that you always play the full five coins for each game. Of course, those that want to play less seriously can play any amount of coins from 1 to 5.

On the next page you'll find the correct strategies for the **9-6 Flattops**.

JACKS OR BETTER: 9-6 FLATTOP STRATEGY

1. Whenever you hold <u>four cards to a royal flush</u>, discard the fifth card, even if that card gives you a flush or pair.

2. Keep a <u>jacks or better pair</u> and any higher hand such as a three of a kind or straight over three to the royal. Play the <u>three to a royal</u> over any lesser hand such as a low pair or four flush.

3. With <u>two cards to a royal</u>, keep four straights, four flushes, and high pairs or better instead. Otherwise, go for the royal.

4. Never break up a <u>straight or flush</u>, unless a one card draw gives you a chance for the royal.

5. Keep <u>jacks or better</u> over a four straight or four flush.

6. Never break up a <u>four of a kind</u>, <u>full house</u>, <u>three of a kind</u> or <u>two pair</u> hands. The rags, worthless cards for the latter two hands, should be dropped on the draw.

7. The <u>jacks or better pair</u> is always kept, except when you have four cards that could result in a straight or royal flush.

8. Keep <u>low pairs</u> over the four straight, but discard them in favor of the four flushes and three or four to a royal flush.

9. When dealt <u>unmade hands</u>, pre-draw hands with no payable combination of cards, save in order; four to a royal flush and straight flush, three to a royal flush, four flushes, four straights, three to a straight flush, two cards to the royal, two cards jack or higher and one card jack or higher.

10. Lacking any of the above, with no card jack or higher, discard all the cards and draw five fresh ones.

(These strategies are not applicable to the 8-5 Progressives).

12. SEEING THE SIGHTS

Okay, now that we've gotten you here, picked out a place to stay, filled your stomach and taught you how to play, it's time to get down to business. Namely, what do you do during the day when you're not gambling? The biggest attractions are, of course, the major hotels, but that doesn't adequately prepare you for what's inside them (or sometimes outside). But that's not all there is to see and do, as you'll soon find out. Please note that all hotel attractions are free of charge unless otherwise noted.

THE STRIP

Las Vegas Boulevard South is the official designation for **the Strip** – one of the most famous thoroughfares in the world and the single most important street in Las Vegas. Covering a distance of about 4-1/2 miles from Russell Road to the Stratosphere Hotel, which is a little north of Sahara Avenue, it certainly ranks as one of the most unusual streets in the world. It is filled with magnificent and sometimes wacky hotel-casinos but it may be even more unusual for what it doesn't have. Where else but in Las Vegas could you encounter the main street of a city on which no one lives, that doesn't have a supermarket or an office building, a post office or many other types of structures that one usually associates with "Main Street"? But that's what makes Las Vegas what it is.

The Strip has been awarded the title of All-American Road by the federal government and is also the only road in the nation to hold the designation of "nighttime scenic byway" and a slow drive along this brightly lit avenue is a must for the first time visitor. Not that it's bad by day, either, but it is after dark when the special quality of the Strip really takes hold. However, the best way to explore the Strip, day or night, is by foot. We remind you at this point of our cautions in the *Getting Around* chapter – be careful when crossing the street and always use the pedestrian bridges where they are available.

We'll divide our exploration of the Strip into two parts. First, the more important hotel/casino attractions, to be followed by the other diversions of the Strip.

HOTEL/CASINO ATTRACTIONS

The hotels are listed in alphabetical order. However, to avoid a lot of unnecessary running around (especially since almost all of the hotels are huge and require a considerable amount of walking), it's best to attack them in a planned manner. Taking into account the amount of time you have available and, therefore, which hotels you are going to see, concentrate on one major Strip section at a time. For example, many are clustered around the intersection of Flamingo Road (sometimes called the Old Four Corners) and Tropicana Avenue (the New Four Corners). All of the following are located on the Strip. To make it easier for you to find your way around we have included the major cross streets or other landmark.

ALADDIN, *near the northeast corner of Harmon Avenue, adjacent to Paris. Tel. 702/736-7114.*

The newest mega-resort on the Strip made its debut in August of 2000 and it certainly ranks as one of the most spectacular casino properties despite the fabulous group of places that preceded it by a year or so. It's a far cry from the original Aladdin which used to occupy this site. While it was a nice place in its hey-day, the old Aladdin never did much of anything with the theme beyond the name. Out of the ashes of the implosion of the old structure has risen a fitting member of the Strip's parade of gorgeous world class attractions. If you remember the original you might see a hint of the architecture of that building in two sections of the new tower that project out from the main portion of the building. That was intentional and we think it makes a nice connection to the past, a past which is usually quickly forgotten in Las Vegas.

The exterior is a delightful and almost fairy-tale like page from the *1001 Arabian Nights* and, indeed, that is deliberate too. Many beautiful touches within the hotel are representative of parts of that famous literary work. The outside also has one of the Strip's biggest waterfalls. The nice facade, however, is only a hint of what comes once you step inside and that's when you'll want to "ooh" and "aah." The Aladdin has one of the most unique and beautiful casino/public areas in town. Yet, despite its size, getting around is relatively easy because of the stacked hotel concept, which means everything is on different levels on top of one another and, in most cases, you can see where you are going without having to look for signs or ask for directions. Also, the different balcony type levels allow you to get great views of the interior from a variety of angles.

The single most striking feature is the 130-foot long "Enchanted Garden", reputed to be the world's largest light board. It is a constantly changing spectacle of lights and patterns representing blooming flowers. If it isn't "on" when you get there, just wait a few minutes. Other interesting aspects of the casino area are the 36-foot long Aladdin's lamp which sometimes has smoke coming out of it, and the giant winged horses (from the Tale of the Ebony Horse) that protrude out from the wall over the race and sports book.

Barely visible from the casino level is the talon and giant nest of the legendary Roc bird, from the tales of Sinbad the Sailor. Go up one level and through Sinbad's Lounge for a better look. Apparently holding up the roof over the bar is the huge egg of the Roc. And from there you can move over a few feet and stand face to face with the watchful eye of the egg's mother! There are many other little touches which grace the Aladdin including colorful circles that represent gems in the structural columns, the hotel lobby with its fantastic Arabian Nights mural, and the costumed characters that you'll almost inevitably encounter as you travel through this magical land.

Above the main casino is the London Club, a European style high-stakes casino. It is the epitome of luxury and elegance. James Bond would have been happy to play there. Since you'll probably be wearing a tee shirt and shorts, you might be intimidated by the surroundings and the casino personnel who are wearing tuxedos and gowns. Don't be. Nevada law allows anyone access to any casino. So just walk in and take a look around. Tell them we told you it was okay to do so!

As beautiful and interesting as the casino area is, the true star of the Aladdin is the **Desert Passage** shopping mall. Individual stores are detailed in *Chapter 15*. We must emphasize that this is not a place you come to just to shop. There's so much to see even if you aren't going to buy a thing so don't make the mistake of missing it because you didn't feel like going shopping. We'll also mention at this time that the same applies to the two other major hotel shopping complexes, those at Caesars and the Venetian. The 130-plus store Desert Passage has entrances at the north and south end of the property directly on the Strip. It slowly loops around three sides of the casino even though as you walk through it you seem to be going straight. It provides casino access from three different places so you can easily alternate your gaming with your shopping.

The Desert Passage is themed to a North African/Arabian motif but, unlike the other major hotel shopping centers, its architecture and style are more varied. That's because it is divided into several sections, each with its own sub-theme. These are called the Morrocco Gate, the Lost City, the Sultan's Palace, Harbor Gate, and India Gate. There's also an unnamed section that separates the casino from the Theater for the Performing Arts. The architecture in each is quite stunning but the most beautiful part is the "Lost City" – here you will see the minarets and domes of Arabia in an array of exquisite colors that is a fitting location for the entertainment that often takes place outside the Alacazam food court.

That entertainment, consisting of acrobats, belly dancers, and musicians, takes place at periodic intervals throughout the day in several different sections of the Desert Passage. The "Hidden Harbor" area is dominated by the front end of a large cargo vessel sticking out into the mall. Rainstorms complete with thunder and lightning occur about every twenty minutes. If you stand close to the pond in which the water collects you can actually get wet! Try it, for most people it will be the only rain you'll see while in Las Vegas.

Within the spacious central court of the Sultan's Palace are chandeliers with gold monkeys and a high ceiling. The mall's customer service desk is also located here and you can get information on entertainment and other goings on throughout Desert Passage. Turning now to the unnamed section, we find this to be a particularly attractive area filled with graceful and colorful arched columns in the Moorish style. It is reminiscent of the famous Mezquita of Cordoba.

BALLY'S LAS VEGAS, *southeast corner of Flamingo Road. Tel. 702/739-4111.*

Bally's was the former MGM Grand (not to be confused with the present MGM a mile to the south). The casino has a thousand slot machines and at 70,000 square feet is big but no longer among the city's largest. The hotel lacks a theme (thereby showing its age) but is still a lovely place and is definitely on the elegant side. This is especially true of its high stakes salon. Bally's also has an attractive shopping arcade on the lower level.

However, Bally's doesn't really have much from an "attractions" standpoint. We were almost going to leave it out of this section entirely but figured a lot of people might think we forgot it, so well known is the Bally's name. So, here goes. There are two towers arranged in an L-shape along the Strip. Everyone thought it was great when first built, but today it looks rather like a modern office or apartment building. The most attractive feature of the exterior are the gardens and topiary that surround the moving walkway that leads from Las Vegas Boulevard to the main entrance that is set far back from the street. Surrounded by glass tubes and towers that are kind of bland during the day, the entire walkway takes on a special appearance at night when the walkway lights constantly go through a changing kaleidoscope of colors.

BELLAGIO, *southwest corner of Flamingo Road. Tel. 702/693-7111.*

Steve Wynn's triumphant vision of elegance brought a degree of class to the Strip that even it's usual worst critics couldn't find much to complain about. You won't find glitz here (even the slot machines are subdued – framed in a fancy marble looking encasement and few bright lights flashing above them); only a well thought out environment that reminds one of a stately European palace. Actually, Bellagio is meant to be the re-creation of a tiny Italian lake district town of that name. We wouldn't be surprised if the hotel is larger than the town. While the exterior fits that bill quite well, the interior is much more elaborate.

The main entryway to the 119-acre Bellagio is via a long winding drive or sidewalk, although pedestrians are more likely to come in via the moving walkway that goes through the marquee – another Las Vegas first, or through the shopping arcade that begins at the Flamingo Road bridges. But more about that part of the hotel later. The massive property is fronted by an artificial lake that covers almost nine acres. It makes for a dramatic and beautiful sight but especially when the fantastic **Fountains of Bellagio** begin their musical act. Spread out along an 1,100-foot long row, the fountains are capable of shooting bursts of water up to a height of 240 feet! A new technology uses very little energy – compressed air forces the water out with a burst that sounds like the popping of a thousand champagne corks!

But the fountains are far more than high jets of water. To the accompaniment of one of nine different musical themes ranging from Aaron Copeland to Frank Sinatra and from a Strauss waltz to Luciano Pavarotti, the mesmerizing waters sway back and forth in a beautiful and gracefully choreographed ballet. While diners watch from the row of upscale restaurants in the hotel that front on the lake, the throngs on the Strip have ample room to spread out and enjoy the show from numerous vantage points. *The fountains play every hour in the afternoon beginning at 2pm and approximately every 15-20 minutes once the sun goes down. Last show is at midnight.* We suggest that you wait until after dark to see them for the maximum effect. During the evening when the lights on the trees that front the lake are on, the Bellagio property becomes an enchanting sea of tranquility along a thoroughfare that is better known for glitz and eye-catching wild attractions. Although we like the glitz, too, one has to admit that the change of pace is simply refreshing.

Step inside the main lobby and you're immediately confronted by a totally different but still beautiful scene. Marble is in abundance. Here, as well as in other parts of the hotel, there is a dramatic interplay of rich, colorful carpeting interspersed with tile. The effect is outstanding. The area behind the ornate registration desk is filled with large plants and trees. However, the area is dominated by the *Fiori di Como*, a unique chandelier designed by noted glass artist Dale Chihully. Covering an area of more than 2,000 square feet and consisting of 2,200 individual pieces of hand blown colored glass (each weighing between 30 and 50 pounds) that are supposed to be flowers but appear more like parasols to some viewers, the $10 million chandelier gives you an idea of how original owner Mirage Resorts was able to spend $1.6 billion on the joint.

Behind the lobby is the fabulous **Conservatory**, a glass roofed paradise of exploding color and beauty. The flowers are contained in 1,200 small bins each measuring 20 x 40 inches. The result is that the floral display is so tightly packed that you can't even see a slither of ground between them. The Conservatory's floral arrangement changes six to eight times a year, according to the season. Whether it's geared to the Spring/Easter season, or Thanksgiving or Christmas or whatever, the sight is a delight to all who pass through this gorgeous facility. (The hotel has even constructed its own greenhouse to grow the flowers for the Conservatory and to serve as a staging area for the next display, which can literally be changed overnight.) A marble staircase to one side of the Conservatory leads to the hotel's spa while several restaurants are located off of the other sides.

Heading back through the lobby and into the casino whose richness we've briefly alluded to, more sights are waiting for you. Everything about the casino exudes a European style and luxury, from the gaming tables and change booths to the rich textured cloth wall coverings. Especially pleasing are the colorful canopies throughout the casino. Each and every one of the several bars in the casino are works of art in themselves. The **Fontana Bar**, a round room fronting the lake is the most spectacular. Outside on the patio is a dramatic view not only of Bellagio's lake but of the Paris Hotel across the street. Because the patio is reached only through the bar, no one under 21 years of age will be able to get to the view from this vantage point. Grown-ups can take a quick look without having to buy a drink, especially earlier in the day. In the evening, however, there is entertainment and casual gawkers aren't welcome.

As you walk around the front portion of the hotel you will pass along many of Bellagio's restaurants. Take a peek in at as many as you can because they're all beautiful and some are of notable architectural design. Two of the nicest, *Prime* and *Picasso* are located downstairs on the **Via Bellagio**, a magnificent glass domed shopping street that leads out from the casino and main restaurant area to the Strip. Those restaurants are the epitome of elegance and the view of the lake from them is simply spectacular. We have always found that the staff doesn't usually mind if you take a quick look. The Via Bellagio itself is reminiscent of the early enclosed European shopping centers, especially like one in Milan, only it is more dramatic. Lined by exclusive shops and restaurants (see the shopping chapter for more details), the Via is filled with potted plants and other dramatic artistic enhancements. In fact, no matter which way you enter the Bellagio from, you'll be amazed the moment you set foot inside.

But we aren't finished yet. To the rear of the hotel is a whole other world of beauty. The walkway leading from the casino leads to the opulent convention area but of more interest to visitors are the pool area and the

Bellagio Gallery of Fine Arts. This outstanding collection of 19th and 20th century masters includes works by Degas, Monet, Picasso, Renoir and Van Gogh. Even Andy Warhol is represented. The collection, compared to most museums, stresses quality rather than quantity. *The Gallery is open daily from 9am until midnight. The admission is $10 ($14 with audio tour). You can reach the gallery without going through the casino if you have children and would prefer them not to enter a gaming area.*

And, finally, the expansive pool area. Covering five acres, the grounds encompass aspects of several styles of Mediterranean gardens. There are six separate pools, some with fountains, trellis lined walkways, statues and plenty of trees. While non-guests cannot enter the pool area itself it can be viewed in all its glory from the Pool Promenade or the Monet Patio. The former is along a small shopping arcade while the latter is in the convention center area.

Strollers and persons under age 18 are not permitted at Bellagio unless they are a registered hotel guest.

CAESARS PALACE, *northwest corner of Flamingo Road. Tel. 702/731-7110.*

Caesars Palace (no apostrophe, please) is now over 30 years old but seemingly constant renovations and expansions have kept it looking spanking new. It was truly the first of Las Vegas' mega-hotel/resorts and set the standards by which all that followed have had to live up to. Despite the fact that Bellagio sits across the street and many other wonderful resorts have taken their place on the Strip, Caesars still competes with any other facility for the most beautiful and amazing place in town. Caesars is everything you ever imagined Vegas was or should be. It's a huge place, with the interior largely done up in neo-Roman luxury, but it has a kind of decadent feel that is in tune with what this town is all about. The theme is carried through in great detail to almost every part of Caesars wonderful empire.

You know it's a special place from the moment you approach it – fabulous fountains and statues grace the main entrance while equally impressive statues line the long north entrance driveway. Among the more famous re-creations at the main entry are the winged *Victory at Samothrace* and *Venus de Medici*. Perhaps the most beautiful of all the statues is the grouping of three figures (including two equestrian) right out in front of the main entrance pool and fountain. The gleaming white life-size sculpture is truly a work of art. Also on the outside, near the central Strip entrance way is an authentic replica of a Thai Buddhist shrine. It supposedly brings good luck. A gift from a wealthy Thai newspaper tycoon, the 14-foot high statue weighs more than four tons.

Three different "people movers" bring guests from the Strip into the casino. Some people refer to them as human vacuum cleaners because they sweep people from off of the Strip and into the casino. One starts at a beautiful circular marble building and passes a holographic display of ancient Rome. Look quickly if you come in this way or else you're liable to miss it – it passes that fast. The Strip entrance to the Forum Shops is highlighted by the magnificent golden **Quadriga Statue**, a charioteer urging on his team of four horses. This is followed by a moving walkway passing under a series of triumphal arches. The statue is lit up at night by gas-lit flames and is spectacular. The final moving walkway comes in from the corner of Flamingo Road and provides a broad panorama of the central area of the Strip. Note that all of the moving walkways (except the one that enters the Forum Shops) are one way: they lead in from the Strip but you have to walk out. Smart, these Romans!

But first let's take a quick tour of the exterior. For many years the architectural style of the older sections of the hotel has been criticized as being, at best, out of tune with the Roman theme and, at worst, ugly. We are referring to the latticed bee-hive look that was popular in the 1960's. This has finally changed as the latest renovation has made the exterior more Roman, like the design of the newer Palace Tower. The latter is still the most spectacular architecturally with its distinctive graceful fluted columns and Corinthian capitals, topped by a lavish Greco-Roman facade on three pediments. The center bears a gold-leaf profile of Caesar himself. If ancient Rome had built near skyscrapers, this is definitely what it would have looked like. One final item of interest is on the outside but we don't know for how much longer. The black dome shaped structure at the north entranceway for many years housed an Omnimax theater (it closed at the end of 2000). At night it is criss-crossed by lights that flash in geometric patterns.

The inside is no less spectacular. The original **Forum Casino** is home to high rollers so you many not want to play there. More casual bettors can be found in the unbelievable **Olympic Casino** where statues, frescoes and a painted ceiling make for one of the most impressive gaming rooms in Las Vegas. You might even see Caesar himself along with Cleopatra, hand maidens and a burley Centurion occasionally walking through the casino and chatting with guests. **Cleopatra's Barge** is a floating cocktail lounge (open evenings only) that's worth a look even if you don't patronize it.

The street level of the **Palace Tower** is a large and magnificent area with so much marble that you would think they had to raid every quarry in the world to get enough. At the rear of the tower is the entrance to the **Garden of the Gods Swimming Pools**. Featuring three large pools and several spas, all with inlaid marble, it is among the top pool areas in the city for beauty. The main pool is round and in the center is a small island with a temple-like structure in the middle. Surrounding the pools are lovely gardens and dozens of classically inspired statues and columns

Even the lifeguard chairs are unique – they look like Caesars' throne! There are also several small Roman style edifices that houses, among other things, a snack bar. Non-hotel guests generally can only enter the pool area during the winter. At other times, however, we can get you to a spot with a great view of the entire area. Take the escalators up to the third floor of the convention area and look out of any of the huge windows along the main concourse. By the way, even the convention area is striking to look at. And while you're still in the Palace Tower area take in the sights of the beautiful open lounge area of the garden-styled Terrazza restaurant, located underneath a magnificent rotunda.

The new and older sections of the hotel are connected by the **Appian Way** that houses a small number of very exclusive shops and galleries. A full size replica of Michelangelo's *David* is located here. The hotel's main lobby is a showplace of gleaming white marble and gold statues.

Had enough? Well, despite all of the wonderful things that we've already mentioned, there is no doubt that the highlight of a visit to the Empire is the incomparable **Forum Shops** – the "shopping wonder of the world." There's much to see and do here, so let's begin. The shopping aspects of the Forum Shops will be detailed in *Chapter 15*, although we have to at least mention at this point **FAO Schwarz** with its imaginative two-story Trojan Horse (you can go inside) whose wooden head moves and eyes shine. The store also has the most delightful mechanical teddy bear display we've ever seen.

Of course, the theme is ancient Rome. The mall itself which (like the other major hotel shopping malls) lacks only department stores. This one resembles an ancient Roman street scene. The ceiling is one of the most realistic sky paintings you're likely to see anywhere. And it gradually changes over a period of about twenty minutes from day to night and then back again. A magnificent **Neptune's Fountain** graces the center court and has to be one of the most photographed sights in town. The **Festival Fountain** contains a large statue of a seated Bacchus, god of wine and merriment, surrounded by smaller statues of Apollo, Venus and others. These seemingly stone monuments come "alive" as part of a laser light show projected on the domed ceiling. Bacchus welcomes guests to his party and tells you a bit about other goings-on in the Forum Shops. Get there early to be sure of a good viewing spot. *Ten minute shows are given daily on the hour beginning at 10am. The last one is at 10pm.*

At the far end of the Forum Shops is the beautiful **Great Hall**, closely modeled after the famous Pantheon in Rome. There's a huge 50,000 gallon semi-circular aquarium with colorful fish to look at, but the main attraction is the **Sinking of Atlantis**. The legend involves the aging Atlas who wishes to turn Atlantis over to either his son or daughter, both of whom are evil and fighting for control. Well, to make a long story short, other gods intervene and destroy Atlantis. It's not the story that counts but the effects. The life-likeness of the mechanical participants is fantastic, surpassing anything you'll see even at Disneyworld. You can even see the folds of their "skin" as they move. (The bad daughter is kind of cute, by the way.) Accompanying the dialogue of the regal family are bursts of fire and water and imaginative videos on huge screens high up on the walls of the rotunda like Great Hall. *Shows lasting about ten minutes are given every hour on the hour from 10am until 10pm.*

There are also several motion simulators in the Forum Shops. The **Cinema Ride**, because it is mild, is for the inexperienced simulator rider and is located on the lower level. *Tel. 702/369-4008. Open daily from 11am to midnight. Prices vary depending upon the ride.* The **Race for Atlantis**, located off of the Great Hall, combines three dimensional IMAX film technology with one of the wildest simulators to be found anywhere. Your "mission" is to save the lost city of Atlantis and it's a lot of fun. On the other hand, if this type of thrill isn't for you, we understand. But you should at least go into the ride's entry area where a mammoth statue depicts a mythological hero slaying an evil dragon. The art work is something that can be appreciated by all ages. *Tel. 702/733-9000. Race for Atlantis hours are daily from 10am until 11pm (to midnight on Friday and Saturday) and the admission is $9.50 for adults, $8.50 for seniors and $6.75 for children age 12 and under.*

CIRCUS CIRCUS, *north of Convention Center Drive at Circus Circus Drive. Tel. 702/734-0410.*

Bigtop Pee Wee meets Nick the Greek at Circus Circus and the result is a wild ride great for both kids and adults. It's one heck of a show with the emphasis on fun, whether it's in the casino, on the Midway or in the theme park. The exterior features a huge marquee in the form of a jolly clown and one of the most glitzy canopies anywhere along the Strip. The main building is shaped like a giant circus tent. Stone gorillas, clowns and other circus characters dot the outside area along Las Vegas Boulevard. The casino is one of the biggest in the city and, after a recent refurbishment, is not quite as pink as it used to be. That may disappoint some but the overall look is much better as the casino was in need of some work. The casino almost always seems to be crowded.

Above the main casino is the **Midway**. This is like a perpetual carnival with games of skill mainly in the old low-tech style – you know, throw the baseball and hit the jar sort of thing. Those interested in more modern electronic versions can go to the big arcade. Then there is the **circus** itself where trapeze artists, clowns and other performers strut their stuff as people watch from a seating area or from around the circular Midway's promenade. The various acts are performed at intervals of approximately 45 minutes and last about ten minutes each. There's a schedule posted but if you hang around long enough you'll likely see just about every type of circus act there is. The circus acts used to be visible from the casino floor but that was changed because it was disturbing to some of the gamblers. *The Midway is open every day form 10:30am until midnight. Circus acts also begin at 11am. Admission is free but there is a charge for each Midway game played. Prices begin as low as 50 cents but most cost at least a dollar.*

The theme park that used to be known as Grand Slam Canyon is now called the **Adventuredome**. It's housed underneath a huge dome (it is the largest indoor theme park in the United States, covering about five acres) with pink glass that gives everything inside a rather unusual color. It has a big roller coaster, log flume and many other rides and attractions along with restaurants, snack bars and live entertainment. The laser tag facility is kind of unusual for a theme park. The Adventuredome is designed to reflect the canyon country of the American southwest (hence, its original name) and the artificial mountains and other landscaping are kind of attractive, making this an interesting place to just walk around for a while even if you don't go on the rides. We like the animated dinosaurs in one part of the theme park. *Tel. 702/794-3939. Theme park open daily from 10am until 6pm (until midnight on Friday and Saturday). Admission is free but there is a fee for rides. You can purchase individual ride tickets ($3-5 each) or passes good for unlimited rides on a single day. These cost $13-17 depending upon the user's height.*

The other main point of interest in Circus Circus is the attractive shopping promenade located outside of the theme park entrance above the hotel's main lobby (which happens to be in the rear of the property). There are some unusual shops and a couple of good places to eat. Circus Circus covers lots of ground and you can save some walking between the Strip side and the theme park side by taking their small monorail.

EXCALIBUR HOTEL & CASINO, *southwest corner of Tropicana Avenue. Tel. 702/597-7777.*

It's fitting that the Excalibur comes up alphabetically right after Circus Circus because it is the other half of the two Las Vegas hotels that are considered to be best for kids. The medieval Camelot theme is done up in great style at this big and fun-filled hotel that seems to be equally appealing to lots of grown-ups. Two L-shaped towers flank a multi-turreted castle of King Arthur. The white turrets are topped in gold, red or blue and make a most colorful sight. It's one of the prettiest hotel exteriors by day but at night is simply fabulous – a sight that is still capable of mesmerizing visitors large and small despite the addition of ever more exotic looking hotels. To get the best view (one that isn't blocked by the tram station) stand on one of the pedestrian bridges that span Las Vegas Boulevard and Tropicana Avenue near to the MGM Grand.

You approach the main entrance to Excalibur via a moving walkway that crosses the moat (a castle has to have a moat, after all). The back entrance doesn't have a moat but is similar in style. Returning to the front, at night you can watch Merlin the Magician do battle with a ferocious fire breathing dragon. Kids will simply adore it but then again, so do we! The huge dragon moves along the water of the moat on tracks that you can't see; its head moves and eyes light up. *The show lasts about eight minutes and is staged nightly on the hour beginning after dark with the last show at 11pm. Shows are subject to cancellation during bad weather.*

Inside, the 100,000 square foot casino is among the biggest in Las Vegas. The medieval theme is continued here with stuffed mounted knights, heavy wrought-iron chandeliers and more. Costumed characters sometimes march around the casino. However, the non-gaming action takes place above and below the casino level. Beneath the casino is the **Fantasy Faire** where kids can play one of the many arcade or carnival type games of skill. Also here are the **Magic Motion Machines**, one of the best motion simulator attractions in town. *Simulators operate daily from 9am until midnight (From 10am on Sunday and to 1am on Saturday night). The cost is $3 per ride. Other Fantasy Faire games have the same hours and cost from 50 cents to about $2 per game.*

Upstairs is the **Medieval Village** with many interesting shops and several restaurants and fast food outlets. Free entertainment is held from time to time on the **Court Jester's Stage** according to a posted time schedule. On this level you'll also find the moving walkway that leads to the adjacent Luxor Hotel. The Excalibur side of the walkway has several more shops that form a continuation of the Medieval Village.

Excalibur is a classic example of Vegas re-creation of suspended reality, replete with knights in shining armor and damsels in distress (those losing at the tables, anyway). Don't expect to find a lot of glitz and glamour at the Excalibur. It's all designed for good fun.

FLAMINGO LAS VEGAS, *just north of the northeast corner of Flamingo Road. Tel. 702/733-3111.*

Way back when, the Flamingo was the first of the modern glitzy casino hotels. It was opened in December, 1946 by the infamous Benjamin "Bugsy" Siegel. Nothing, however, remains of the building that Bugsy built. Acquired by the Hilton chain and now Park Place Entertainment, the Flamingo has undergone a series of enlargements and enhancements that has put it among the biggest and most beautiful of all Strip hotels. The exterior of the L-shaped glass and concrete tower features the unmistakable floral Flamingo logo as well as a glass facade of pink flamingos. The interior boasts a large and elegant casino as well as a small but attractive shopping arcade.

However, from an attractions standpoint, the real star is the magnificent grounds, which we rate as among the very best of any Las Vegas hotel. All of the grounds are in the rear as the hotel itself sits right on the Strip and does not have any fronting property. The large tropical garden is filled with palm trees and other vegetation that covers 15 acres and are threaded by winding paved paths. They lead first past the small animal habitat that contains a dozen Chilean flamingos and a pond that houses a colony of African penguins. The latter are small (only 18 inches high) and are so cute to watch. Twice-daily feedings *(at 8:30am and 3pm)* are popular, especially with kids.

Beyond the habitat is a large waterfall, artificial lake and a fountain surrounded by four pink stone flamingos spraying water into the fountain. The pool area sits behind all of this and is an elaborate maze of interconnected pools, water slides and lagoons. A bridge crosses this marvelous landscape and is a great spot for pictures. The grounds also house the Flamingo's pretty wedding chapel which fronts the upper level pool area. Opposite the wedding chapel entrance is a short trellis lined walkway which ends at a stone cairn that holds a monument which pays tribute to the role played by Bugsy Siegel in developing this resort city. Only in Las Vegas!

HARRAH'S LAS VEGAS, *between Flamingo Road and Sands Avenue. Tel. 702/369-5000.*

It wasn't that long ago that Harrah's used to be recognized by its showboat facade. That's all gone now as this older property made extensive additions and changes to make it more competitive with the mega-resorts that surround it. The new carnival theme is colorful and quite attractive, although Harrah's doesn't exactly have a true attraction appeal. Harrah's does combine style with a fun atmosphere in a pleasant sort of way. The exterior is highlighted by a huge facade consisting of hundreds of large brightly colored lights surrounding a fantastic mural that depicts traditional Las Vegas entertainment. Also decorating the outside are big blue Harrah's logo globes, life size gold court jesters and the **Carnival Court**. What looks like an old style carousel from a distance is actually a covered stage area where you can watch live entertainment, mostly in the form of bands. The Carnival Court is surrounded by several interesting shops.

The interior of Harrah's casino is large and equally colorful. We especially like the ceilings in some areas of the casino that feature thousands of tiny bulbs that create a dazzling atmosphere. Also be sure to hunt down the colorful and life-like statue in the casino that is themed around gambling. The statue changes periodically as they are rotated to other Harrah's locations. To the rear of the hotel near the attractive check-in area are several more interesting shops.

IMPERIAL PALACE, *north of Flamingo Road, adjacent to Harrah's. Tel. 702/731-3311.*

This palace doesn't measure up to the standards of its neighbors when it comes to eye appeal. The Oriental theme inside and out is alright but isn't done with any particular style or grace. This doesn't seem to detract from the Imperial's popularity with players who always make the casino one of the busiest and liveliest places on the Strip. The one real attraction for visitors who aren't coming here to play is the world class **Imperial Palace Auto Collection**, one of the foremost museums of its kind. Located on the fifth floor of the main parking garage (elevators in the rear of the hotel), it has one of the biggest collections of antique and customized cars in existence. More than 200 cars are on display at any one time (some are always on view while others are rotated from storage). Many of the vehicles were owned by celebrities or world leaders. Included in the latter are Hitler's custom built Mercedes and Mussolini's Alfa Romeo. Several cars used by American presidents are also on display as well as Model T's, a 1947 Tucker (only 51 were made) and several 1930's Caddies. A separate room houses the largest collection of Duisenbergs in the world. *Open daily from 9:30am until 11:30pm. There is, in theory, a $7 adult admission charge. However, the majority of visitors never pay this because of the widespread availability of free coupons. You'll likely be able to get coupons entitling you to free entry in many visitor magazines or frequently from hotel employees outside on the Strip.*

LUXOR, *southwest corner of Reno Avenue (one block south of Tropicana Avenue). Tel. 702/262-4000.*

Originally built in 1993 at a cost of $375 million, an additional $240 million was pumped into expansion and renovation that turned what was previously an unfulfilled great idea into one of the most spectacular properties on the Strip. In a city of unique hotels, the Luxor may well be the most unusual of them all, despite competition from places like New York, New York and the Venetian.

Set behind a tall, slim obelisk and a man-made lake with temple "ruins," the Luxor is a 350-foot high glass pyramid, actually the fourth largest pyramid in the world. In front of the pyramid, which is the main building, is a ten-story high Sphinx that doubles as the hotel's *porte cochere* and main entrance. The pyramid is placed far enough back from the Strip so that you can approach it on foot via walkways lined with dozens of lion statues. To the north are the twin stepped pyramid towers. All over both the exterior and interior are authentic Egyptian hieroglyphics and beautiful art works. It is important that during your visit to Luxor that you shouldn't move along too fast – take some time to really appreciate the stunning detail that has been incorporated into the design. Almost everything is a true copy of something that existed in ancient Egypt. The pyramid is topped with what is said to be the brightest light in the world. Attention is focused on it by blinking lights that run up and down the four corners of the pyramid. It's a good thing they have those lights, too, because with its dark glass exterior, you would have trouble seeing the Luxor at night.

Stepping into the fabulous lobby is an eye-popping experience. The beauty is awesome and lovers of ancient Egyptian architecture will go insane. Huge Pharaoh figures standing five stories high sit in front of subtly lit pools flanked by heroic lions. Off to the right is the equally dramatic registration lobby that contains more monumental statues as well as gorgeous and life-like paintings of ancient Egyptian scenes. Generous use of marble and tile adds to the luxurious surroundings. The beautiful 100,000 square foot casino is round and also features an Egyptian motif.

Some of the things you should look for around the casino perimeter are the gold statue of Queen Nefertiti outside the lounge that bears her name; the reclining figure of a topless Cleopatra in the middle of the **Nile Bar**, and the fabulously ornate entrance to the **Ra Nightclub**. (More about the latter for nightclub patrons in *Chapter 13.*) Since costumed characters in line with the theme of the hotel have become such a hit, the Luxor has recently joined the act. You'll encounter Pharaoh and Queen Nefertiti in various public areas of the hotel beginning around noon on Thursdays through Sundays. Also take a peek on the lower level at the entrance to the buffet area even if you aren't going to be eating there. It's a highly imaginative re-creation of an Egyptian archaeological site complete with unearthed mummies. And for visitors who aren't going to be seeing a show at the Luxor, we'll mention that the theater is, along with the one at Bellagio, the most lavish and beautiful in Las Vegas. So try taking a peek if you can (although if you're chased out we'll adamantly deny sending you on this secret mission.)

The Luxor's shopping area is known as the **Giza Galleria** and features several interesting shops with Egyptian art works, most notably the **Cairo Bazaar**. Outside the entrance to the shopping area are two talking camels who'll be glad to tell you a bit about the hotel. Again, further details on the individual stores will be in the chapter on shopping, but, just as an attraction, some of the stores are well worth seeing for their beautiful wares and the same can be said about the tomb-like surroundings of the Galleria itself with its statues and deliberate ruined look. The Giza Galleria is off to the side of the hotel where the moving walkway to the Excalibur begins. Again, the decor in this section is mind boggling. A larger shopping mall more on the scale of those at Aladdin, Caesars or the Venetian is planned to be added between the Luxor and Mandalay Bay.

Upstairs via the escalators to the left of the main lobby as you come into the hotel is the so-called **Attractions Level**. This level offers the best views of the massive interior of the pyramid, an atrium covering 29 million cubic feet and which is capable of housing nine Boeing 747 aircraft. Of course, they might have a little difficulty getting them through the front doors! You can also get a good look at the lobby area from up here. The Attractions Level houses several shops, a restaurant, food court and the hotel's big arcade in addition to its main visitor attractions.

The first and best of these is **In Search of the Obelisk**, a wild motion simulator ride housed inside a structure designed to resemble the exterior of an ancient temple. The second is the **Luxor Imax Theater** where different high-tech motion pictures are shown. The theater is a modern black glass structure that is decidedly futuristic looking for this Egyptian themed hotel except for the two large Pharaoh statues that stand guard at its entrance. Another venue for changing films during the afternoon is the **Pharaoh's Theater**.

Finally, **King Tut's Tomb and Museum** is a highly imaginative walk-through journey of an exact replica of the famous young king's tomb as it was found in 1922 by Harold Carter. High quality re-creations of many of the artifacts found in the tomb are on display. *Attraction hours are daily form 9am until 11pm (until midnight on Friday and Saturday). IMAX sometimes has different hours and Pharaoh's Theater closes at 4:30pm* (because that theater is used for a show during the evening). *The admission is $7 for the simulator ride and $5 for King Tut's Tomb. Prices for the IMAX theater is $9 while films in the other theater are $4. Call Tel. 702/262-4555 for exact IMAX show schedule and information on all attractions.* Also on the Attractions Level is the hotel's food court. This is at the bottom of an area featuring the facade of an Egyptian city of the early 20th-century. It is quite attractive.

That about concludes the inside of Luxor but you're not quite finished with your tour as yet. The pool area is also quite a sight with cascading waters and plenty of other big statues to remind you what hotel you're in. Although access to the pool area is usually restricted to hotel guests, you can get a good view of it from the bridge at the rear of the hotel that crosses over to the parking garage or from near the entrance to the hotel spa located in the west tower.

MANDALAY BAY, *north of Russell Road, adjacent to Luxor. Tel. 702/632-7777.*

Although this is an upscale hotel, it doesn't mean that it isn't a fun place to visit or stay. A lot of that has to do with their entertainment program and some of the wild restaurants that were previously described. Going one better on the tropical theme in evidence at several Las Vegas hotels, Mandalay Bay reaches well beyond tropical to exotic. It could easily have been called Shangri-La and have been well named, for it even takes exotic to new, mysterious levels. The 950-million dollar mega-resort covers more than 40 acres at the southern end of the Strip and has been delighting folks since it opened in March of 1999.

Exploring its sights isn't always that easy. Not only is it huge, like so many of its neighbors, but the layout can be kind of confusing. You should pick up a map at the reception area to help you get around. For now, we'll do our best to be your guide, starting with the Strip pedestrian entrance at the hotel's north end. Two huge winged gargoyles (frequently found throughout Mandalay Bay) stand guard at a colonnaded entrance way. The walkway winds through an enchanting area of waterfalls surrounded by round pagoda-like mythical temples. One of the larger temples has a dozen elephants on its facade. The 40-plus story golden glass Y-shaped tower of the hotel stands proudly behind the almost jungle-like landscape and the whole scene is imposing by either day or night. We need to mention that most Mandalay Bay visitors will arrive by the covered walkway from Luxor or via the tram or by car. All of these methods do not take you through the main entrance. Therefore, even if you come by one of those ways, you should take the extra time to walk out to the main entrance and see this beautiful area.

On the lower (or Beach level) of the hotel are escalators that will take you up to the main hotel, but while you're down here go past the elaborate spa and outside where you'll reach the **Lagoon Entry Pavilion**. This 11-acre area contains Mandalay Bay's wedding chapels, several pools, a sand beach, lazy river ride, eating places and more. Unfortunately, only hotel guests are admitted to the Lagoon area. There's a perimeter walkway around it where you can catch glimpses of it but better views are available from the registration lobby and along the promenade to the Shark Reef (about which more will be said shortly).

The casino level carries out the exotic theme quite well. Within the casino, tiered ceilings and statues make for an attractive place to play. The centrally located **Island Lounge** is a great spot to sit, have a drink, and watch the action. The pretty **Coral Reef Lounge** features even nicer statuary and colorful aquariums. Rattan furniture helps to get you in the right mood. Just off of the *porte cochere* on the casino level is the hotel's registration area. Lush tropical foliage and small waterfalls line the wall behind the registration desk. The lobby itself is luxurious and has cages containing colorful exotic birds as well as a beautiful aquarium that resembles a pagoda.

But more about those birds. The hotel has a resident population of 40 tropical birds including parrots, macaws and cockatoos. Between four and six are in residence in the lobby cages at any one time (except for their day off on Tuesday) and they're rotated every hour. Try to be in the lobby during one of their four exercise periods (*11am, 1pm, 2:30pm and 4pm*) when their sexy and scantily attired handlers put them through their paces to the delight of visitors. And men, if your wife or girlfriend is present, do at least try to keep your eyes on the birds at least some of the time. At the far end of the lobby is a large glass wall that looks out on the Mandalay Bay lagoon. From this vantage point there is a fabulous view of a magnificent fountain flanked by six large lizard-like creatures paying homage to a central winged gargoyle. Waterfalls are an integral part of the fountain.

On the opposite side of the casino from the lobby is the **House of Blues**, an unusual looking restaurant and entertainment complex that looks more Arabian than far-eastern. Even if you don't go here for a show or a meal, it's worth taking a walk through for the odd "art" that lines the exterior as well as the restaurant itself.

To the rear of the hotel is a broad promenade that lacks the exotic theme of the rest of the hotel. It is here that most of Mandalay Bay's restaurants are located. It pays to walk around this area regardless of whether or not you're going to be patronizing the restaurants. Among the things you'll see are the big statue of Lenin outside of *Red Square*. His head is missing, although the top is "delicately" covered with faux pigeon poop. The statue did have a head when the hotel first opened but, after less than a month, it was removed because too many people thought that having Lenin around was a bit offensive. We thought it was great – the personification of communism in the most capitalist city in the world!

Anyhow, if you're here during the evening you can stand outside of *Aureole* and join people craning their necks at the small round window to see the wine stewards being hoisted like rock climbers in order to retrieve a bottle from the 40-foot high wine cellar tower; *rumjungle's* fire and water wall is another site. On the wall past *Aureole* and the adjacent Oriental restaurant is a pop-art sculpture collection of various body parts in white plaster. Strange. Odd. We could think of a few other terms too but we'll let you add them yourself.

Now continue beyond restaurant row and past the entrance way to the Special Events Center (a 12,000 person capacity concert and sports venue) and the convention center. Shortly after you'll also pass by a windowed area that has great views of Mandalay Bay's wave pool. Eventually, you will get to the end and the entrance to the spectacular **Shark Reef**. This 90,000 square foot aquarium is educational and interesting as well as visually stunning. With nearly a hundred species of sharks, tropical and fresh water fish and other marine life, the Shark Reef contains almost two million gallons of sea water in a specially controlled environment. There are touch tanks for children and many other informative exhibits. Rather than having signs by each tank, a visitor's approach automatically activates the latest in flat-screen television technology that will display a short informational program on the fish in nearby areas. But the thing that most impressed us about Shark Reef is its elaborate setting. This isn't simply an aquarium with tanks. Rather, it is a themed environment which represents a sunken mystical city. You enter through an area of "ruins" and slowly descend via a ramp to beneath the sea which has engulfed the temples and other buildings of the city. There's even the deck of a sunken ship in a darkened area of the aquarium. *The Shark Reef is open daily from 10am until 11pm with the last admission at 10pm. The admission price is $13 for adults and $10 for children ages 4 to 12. Nevada residents pay $10. Credit cards.*

MGM GRAND, *northeast corner of Tropicana Avenue. Tel. 702/891-1111.*

The MGM is one of those places that, despite not being old, is always undergoing a major overhaul. For the time being, at least, it seems to be done. In the process they've transformed the place from the World of Oz to what is now billed as "the City of Entertainment," an appropriate name for the world's largest hotel with more than 5,000 rooms. Walking from one end to the other it does, indeed, seem city-sized. It covers 114 acres.

If you saw this place when it first opened, you'll hardly recognize it today. Even the main entrance has completely changed. You used to enter through the mouth of a gigantic lion that sat on the corner of the Strip and Tropicana Avenue. People complained that it looked like a paper-mache lion and was childish. So they've replaced it with a smaller gold lion (which we still think looks kind of cheap – like gold aluminum foil). On a more positive note, however, the lion is surrounded by fountains and impressive statues holding lighting fixtures that look something like Atlas holding up the world. Huge electronic message screens flank either bridge entrance and the whole thing is rather impressive, especially at night, despite the chintzy lion.

The other complaint in the past was that the entirely green building, because of its size, was ugly. They've softened the green with touches of beige and by putting big yellow lettering and more lion symbols along the top. This is an improvement even though it still is far from being the most striking edifice on the Strip. The size, however, is definitely notable.

Walk inside and the picture improves immediately. A huge rotunda like area that's actually part of the casino is exquisitely adorned with fabulous statues and show business themed murals in an attractive art deco style. The huge ceiling makes it seem even bigger than it already is and various MGM movies, advertisements and other things constantly play on a huge overhead screen. The exception is when one of the live legends of rock and roll shows is being performed on the high stage behind the Entertainment Dome's Showbar Lounge. Most people watch the show from the casino so you don't have to even buy a drink for some first-rate musical entertainment. The show, and the entire scene of this immense area, can also be seen well from one of two balconies that can be accessed via escalator from the main level or directly from the two pedestrian bridges that lead into the MGM from New York, New York or the Tropicana.

Adjacent to one of the entrances is the Las Vegas home of the wacky **Rainforest Care**. Even if you don't eat here it's definitely an interesting place to look at. You can see the extravagant jungle setting, watch the "animals" (or people) and just rejoice in the remarkable color and detail of the scene. Their gift shop is equally wild and something you shouldn't miss. Be careful, though, because the shop contains big snakes and an alligator, among other creatures. We're just kidding – they're all fake despite their life-like appearance.

But, speaking of real animals, on the opposite side of the Entertainment Dome is the MGM's **Lion Habitat**. This large glass enclosed facility is home to a half dozen or more lions, of which at least two will always be there during operating hours. Trained staff play with the beasts even though they usually seem to be more interested in lying around. The environment is designed to resemble a jungle temple setting and is beautiful. Visitors can observe the lions from the outside glass-walled perimeter or actually walk through a glass tunnel that enters the habitat. Sometimes the lions will be walking on the tunnel roof right over your head. Adorable lion cubs are available for posing for pictures for a hefty fee, of course. However, most visitors just like to stop for a few minutes and watch the playful cubs cavorting in their little den. The Habitat exit is via a gift shop themed to lions. *The free Habitat is open daily from 9am until 11pm.*

The 172,000 square-foot casino is one of the more attractive gaming establishments in town. Covering the equivalent of four football fields, you have to take a stroll around it to get a real feel for how big it is. The high stakes area is particularly beautiful and is reminiscent of a lavish European casino for the jet set. The walls around the perimeter of the casino and many other public areas are filled with large black and white photographs of celebrities from years gone by. Unfortunately, they aren't labeled and many younger visitors won't be able to recognize who the person is. Even more pictures, these in color and of contemporary celebrities, line the walls of the promenade that connects the end of the Studio Walk with the Convention Center. Also of interest on the inside is the huge registration lobby with tons of white marble, another gold lion (this one is real nice), elaborate "draperies" of plaster that look like the real thing, and a massive multi-screen area behind the desk that advertises the hotel's shows amongst other things.

Two places to shop in the MGM are **Star Lane** on the lower level and the bigger and much nicer **Studio Walk** that connects the casino to the hotel's convention area, pool, and arena. The Studio Walk has many unusual shops and also houses a good number of the hotel's fabulous restaurants. MGM has recently signed a marketing agreement with a racing company and they plan to put a model of their racing car in the Studio Walk. Off to one side of the Studio Walk is the passage leading to the **Grand Garden Arena**. Home to major concerts and sporting events, the 13,000-seat arena is the largest venue of its type that is part of a Vegas hotel.

The pool area is quite attractive but is off limits to non-guests. You can get a pretty nice view of at least part of it from the large glass window wall at the very end of the Studio walk. The seven-acre facility consists of a series of five interconnected pools, a flowing river, several bridges, fountains and waterfalls. This is also the area from which you enter the **Park at MGM Grand**. Formerly known as the MGM Grand Adventures Theme Park, this mini-Disney type attraction was built in the era when Las Vegas decided it was going to transform itself into a family place. Well, that didn't exactly work and the theme park was never a financial success. In fact, it continually shrunk over the years. Now, although some of the more popular rides remain (the *Sky Screamer*, for instance, a hybrid bungee jumping and sky diving ride that lets screaming nuts...oops, we mean brave souls...fly through the air), the theme park itself has been "repositioned" to be a promotional item for groups of from 50 to 700. There is no longer any general admission to the public. Only groups who reserve it can use it. So, don't say anything about the Park at MGM Grand to your kids unless you're a part of a big group!

THE MIRAGE, *west side of the Strip between Flamingo Road and Spring Mountain Road. It is between Caesars and Treasure Island. Tel. 702/791-7111.*

If Caesars Palace was the birth of the Las Vegas mega-resort, then the Mirage represents its coming of age. It is a tropical paradise that can rival any resort in the world. The building is a beautiful white and gold structure that brilliantly captures the strong desert sun in a multitude of ways depending upon the time of day. It is set back quite far from the Strip via an arc-shaped driveway. Between the drive and Las Vegas Boulevard is an immense landscaped area with beautiful palm trees, waterfalls, statues and much more.

It is these waterfalls, gorgeous by day, that turn into the famous smoke and fire belching **volcano** attraction each evening. You'll first hear the rumbling of the volcano and see it begin to smoke before it explodes in a fiery eruption that looks an awful lot like the real thing. Even if you're standing far away you'll be able to feel the heat of the gas-generated flames that set the waters of the lake ablaze. The show can be seen from just about any vantage point along the Strip that fronts the Mirage. You can also watch from in front of the main drive-up entrance although there's far less room there. Although it attracts big crowds you usually won't have a problem finding a good spot because there is so much room to watch. (If you happen to be across the street at the Venetian, the balcony of the "Doge's Palace" is also a fabulous place to watch the volcano from.) *"Eruptions" take place approximately every 15 minutes beginning after dark and last until midnight. The spectacle lasts about five minutes. It will be cancelled during periods of heavy rain or high winds.*

One other thing to see outside on the Strip side of the Mirage is the larger than life sized heads of Siegfried and Roy with one of their famous white tigers. It's nice during the day but is even better at night when it is illuminated.

The interior of the Mirage has its own share of wonderful sights. Upon going through the main entrance, turn right into the hotel check-in area. Behind the desk is a 53-foot long, 20,000 gallon aquarium filled with colorful and often unusual species of fish as well as sand sharks. Then turn around and head into the 90-foot high glass dome that houses a lush tropical paradise. You'll think you're in the South Seas, a theme that is carried out in many areas of the hotel's beautiful interior, including the large and elaborate casino. Another big attraction is the **tiger habitat** located on the south side of the casino near the moving walkway entrance out to the Strip. There is almost always at least one of the rare big white cats on hand behind a sturdy glass wall. Visitors pack the area to get a glimpse. If you're lucky the animals will be in an active mood and not just lying around their attractively designed Indian-themed white jungle den. Overhead monitors continuously play a video with Siegfried and Roy that explains how they are protecting this endangered species.

If you really want to see animals, however, you'll have to fork over some money to visit **The Secret Garden of Siegfried and Roy**. This tropical setting sits behind the hotel adjacent to the Mirage's very attractive pool area. Besides white tigers there are many other types of animals roaming around a beautiful natural setting. There's also a large dolphin habitat and visitors can observe the animals from both above and beneath the water's surface. Proceeds from admission tickets are used to fund educational and conservation programs. *The Secret Garden is open daily except Wednesday from 11am until 5:30pm. Admission is $10 for everyone over age 10. You can visit the dolphin habitat alone on Wednesday for $5.*

Strollers are not allowed in the Mirage unless they are the property of registered guests. However, this doesn't seem to be as strictly enforced as at the Bellagio.

MONTE CARLO, *between Tropicana and Harmon Avenues. Tel. 702/ 730-7777.*

The French Victorian styled hotel is modeled after the famous Place du Casino in Monte Carlo, Monaco. While it doesn't have anything wild or crazy like most of the other major hotels, it does have a degree of class and elegance about it. That includes the beautiful 90,000 square foot casino with its magnificent chandeliers and immense potted plants. The exterior entrances at both the north and south ends are graced by a central fountain that is flanked by large statues in niches that are brilliantly illuminated at night. The "main" entrance, located in between the two access points just described, is hardly ever used because just about anyone approaching from either north or south will use one of the two fountain entry points. However, it's worth taking a look at if you like beautiful architecture.

Of interest, if you can get in, is the lovely pool area that includes various wave pools, mini-waves crashing against artificial rocks, and the sight of people riding an inner tube along the long and winding "Easy River." The **Street of Dreams** shopping arcade is a pleasant place for a stroll and has some interesting shops. It ends at the tram station for those desiring to go next to the Bellagio. The view of the pool area from the station is quite good.

NEW YORK, NEW YORK, *northwest corner of Tropicana Avenue. Tel. 702/740-6969.*

Since it opened at the beginning of 1997, New York, New York has been "wow-ing visitors and has become one of the big must-sees in Las Vegas. This is likely to continue regardless of what else is built on the increasingly unbelievable Strip. The exterior re-creates the skyline of Manhattan Island with replicas of some of the most famous structures. Each one is approximately a one-third scale of the real thing.

The tallest point of this "skyline" is the 48 story high Empire State Building. Other buildings include the AT&T, CBS, Chrysler and Seagram's towers. The casino low-rise building is also composed of replicas. Some of these are the Soldiers & Sailors Monument, the immigration station on Ellis Island, and Grand Central Terminal. However, the absolute highlight is right on the corner of the Strip and Tropicana Avenue. Dramatically angled in front of the whole structure is the 150-foot high Statue of Liberty replica. It's even on its own "island," flanked by two New York City fire boats that spray water into the air. Visitors can enter the casino through one of the of the pedestrian bridges or through entrances located on the Strip side of the property where a 300-foot long version of the Brooklyn Bridge, complete with East River, sits.

If that wasn't enough, the whole thing is surrounded by the **Manhattan Express** roller coaster. It rises to a maximum height of more than 200 feet, goes 65 mph and has a 144-foot drop at one point in addition to a gravity defying loop! Only thrill seekers need apply. *Operating hours are daily from 10am until 10pm (until 11pm on Friday and Saturday) and the cost of a ride is $7.* All in all, New York, New York probably possesses the most architecturally diverse exterior landscape on the Strip, both modern and eclectic – but mostly beautiful! It's advertised as the "greatest city in Las Vegas."

Unfortunately, we aren't as enthusiastic about the interior of this hotel as we are about the outside, although it does have its good points. The biggest negatives are the overall crowded atmosphere (maybe that's appropriate because New York is, after all, that way) and the drab and dark ceiling. The best features begin with the re-creation of a part of Grand Central Terminal. From the second floor balcony you get a great overview of the inside of the casino. Other parts of the interior are re-creations of such other famous New York landmarks as Central Park, Rockefeller Center (complete with Prometheus fountain statue) and the New York Stock Exchange. Another area is designed to look like Greenwich Village or Soho, complete with fake subway station entrances, graffiti, smoking sewer covers and garbage cans. However, there's no foul smell and no one has reported being mugged except by a slot machine. A cute thing to take notice of are the casino change carts which are made to look like New York City yellow cabs.

There's a big game arcade on the mezzanine level which is also where the Manhattan Express leaves from. And what would a miniature New York be without a branch of Nathan's Famous? Nothing, of course, so you'll find that here as well.

PARIS LAS VEGAS, *just south of the southeast corner of Flamingo Road, adjacent to Bally's. Tel. 702/739-4612.*

Joining the other "cities" on the Strip in September of 1999, Paris already has a special allure to Strip visitors, just as the romantic appeal of the real "Pah-ree" is world famous. This reincarnation of the city by the Seine in the desert is nothing short of marvelous and the exterior has quickly become a magnet for the photographic-minded visitor.

What would Paris be without the **Eiffel Tower**? Not the same, of course, so a 50-story high replica stands out front right on the Strip. You can even dine at the tower, just like the real thing – a gourmet restaurant is located about ten stories up. Or, for a panoramic view that is simply marvelous, take a ride in a glass elevator to the observation deck atop the tower! *Elevator operates daily from 10am until 1am. The admission is $9 for everyone over age 5 except that seniors pay $7. The charge is waived for Eiffel Tower Restaurant patrons.* Other famous Paris landmarks that have been re-created to form the hotel's exterior facade are the Opera House, the Louvre, and the Hotel de Ville (Paris' city hall which here in Las Vegas is the actual hotel tower. There's also an **Arc de Triomphe** that serves as the place where cars turn around to the hotel's drive-up entrance and *porte cochere*. The replica structures range in scale from about half actual size to about two-thirds. Finally, the exterior sights include a huge and colorful "hot air balloon" that serves as the hotel's signature marquee. In a city of unusual marquees, this may be the best yet, especially at night. The balloon's "basket" is a four sided electronic message board.

The interior is no less fascinating. First of all, three legs of the Eiffel Tower come through the casino. There's a replica of the Pont Alexander III, a famous picturesque bridge. At this Paris the bridge overlooks the casino and serves as the entry way to the Eiffel Tower elevators. The casino itself is lovely with the table pit areas covered by structures that look like the entrance to some of Paris' metro stations. There's a feeling of romanticism and elegance in the air when you're inside Paris, enhanced by the facade of "buildings" around the casino perimeter which house shops and restaurants, among other things, but have an authentic Paris look and feel.

The care taken in designing this place boggles our minds and we think you'll react the same way. There are lots of nice little touches throughout but none are more amusing than the many life-size statues of Paris people – from painters working on the Pont Alexander to lovers. You might find yourself sitting next to one on a bench on **Le Boulevard**, Paris' shopping arcade. Even here the Parisian style and atmosphere are in strong evidence. The aroma of fresh baked bread from J.J.'s Boulangerie permeates the area and you might even see bread deliveries being made by a bicycle riding delivery boy in a red and white striped shirt. We also love the blue "police" outfits worn by the cocktail waitresses and the way that the staff always greets you with a few words of French. The hotel's lobby, although not overly big, is the epitome of elegance with its white and gold colors and crystal chandeliers. It looks like a European palace.

Two other areas of the hotel are a little more off the beaten track but worth a look if you can do so. We don't often recommend strolling through a hotel's convention area but make an exception for Paris. You see, the outer area of the main ballroom is designed in the style of the elaborate **Hall of Mirrors** at the Palace of Versailles. This is a beautiful spot. (It's located at the end of Le Boulevard). This section of the shopping arcade also extends into a short walkway that connects directly with the casino at Bally's. Finally, the third floor pool area of Paris is just delightful. Technically, its open only to guests but during the off season you should be able to get out there for a look. Covering two acres, it's a French garden complex with flower beds and sculpted hedges. It also has one of the best views of the Eiffel Tower that you can get from anywhere.

RIVIERA HOTEL, *opposite Circus Circus at Riviera Avenue. Tel. 702/ 734-5110.*

One of the older hotels on the Strip, the Riviera is nothing to rave about but it does have two things worth looking at. The front section of the building that faces the Strip is a dark green glass wall with huge advertisements for the shows and restaurants to be found inside. When lit up at night it makes for one of the more spectacular electrical displays of any Strip hotel. Outside the entrance is a life-size bronze sculpture of the cast of one of the Riviera's shows – *Crazy Girls*. The statue depicts seven half-naked girl dances (with bikini bottoms) facing toward the wall and duplicates what has become one of the more famous billboard advertisements in town. No one we know finds the sculpture itself objectionable although a few women's groups complain that men were touching the girls for good luck. They would prefer to have the statue moved to a place where you look but don't touch. Whatever your view, it's very Las Vegas!

SAHARA HOTEL, *northeast corner of Sahara Avenue. Tel. 702/737-2111.*

The traditional end of the Strip before the construction of the Stratosphere tower, the Sahara dates back to Las Vegas' early days as a gaming resort. It has been redone quite a bit and the casino and most other public areas are now quite attractive although certainly nothing special. In fact we don't even recommend coming here to see the place unless you're interested in a new area of the hotel that appeals to racing and roller coaster enthusiasts.

Speedworld is a fantastic place for kids and kids of all ages who like auto racing mixed in with their thrill rides. This section of the hotel features the **NASCAR Cafe** (which won't make our dining list), a large gift shop with racing car items, and 20 NASCAR stock cars. The batch includes "Carzilla," reputed to be the largest stock racing car in the world. The area is filled with giant TV projection screens and surround sound that literally put you in the middle of the racing action. So does the **Las Vegas Cyber Speedway** with its virtual reality racing. The newest addition and, perhaps the star, is **Speed**, a wild roller coaster that drops 200 feet at the astonishingly frightening speed of 70mph! Since the track is only about a quarter of a mile long the ride is, unfortunately, over in about 50 seconds. (Some might say fortunately – those who don't will be back in line for seconds.) *Tel. 737-2471. NASCAR/coaster attractions are open daily from 10am until 10pm (until 11pm on Friday and Saturday). Prices vary according to attraction but are around $8 for the Cyber Speedway and Speed.*

STRATOSPHERE, *at the intersection of Main Street about two blocks north of Sahara Avenue. Tel. 702/380-7777.*

The 1,149 foot high Stratosphere Tower is not only the tallest structure in Las Vegas, but it is the biggest free standing tower in the

United States. The locals are sharply divided as to whether it's an eyesore or a thing of beauty and grace. We tend to lean slightly towards the latter. The location of the Stratosphere has caused some problems for the giant complex. It is only a few blocks north of where the Strip traditionally ends but those few blocks make a big difference. Las Vegas Boulevard at this point is no longer an attractive place when compared with the fabulous four miles to the south of it. The city is attempting to improve the area with landscaping and by razing some of the run-down buildings. All of that, of course, is a long term project. In addition, the northern part of the Strip is mainly comprised of the older hotels. The real action (with the exception of relatively nearby Circus Circus) is definitely further south.

The Stratosphere has a large and fairly attractive casino with all the things you would expect from a Strip operation. But many people just come to take the ride up to the top of the **Stratosphere Tower**. The views from either the indoor or outdoor observation decks or the revolving restaurant are, on clear days, simply spectacular. The nighttime view is absolutely unreal.

Thrill seekers want much more than just a fast elevator ride and they'll find it here, too. The appropriately named **High Roller** is a roller coaster that spins around the pod portion of the tower about a quarter of a mile above the street! You might think that such a setting would make it one of the more hair-raising roller coasters in and of itself, but riders say it goes too slow to put it in that category. It sure scares the heck out of us! Definitely more gut wrenching is the **Big Shot** that shoots fruitcakes – oops, we mean visitors – 160 feet into the air through a metal gantry at the top of the tower before it drops them, free fall style, back to the launching pad.

Smaller children aren't neglected at the Stratosphere either. The **Strat-O-Fair** is a new midway type attraction with ferris wheel, bumper cars and more. It even has a **Little Shot** version of the famous thrill ride. It's 1960's World's Fair theme is attractive. *The elevator ride to the top of the tower costs $6. The tower elevators, thrill rides and Strat-O-Fair are open daily from 10am until 1am (until 2am on Friday and Saturday). Fees for the thrill rides vary from $3 to $8 per ride and there are also combination passes available which offer a discount on the cost of multiple attractions. Entry to Strat-O-Fair is free but there is a per ride fee with combination tickets available.* Rumors have been circulated (mainly by owner Carl Icahn) that a third thrill ride will soon be in the works but we haven't seen anything definite yet.

More sedate activities at the Stratosphere can be pursued along the **Tower Shops** promenade. It's an OK shopping area that is separated into areas representing Paris, New York and Hong Kong. It's definitely no match for the shopping malls at Aladdin, Caesars or the Venetian.

TREASURE ISLAND, *southwest corner of Spring Mountain Road. Tel. 702/894-7111.*

The Strip side entrance to this hotel is via a boardwalk that crosses a small artificial lake and passes through **Buccaneer Bay Village**. Several colorful "buildings" are on the edge of the bay and look like an authentic Caribbean town of the late 17th century. The 80-foot long *Hispaniola* pirate ship is moored there, while the frigate *HMS Britannia* is docked past "Skull Point" out nearer to the Strip, which brings us to the nightly **Battle of Buccaneer Bay**, perhaps the wildest, most extravagant and popular of Las Vegas' free hotel attractions. It alone is worth coming to TI for. The show packs in the crowds almost without fail so you should plan to arrive early in order to get a good spot. Unlike their neighbor with the volcano, viewing space is somewhat limited.

The ten minute show begins with the British warship sailing into Buccaneer Bay where it finds the pirates unloading their treasure. After some humorous dialogue between the staid British captain and the plucky pirate leader, the battle begins. Each side fires cannon at the other; there are explosions on both ships and in the village behind. Flames leap out and spectators can feel the heat as masts tumble. Just when it looks like the pirates have had it, a lucky salvo at their enemy's magazine sinks the British ship to the delight of the crowd. Stay around for a minute and you'll see it reemerge from the Bay. *Performances are held every day (weather permitting – no shows when winds are high) beginning at 4pm and then every 90 minutes through 10pm with an extra show at 11:30pm on Friday and Saturday nights.*

Now for the rest of the place. This *used* to be one of our favorite hotels but we are sorry to say that is no longer the case. Aside from the pirate ship battle, management has decided to "upgrade" the hotel and make it more sophisticated. This has done wonders for the hotel as a place to stay but, alas, not as a visitor attraction. So many of the cute pirate touches that abounded throughout the casino and other public areas are history.

All that's left that is worth seeing is the area where you come in from Buccaneer Bay which still has huge pirate ship figures and the **Gold Bar**, located in the casino and which is almost buried in treasure. The hotel's small shopping arcade is also pleasant enough as is the elegant lobby. **Mutiny Bay** is one of the better arcades on the Strip. Besides the fun and games for kids, adults will appreciate the detail in the Caribbean village setting. We're especially fond of the talking skeletons at the entrance. Oh, yes, there's one other thing we still love about Treasure Island – their gift shop sells one of the cutest hotel mascot teddy bears around – a little pirate teddy complete with eye patch and leather vest.

TROPICANA, *southwest corner of Tropicana Avenue. Tel. 702/739-2222.*

Bring your lucky Hawaiian shirt to the Tropicana. One of the oldest joints on the Strip (its nickname for years was the "Tiffany of the Strip"), the Tropicana is now called the "Island of Las Vegas." Oh, those marketing people. What would we do without them? Anyhow, while parts of the main casino are beginning to show their age, it remains a lovely place and there are several things worth seeing, beginning with the outside garden area that has the best view of New York, New York. Catching the animal fever of the Mirage and MGM, there is a tiger cage outside as well where you can take a look at the beautiful animals that are used in an afternoon magic show (see the entertainment chapter for details on that).

Stepping inside, the main pit area of the Tropicana casino is still one of the more attractive places in the city. We especially like the huge Tiffany glass ceiling over the main table game area but have mixed emotions about the green and red floral carpet design. A relatively recent addition to the Tropicana interior is the **Casino Legends Hall of Fame**. The collection has more than 15,000 objects, including casino items, clips of movies about Las Vegas, costumes of performers, photographs and more memorabilia that brings the history of Las Vegas and its gaming to life.

There's even a section on showgirls, naturally, since this is the Tropicana, home of the Folies Bergere! So far more than 60 people have been inscribed as members of the Hall of Fame. The list includes entertainers, gaming figures, movie personalities and others. Elvis, of course, is included. *Hall of Fame open daily from 8am until 9pm (until midnight on Friday and Saturday). The cost of admission is $4 for adults and $3 for seniors, but with just a little effort you can easily get free passes from magazines and often at the hotel entrance.*

Besides the Hall of Fame, the biggest reason to visit the Tropicana is its lovely grounds. Take the escalator up from the casino and walk across what used to be the Wildlife Walk but has since been turned into a bazaar like shopping area with carts and kiosks. There are still a few birds on display at the far end. The walkway leads to the hotel's newer tower but also provides access to the pool area. There is plenty of wildlife on the grounds including flamingos, ducks, and several unusual species of birds.

Also in this area is the hotel's wedding chapel which looks like a big Polynesian styled hut from the outside. There are good views of the grounds and the towers of adjacent hotels from this vantage point. Although the Wildlife Walk is gone you can still see colorful birds strut their stuff. The Tropics Lounge hosts Joe Krathwohl, better known as the "Bird Man of Las Vegas" in a free show. This guy is a little on the looney side but it makes for a fun affair for all ages. He's been on Letterman and Leno. *Daily except Thursday at 11am, 12:30pm and 2pm.*

A final Tropicana claim to fame is that it is one of only two places in town (and the only one on the Strip) where you can gamble from the inside of a swimming pool. The "swim-up" black jack area has special machines that will even dry out your money! This privilege of losing your trunks at the gaming table is reserved for registered hotel guests but anyone can watch.

THE VENETIAN, *just south of Sands Avenue. Tel. 702/733-5000.*

Simply spectacular. We could leave it at that but, since you bought the book you're entitled to find out why. Las Vegas is unreal in many ways. Paradox after paradox presents itself to the observant visitor and perhaps none is greater than the theme of the Venetian. For the famous city of water has been meticulously re-created in the parched desert. Unlike many other Vegas hotels that have scale replicas of famous buildings, statues, or whatever, the Venetian took a different approach – they went for full scale reproductions. So, the **Campanile Tower**, for instance, is the same as the real 315-foot high, golden angel topped architectural master-piece. In fact, except for the moving walkways leading from the Strip and through the Campanile, you could well think you're in the real Venice. Everywhere are graceful arches, colorful Old World facades, and huge reliefs of the heroic winged Venetian lion.

No one thing dominates the scene as you enter from the Strip, but the graceful **Rialto Bridge** comes close. While the real bridge crosses the Grand Canal, this one spans the main roadway into the hotel. The lagoon along Las Vegas Boulevard (550,000 gallons of water) fronts some of the other notable re-creations. These include the fabulous colonnaded **Doge's Palace**, the **Ca D'Oro (Palace of Gold)**, **St. Mark's Library** and the **Bridge of Sighs**. The latter is so called because prisoners had to cross the bridge from the Palace to get to the prison. Fortunately, the hotel doesn't re-create that unpleasant part of Renaissance Venice but today's sighs might be a result of losing one's shirt in the casino. Before heading inside you should take some time to carefully examine the many statues, of which no two are alike, and the other details that have been researched and re-created with the greatest degree of authenticity possible.

A re-creation of Venice could never be complete without the famous pigeons. We're glad to report that even that small detail hasn't been forgotten in the Las Vegas version, although it has been modified a bit. Dozens of white doves are released several times a day *(beginning on the hour at 2pm and again at 3:00 and 4pm)* from outside in front of the Doge's Palace. The doves streak across the facade on their way back home in the rear of the hotel. This is a nice touch but the only problem with the mini-spectacle is that you have to be sharp and look quickly because the whole thing is over in a matter of seconds. Although their flight pattern is such that you probably won't get "dropped" on like in the real Venice, do keep in mind that if it does happen it is reputed to be a sign of good luck. Sure!

Fabulous, too, are the interior features. So let's go inside. The casino is, of course, the usual dazzling room you would expect from a major Strip hotel. We also love going upstairs to the second level and stepping outside on the balcony that overlooks the lagoon and also provides a wonderful panorama of the nearby areas of the Strip. Even better than that are the remarkably vivid hand painted frescoes, surrounded by gold moldings that adorn many of the ceilings in the Venetian's public areas. They are equalled only by those found in the great palaces of Europe. One would have thought that such skills were a lost art but apparently, to our good fortune, can still be done with amazing artistry. The **Gallery**, which connects the hotel's main entrance and registration area with the casinos, is the best example of this kind of work. The lobby has a beautiful fountain beneath a domed ceiling, while the Gallery itself is a spacious arched room where you can just stand there and stare almost endlessly at the elegant scene.

But as wonderful as all this is, perhaps the best piece of re-creation is the huge **Grand Canal Shoppes**. The main entrance to the shopping mall is above the casino and behind the Strip-facing balcony via the Great Hall and its magnificent ceiling. But the biggest highlight of the mall is the 1,200-foot long Grand Canal that runs almost the entire length of the Shoppes and has its own fleet of authentic working gondolas – and the gondoliers will even sing for you. Along either side of the canal are fashionable shops and restaurants. The ceiling re-creates the Venetian sky before sunset. Also within this magnificent shopping realm is a replica of **St. Mark's Square**. Those who have been to Venice will immediately recognize it – the re-creation is that good. To many onlookers, the colorful Venetian facades and painstaking detail will be enough to make a walk along the Grand Canal a delightful experience. The historian, however, will be pleased to note that several real Venetian neighborhoods are represented in the various passages of the mall.

Live entertainment is held at various places and times throughout the Grand Canal Shoppes according to a posted schedule. This takes the form of colorfully costumed performers of the type that entertained Venetian big-wigs seven centuries ago. They're called the *Artiste del Arte & Opera Trio*. Also be sure to check out the Venetian Living Sculptures, two individuals clothed in snow white outfits and make-up that look like marble statues. They'll be glad to pose with you for pictures. It's custom-ary to give them a tip of a dollar. *Gondola rides are available during the regular operating hours of the shopping center (daily from 10am through 11pm and to midnight on Friday and Saturday). The fare for the 12 minute ride is $10* *per person.* Outdoor gondola rides are going to be added soon. The Venetian also has added the **Theaters of Sensation** which combines 3-D film technology with the ride. Subjects for the films change periodically (there are five different ones to choose from) and while the ride isn't bad at all, it certainly doesn't break any new thrill barriers or technological ground. One can only wonder if the demand for so many of these rides is enough to keep them all operating. *Hours are daily from 10am until 11pm and until midnight on Friday and Saturday. The adult admission fee is $9 for a single film and ride while discounts are offered on multiple rides.*

Another point of interest in this $1.2 billion dollar mega-resort is a branch of the world famous London-based wax museum, **Madame Tussaud's**. Approximately half the size of the one in London, the Vegas version occupies two floors of a re-creation of the **St. Mark's Library Building**. The museum features approximately a hundred figures in settings appropriate to the person depicted. There is some emphasis on people who have been important to Las Vegas such as Frank Sinatra and Tom Jones, among many others. Although all of this may sound a bit corny or even childish to you, don't dismiss it out of hand. It's a high quality museum done by the best in the business and the result is an entertaining experience. *The wax museum is open daily from 10am until 11pm and the admission price is a rather hefty $13.50 for adults and $11.50 for seniors. Children between the ages of 4 and 12 pay $10.75. Credit cards.*

Not to be outdone by the Bellagio when it comes to art, the Venetian recently announced that it had signed an agreement with the prestigious Guggenheim Museum of New York and St. Petersburg, Russia's Hermitage, to open a permanent museum collection at the hotel. It will be housed in a separate building with an as yet undetermined opening date, but probably not before 2002. In the shorter term visitors can look forward to temporary exhibits in a gallery near the hotel's main entrance. Details were still a little sketchy at press time so, if this is of interest to you, do make inquiry when visiting the Venetian.

OTHER STRIP DIVERSIONS

SHOWCASE, *north of Tropicana Avenue immediately adjacent to the MGM Grand.*

This is a difficult attraction to categorize. On the mundane side are some movie theaters and a huge gift shop. However, even the latter is somewhat different because it is designed to look like the Grand Canyon. Well, that can't be re-created even in Las Vegas, but the overall effect isn't that bad. Coca-Cola used to have a big exhibit at Showcase but that has closed down and all that remains is a big gift shop with lots of Coca-Cola items and memorabilia. Also, the huge Coca-Coca bottle shaped glass elevator is an interesting sight. Two completely different attractions within the Showcase complex are GameWorks and M&M's World.

Gameworks is a 45,000 square-foot arcade on the lower level where kids and adults will be in high tech game heaven. It even has it's own restaurant and bar for the grown-ups. For a change of pace you can go mountain climbing. Sort of. Two artificial rock towers are said to be the tallest indoor climbing mountains in the world. Beginning on the lower level they rise to a couple of stories above. There's usually no shortage of people attempting to make the climb but they're always greatly outnumbered by the hordes of visitors who come to watch from the street level overlook. *Tel. 702/432-4263. GameWorks is open daily from 10am until 4am. The admission is free but there is a charge for each game or activity.*

COMING SOON...

The period from the autumn of 1998 through the summer of 2000 was one of the most momentous and exciting in the history of Las Vegas. It saw the opening of five of the greatest resorts on the Strip – Bellagio, Mandalay Bay, the Venetian, Paris and the Aladdin. Several notable off-strip resorts also made their debut during this time. That kind of pace simply can't be sustained, even in Las Vegas, so we can now expect a few years of far less frenzied activity. However, Vegas never stands still so there is more out on the horizon.

Among projects in the talking stages is a replacement for the Desert Inn with a high-rise mega-resort in the elegant tradition of Bellagio. Steve Wynn is behind it so it's sure to be spectacular. A San Francisco themed hotel may be in the works (actually two competing moguls are each thinking about such a project). Either or both would be on the north side of the Strip. And, although it could be as much as five years off, it is considered to be a sure thing that MGM/Mirage will eventually tear down the Holiday Inn Boardwalk and replace it with a huge property that will effectively connect the Bellagio and Monte Carlo. We've also been hearing talk of a mega-resort (theme undetermined) to be built on the south Strip opposite Mandalay Bay.

*Now under construction is **The Palms**, a semi-themed resort that is slightly off-Strip (practically across the street from the Rio). The first phase will open in late 2001. Also planning for a 2001 debut is the **Resort at Green Valley Ranch** in Henderson. It will have a "Santa Barbara" theme, whatever that means. It's going to be located right by a beltway exit and will be merely a ten minute ride from the Strip. A London-themed hotel on the former El Rancho site also seems like a strong possibility.*

M&M's World starts out from the big gift shop and proceeds through cute exhibit areas. Highlighting this adventure that is best for the young ones is the *M&M Academy* where you'll walk through a fantasy tour of how the little candies are made. It's not like a real factory – just a highly imaginative and oversized piece of fun that even a majority of adults are likely to have to admit they enjoyed. A professor conducts you through the M&M "labs" and you'll see a ten minute movie featuring the misadventures of Red and Yellow (two pieces of candy, of course), in a very effective 3-D mode. *Tel. 702/597-3122. Operating hours are 10am through midnight. The M&M Academy is open Thursday through Monday from 11am until 7pm (until 9pm on Friday and Saturdays). There is a $4 admission charge for the Academy only.*

Also on the premises of the M&M's World is an outlet for **Ethel M Chocolates**, which is manufactured by the same company. Tours to their factory in Henderson leave periodically from this location; see the Henderson section for more information on that attraction.

There are a few other attractions on the Strip that might be of interest to some visitors. The **Don Pablo Cigar Company**, *3025 Las Vegas Blvd. South*, is interesting if you want to see how the pros roll cigars the old-fashioned way. The rollers are mostly Cuban and if you've never seen one of these babies being rolled by an expert, you're in for a treat. *Tel. 702/369-1818. Open Monday through Saturday from 9am until 6pm and on Sunday from 10am until 4pm. Admission is free.*

The **Guiness World of Records**, *2780 Las Vegas Blvd. South*, features both Vegas and real-world feats displayed through mock-ups, life-size dolls, photos, computers and TV screens. See what some people will do to get their name into the record book. *Tel. 702/792-3766. Open daily from 9am until 6pm. The admission is $5 for adults, $4 for seniors and $3 for children.*

Finally, the **Magic and Movie Hall of Fame**, *3555 Las Vegas Blvd. South (on the upper level of O'Sheas's Casino)*, tells all about magic, the movies and ventriloquism through exhibits and memorabilia covering 20,000 square feet. It's mildly interesting if you like this sort of thing (magic, that is). The admission includes a magic show but the latter is only held once a day at 3pm. *Tel. 702/737-1343. Hours of operation are Tuesday through Saturday from 10am until 6pm. Admission is $5 for adults and $3 for children age 12 and under.*

OFF-STRIP

Besides several museums there are some hotels in the immediate off-Strip area that are definitely worth visiting – the Rio, Las Vegas Hilton and the Hard Rock Hotel. All have something special in their own way but the Rio is definitely one of Las Vegas' must-sees. Let's look at the hotels first.

HARD ROCK HOTEL, *Harmon Avenue at Paradise Road, about 3/4 mile east of the Strip. Tel. 702/693-5000.*

You can't miss either the hotel or the adjacent **Hard Rock Cafe** – both can quickly be identified by their giant guitars. In the case of the hotel itself the guitar goes right through the porte cochere. As it says by the entrance, "when the place is rockin', don't bother knockin'." And this place is quite likely to be rocking. The casino is one of only a handful in Las Vegas that is round. It's not one of the bigger gaming areas but it is attractive with its overhead globe (the world of rock, of course) and saxophone shaped chandeliers. Harley Davidson motorcycles and other interesting items dot the casino. Many TV screens are scattered throughout and show music videos.

But the big attraction is the veritable museum of rock and roll that completely surrounds the casino. Here you can see the original gold records, costumes and instruments of more than a dozen famous rockers going all the way back to the 1960's. There's also a special Beattles display and a sports memorabilia collection. If you would like something more than just circling the casino and looking at the exhibits then stop by the hotel's Concierge desk to pick up a brochure which will make your self-guided tour more enjoyable. You may also be interested to know that Hard Rock's management donates a portion of the proceeds from slot play to help save the world's rain forests.

LAS VEGAS HILTON, *Paradise Road immediately north of the Las Vegas Convention Center. Tel. 702/732-5111.*

This used to be the largest hotel in the city before the building boom of the late 1980's began. It's still huge. In fact, it is one of the more easily recognizable structures in town as is the big gold colored marquee. The casino is big and elegant but somewhat understated and refined. The showroom used to play host to Elvis Presley when the place was called the International and that era is still commemorated to this day with a wonderful life-size statue of the King with guitar and microphone in hand on display in the main entrance lobby. Also of interest is the Race and Sports Book. Called SuperSports, it is Las Vegas' biggest such operation and looks like it could substitute for NASA Mission Control. Actually, after NASA, it has the largest display of big screen monitors in the world. Late in the evening when sports action is over for the day, those monitors are used to show music videos.

The big attraction at the Las Vegas Hilton is **Star Trek: The Experience**. This 40,000 square foot, $70 million extravaganza has Trekkies from all over the world salivating. It's about as close to the "real" thing as you can get. The entrance area of the Experience is quite dramatic with its large models of Starfleet ships suspended from a painted ceiling that looks like outer space. The attraction itself consists of several sections but the two main parts are the *History of the Future*, which displays Star Trek memorabilia and the *Voyage Through Space*. The voyage includes an unusually long (22-minute) motion simulator ride. Portions of the "journey" are mild and others are quite a ride. Visitors are "beamed" aboard the USS Enterprise and taken on an adventure through the 24th century. You can get dressed up as a Starfleet officer or as an alien.

Also within the Star Trek attraction area is a re-creation of the promenade from *Star Trek: Deep Space Nine*. It houses, among other things, a big gift shop with all sorts of ST merchandise and *Quark's*. The latter is an interesting restaurant and even has a Ferengi wait staff. Details were in the *Where to Eat* chapter; *Tel. 888/462-6535. The Experience is open daily from 11am until 11pm. The admission price is $25 per person (for an all day pass but we fail to see how you could spend all day here). Senior and Nevada resident discounts are available. Credit cards.*

Despite the fact that Star Trek enthusiasts generally love this attraction, its off-Strip location and the out-of-this-galaxy price have made the attraction less than a financial bonanza for the Hilton. We have even heard rumors that its future is in doubt. Parents are advised that the Experience can be accessed without having to enter the casino. However, outside the Star Trek area is the **Spacequest Casino**, a real casino that gives you a possible taste of what gambling will look like in the future. For example, you can activate the slot machines by passing your hand through a light field. Just what the world needs, right?

THE RIO, *Flamingo Road, about 3/4 of a mile west of the Strip. Tel. 702/252-7777.*

Rivaling anything you can see on the Strip, the Rio has been popular since it opened with both visitors and locals alike because it's such a fun place. It has an intangible quality to its atmosphere that is hard to describe but seems apparent to just about every visitor we've taken there. Maybe it's the little things, like Rio Rita, a Carmen Miranda type character who roams through the casino greeting guests that make the Rio special. The carnival and tropical theme is most evident in the original part of the casino. The very attractive pool area is also worth taking a stroll through.

The 51 story tower is the highest hotel structure in Las Vegas (if you don't count the Stratosphere) and is clearly visible from the Strip with its blue and red glass facade in geometric patterns. The top floor is the **Voo Doo Lounge** and it offers a panorama of the Strip that we feel is even better than from the Stratosphere because it's closer. There have been times in the past when the lounge was open during the afternoon and you could sneak out to the observation deck for the view without having to buy a drink. At the present time the lounge opens at 5pm and you will have to patronize the bar in order to take in the magnificent panorama. On the other hand, this isn't necessarily a negative. There are few places in town that can compete with the atmosphere here for sitting around and watching the world as you sip on an exotic drink of some kind. Children are not allowed on the deck at any time since it is considered to be a part of a drinking establishment. However, the floor beneath the lounge is a restaurant of the same name and offers the same view from behind glass. Although it's an adult oriented restaurant (see the *Where to Eat* chapter), children are allowed. It opens at the same time as the lounge.

The first two levels of the tower are the glitzy and exciting **Masquerade Village**. More than twenty stores and eateries line both sides of each level. In the middle of it all is another casino. Shopping or window-shopping is nice but the real reason to come to Masquerade Village is for the fabulous **Masquerade Village Show in the Sky**. This definitely rivals the pirate ship battle at Treasure Island as the best free show in town. While live entertainment in the form of ornately costumed dancers and acrobats takes place on and above a stage in the middle of the casino, performers are circling above the village on exotic "floats" suspended on tracks from the ceiling and traveling along a 900-foot journey. For a fee of $10 visitors can get dressed up and join the performers on one or more of the floats. The cast of almost 40 performers are high energy all the way. The Shows last approximately 15 to 20 minutes including the pre and post-show goings on.

Four similar shows rotate. They have different themes such as Carnival in Rio, a Venetian carnival and New Orleans, but the floats are the same. Only the costumes and music change. At the end of each show as the floats make their way back to their hidden "garage," the performers throw colorful beads to people on both levels and managing to secure one seems to be a big priority for lots of visitors. We have quite a collection at home! It's terrific fun and attracts big crowds so you should arrive early in order to get a good viewing spot. The main viewing area is the upper level on the side of the casino facing the main stage. However, if you've already seen the show once (or more) and would like to concentrate on the stage performers, then watching from downstairs nearer to the stage is also a good idea.

The area opposite the stage is part of the casino and for the half-hour preceding each show the Rio has a slot "tournament" of sorts – you play for pay in order to secure a near front-row seat for the show. Rio Rita is on hand to give out gifts in addition to the cash you get from the machines every time you hit the required jackpot. There's a good chance you'll get one if you play the full half-hour. Whether you take the free route from upstairs or are snared by their offer to play, it's a great show that shouldn't be missed. *Performances are given Thursday through Monday, every two hours from 4pm until midnight. Children must watch the show from the upper level only.*

Before leaving the Masquerade Village you might want to take a few minutes to visit the **Wine Cellar Tasting Room** located by the Napa Restaurant. Even if you don't want to taste or purchase wine (or don't even like alcoholic grape juice for that matter), this is an interesting little stop. Their collection of wine is the largest in the United States and it's fun to browse around.

Now here's the rundown on several non-casino/hotel attractions of interest not far from the Strip. All are museums but two of them aren't ordinary museums but, rather, tributes to two of Las Vegas' most famous and beloved performers, Liberace and Elvis Presley. The ever-popular **Liberace Museum**, *1775 E. Tropicana Avenue, about 1-1/2 miles east of the Strip*, gets rave reviews from just about everyone, including those who weren't even particularly fond of Mr. Showmanship himself. The extensive collection includes several of his pianos – one of them a rhinestone encrusted Baldwin; about a half-dozen of his one-of-a-kind automobiles; stage jewelry and his lavish costumes and furs. Among the latter are a full-length Black Diamond Mink cape and a King Neptune costume that weighs an incredible 200 pounds. The museum also has an excellent gift shop with many musically oriented items. *Tel. 702/798-5595. Hours of operation are daily from 10am until 5pm (opens at 1pm on Sunday). The admission is $7 for adults, $5 for seniors. Children under 12 are admitted free.*

The **Elvis-A-Rama Museum**, *3401 Industrial Road (one block off of the Strip behind Treasure Island)* is less well known than the Liberace Museum, mainly because it hasn't been open that long. It is, however, a fitting tribute to the King. The world's largest collection of authentic Elvis items is housed in this $3.5 million facility which began when Elvis admirer Chris Davidson began collecting memorabilia. The museum displays almost two thousand items, including Elvis' 1955 Fleetwood Cadillac touring car. An 80-foot long mural depicting scenes from the King's career is also of interest. Any Elvis lover will thoroughly enjoy the place and will also want to check out the gift shop. *Tel. 702/309-7200. Open daily except Monday from 10am until 6pm. The admission price is $10 for those age 12 and over while seniors and Nevada residents pay $8. Credit cards.*

Finally, a more traditional museum can be found on the University of Nevada-Las Vegas campus. The **Marjorie Barrick Museum of Natural History**, *use the entrance at Harmon and Swenson,* houses a number of exhibits which change from time to time. The permanent collection emphasizes the natural history, archeology and anthropology of the desert southwest. *Tel. 702/895-3381. Open Monday through Friday from 8am until 4:45pm and on Saturdays from 10am until 2pm. Admission is free.*

DOWNTOWN

The downtown hotels are unlike their Strip counterparts in lots of ways, but especially when it comes to their appeal as attractions. Maybe unappeal would be more fitting because there isn't too much to see in these hotels unless you just like to look at casinos. Several, however, do have an old-time atmosphere and feel to them which might well be of interest to some visitors. Despite our unenthusiastic opening there are a few things worth seeing in a couple of the hotels.

The **Golden Nugget** displays the *Hand of Faith Nugget*, the largest solid gold nugget on public display in the world. It weighs in at 62 pounds. Try putting that on your finger! A number of other sizable specimens are also on display. The Golden Nugget's pool area and casino are the nicest to be found downtown.

But of greater overall interest is **Main Street Station**, a couple of blocks north of Fremont Street. It is filled with authentic antiques and is second only to the Golden Nugget in the downtown beauty pageant. The theme is generally Victorian. The lamp posts out front are from Belgium and date from World War I. There's a lot of stained glass and fine wood paneling all around. Also of interest is a small section of graffiti covered stone from the Berlin Wall. Unfortunately, it can't be seen by the ladies since it is housed over one of the urinals in the men's room off the casino.

Despite that setback to equal access, both men and women should take some time to stroll around and appreciate all the little art things to be found. You can pick up a brochure which will direct you to and explain 19 different antiques, artifacts and other points of interest. Either on your way to or from the hotel, do take a look at the several historic railroad cars lined up alongside the west side of Main Street. Although you can't enter the cars you can look in and see how well preserved they are. Many of these cars, now the property of Main Street Station, were used by famous people ranging from Buffalo Bill to Teddy Roosevelt.

The majority of downtown's hotels line up on either side of a four-block stretch of Fremont Street. Besides the hotels there are lots of gift shops and other assorted businesses on this street, including Las Vegas's most famous topless bar – **The Girls of Glitter Gulch**. The street has been closed off to automobile traffic and, when busy at night, has a rather festive atmosphere. There are many vendors selling a variety of goods from carts in the tree lined mall. This area is also home to one of the more spectacular attractions in town – the **Fremont Street Experience**. The mall is covered by a curving white canopy. Each night one of the greatest sound and light shows takes place when more than two million lights are computer synchronized into a show that travels across the canopy accompanied by music from numerous speakers. It's quite a sight to see all the hotel lights of Glitter Gulch go off and leave you in momentary darkness until the Experience begins. At the end the lights come back on and Fremont Street returns to normal – everyone goes back into a hotel to gamble, eat or whatever else you want to do.

There are several different shows that rotate but they're all highly colorful and imaginative. During certain periods there are special Experience shows geared to the season or important in-town events, such as the National Finals Rodeo. *Tel. 702/678-5777. The shows are free of charge and begin on the hour after sunset.* Fremont Street is also the scene of live and usually free entertainment from time to time. This is more likely to occur around holiday periods or, again, important special event times. Check the usual sources of information for what's going on in town.

At the corner of Fremont and Main is the old **Golden Gate Hotel**. This is a small and rather unglamorous looking place but it is notable as the oldest hotel in Las Vegas, dating all the way back to 1906. It's also the home of one of the most famous shrimp cocktails in town, more of a bargain than ever at only 99 cents (although who know's how much longer that can last).

The Fremont Street Experience was supposed to be downtown's answer to the glamour of the Strip. While it has been helpful, one attraction can't compete with the myriad stars along Las Vegas Boulevard South. So, other things have been done or are planned to try and help things a bit more. One is a multi-story entertainment center called **Neonopolis**. It was supposed to have been finished by the time this book came out but construction was halted for a time because the project ownership has had financial problems. Things are supposed to be back on track now. The **Neon Museum** is, so far, a collection of several marquees from old hotels that have been restored and placed along Fremont Street between Las Vegas Boulevard and the canopy. These include the old lamp from the original Aladdin and the horseback riding matador from the Hacienda. They're lit up at night and are an interesting piece of history. The "museum" is trying to acquire, restore and place additional items. If it ever fulfills its plan it could become a major attraction.

Several museums and historical points of interest are located within a few blocks to the north of the downtown casino center in the vicinity of Cashman Field. First in this group is the **Las Vegas Natural History Museum**, *900 Las Vegas Blvd. North.* This nine-year old museum has finally come into its own as a quality cultural attraction. Exhibits concentrate on the desert southwest and Nevada. The dinosaur exhibit and live shark are probably the most popular features. *Tel. 702/384-3466. The museum is open daily from 9am until 4pm and there is an admission charge of $5 for adults, $4 for senior citizens and $3 for children ages 4 through 12.*

The **Lied Discovery Children's Museum**, *833 Las Vegas Blvd. North*, has interactive exhibits and is especially good for youngsters up to the age of 12. *Tel. 702/382-5437. Open daily except Monday from 10am until 5pm. The admission is $5 for adults and $4 for children ages 2 through 17.*

Finally, the **Old Mormon Fort**, *908 Las Vegas Blvd. North*, contains the oldest surviving building in Nevada. It will give you an idea of what Las Vegas was like when it was first settled by Mormons from Utah in 1855. The fort has been undergoing a lengthy restoration process and it is subject to temporary closures. *Tel. 702/486-3511 for hours and more information.*

AROUND LAS VEGAS

While there are quite a few attractive casino/hotels in this geographic division, such as the **Regent Las Vegas** and the adjacent **Suncoast**, there is only one that is worth a visit from a sightseeing point of view and that is **Sam's Town**, *Boulder Highway at Nellis and Harmon, Tel. 702/456-7777*. As the name implies, it is mostly a western or cowboy themed property that is popular with locals as well as visitors. As the property has grown and matured it has, to some extent, been shedding its cowboy look for a somewhat more sophisticated image.

Of most interest is the beautiful atrium known as **Mystic Falls Park**. Surrounded by the hotel tower and designed to look old, the park is bordered by several of the hotel's restaurants and shops. Within the park are meandering pathways that take you past small streams and automated animals of all sizes that sure look like the real thing. You have to be quick-eyed to catch some of the smallest ones. At night the little lights on the park's many trees give a perennial Christmas appearance. Also in the atrium is the **Sunset Stampede**, a lively high-tech display of lasers, sound, light and water. *Free performances lasting about ten minutes are given daily at 2:00, 6:00, 8:00 and 10pm.* The effect is more dramatic in the evening so try to get to one of the later shows if you can so arrange your schedule. If you happen to be visiting Sam's Town from late November through shortly after the New Year, then you're in for a special treat because Mystic Falls Park is wonderfully decorated with the spirit of Christmas. It's a thrill for all ages and we think even a real Scrooge would have to manage a smile at its sight.

The remainder of the attractions are scattered all about the valley and your interests will dictate which ones are appropriate for your available time. For a little scenery you might want to get a close-up look at **Sunrise Mountain** on the east side of the valley. The natural area that encompasses this distinctive and colorful peak can be reached via Lake Mead Boulevard (Highway 147). If you continue east on that route, you'll eventually reach the Lake Mead National Recreation Area, which is described in the chapter on excursions.

Desert Demonstration Gardens, *3701 W. Alta Drive, off of Valley View*. This facility is run by the Las Vegas Valley Water District and was designed to acquaint residents new to the desert with ways to landscape their homes using low-water techniques. Called xeriscaping, you don't have to live in the desert to find this interesting. The displays of desert flora are attractive, too. *Tel. 702/258-3205. Gardens open daily (except holidays) from 8am until 5pm and there is no admission fee.*

Gilcrease Bird Sanctuary, *8101 Racel Road, 1-1/4 miles north of US 9. (Rancho Road) via Durango to Racel*. The sanctuary is home to a large number of game and exotic birds as well as birds of prey. They are all here through the efforts of the Wild Wing Project and are being rehabilitated from injury. *Tel. 702/645-4224. Open 11am until 3pm, weather permitting, from Wednesday through Sunday. The admission fee is $3 for adults and $1 for children.*

Chinatown, *along Spring Mountain Road west of I-15*. You won't confuse this with Chinatown in New York or San Francisco but if you want a small taste of the Orient then this can be an interesting little diversion. **Chinatown Plaza**, *4255 Spring Mountain Road*, is the heart of the area and has a number of shops and restaurants. The architecture is Chinese and includes a pretty ceremonial gate and statues.

Las Vegas Art Museum, *9600 W. Sahara Avenue*. Yes, there is art in Las Vegas besides what you can find in the Bellagio. This isn't one of the great art museums of the world but it does have a number of interesting works in its permanent collection, including some by Salvador Dali. *Tel. 702/360-8000. Hours of operation are Tuesday through Saturday from 10am until 5pm and Sunday from 1pm until 5pm. Admission is $3 for adults, $2 for seniors and $1 for children.*

Las Vegas Mormon Temple, *827 Temple View Drive (off of the east end of Bonanza Road)*. Visiting religious shrines may not come to mind to many people planning a trip to Las Vegas, but like all Mormon temples, this one is an architectural work of art surrounded by nicely landscaped grounds. The temple itself is closed to non-Mormons. Excellent views of the Strip and mountain background can be had from this high vantage point in the eastern foothills.

Nevada State Museum, *700 Twin Lakes Drive, in Lorenzi Park*. This museum has exhibits on both the natural and human history of Nevada with special emphasis on the Las Vegas area. Of greatest interest is the exhibit which shows what Las Vegas was like in the 1940's – quite a contrast from today. Another exhibit on how animals adapt to the brutal conditions of life in the desert is highly educational. *Tel. 702/486-5205. Open daily from 9am until 5pm. There is a $2 admission charge for those over 18 years of age.*

Shelby American Factory & Museum Tour, *6755 Speedway Blvd. (adjacent to the Las Vegas Motor Speedway)*. This interesting facility provides visitors with a look at the world of high speed racing through a museum and display area that houses a collection of Shelby's high performance race cars that span almost 40 years. Of even more interest is the factory tour. *Tel. 702/643-3000. Open daily from 10am until 5pm. There is no admission charge. Free tours of the assembly area begin at 10:30am or 3:30pm (the latter time by appointment only).*

Southern Nevada Zoological Park, *1775 N. Rancho Drive.* While not terribly large, Nevada's only zoo (if you don't count some of the animal collections in some of the Strip hotels) is a nice place to get some fresh air and see some wildlife. The zoo features a mix of animals from all over the world, with emphasis on the southwest. A petting zoo for children is a good place to take the little ones. *Tel. 702/647-4685. Open daily from 9am until 5pm and the admission is $6 for adults and $4 for children ages 2 through 12.*

And, finally, here's a little tip if your flight home is delayed and you need something to do at the airport besides eating at bad overpriced restaurants or playing on the tightest machines in town. McCarran has a free **Aviation Museum** that traces the history of flight in Las Vegas through models, pictures, uniforms and artifacts. It is located on the second level beginning above the baggage claim area and is open at all times.

HENDERSON

The city of Henderson occupies the southern portion of the Las Vegas Valley. More than half of it is surrounded by colorful mountains. The Lake Mead National Recreation Area forms a part of its eastern boundary. Henderson covers a big area (larger than the city of Las Vegas) and stretches for more than 15 miles from east to west.

Getting to Henderson from the Strip is easy. You can take either Flamingo Road or Tropicana Avenue east to I-515 and then go south to Henderson. (From downtown just hop I-515 all the way). From the southern end of the Strip you can drive east on Sunset Road right into Henderson or take I-15 south to I-215. That road has several exits within Henderson.

Most of the casinos in Henderson are rather small and geared towards the locals. However, there are two casino/hotels that are worth taking a look at if you're in the area. **Sunset Station**, *Sunset Road at Stephanie Street, two blocks west of the intersection of I-515, Tel. 702/547-7777*, is the most elegant of Station Casino's properties to date. It would fit in nicely on the Strip with its Spanish Mediterranean design, painted "sky" ceiling and other attractive features. The focal point is the main table gaming area and its central **Gaudi Bar**. Named for he noted Spanish designer, a fabulous multi-colored glass ceiling has been fashioned that looks like waves and has no straight lines in it.

The Reserve, *Lake Mead Drive at I-515, Tel. 702/558-7000*, is the only African safari themed hotel in the Las Vegas Valley. The outside is highlighted by colorful murals of wildlife and large monkeys up on the towers. Inside is even more colorful with tusk-framed change booths (the outside marquee is also designed to look like two giants tusks), a brilliant elephant mural behind the registration desk and a bunch of naughty simians who inhabit the appropriately named *Funky Monkey Bar*. Also be sure to see "Congo Jack's" plane wreck. Sometimes Congo Jack himself along with Monsoon Mary can be seen strolling through the casino.

Among visitors Henderson's best known non-hotel attractions are two free factory tours that are in close proximity to one another and can make an interesting little trip in and of itself, or a combination with a Hoover Dam day excursion. These are Ethel M (fine chocolates) and Ron Lee (porcelain clown figures). All are suitable for children but can be thoroughly enjoyed by adults, too. The food manufacturer provides free samples and has a gift shop which feature company logo items and more. There used to be four factory tours but, alas, two have closed down their visitor facilities. The Ocean Spray and Favorite Brands factories no longer give tours.

Ethel M, *2 Cactus Drive (off of the intersection of Sunset Road and Mountain Vista)*. A subsidiary of the folks at M&M's, Ethel M manufactures more expensive boxed chocolates. The self-guided factory tour leads you past all of the stages in the making of their delicious morsels. Signs and videos explain the process in more detail. There is a nice gift shop that sells all sorts of southwestern items plus a factory store where you can purchase any Ethel M product. Outside the factory is a beautiful cactus garden with winding paths that lead you past a variety of desert flora. During the Christmas season is an especially time to visit as the gardens are illuminated with thousands of tiny white lights. *Tel. 702/433-2500. Hours are daily from 8:30am until 7pm.*

For a change of pace **Ron Lee's World of Clowns**, *330 Carousel Drive (off of Warm Springs Road just west of Gibson)*, isn't a food maker. Rather Ron Lee produces hand made pewter, porcelain, and other figurines, all with a clown theme. Their workmanship is beautiful and will delight adults as much as children. In addition to the self-guiding factory tour that takes you through each phase of the production process, the lobby has on display Mr. Lee's own personal collection of figurines. Many are elaborate works of art. The gift shop, too, has fine specimens that you can look at to your heart's content. They're available for purchase but, be fore warned, the prices are quite high. It's best to visit during the week if you can because the most interesting part of the factory tour is to see the employees painstakingly at work. There is an old time carousel on the premises that your children will just have to take a ride on. *Tel. 702/434-3920. The operating hours are Monday through Friday from 8:30am until 4:30pm and on Saturday from 9am until 4:30pm. There is a nominal charge for the merry-go-round.*

AMERICA'S FASTEST GROWING CITY

What is now **Henderson** *began as a small town called 'Basic' back during World War II. It was built to provide housing for the titanium plant that made the light-weight and durable metal for aircraft. The plant is still there (in a larger industrial park that is actually on a plot of land that isn't part of Henderson but is surrounded by it), but there are few other remnants of the old Basic. A walk down Water Street in the old "downtown" is like a stroll through an earlier period except for the modern City Hall and other public buildings that cover a portion of upper Water Street.*

Henderson had only 6,000 residents back in 1950 and a mere 50,000 as recently as 1988. However, recent growth has been phenomenal. The 2000 population is estimated to be about 180,000 people, surpassing Reno and making Henderson the second largest city in Nevada! There is little sign of any significant slowdown as building continues at a torrid pace. They don't build new houses in Henderson, they build whole neighborhoods at a single time.

In addition to the old Basic area, Henderson has sizable new residential areas on the east side. However, the best known and heaviest populated areas are in the west where the established communities of Green Valley and Whitney Ranch have recently been joined by a number of award-winning master-planned communities like Green Valley Ranch, McDonald Ranch, Seven Hills, Anthem and others.

The **Clark County Heritage Museum**, *1830 Boulder Highway*, is conveniently located on the way to Hoover Dam. This museum has exhibits on the Native American inhabitants of the area and then moves on down through the ages to the first settlers. The mining era is then traced before you reach a number of exhibits on Las Vegas since the legalization of casino gambling. Of even greater interest are the outdoor exhibits that have actual houses along "Heritage Street." These were moved here from various locations in southern Nevada. There's also a re-created ghost town, railroad terminal complete with 1905 Union Pacific Steam engine, and mining equipment. *Tel. 702/455-7955. Hours are daily* *from 9am until 4:30pm. The admission charge is $1.50 for adults and $1 for children.*

The **Henderson Bird Preserve**, *3400 Moser Street (off of E. Sunset Road & Boulder Highway)* is a 147-acre migratory bird stop encompassing an area of wetlands and ponds. Handicapped accessible boardwalks and easy trails cross the entire preserve and there are blinds for viewing the birds. The fall migratory season (October) is the best time to visit. During the summer you should come early to avoid the hottest part of the day. *Tel. 702/565-2063. Hours are daily from 6am until 3pm and there is no admission charge.*

Finally, the Green Valley section of Henderson has commissioned many life-size sculptures such as people waiting for a bus, children playing, and so on, that are scattered throughout the area. They're especially concentrated in the area along Green Valley Parkway south of Sunset Road. For a listing of all the sculptures and their locations, ask for a brochure available in many Green Valley retail shops.

When you're ready to work your way back to Las Vegas you might consider taking a different route from whence you came. **Horizon Ridge Road** is our suggestion. It curves along near the mountain foothills, providing a good a good view of both the mountains and some of the many attractive planned communities in Henderson. The road begins at the intersection of Horizon Road and the I-515 highway exit of that name. As you swing around the first turn there is, on clear days, a stunning panorama of the distant Strip and the entire Las Vegas Valley. The nighttime view is equally wonderful. As the road dips and rises the mountain and city views will keep disappearing and reappearing. Take Horizon Ridge to Eastern and then go north to I-215 which will bring you back to the Strip.

13. NIGHTLIFE & ENTERTAINMENT

Las Vegas rightfully claims its place as the "capital" of many things, but perhaps nowhere is their leading status more evident than in entertainment. There is so much nightlife on or near the Strip that your biggest problem will be trying to see and do everything you want in the time available. There's surely something for every taste. Glitzy revues with gorgeous showgirls, high-tech production shows, magic and the biggest celebrities in show biz are only the start. There are also sophisticated nightclubs, western dance halls and wild strip joints. Throw in comedy improv clubs and countless hotel lounges for good measure and you get the idea.

Show-going is a big part of a trip to Las Vegas for millions of visitors so it should come as no surprise that getting into the show of your choice isn't always an easy thing to do. If possible, try and purchase your tickets for the most popular shows before your arrival. Unfortunately, this isn't always possible to do because some shows only sell tickets three days to a week in advance. On the other hand, many shows have advance sales of six months or even more. Be prepared to pay dearly for some of the better known acts. Prices typically start at around $35 but do go up to in excess of $100. Big name celebrities will often garner even higher prices, especially during major holiday periods. Alas, entertainment isn't as cheap as it used to be in Las Vegas, but comparable shows elsewhere would still likely cost you even more.

The last several years have seen several trends in showroom policies that are mostly better for the visitor. First of all, almost all showrooms have pre-assigned seating. Not only do you know where you're going to sit before you enter the room, but you no longer have to give a bribe – er, excuse us – a tip to an unfriendly maitre'd in order to be assured a good seat. There are no dinner shows left anymore (with the exception of the Tournament of Kings and that's a special case to be described later). This is probably good too because the small tables and so-so food served weren't a great dining experience. Even cocktail service has changed quite a bit. While table service is still available in a number of showrooms, the trend is to have an open cash bar just outside the theater. One of the reasons for this is due to another trend. That is the replacement of nightclub style table seating with theater style seats. The result is that you're less crowded in, don't have to cram your neck to see the stage, and generally have a more comfortable place to watch the show.

In addition to the "dark" night or nights that most shows have, we want to reiterate that many of the larger shows close up shop during traditionally slow show-going periods. The two biggest entertainment gaps are during the November Comdex convention and from early December to just before the holiday season gets in full swing. If shows are an important part of your Las Vegas plans, you may want to think twice before arranging your trip during one of those periods.

While the information that follows was accurate at press time, be advised that shows can often change suddenly. Even shows that have been around for years tend to close on short notice when the decision is made to pull the plug. And the hotels, constantly striving for bigger profits to satisfy the stockholders, are less likely than ever to stick with a show that hasn't been bringing in big audiences. So, especially for the lesser known shows, always check the current magazines to see what's new in town on the show scene.

PRODUCTION SHOWS

Twenty years ago if you asked for the definition of a production show it would simply have been the traditional Las Vegas revue – showgirls, feathers, brilliant costumes, colorful sets, specialty acts (singers, magicians, etc.) – in short, lavish spectacle. That still exists but this high-tech world has spawned shows that are minus (or mostly minus) the showgirls and related specialty acts. Big magic shows and shows heavy with acrobatic performances are also included in this major category.

AMERICAN SUPERSTARS (Stratosphere/Broadway Theater). While *Legends in Concert* (see below) is considered to be "the" celebrity impersonator show, American Superstars has become a worthy rival. I started as a lounge act and has been considerably upgraded. The talented and energetic performers do rock, country and pop celebrities with incredible realism. The dancers are also quite good. This may well be one of the better entertainment values on the Strip. *Tel. 702/380-7711. $27 for adults, $22 for children ages 5 through 12, plus tax. Nightly except Thursday at 7pm with an additional 10pm show on Wednesday, Friday and Saturday. No one under age 5 admitted.*

AN EVENING AT LA CAGE (Riviera/La Cage Theater).
This show has been around for about a dozen years so it must be pretty good. Well, it is, if you like female impersonators. The star of the show is Frank Marino, who is excellent. He does a Joan Rivers that's better than the real thing. The supporting cast is also good. We do want to emphasize that despite the nature of the performers, the audience is definitely mainstream, so you don't have to feel embarrassed about showing up. *Tel. 702/794-9433. $22 and up plus tax and tip. Nightly except Tuesday at 7:30 and 9:30pm. No one under age 8 admitted.*

THE BEST OF THE FOLIES BERGERE...SEXIER THAN EVER (Tropicana/Tiffany Theater).
A long name for a show so just call it the *Folies Bergere* like everyone in Las Vegas does. This show opened in 1959 and has the distinction of being the longest running show on the Strip (or anywhere in Las Vegas for that matter). This version takes the most popular acts from over the years, including the famous "Can-Can" number, and combines them in a fast paced tempo that improves on past editions of the show. The costumes and sets are excellent – lots of those feathers – but not as elaborate as in "Jubilee" (see below). It lacks the technical wizardry of most other shows these days and the Tiffany Showroom could use a major overhaul. Despite these few small shortcomings, it is the most traditional of all Vegas revues and that alone makes it worthwhile. So do the gorgeous showgirls! However, the early show is not topless and, to us, it definitely loses something in the process. *Tel. 702/739-2411. Nightly except Thursday at 7:30 and 10pm. No one under age 5 is admitted to the early show and you must be at least 21 for the late show.*

BLUE MAN GROUP (Luxor/Luxor Theater).
Many of the "knowledgeable" critics just love this show. We surmise that it is difficult for anyone who writes professionally about show-biz to criticize anything that is labeled "avant-garde" and originated in New York. We don't think it's all that funny or entertaining. Maybe the cast paints their faces blue so that no one will recognize them on the street. Funny, the same critics who pan someone like Gallagher find the not-so-different antics of the Blue Man Group to be hip. Well, there's no accounting for taste – we've actually seen people come out of the theater smiling. This is definitely not a show that will appeal to all tastes and you're likely to either love it or hate it with few patrons coming much in between. Try it if you have an open mind. Maybe you'll be able to explain to us why the critics like it so much. *Tel. 702/262-4400. $55-65. Nightly except Wednesday at 7pm and also at 10pm on Tuesday and Friday.*

DE LA GUARDA (Rio/de la Guarda Theater).
Originating from Argentina by way of New York, de la Guarda is an experience, to be sure. Whether it is great entertainment is another

matter. The specially designed "theater" requires that the audience stand while most of the action takes place above your head. The cast of dancers is energetic and talented but the whole thing, even though the show is rather short, can get a little tiresome after the first part of the show. Maybe because the beginning is the best part. Also, the noise level is far too high for many people. Undoubtedly a lot of younger theater goers will love this show but there's an equally good chance that you may hate it. *Tel. 702/252-7776. $45. Tuesday through Saturday at 9pm and also at 11:30pm on Friday and Saturday. No one under age 8 is admitted.*

EFX ALIVE!! (MGM Grand/EFX Theater).

This show can now be considered to be in its fourth edition since it is considerably revised each time the main star changes. The headliner now is Australian rock star Rick Springfield. Previous stars were Tommy Tune, David Cassidy and Michael Crawford. It seems that the role is just too much for any one person to handle for much more than a year or so. The biggest and most technically oriented of the new style Las Vegas production shows, EFX dazzles the audience with its sets and costumes, but especially the wonderful special effects that gives the show its name. The cast of more than 70 fills a tremendous stage in this huge 1,600 seat theater with an array of elaborate dance numbers. It's entertainment that is well suited to all ages.

The latest version adds "Alive" to the EFX moniker and although the show has demonstrated that it's bigger than whoever the star is, the current version does, indeed, seem to have a more lively flow than in the past. There are more rock numbers in the Rick Springfield edition of the show. The H.G. Wells "Time Machine" sequence is still the show's highlight and compares favorably with any show in town. The rest of the show is also good but doesn't quite live up to the hotel's promotional claim that to miss EFX is to "miss Las Vegas." *Tel. 702/891-7777. $55-75 for adults and $40 for children ages 5-12. All prices include tax. Tuesday through Saturday evenings at 7:30 and 10:30pm. No one under age 5 admitted.*

JUBILEE! (Bally's/Jubilee Theater).

The city's biggest traditional revue, Jubilee! features the largest cast, the most elaborate costumes, and the greatest sets of any show. A couple of acts stand out in particular for their overwhelming beauty and artistry. These are the destruction of Delilah's temple by a revengeful Samson and the sinking of the Titanic. Just for the record, this show has been putting the famous liner into a watery grave each night long before the current Titanic craze. For feathers and costumes, beautiful long-legged showgirls, and top notch dancers, Jubilee has never had an equal and probably never will. *Tel. 702/967-4567. $50-66 including tax. Nightly except Tuesdays at 7:30pm and 10:30pm. No one under 18 admitted.*

LANCE BURTON: MASTER MAGICIAN (Monte Carlo/Lance Burton Theater).

Wholesome family entertainment is the best way to characterize this show. Mr. Burton is definitely one of the most accomplished magicians in the world, so anyone who likes magic is sure to thoroughly enjoy this show. If you're not a real enthusiast of this kind of art, you should still leave the theater with a smile on your face. That's because Burton is an entertainer who is very at home interacting with the audience. A supporting cast of six female dances are pleasing to the eyes and helps keep things moving along at a nice pace. The star gets a break to allow some time for a comic juggler who is also quite good. *Tel. 702/730-7160. $50-55. Tuesday through Saturday evenings at 7:00 and 10pm and at 7pm on Sunday.*

LASTING IMPRESSIONS (Flamingo Las Vegas/Flamingo Showroom).

We could have listed this show in the celebrity category because it is dominated by its star, talented impersonator Bill Accosta. However, unlike Danny Gans over at the Mirage (see review below), this show is more in keeping with the traditional Las Vegas production show. Accompanied by a lively orchestra and eight talented and sometimes topless dancers, Lasting Impressions will do exactly that – you'll leave the theater with fond memories of the show you have seen. Mr. Accosta concentrates his impressions on performers of the past rather than contemporary names but all of them will be familiar even to young audiences. He handles the job with great skill. *Tel. 702/733-3333. $40-70. Nightly except Friday at 10pm with an additional show on Tuesday at 7:30pm. No one under age 18 is admitted.*

LEGENDS IN CONCERT (Imperial Palace).

This was the original celebrity impersonator show. When it opened it was supposed to run for six weeks. Instead, it has been around for twelve years, has spawned offspring in other cities as well as numerous imitators within Las Vegas. It is, however, still the best of its genre. In most cases you'll be hard-pressed to tell the impersonator from the real thing. The band is one of the best in town and special kudos also go to their dance team which definitely enlivens the proceedings. The costumes, which in the early days of the show left something to be desired, have also gotten a whole lot better over the years. The celebrity line-up changes from night to night but a typical evening could well be a cast of Gloria Estefan, Rod Stewart, Diana Ross, Garth Brooks, the Four Tops and, of course, Elvis. *Tel. 702/794-3261. $35 including tax, tip and two drinks; $20 for children under age 12. Nightly except Sunday at 7:30 and 10:30pm.*

MEN ARE FROM MARS, WOMEN ARE FROM VENUS (Flamingo Las Vegas/Flamingo Showroom).

It seems that Las Vegas never completely gives up on trying Broadway type shows. Perhaps encouraged by the success of *Chicago* in its 18-month run at Mandalay Bay, this slightly off-beat but mildly entertaining show about relationships is being given a chance to strike it big in Glitz City. Although many people will enjoy the talented cast we doubt if you'll ever have trouble finding a ticket. *Tel. 702/733-3333. $28-52. Nightly except Tuesday at 7:30pm with an additionals shows at 10pm on Friday and a Sunday matinee at 3pm (lowest price).*

MICHAEL FLATLEY'S LORD OF THE DANCE (New York, New York/Broadway Theater).

Don't expect to see Mr. Flatley in this show. He lends his name but not his presence to the proceedings. The cast of 40 dancers accompanied by several musicians is talented and energetic, but unless you are stimulated by the thought of ninety minutes of Celtic dancing, it can become rather tedious after the first third. *Tel. 702/740-6815. $50-70 with the higher prices being on weekends evenings, all including tax. Shows 7:30 and 10:30pm on Tuesday, Wednesday and Saturday; 9pm only on Thursday and Friday.*

MYSTERE (Treasure Island).

The first and, in many ways, still the best of the "new-age" surreal production shows, Mystere is a delightful time for audiences of all ages. The effects and costumes are all wonderful and some of the acrobatic performances border on the unbelievable. To make things even better, Mystere has something that most shows of its type lack – a true sense of humor and comic relief. Staged in an excellent theater that was specially designed for this show, it is something that you will always remember, even if you have a difficult time in describing what you saw. We can best summarize it by saying that it is one part circus, one part Las Vegas production show, and one part sheer imagination. The sum of it all is possibly the best evening of theater entertainment you are ever likely to experience. Even after many years this is still a hot show and tickets are sometimes difficult to get. *Tel. 702/894-7722 or 800/392-1999. $75-88 plus tax. Wednesday through Sunday evenings at 7:30 and 10:30pm.*

"O" (Bellagio).

A short name for a big show. And an unusual name as well. "O" is the pronunciation of the French word *eau*, which means water. And water is at the heart of this $92 million production extravaganza created by the always imaginative folks at Cirque du Soleil. The stage is often covered by a movable platform but is essentially a lake that reaches a depth of up to 25 feet and contains 1.5 million gallons of water. Designed around a loose framework of a tribute to the theater, "O" is much more than a water-borne version of Cirque's fabulous Mystere, although it does have some of the same surreal atmosphere, acrobatic performers and other things common to their shows. This is a fast paced ten act show with a talented and active cast of 74 in colorful costumes that is sure to please viewers of all ages. The magnificent three-tiered theater holds 1,800 people and, with it's brilliant oval shaped domed ceiling, is about on a par with the magnificent theater at the Luxor. This one, though, has some of the feel of a gracious European opera house. If you think getting a ticket for Mystere is difficult, wait to you try and procure one for "O". It is a formidable task, especially if you aren't staying at an MGM/Mirage property. *Tel. 702/693-7722. $99-121 including tax. Friday through Tuesday evenings at 7:30 and 10:30pm.*

SIEGFRIED & ROY (The Mirage/Siegfried & Roy Theater).

The masters of the disappearing white tiger have been doing their thing at the Mirage since 1990. Long considered by many as the "best" show in town and as the one "must see," we don't think it meets those exceedingly high standards. An excellent show to be sure, Siegfried & Roy doesn't quite justify it's place as the second most expensive show in town (after "O"). There are several others that are better. The magical gifts of the German dynamic duo are not in question, nor is their ability to communicate well with the audience. They are indeed master showmen who have earned an almost legendary place in the annals of Las Vegas showdom. It is far more than a magic show as all of their work is either accompanied by or sandwiched in between rather lavish production numbers featuring a large supporting cast.

Some people are a little disappointed in the relatively small role that the famous white tigers play in the show. Over the years several new acts have been introduced into the show so if you haven't seen it in quite a few years, an encore may be in order. The two stars are beginning to show their age a little and one wonders how much longer they can keep it up. *Tel. 702/792-7777. $95 including tax, tip and two drinks. Friday through Tuesday evenings at 7:30 and 11pm. No one under age 5 admitted.*

SPLASH III (Riviera/Splash Theater).

This show has consistently been quite popular among visitors to Las Vegas. Locals (and especially the critics) tend to pan it as one of the worst things to ever have hit the Strip. The truth lies somewhere in the middle. Now in its third version (thus the Roman numeral that has been added to the name of the show), it features much less of the water-based acts that made the show famous. That part of it was one of the most criticized but, apparently, it is alright to do things with water at Bellagio. We never understood the double standard.

However, many of the most popular acts have been retained from previous versions and the current show might well be the best since it premiered. The male dancers are handsome, the female dances beautiful and well endowed, and the costumes are good – all necessary ingredients for a successful revue. On the other hand, there is nothing to fill you with awe and you may well leave the theater with the mixed emotions we have. Overall, it's a relatively good value. *Tel. 702/477-5274. $50 plus tax. Nightly* at 7:30 and 10:30pm. The early performance on Sunday is the family show; no one under 18 will be admitted for all other shows.

STORM (Mandalay Bay).

This show was set to make its debut in March 2001 just as we were going to press, so we can't offer a personal review. However, it appears that it's going to have all the ingredients for a mega-show in a mega-hotel. With a loose "Latin" theme, Storm will feature a cast of about 50 dancers, acrobats and other performers who will sing and dance up a storm. To top things off, there will be plenty of special effects to accompany the storm theme. Expect rain, thunder, lightning and other atmospheric occurences. *Tel. 702/632-7777. $55-65 plus tax. Sunday, Monday and Thursday at 7:30pm; Friday at 10:30pm; Wednesday and Saturday 7:30pm and 10:30pm.*

TOURNAMENT OF KINGS (Excalibur).

This is now the only dinner show in a major Las Vegas hotel and it offers an evening of fun for all. The basic concept involves guests sitting around a medieval style arena and they cheer on their own knight in

THE LATEST ENTERTAINMENT SCENE

The only thing changing faster than restaurants or the face of the Strip itself is entertainment. Shows here one day are gone the next. Or a show might move from one hotel to another. We've been as up to date as we possibly can be in this chapter. Here's a rundown on rumors and reports on the entertainment scene. You might encounter some of these when you visit.

A virtual lock (except for details like the debut date, schedule and pricing) is a show to be called **Lumiere** *at the Aladdin. It will star ex-Baywatch babe* **Carmen Electra** *who will be the lead character in a high-tech show with a story line. The show will also feature a well-known European magician but it won't be a magic show. Hmmm – lot's of guys might be interested in seeing Carmen's magic – she is reputedly a good dancer but that's a side of her that the public hasn't seen up to now. The Aladdin, by the way, is also reputedly working on a late night show that would strictly cater to the adult audience. This showroom will also convert to a nightclub (see the listing later in this chapter)*

Now that Caesars Magical Empire is gone the rumors that it would be converted into a Latin-themed nightclub (possibly owned by Jennifer Lopez and Jimmy Smits) seems much more likely to occur. It could happen before the end of 2001. It would replace the Magical Empire.

And, finally, **Celine Dion** *wants to return from her two year family making hiatus by starring in her own Las Vegas show. Her business people are negotiating with several hotels. Interesting possibilities all. Well, you'll be able to say you saw it here first!*

shining armor in this elaborately staged feast of chivalry and jousting. It's a natural for children but we've seen plenty of adults get really caught up in the fun and action.

The latest version of the show has been further enhanced by new and more elaborate sets and colorful costumes. The finale depicts a coronation in a cathedral set and is definitely a great conclusion to the evening's festivities. Oh, yes, the food isn't anything to rave about but you get to eat your meal in authentic medieval style – soup sipped from a tureen and a main course without the civility of utensils. It brings new meaning to "finger lickin'" good. *Tel. 702/597-7600. $37 for the dinner show plus tax. Nightly at 6:00 and 8:30pm.*

CELEBRITY ENTERTAINMENT

You have to scan the newspapers or events magazines (as well as the hotel marquees) to find out who is in town when you're there. Smart advance planners will even go so far as to call for a schedule well before their departure since the biggest stars often sell out quickly. Most of the name entertainment, especially the bigger names, is scheduled well in advance. In addition to the celebrities who come to town for short stints (ranging from a single performance to a couple of weeks), there are several on-going celebrity shows. Let's take a look at those first.

DAVID BRENNER (Golden Nugget).

How long has this guy been around? Forever, it seems, but the story is still the same. If you liked his style of comedy in the past you will like this show. Otherwise, don't even bother. *Tel. 702/796-9999. $35. Nightly except Monday at 8pm with an additional 10pm show on Saturday.*

ANDRE-PHILIPPE GAGNON (The Venetian/Showroom at Venetian).

Mr. Gagnon is a French-Canadian impressionist who has a lot of talent and charm. The show has both comic segments and singing which results in a generally entertaining evening that is in no way especially memorable. This is also one of the most over-priced shows in town. *Tel. 702/948-3007. $45-84. Wednesday through Friday at 8:30pm and Saturday and Sunday at 6:30pm. No one under 21 will be admitted.*

DANNY GANS (The Mirage/Danny Gans Theater).

Mr. Gans has become a celebrity from his Las Vegas career, several times having been named Entertainer of the Year. Beginning at the long-gone Hacienda, he moved to the Rio for several years before finally coming to the Mirage a short time ago. Danny-boy is an extremely talented individual but, in our opinion, the show is good although not worthy of any special honors. He can project an incredible number of voices and that, in a way, is the show's biggest problem as he tries to cover too many different people and the show loses some focus. In addition, considering the lack of any big production values, the show is quite overpriced. The plus side is that few people will leave the theater saying that they didn't like the show. *Tel. 702/791-7111. $74-99 including tax. Nightly except Monday and Friday at 8pm. No one under age 8 will be admitted.*

CLINT HOLMES (Harrah's/Harrah's Showroom).

The subtitle of this show is **Takin' it Uptown** and Clint Holmes is a capable and affable performer who sings and dances his way through this largely one person show. The question is whether one person can entertain today's audiences in this manner without having real star power. We believe that Clint is up to the task so long as you don't set your expectations sky high. *Tel. 702/369-5111. $45. Nightly except Wednesday at 7:30pm with an additional 10pm show on Thursday and Saturday.*

WAYNE NEWTON (Stardust/Wayne Newton Theater).

Mr. Las Vegas has returned to the city that made him a household name. Ol' Wayne still has the charm to turn an audience and what he now lacks in vocal range and physical energy he mostly makes up for through savvy stage experience, not to mention some excellent back-up singers and a large orchestra. If you always liked Wayne Newton then there is no reason to think that you won't come away from this show completely satisfied. However, if the younger Newton wasn't your cup of tea it isn't likely that the senior version will do much better for you. *Tel. 702/732-6325. $50 including tax and one drink. Sunday through Thursday at 9pm and Saturday at 8:00 and 11pm. Mr. Newton is in the house 40 weeks out of the year so check in advance to make sure he is appearing when you want to see him.*

STEVE WYRICK (The Sahara/Sahara Theater).

It seems you can't go two blocks on the Strip without running into a magic show, whether it is of the traditional type or the more spectacular Las Vegas version of the genre. Steve Wyrick is a capable magician and this is a good show if you like magic. Since the star isn't nearly as well known as many other Vegas magicians, such as Lance Burton, this show has to compete by offering lower prices. And that's good news for you because this is a good value. We also like the elaborate sets that Mr. Wyrick uses for his biggest acts. Given the price, that comes as something of a pleasant surprise. *Tel. 702/737-2111. $35. Nightly except Tuesday at 7:000pm and 10pm.*

Short-term celebrity entertainment is presented at many hotels including, among others, **Caesars Palace, Mandalay Bay** (in the arena and House of Blues), **MGM Grand** (Hollywood Theater and Grand Garden Arena). In addition, many of the Strip hotels with regularly scheduled production shows have celebrity entertainment during the "dark" nights for the on-going show or when the cast of the show has a week or two off for a well deserved rest. Off-Strip hotels with name entertainment include the **Orleans** and **Arizona Charlie's** but perhaps the best known in this category are the major names in rock who appear at the **Hard Rock Hotel** in *The Joint*. Many "locals" casinos also have celebrity entertainment at a bargain price. The biggest genre in this group are rock groups from the 60's and 70's who still have a faithful following. A new state-of-the-art venue at **Sam's Town** also appears to be headed towards star-attraction power.

Of all the venues just mentioned, the **House of Blues** is the most unusual. Featuring decor that can only be described as outrageous, the facility is a mixture of theater and nightclub and is ideally suited to all types of audiences. The more sedate concert-goer can sit in the upper level in comfortable theater style seating. Those who never bother to sit during a performance can choose downstairs where there aren't any seats to get in the way – the pit-like floor fronts the stage and has plenty of room to move about to the beat of the music. Railings provide some support and help to keep the crowd organized.

LOUNGE ACTS & OTHER SHOWS

This category includes a wide range of shows. The true "lounge" act is a Las Vegas fixture that goes back to the town's earliest days as a casino Mecca. All of the major hotels have a lounge show in addition to their main showroom. These are listed in the entertainment summary of the hotels in the *Where to Stay* chapter. Lounges are much smaller than showrooms, often containing fewer than a hundred seats although some cat fit in several hundred. (By comparison, the major showrooms accommodate anywhere between 500 and 2,000 people.) There is generally no admission charge to a lounge show but there is a cover charge, usually in the form of a two-drink minimum, so this can be an inexpensive way to take in some entertainment.

Lounges are traditionally located in or right off of the casino and in almost all cases you can see the goings on in the casino from them – a reminder to come out and gamble. Some lounge acts stay around indefinitely while others are only booked for a short time. Because of that, it is always best to check current magazines or newspaper listings to see who is appearing. However, more often than not it is likely that you will not have heard of the performer. This doesn't mean that they aren't talented. One must remember that many of the biggest name performers in show business got their start in lounge acts. In a lounge act you'll usually se a singer (or singing group) backed by live musicians although other forms of entertainment can also be featured. You'll also find that quite a few hotels have, in addition to one or more lounges with entertainment, a piano bar.

The shows in the listing that follows aren't easy to fit in any particular category. While they certainly aren't like the lounge acts just described, they also aren't the type of show that can be said to be a major production show. So, read the descriptions and decide if they're for you.

THE DREAM KING (Holiday Inn Boardwalk).

This Elvis show was the first of several Elvis shows in town and, although not great by any means, is still the best of the lot. Show-star Trent Carlini is one of the better Elvis impersonators and if that is what you want to see, then we recommend you do it here. *Tel. 702/730-3194. $28. Tuesday through Saturday at 8:30pm.*

FOREVER PLAID.

No, we didn't forget to tell you which hotel this show is at. Here's the story: this highly entertaining little show about a bunch of '50's nerds managed to please audiences of all kinds for many years at the Flamingo. In fact, it was still doing relatively well there when it was decided by the powers that be that it was time for a change. (The Second City took its place.) As we went to press the show's producers were in the process of trying to secure a new home for it and the inside scoop was that it was going to be accomplished within a short time so you should scan the weekly magazines to see where it's at. While at the Flamingo the cost was only $25 and since it probably won't wind up at one of the more luxury hotels, it can be safely assumed that the price will be in that range once again.

HAWAIIAN HOT LUAU (Imperial Palace).

This show makes for a fun-filled evening. Held at poolside from March through October (weather permitting, which is almost always), the festivities begin with a buffet that features the food of the islands. This is followed by a Hawaiian style revue. While it isn't like being in Hawaii (the slab-like construction of the Imperial Palace hotel that surrounds the pool area isn't a particularly great atmosphere), it is a decent show and the food is alright too. Price includes island drinks. Tickets must be purchased in advance. *Tel. 702/794-3261. $30 for adults; $16 for children ages 3 through 12. Tuesday and Thursday evenings. Seating begins at 6:30pm.*

HIP-NOSIS (O'Sheas Casino and Flamingo Las Vegas).

We wouldn't give a ticket to this show to our worst enemy but, in the interest of being as thorough as possible, we include it here for those who may need hypnosis to get a good night's sleep. Audience participation is optional but we suggest that you do try it if you want to stay awake. *Tel. 702/737-1343 (O'Sheas) or 702/733-3333 (Flamingo). $25. Tuesday through Saturday at 9pm at O'Sheas and Friday and Saturday at midnight at the Flamingo.*

HONKY TONK ANGELS (Gold Coast).

Self-described as a "tribute" to some of the biggest female stars of country music (including Patsy Cline, Reba McEntire, Dolly Parton, and Tammy Wynette), the show is quite entertaining if you like an evening filled with popular tunes from the world of country music. The show does keep up to date as is evidenced by the fact that they already have a Faith Hill impersonator. The cast is generally good with the individual performances ranging from adequate to excellent. One thing is for certain – at the prices the Gold Coast gets for this show you can't possibly go far wrong. *Tel. 702/251-3574. $10 or $15 with dinner package. Nightly except Tuesday at 8pm.*

LEGENDS OF COMEDY (New Frontier).

The impersonation tribute genre is alive and well in Las Vegas! Here's another one for you to consider. Actually, we shouldn't be so hard on this kind of show since some of them (like Legends in Concert) are among the better shows in town. This low-tech and relatively low-priced entry in the field is quite good. Some of the biggest names in American comedy are well portrayed by a talented group of hopeful comics. Among the "stars" you'll laugh at are Jack Benny, George Burns and Bill Cosby. There's even a Jay Leno for the late night TV set. On a personal level we could do without the Roseanne impersonator. Not that she doesn't do a credible job, but the copy is as un-funny and obnoxious as the original. *Tel. 702/794-8200. $27. Nightly except Tuesday at 7:00 and 10:30pm.* There have been reports that this show might be moving to O'Sheas Casino, so check the local papers to be sure you're going to the right place.

MELINDA, FIRST LADY OF MAGIC (The Venetian/Showroom at Venetian).

Melinda is a pretty lady and a talented magician. She has been in and out of starring roles in many smaller Las Vegas hotels, so the Venetian is her biggest career opportunity. As a magic show it is just so-so. On the other hand, if you doubt whether you can enjoy sitting through ninety minutes of magic, the lengthy on-stage presence of a team of excellent high energy dancers will likely add to your enjoyment of this show. *Tel. 702/948-3007. $35-70 for adults and $20 for children under 12. Friday through Monday at 6:30pm and at 8:30pm on Tuesday and Thursday.*

MIDNIGHT FANTASY (Luxor/Pharaoh's Theater).

Based on the name and ads for this show you might think it is a throwback to the traditional topless Las Vegas revue. Well, it is topless, but the similarity ends there. It is, however, further indication that topless is back in style in Las Vegas and this may well be one of the better shows of its type – that is, the scaled back production show genre. What we like most about Midnight Fantasy is that the eight member women's dance team is excellent. They display grace and talent in addition to their beauty.

On the other hand, the show lacks the elaborate staging that this kind of entertainment needs. The recent addition of a comedian and a singer has made the show better. All in all, not a bad buy. By the way, most of the audience is couples and that's appropriate because the show is definitely not raunchy in any way. *Tel. 702/262-4400. $30 including tax. Nightly except Monday. Shows at 8:30 and 10:30pm except only 10:30pm on Wednesday and only 8:30pm on Friday. No one under age 21 will be admitted.*

NAKED ANGELS (Jackie Gaughan's Plaza).

This show was originally called Hot Trix but they changed it to give it more sex appeal. While it generally follows the format of the budget topless revue genre, Naked Angels does go a bit further than other shows of this type on the Strip, which should make it quite popular during Comdex and other big conventions when men are the primary guests in town. As a matter of fact, at the end of the late show the female members of the cast are available for private dances almost like those in the "gentlemen's clubs" found off-Strip.

We don't consider this show good to be solid entertainment for most couples, as they may just have gone slightly past the line of good taste. That's not surprising to us because some downtown operators will do just about anything to lure people away from the Strip. You might have noticed the dearth of entertainment in downtown. But the main question is whether this more risque show is good entertainment? In this case the answer, unfortunately, is not really. The female cast are strippers rather than dancers and it shows. The comedian is alright. *Tel. 702/386-2444. $29. Nightly except Monday at 8:00 and 10pm. No one under age 21 will be admitted.*

THE RAT PACK IS BACK (Sahara/Congo Room).

If you liked Franky, Sammy, Deano and Joey (and it seems that there aren't that many people who didn't), then this retro of old Las Vegas should appeal to you. It is loosely themed around a birthday party for the Chairman of the Board which allows the star impersonators to have a good reason to sing all of the old favorites. They do a more than credible job. *Tel. 702/737-2111. $35. Shows at 8pm on Wednesday through Friday and Sunday; and at 7:30pm and 10pm on Tuesday and Saturday.* The show's producers have not had a great relationship with the Sahara and, as we went to press, rumors abounded that they were looking for a new place to stage their production.

SCINTAS (Rio/Copacapana Showroom).

Three men and one woman combine in this lively budget show that proves just how popular celebrity impersonation is these days. While mimicry is the focus of the show it has a little of everything as the troupe can handle both comic and musical impressions. While it doesn't rank up there with the big shows, it's definitely a good way to make for a rather pleasant evening. Scintas played to receptive audiences for a year at the Las Vegas Hilton and the show was slated to move to the Rio as we went to press. What changes were planned, if any, was unknown as were details including the show schedule and pricing. *Tel. 702/364-9192 for all further information.*

SECOND CITY (Flamingo Las Vegas/Bugsy's Theater).

The brand new Las Vegas version of the original Chicago hit, this audience "interactive" comedy show has launched several now well known comedians from obscurity to stardom. The show was scheduled to open after we went to press so we can't offer any details or opinions. *Tel. 702/733-3333. $25 plus tax. Nightly except Monday at 7:00 and 9:30pm.*

SHOWGIRLS OF MAGIC (San Remo).

The San Remo has for many years presented a series of shows that have never quite been successes. They all involve a small cast (because of the small theater and stage) of nice looking ladies who sing, dance and even perform a few magic tricks. If you're looking for low cost entertainment this might do but it certainly isn't going to set any records for longevity at the San Remo. Incidentally, the name of the show was used once before, which gives you an indication of how this hotel keeps on trying. The late show is topless while the early show can hardly be termed family entertainment with its minimally clad cast. *Tel. 702/597-6028. $26 including one drink. Nightly except Monday at 8pm and 10:30pm. No one under age 21 will be admitted to the late show.*

SKINTIGHT (Harrah's/Harrah's Showroom).

Another of the new topless revues in the tradition of *Midnight Fantasy.* This one isn't quite as entertaining as the former but it does have a higher talent level than *Crazy Girls.* Again, it is suitable for couples as the emphasis is really on dancing. *Tel. 702/369-5111. $40. Nightly except Thursday at 10:30pm with additional shows on Wednesday at 7:30pm and Saturday at midnight. No one under age 18 will be admitted.*

CRAZY GIRLS FANTASY REVUE/ (Riviera/Mardi Gras Plaza).

The two names is because for many years this show was known as "Crazy Girls" and was one of the more popular of the good natured jiggle shows (except for when it was spiced up at Comdex time). Because there has been a lot of new competition in the low-budget topless show genre such as Midnight Fantasy and Skintight (shows where the talent level was also higher), Riviera management has decided that it was time to make the show even more adult in nature.

The new show with the "Fantasy" name was set to debut in April of 2001 after we went to press. Therefore, we aren't able to offer any details or critique but we doubt if it will achieve much if any praise. Crazy Girls never did although we always felt it was a reasonably priced bit of entertainment if you had low expectations. *Tel. 702/794-9433. Crazy Girls prices began at $20 but it has been reported that prices for the new version will be in the neighborhood of $40. Nightly except Monday at 8:30 and 10:30pm and additional midnight show on Saturday. No one under age 18 admitted.*

ALL THAT JAZZ

Lovers of jazz will find that this art form is alive and well in Las Vegas. And, even better, you can combine it with fine dining that is good enough for us to have included it with our listing of restaurants. We could only put it in one place and this is where we felt it to be most appropriate.

*The **Blue Note Cafe**, in the Aladdin, Tel. 702/862-8307, is the second such place in the country, the original being in New York. This cabaret is a little too big to be called intimate (450 seats) even though it has a smaller feel. Some of the biggest names in the jazz world perform here on a nightly basis. Club patrons are served an excellent dinner during the show or you can dine in the adjacent grill cafe. While the latter doesn't have live entertainment, patrons will be kept amused while waiting for their food by the videos of jazz's greatest performers, past and present. There are plans to use the Cafe as a more traditional nightclub venue after-hours.*

***Tres Jazz**, in Paris (in the arcade leading to Bally's), Tel. 702/946-4346, also features live jazz entertainment. The cuisine is a combination of Caribbean (try the marinated Bahamian grouper) and nouvelle American. The lovely room is mainly in the art deco style but it has the atmosphere of a sophisticated Parisian supper club, which is appropriate given its Paris-Las Vegas location.*

COMEDY ACTS

We have mixed feelings about all of the comedy shows. Sometimes they can be hilarious and other times, well, real duds. It all depends on how good the line-up is on a particular evening and you never really know for sure before entering the theater. We're acquainted with people who regularly seek out the comedy shows while others have had their fill of them after one or two attempts. You'll have to be your own judge as to whether this type of entertainment is for you. There are usually age restrictions as most of the acts feature adult oriented humor.

The main comedy shows are:

BOURBON STREET COMEDY THEATER (Bourbon Street). *Tel. 702/228-7591. $20. Nightly at 7pm with an additional 9pm show on Sunday.*

CATCH A RISING STAR (Excalibur). *Tel. 702/597-7777. $17. Two shows nightly.*

This is a "re-make" of the show of the same name that used to be at the MGM Grand. It was scheduled to begin performances in its new home sometime in the spring of 2001.

COMEDY STOP (Tropicana). *Tel. 702/739-2714. $18 all inclusive. Nightly at 8:00 and 10:30pm.*

THE IMPROV AT HARRAH'S. *Tel. 702/369-5111. $25 plus tax. Nightly except Monday at 8:00 and 10pm.*

RIVIERA COMEDY CLUB. *Tel. 702/794-9433. $15 plus tax and tip. Dinner options available. Nightly at 8:00 and 10pm with an additional show at 11:45pm on Friday and Saturday.*

AFTERNOON DELIGHTS

While Las Vegas has earned its entertainment reputation as a night town, there are several shows that have found a home during the daylight hours. These are low cost, low-tech shows with smaller casts and not a lot of extravagant staging. But, then again, if you don't have enough money in your budget for the big shows, a matinee performance may be the way to go. If your expectations are reasonable, there's no reason why you shouldn't enjoy them. Daytime shows seem to come and go even quicker than some of their sister night acts, but these are the ones that are currently on the scene.

Bottoms Up *(Flamingo Las Vegas/Flamingo Showroom). The only "topless" afternoon show, this is a good-natured revue with all of the elements of a big revue, but just on a much smaller scale. There is a large emphasis on comedy. Tel. 702/733-3333. $13. Daily except Sunday at 2:00 and 4pm. No one under 21 admitted. Coupons available for 2 for 1 admissions with purchase of drink.*

The Illusionary Magic of Rich Thomas *(Tropicana). A low-tech and low-keyed Siegfried & Roy genre show, complete with tigers. Need we say more? Tel. 702/739-2411. $17-22. Daily except Fridays at 2:00 and 4pm.*

Stars of the Strip *(Lady Luck). The stars that are impersonated include Liberace, Elvis (of course) and many others but the talent is definitely better at the Stratosphere or Imperial Palace. Tel. 702/477-3000. $15 (or free admission with purchase of drink). Monday through Friday at 2:00 and 3:30pm.*

Viva Las Vegas *(Stratosphere). Tracing its origins all the way back to the Sands Hotel, it is the longest running daytime show in Vegas. Again, don't expect Jubilee!, but it is good fun for the price and the hard working cast is more than adequate. Tel. 702/380-7711. $12 plus tax (discount tickets readily available). Daily except Sunday at 2:00 and 4pm. No one under 5 admitted. Discount coupons available.*

NIGHTCLUBS & DANCE HALLS

BABY'S NIGHTCLUB, *Hard Rock Hotel, Tel. 702/693-5555. Thursday through Saturday.*

This is literally an "underground" club and features two large rooms with state-of-the-art technical facilities and nationally known DJ's and performers. It's as sophisticated and expensive as some of its Strip bretheren such as Studio 54 or Ra.

THE BEACH, *365 Convention Center Drive, Tel. 702/731-1295. Nightly.*

Dancing all the time to the sounds of semi-name live entertainment in a colorful atmosphere. That has been the secret of this club's success. It is also well known as one of the best places to go if you're looking to hit it big with the opposite sex. That goes for the picker uppers as well as the picked up.

CLEOPATRA'S BARGE, *Caesars Palace, Tel. 702/731-7110. Nightly.*

Live music and dancing. This place specializes in keeping people entertained during the wee hours. Classy setting on a modern day version of the Nile queen's pleasure barge. It actually floats!

CLUB RIO, *The Rio Hotel, Tel. 702/252-7977. Wednesday through Saturday.*

This 900-person capacity room led to numerous other dance clubs being established in some of the big hotels. This is, however, still among the best. It certainly is popular. DJ, boogie nights, some top 40 acts and almost anything else you can think of. Lots of locals in the crowd.

C2K, *The Venetian, Tel. 702/933-4255. Friday and Saturday.*

The unusual name stands for Carnivale 2000. It was so named because it opened in the millenium celebration year and at that time every other word out of someone's mouth was Y2K so they figured it would be a good idea to capitalize on. Well, the Y2K furor has passed but C2K remains one of the hottest spots in Vegas. In fact, it was a little too hot to handle for a time. It was briefly closed in order to institute new management that wouldn't always turn the other cheek to drug offenses and other goings on that are found in clubs of this type throughout the country. We don't mean to pick on C2K because, let's face it, if you're looking for that kind of action, it is easy enough to find anywhere. On the other hand, C2K has definitely gotten a tough reputation. We've been hearing rumors that the Venetian might just shut down C2K and reformat it into a theater that will have Broadway style shows. However, this is probably down the road a bit.

DRAI'S, *in the Barbary Coast Hotel.*

Sophisticated late-evening entertainment. See the restaurant listing for more information on their after-hours club.

DYLAN'S DANCE HALL, *4600 Boulder Highway, Tel. 702/451-4006. Thursday through Saturday.*

A combo western and rock palace. Good fun. It mostly attracts a locals crowd but visitors will find a warm welcome. The place is likely to be busier than ever now that the nearby Rockabilly's has been turned into a gentleman's club called The Library.

GOLD COAST DANCE HALL, *Gold Coast Hotel, Tel. 702/367-7111. Sunday afternoon and Tuesday evening.*

This is a simple but good venue for older folks as well as younger ones who appreciate the sounds of the big band era. There's nothing high-tech (or even overly loud) about the dance hall – just a place to go for serious old-fashioned dancing. The cover charge even includes a ballroom dancing lesson.

THE HOP, *1650 E. Tropicana Avenue, Tel. 702/310-5060. Nightly.*

A popular place with the locals that caters to a mostly younger crowd, the Hop features live music and a disc jockey. Celebrity entertainment is featured on occasion and, while not the biggest headliners in the business, those appearing are often recognizable names. The location is only a short distance from the Strip.

HOUSE OF BLUES, *Mandalay Bay, Tel. 702/632-7607. Friday and Saturday.*

It seems that this multi-purpose facility can be listed in just about every category – restaurant, theater, nightclub. It turns into a dance hall on weekend evenings and features, in addition to the blues, both rock and country music.

NAUGHTY LADIES SALOON, *Arizona Charlie's, Tel. 702/258-5200. Nightly.*

Live entertainment and dancing with plenty of locals in attendance. The place isn't high tech or fancy like its Strip bretheren but for those who don't go for the "sophisticated" atmosphere of those other clubs, this is a good alternative. It may well be best known for their great Monday Night Football parties.

THE NIGHTCLUB, *Las Vegas Hilton, Tel. 702/732-5422. Nightly.*

One of the more elaborate and sophisticated of the major hotel clubs, this one often has some fairly big names performing. Full choreographed shows. The action starts late since this room is used for other forms of entertainment earlier in the evening.

RA, *Luxor, Tel. 702/730-5900. Wednesday through Saturday.*

Truly one of the city's pleasure palaces and, along with the aforementioned *C2K* and *Studio 54* (see below), one of the exquisite *in* places for the *beautiful* people. Trendy, with semi-big to big name rock entertainment. The decor is the wildest ancient Egyptian you could imagine. It starts at the main entrance where you're greeted by two golden (and topless) statues of trident-wielding wild ancient Egyptian women. However, the high boots and platform heels adds a definite touch of modernity. The blue lit entryway is flanked by eight statues of Egyptian gods complete with human bodies and animal heads. Upon reaching the club itself you're overwhelmed by a huge winged statue of Ra, the Egyptian sun god. The 900-person capacity club's walls are covered with silver and features high tech lighting, dramatic sound, laser lights and other special effects to go along with several caged dancers. This is most definitely much more than simply a place to go dancing. Dress code.

ROXY'S, *Sam's Town. Tel. 702/456-7777. Nightly except Monday.*

Live bands provide the sound for dancing with a variety of music ranging from country to rock. A fun atmosphere that is a cross between the more lavish Strip pleasure palaces and the usually far simpler locals clubs.

RUMJUNGLE, *Mandalay Bay. Tel. 702/632-7408. Thursday through Sunday.*

Starting around eleven in the evening, *rumjungle* converts from restaurant to high energy club with a dance show on an elevated stage. It attracts the sophisticated younger set much like those who go to Ra or Studio 54 even though it isn't really the same kind of facility. We think it's one of the more fun evening spots in town.

STUDIO 54, *MGM Grand, Tel. 702/891-7254. Tuesday through Saturday.*

A latter-day reincarnation of the famous late 70's pop culture club in New York that started it all. It's just as picky about what you wear and who they will let in. If you're the type that wants to "be seen," then this is the place. Some big name entertainment appears here. The place definitely rocks. The three-story club features state-of-the-art sound and lighting, four separate dance floors, four bars, private club rooms and a gallery of celebrity photographs taken at the original Studio 54. Dress code.

UTOPIA, *3765 Las Vegas Blvd. South, Tel. 702/740-4646. Wednesday through Sunday.*

The Club Utopia was definitely one of the most *in* hot spots on the Strip (and certainly the most popular outside of the main hotels) before it had to close down due to fire damage. It has now reopened (over the 2001 New Year's weekend), thoroughly refurbished and nicer than before the remodeling. It is more casual than the best known of the Strip hotel clubs but is still definitely on the sophisticated side. It has always been known for its great rock music.

VOODOO CAFE & LOUNGE, *The Rio Hotel, Tel. 702/252-7777. Nightly.*

Good bands and good fun in addition to an unforgettable nighttime view of the Strip. There's always live music and enthusiastic patrons. It most certainly is in keeping with the well deserved reputation of the Rio as a place to go to have a good time.

THE VORTEX, *Aladdin*. This combination showroom and nightclub facility was still incomplete at press time but is going to be called **The Vortex**. The nightclub aspect will be in line with some of Las Vegas' other pleasure domes like *Ra*, *C2K* and *Studio 54*. The entertainment seeker coming into town will, therefore, definitely want to check out how developments here play out. This club was scheduled to open sometime during 2001 and, based on reports we've received, should take its place as one of the city's biggest night spots.

Several "local" casino/hotels also have nightclubs that aren't as well known among visitors as the ones we've just listed. Palace Station (**Trax**) and Boulder Station (**Railhead Junction**) are in that category. In addition to the above venues, microbreweries are a popular place to pass some time during the evening when in Las Vegas.

The Monte Carlo was the first of the Strip resorts to have one (**Monte Carlo Pub & Brewery**, *Tel. 702/730-7777*). While that hasn't set a big trend, there are plenty of other of these pubs around. These include the **Holy Cow!**, *2423 Las Vegas Blvd. South, Tel. 702/732-2697*; **Gordon Biersch Brewery**, *3987 Paradise Road, Tel. 702/312-5247*; **Triple 7 Brewpub**, *Main Street Station Hotel, Tel. 702/387-1896*; and **Sunset Brewing Company**, *Sunset Station Hotel, Tel. 702/547-7777*.

GENTLEMEN'S CLUBS

There's no doubt that quite a few men come to Las Vegas with their buddies for a raunchy good time. And Las Vegas obliges as there is no shortage of "gentlemen's clubs" – a nice euphemism for topless go-go bars, nudie clubs or whatever other term you wish to apply.

Clubs are of two basic types: the first is the **topless** joint, indicated by **(T)** in the listings that follow; the other is those where the dancers are totally **nude (N)**. All offer lap dancing. In general, the topless clubs serve all alcoholic beverages while the nude clubs aren't allowed that privilege.

Some of these clubs advertise that they welcome couples. While we're sure they do, you won't find many women guests and we certainly don't recommend that in general. There are, however, a couple of clubs that are "higher class" and do, indeed, see couples in attendance. These more sophisticated clubs are the **Club Paradise** (T), *4416 Paradise Road, Tel. 702/734-5848* and the **Olympic Gardens** (T), *1531 Las Vegas Blvd. South, Tel. 702/385-8987*. Both of these establishments offer, in addition to the usual things found at these clubs, cabaret style entertainment that isn't too bad, talent wise.

Some other popular men's clubs near the Strip and downtown are:
- **Cheetah's** (T), *2112 Western Avenue, Tel. 702/384-0074*
- **Crazy Horse Too** (T), *2476 Industrial Road, Tel. 702/383-8003*
- **Girls of Glitter Gulch** (T), *20 E. Fremont Street, Tel. 702/385-4774*
- **Little Darlings** (N), *1514 Western Avenue, Tel. 702/366-0959*
- **Palomino Club** (N), *1848 Las Vegas Blvd. North, Tel. 702/642-8587*
- **Showgirls** (N), *3247 Industrial Road, Tel. 702/893-3409*
- **Spearmint Rhino** (T), *3344 S. Highland Drive, Tel. 702/796-3600*
- **Talk of the Town** (N), *1238 Las Vegas Blvd. South, Tel. 702/385-1800*
- **Tally-Ho** (N), *2580 S. Highland Drive, Tel. 702/792-9330*
- **Tender Trap** (T), *311 E. Flamingo Road, Tel. 702/732-1111*

And for the Ladies...
With fair play in mind we would be happy to present the flip side of gentlemen's clubs and offer some suggestions for the ladies on the prowl for a fun time. Unfortunately, there aren't any permanent clubs of that genre to choose from. Some of the better-known shows, *Thunder from Down Under*, is not totally nude.

CULTURAL OFFERINGS
While some of the Strip shows (as opposed to strip shows) are truly artistic presentations, the high-brow visitor may still consider them a tad beneath their demeanor. For those unfortunate souls (and others who occasionally like to cultivate their finer side), here's a quick rundown on some other entertainment possibilities.
- **Charleston Heights Arts Center**, *Tel. 702/229-6383*. Theater.
- **Las Vegas Civic Ballet**, *Tel. 702/229-6211*
- **Nevada Dance Theater**, *Tel. 702/895-3827*
- **Nevada Symphony Orchestra**, *Tel. 702/792-4337*
- **University Dance Theater**, *Tel. 702/895-3827*

Two venues for various types of performances are the **Artemus W. Ham Concert Hall**, on the University of Nevada-Las Vegas campus, *4505 S. Maryland Parkway, Tel. 702/895-3801* and the **Nicholas J. Horn Theater** at the Community College of Southern Nevada, *3200 E. Cheyenne Avenue, Tel. 702/651-5483*. Major hotels sometimes present Broadway style productions as do other venues throughout the city. The Aladdin Theater for the Performing Arts is a good example. Scan the entertainment pages of the newspapers for current happenings.

And, while not really a cultural event, we want to report that at press time we have word that **Caesars Magical Empire**, a combination magic show and gourmet dinner ($75 for adults), was scheduled to close in June 2001. However, there is a possibility that it will remain open. Magic lovers might want to check out its status.

14. SHOPPING

As recently as seven years ago there was nothing too special in the way of shopping in Las Vegas. Besides the hotel gift shops and plenty of souvenir joints (most of them offering cheap, tacky merchandise), there wasn't much else to choose from. Oh, sure, you could go to one of a few local malls, but they had the same stores you could find anywhere. In short, Las Vegas was definitely not a shopper's paradise. Boy, has that changed!

Beginning with a few upscale shops called the Appian Way in Caesars Palace and Bally's Avenue Shops arcade, the hotel owners soon realized they had a good idea on their hands. There has literally been an explosion in the growth of hotel shopping on the Strip as well as concurrent growth in malls, outlets, and other types of specialty shopping throughout the Valley. Las Vegas has become a true shopping destination that rivals any city in the world. Yes, the world because you have everything from flea markets like Istanbul's bazaar to the most sophisticated stores that are usually found only on New York's Fifth Avenue, Rodeo Drive in Beverly Hills, or in Paris. The best is on the Strip but the avid shopper will also find much else that is of interest in many other locations throughout Las Vegas. And if you still want that inexpensive trinket to bring back to the folks at the office, you can still find that with great ease.

First we'll take a look at the major shopping arcades, malls and so forth by our usual geographic breakdown. Then we'll move on to some specific store suggestions for the most popular categories of goods that Vegas visitors usually look for.

THE STRIP

Hotel-Based Major Shopping Centers
DESERT PASSAGE (Aladdin).

The newest and largest of the hotel shopping malls, Desert Passage is a fantasy world for both the casual visitor or window shopper and the shopaholic. Although there are quite a few stores with moderate prices the majority are definitely of an upscale nature. Many retailers at the Desert Passage are making their Las Vegas or even American debut at this locale. The choice of restaurants is outstanding, ranging from fast food to gourmet.

Some of the many well known names to be found as you walk through the Desert Passage are **Aveda** and **Bath & Body Works** for your physical well being, **Ann Taylor** and **Eddie Bauer** for clothing and such specialty shops as **Victoria's Secret** (you will see many of the same stores in two or even all three of the big Strip shopping palaces), the **Discovery Channel Store**, **Godiva Chocolates** and **Toys International**. You'll also find some of the finest names in European designer fashion such as **Herve Leger** and **Cesare Paciotti**. Perfume seller **Sephora** has also opened up a branch here. The mall is also filled with kiosk-based retailers who sell everything from the whimsical to the magical. The Dessert Passage charges a $2 fee for valet parking, the only such charge in town to our knowledge. We hope it isn't the start of a new trend.

THE FORUM SHOPS (Caesars Palace).

This was the first of the Strip's premier shopping destinations and is still a number one choice for many shopping-minded visitors. Beyond the spectacular street scene, the talking statues and the impressive fountains that were detailed in the chapter on sightseeing, there are more than 90 stores and restaurants covering just about anything you could imagine. By all accounts the Forum Shops, measured on a sales per square foot basis, is the most successful shopping center in the world. The only thing missing here (and in the other hotel-based malls) is department stores, but who needs them? The unusual is just as easy to find here as is the ordinary, maybe even easier.

Among the most notable and recognizable stores are **Gucci**, **Victoria's Secret**, **FAO Schwarz**, **Gap/Gap Kids**, **The Museum Company**, **Polo Store/Ralph Lauren** and **Ann Taylor**. Other significant merchants include the **Virgin Megastore** and **Nike**. Numerous fine arts stores are located throughout the Forum Shops. You'll find prices reaching to $25,000 or even much higher! There are also many restaurants in the Forum Shops, ranging from **Planet Hollywood** to European style "outdoor" cafes. There's also a deli and ice cream shop. One of the most unusual stores in the mall is **Antiquities**, a natural for the Forum Shops. It features photographs, old time gadgets, movie posters and the like. Much of the merchandise is limited editions signed by famous celebrities (e.g., a negligee worn by Madonna).

The Forum Shops certainly isn't intending to rest on its laurels. A Phase III expansion of the Forum Shops is scheduled to be underway in the very near future and should take about 1-1/2 years to complete.

GRAND CANAL SHOPS (The Venetian).

As was just the case with the two previous listings, we won't bother to repeat from the Seeing the Sights chapter what this place has to offer for the non-shopping visitor's standpoint. If you can drag yourself away from looking at the Venetian street scenes and riding the gondolas along the Grand Canal, you'll notice almost a hundred different places to shop for all sorts of things. Of course, like all good Strip shopping centers, the stores are almost entirely of an upscale nature, so be prepared to spend big bucks. Located above the Venetian's casino, some of the major retailers here include **Movado**, **Cesare Paciotti** (Italian designer fashions), **Donna Karan Coutoure**, **In Celebration of Golf**, **Gallerie San Marco** (art gallery), **Marshall Rousso**, **Toys International**, **Ann Taylor**, **Banana Republic** and **Kids Karnivale**. A place for gorgeous works of porcelain art is **Lladro**.

Two unique stores are worth mentioning here because they offer a true taste of the real Venice. **Il Prato** has a collection of masks and costumes that would make a Renaissance theater patron swell with joy. Then there's **Vipa de Monti**, a store that sells fine Venetian glass in all shapes, sizes and colors. Several of the Venetian's finest restaurants are located within the Grand Canal Shoppes as is a large food court which includes, among many other choices, a kosher-style New York deli. Many of the stores are first timers on the Las Vegas scene and are unknown to shoppers who haven't been to Europe. The Shoppes is also the location for a group of roving entertainers called *Artistie del Arte* who perform Renaissance-style music and comedy in colorful costumes. There are also many fashion related events held here. In addition to the Grand Canal Shoppes, the Venetian also boasts **Sephora**, a leading perfume and cosmetic store from France. Among the treasures here that will certainly interest women shoppers are the *Lipstick Rainbow* collection that offers 365 different shades – one for each day of the year.

TOWER SHOPS (Stratosphere).

The **Tower Shops** were designed by the same folks who brought you the Forum Shops. But the comparison ends there. It is not on the same elaborate level as the Forum Shops or the others listed above. It is not beautiful by any means but we include it here with the major hotel shopping centers because it is the fourth largest – containing more than 50 stores. There is a street theme that has sections for Paris, New York and Hong Kong, but there is a definite down-scaling to the atmosphere. On the other hand, that also applies to the stores so if you're looking for a place to shop that is more affordable, the Tower Shops do present an opportunity for that. Many are recognizable national chains in the moderate price category and the nature of the stores runs the gamut from gifts to clothing. There are also several fast-food establishments.

Other Hotel Shopping Arcades

There's hardly a major hotel that doesn't have some shopping and the failure of an establishment to be listed here isn't meant to imply that there aren't any stores to be found. However, this compilation represents those with at least 20 shops except for a few smaller ones that are notable for some other reason.

Bally's: The **Avenue Shops**, with about 40 stores, is the biggest hotel shopping arcade other than the four major centers just explored. You'll find a slower paced environment to shop for high quality goods. There are also several fast-food eateries located here.

Bellagio: Via Bellagio is the name given to this small but elegant sky-lit shopping street built on the style of the early enclosed shopping malls in Italy. The all-upscale shops here include such famous names as **Tiffany, Georgio Armani, Chanel** and **Hermes**. Several fine restaurants lie either on or beneath the Via Bellagio but this is most definitely not a place for fast-food or snacking.

Excalibur: A range of interesting stores can be found in the **Medieval Village**. This extends onto a promenade that ultimately leads to the moving walkway that connects with the Luxor Hotel. Many of the stores feature gifts themed to the hotel's design, but you will also find clothing stores and other forms of general merchandise. There's a small food court and restaurants.

Luxor: The relatively small but attractive **Giza Galleria** concentrates mostly on Egyptian themed gift items. While a couple of places here have prices that are in outer space, a more reasonable range can be found at the colorful **Cairo Bazaar**.

MGM Grand: This gigantic hotel has two separate shopping areas. **Star Lane** is located on the lower level from the main lobby and connects the hotel with the monorail station. It contains about a dozen shops of varying types but is geared mainly toward the souvenir hunter. Nicer and pricier is the **Studio Walk**. This promenade has clothing and gift shops as well as art galleries and assorted other retailers along with many of the hotel's better restaurants. There's also a large food court.

Paris: There are more than a dozen shops along **Le Boulevard**, which has an assortment of retailers in a lovely atmosphere that does a fine job of continuing the French theme at this hotel. Many of the shops have French names with cute plays on words that incorporate the type of merchandise sold.

Riviera: This venerable hotel has more than 20 stores in a shopping arcade behind the main casino. It's not anything visually but there is a good mix of pricing and merchandise to be found.

While the above constitute the rest of the biggest and the best of the hotel shopping arcades, they aren't the only ones by any means. Shopping can be found in just about all of the major hotels. Those with the next tier of good shopping include Circus Circus (on the promenade outside of the theme park entrance), the Flamingo Las Vegas, the Mirage, Monte Carlo (**Street of Dreams**), New York, New York, and Treasure Island. We also need to mention that shopping at Caesars is not limited to the Forum Shops. You can also visit the highly upscale **Appian Way** shops for fine fashions and art works.

Non-Hotel Strip Shopping

The hotels definitely offer the most interesting shopping on the Strip. The remainder generally consists of cheap gift shops and the like. However, one big exception to this is the **Fashion Show Mall**, *3200 Las Vegas Blvd. South, across the street from Treasure Island, Tel. 702/369-8382.* Here you will find mostly upscale shopping in an attractive setting that houses more than 130 stores including small boutiques and large department stores like **Saks**, **Nieman-Marcus,**, **Macy's** and **Dillard's**. The Strip entrance to the mall has a few visual novelties including an Italian restaurant with a huge painting of the Mona Lisa. On the opposite side is the **Dive!** restaurant, which is shaped like the front of a submarine and periodically makes diving sounds. The mall has a large food court.

The Fashion Show is now in the process of a major expansion which is supposed to include, besides many other stores, several Strip style "attractions." We await further word on the details. The expansion will more than double the size of the mall and will be completed in phases from late in 2001 through 2003.

The **Showcase** isn't exactly a shopping center in the usual sense of the word, but you can refresh your memory by referring back to the Seeing the Sights chapter for what's inside. There is also a multi-screen cinema on the premises, but why anyone would come to Las Vegas and want to take in a movie is quite beyond us.

OFF-STRIP

Other than some typical local strip malls there isn't too much in the vicinity of the Strip to offer shoppers. The notable exception is the 22 store shopping center in the Rio's exciting **Masquerade Village**. If you're not to busy watching the Sky Parade or gambling, you can check out some of the nice and mostly very upscale shops. There's also a small food court as well as some better restaurants. The **Las Vegas Hilton** has a nice selection of stores that include several for children's items such as clothing and toys. And most of them aren't *Star Trek* linked.

DOWNTOWN

The Fremont Street Experience is home to, besides hotels, plenty of small stores that specialize in gifts and souvenirs. Not far from downtown lies Vegas' antique row, although most of the stores are scattered over a fairly broad area. Many are located along **East Charleston Boulevard** and they sell all manner of collectibles from all over the world, not just from Las Vegas' short but glorious past.

AROUND LAS VEGAS

Two major regional shopping malls are located not far from the Strip or downtown. The first is **The Boulevard Mall**, *3528 Maryland Parkway, Tel. 702/735-8268*. The stores are mostly the usual national chains but they are generally less expensive than shopping at Strip hotels. The department stores are **Dillard's, Macy's, Sears** and **JC Penny**. The mall has a huge food court if you get hungry. The **Meadows Mall**, *4300 Meadows Lane, Tel. 702/878-4849*, has 150 stores on two levels, including four department stores and a food court. For the most part the stores at the Meadows are a little more down-scale from those at the Boulevard but, again, most are the usual national chains.

If you're looking for outlet stores then try the **Belz Factory Outlet World**, a little south of the Strip at *Las Vegas Boulevard South and Warm Springs Road, Tel. 702/896-5599*. With about 160 stores, this is one of the biggest outlet malls in the country. A lot of people swear by the great buys at these type of places. We're not so sure about that but if you just like to shop then it's worth taking the short ride to Belz. It's especially good for apparel shopping. **Saks Fifth Avenue** is among the stores having an outlet here. There are two food courts in this very long single level mall. The 60 stores of **Vegas Point Plaza** are located at *9155 Las Vegas Blvd. South*. One of the problems here, besides the fact that it is a little further from the Strip than its neighbor Belz, is that it isn't enclosed so that summer shopping is definitely on the toasty side.

We also have to mention the **Fantastic Indoor Swap Meet**, *1717 S. Decatur Blvd. at Oakey, Tel. 702/877-0087*. Open only on weekends (extended days during the Christmas shopping season), this gigantic flea market houses hundreds of booths. You can find clothing as well as gift items, and a plethora of unusual things. It makes a great place to browse even if you aren't planning on buying anything. Locals shop here in droves because you can often get some really good buys. Food court on the premises. Las Vegas has several other flea markets but this one is the best.

HENDERSON

The Henderson building boom has certainly included plenty of new shopping areas. For the most part the opportunities are the major national retailers that you see just about everywhere else. The major shopping area is located along **Sunset Road** from Green Valley east to I-515. **Stephanie Stree**t both north and south of the intersection of Sunset also has lots of stores. Within the Sunset corridor is the **Galleria at Sunset Mall**, *Tel. 702/434-0202*. The two-level mall has about 130 stores in a brightly sky-lit facility that is the most attractive of the regular malls in the Valley. The decor is colorful with a hint of southwestern. They also have a 600-seat food court with pretty topiary and other plantings.

I'M LOOKING FOR....

Besides the usual souvenirs that travelers are always hunting for (and which we'll make some suggestions on in the section that follows), visitors to Las Vegas seem most interested in apparel, works of art, jewelry, Native American and southwestern items, and western wear. We won't even bother mentioning any apparel stores beyond the one's previously listed in the bigger Strip hotel malls because there are so many. They include all of the national names plus scores of local places in addition to the fanciest names in the industry. However, we will remind you that unless you're looking to make an expensive fashion statement, you're better off shopping for clothing away from stores in Strip hotels.

Art

The Forum Shops are home to some of the finest art galleries in Las Vegas. These include the **Galleria di Sorrento** and the **Galierie Lassen**. Caesars Palace also has the **Gallerie Michelangelo**, located near the entrance to the Palace Tower. Another excellent place to purchase fine art is the **Passman Gallery** located in the Masquerade Village of the Rio Hotel (another branch at the Aladdin). Desert Passage has **Addi Galleries**, **Z Gallerie**, **Gallery of Legends** and **Thomas Kinkade at Le Gallerie Luministe**. Luministe also has locations at the Fashion Outlet and at the Galleria at Sunset in Henderson. Las Vegas-based **Ron Lee's World of Clowns**, who you read about in Chapter 12, is also represented at the Desert Passage. Besides the aforementioned **Lladro**, you'll find **Wentworth Gallery** and **Regis Galerie** at the Grand Canal Shoppes.

Getting away from hotel shopping, you can choose from a wide selection at **Debora Spanover Fine Art**, *1775 E. Tropicana Avenue*; the **Art Encounter**, *3979 Spring Mountain Road*; and **Carrara Galleries**, *1236 S. Rainbow Boulevard*. If you're specifically looking for Egyptian artwork then there are several places in the Luxor. Not to be left out, neighboring Mandalay Bay has the **Galerie Renaissance**. The **Crystal Galleria** in the

Forum Shops has a wonderful selection of beautiful items if you're looking for quality glass and crystal.

Jewelry

Every hotel shopping mall and arcade seems to have several jewelers, as do all of the local malls. **Jewels of the Nile** in the Luxor and **Tiffany & Company** or **Fred Leighton**, both in the Bellagio, are among these. The Forum Shops has **Hyde Park Jewelers**, and the Grand Canal Shoppes has at least a half dozen fine jewelry stores including **Ca'd'Oro** and **Venetzia**. In case you don't have a fortune to spend, try **Agatha** which features beautiful versions of fine European jewelry that are too nice to call costume jewelry. Not to be left out of the fine jewelry scene is the Desert Passage that boasts **Ancient Creations** and **Clio Blue Paris**.

The Rio has several fine jewelers including **Diamonds International**. However, assuming you're not in the category of the visitor who has thousands or maybe tens of thousands to spend on the finest jewelry, you can turn to **M.J. Christensen** with locations in most major area malls, and the **Tower of Jewels**, several locations in malls. You can also find a good selection at reasonable prices at **Tiffin's** in the Boulevard Mall.

Native American Goods/Southwestern Crafts

The selection is not that great in Vegas. This is the southwest but it isn't Arizona or New Mexico. A few places that come to mind are **Amanda's**, *9155 Las Vegas Blvd. South;* **Viva Southwest**, *1226 S. Rainbow Blvd.*; **Nava Hopi Gallery**, *Galleria at Sunset Mall;* and **West of Santa Fe** in the Forum Shops. You can also find several merchants selling this genre of goods in the **Fantastic Indoor Swap Meet**. Finally, **El Portal Gifts**, downtown on the *Fremont Street Experience*, has an excellent selection.

Western Wear

Two places with boots in their name sell a lot more than footwear. These are **Cowtown Boots**, *2989 Paradise Road*, and the **Boot Barn**, *7265 Las Vegas Blvd. South*. Three well known places with the local western shoppers are **Sheplers**, *3025 E. Tropicana Avenue or 4700 W. Sahara Avenue;* **Adam's Western Store**, *1415 Western Avenue;* and **Miller Stockman**. The last retailer has locations in the Fashion Show, Meadows and Galleria Malls. **West of Santa Fe** (Forum Shops) also has a decent selection of western wear in addition to southwestern and Native American goods.

HOW ABOUT THOSE SOUVENIRS?

It's only natural to want to bring home a souvenir of Las Vegas for your friends and family or to put on display in your own home. The choices are endless. Just about every hotel has a gift shop which has their logo on everything from tee shirts to glasses to you name it. Prices do vary quite a bit and, surprisingly, things aren't always the highest in the more expensive hotels. Shop around and look for your favorites before you buy.

You can get "generic" Las Vegas stuff in scores of gift shops that are scattered on the Strip but even more so in downtown on Fremont Street. Although some of the merchandise is quality, things are generally chintzier in these stores than in the hotel shops. A store that bills itself as the world's largest gift shop is **Bonanza**, *2400 Las Vegas Blvd. South at the intersection of Sahara Avenue*. We don't know if it actually is the largest but the size of the selection (which ranges from junk to good quality) is impressive. When our visitors have been having trouble finding what they want we usually wind up at Bonanza and, more often than not, they find what they're looking for.

GAMBLING PARAPHERNALIA

If you're looking for something to bring home, how about a slot machine (either mini or full sized)? Or a poker table. Maybe just some authentic Las Vegas chips. They're all available for sale in several places that sell to the pros as well as to the casual visitor. When buying gaming equipment please be aware of restrictions that may be imposed by the state in which you live, even if it's for private use. Store personnel can assist you with this.

*The biggest gaming equipment emporiums are the **Gambler's General Store**, 800 South Main Street, Tel. 702/382-9903; the **Bud Jones Company**, 3640 S. Valley View Blvd., Tel. 702/876-2782; **Showcase Slots & Antiquities**, 4305 Industrial Road, Tel. 702/740-5722 and **Paul-Son Gaming Supplies**, 2121 Industrial Road, Tel. 702/384-2425. All of these places can sell you slot machines, chips, dice, gaming furniture, books and much more. Speaking of books, if you want literature on gaming or Las Vegas, then check out the **Gambler's Book Club**, 630 S. 11th Street, Tel. 702/382-7555. Serving gamblers since 1964, it has the best and most extensive selection of gaming books in the country. The staff is friendly and knowledgeable and can direct you to just what you're looking for.*

*Finally, if you're looking for old time slot machines then you should visit the **House of Antique Slots**, 1243 Las Vegas Blvd. South, Tel. 702/382-1520. Casino clothing is available from **Dealers Room Casino Clothiers**, 3507 S. Maryland Parkway, Tel. 702/732-3932. This is a great place for those of you have fantasies of dressing like a real-live dealer or croupier on Bingo Night or poker night with the folks back home.*

15. SPORTS & RECREATION

For fun in the sun there are few other major cities in America that can offer the variety of sports and recreational activities that Las Vegas does. There are even some professional and college spectator sports. Whichever sport you like to play, or whatever sport you like to watch, you should have no trouble finding something fun to suit your needs...assuming it isn't ice fishing!

And to make things even more enticing to the recreational enthusiast, Las Vegas is a place where you can partake in outdoor activity at any time of the year. It's possible to go skiing down the snowy slopes in Lee Canyon on a winter morning and to water ski that same afternoon on Lake Mead. Such are the pleasures of Las Vegas. The winters are mild enough to get out on the golf course and even the summer, with its dry heat, doesn't deter too many people from physical activity. We should, however, remind and caution those who aren't accustomed to the heat to take it slowly and try, whenever possible, to restrict strenuous activity to the morning hours (or after dark where available).

Here's a sport-by-sport rundown on the action.

BICYCLING

We don't suggest taking a casual bike ride up the Strip. But, if you do like to ride your bike, the Las Vegas area does have some great places. Red Rock Canyon is a fabulous spot to pedal as are many of the less crowded portions of the Lake Mead National Recreation Area. Bike lanes are common throughout the area but many of the Valley's residential communities have bike paths. These can be found in Summerlin and to an even greater extent in Henderson which has miles of trails already in use and many more under construction or in planning. For information on the latter, contact the **Henderson Department of Parks and Recreation**, *Tel. 702/565-2063.*

An interesting biking adventure is provided by **Downhill Bicycling Tours**, *Tel. 702/897-8287.* They'll bus you 18 miles from Las Vegas to the 8,000-foot elevation and from there you return by bike, all either downhill or on level ground.

BOATING

Boating choices in the greater Las Vegas area are pretty simple: if you want it close by then go to **Lake Mead**. There are six marinas to choose from within the National Recreation Area. For those without their own boat, the **Lake Mead Lodge**, *322 Lakeshore Road, Boulder City, Tel. 702/ 293-3484*, is very accessible and has a good selection of watercraft for rental.

If you're willing to drive a little further, boating is also available either on Lake Mohave or on the Colorado River, both accessible from Laughlin, about a 90-minute drive from Vegas. Call or visit the **Laughlin Visitor Center**, *1555 S. Casino Drive, Tel. 702/298-3321 or 800/LAUGHLIN.*

BOWLING

The biggest and best bowling alleys in the Las Vegas area are located in some of the casino hotels. Although none are on the Strip itself, there are several that are within a short distance. All of them are open 24 hours a day, just in case you get the urge to throw a few strikes at three in the morning:
- **Castaways**, *2800 Fremont Street. Tel. 702/385-9153.* 106 lanes. Site of some major tournaments.
- **Gold Coast**, *4000 W. Flamingo Road. Tel. 702/367-4700.* 72 lanes.
- **The Orleans**, *4500 W. Tropicana Avenue. Tel. 702/367-4700.* 70 lanes.
- **Sam's Town**, *5111 Boulder Highway. Tel. 702/454-8023.* 56 lanes. Between midnight and 4am this bowling alley takes on the atmosphere of a night club with laser lights and music. That's sure different but if you're a serious bowler we don't see how it can help improve your game.
- **Santa Fe Station**, *4949 N. Rancho Drive. Tel. 702/658-4995.* 60 lanes. This one is a little bit further from the Strip than the others but it isn't far if you're staying downtown.
- **Suncoast**, *9090 Alta Drive. Tel. 702/636-7111.* 64 lanes. Saturday nights are a little on the style of the "nightclub" bowling at Sam's Town.
- **Texas Station**, *2101 Texas Star Lane. Tel. 702/631-1000.* 60 lanes. In keeping with the latest trend, this newest of the hotel bowling facilities also has "nightclub" aspects after hours on the weekends.

BUNGEE JUMPING

Las Vegas isn't New Zealand when it comes to bungee jumping but you can try out **A.J. Hackett Bungee**, *810 Circus Circus Drive (adjacent to the Circus Circus Hotel), Tel. 702/385-4321.* They have a 201-foot high tower with a double bungee deck. An elevator takes you up to the jump-off point. Jumping is available day and night. The price is $49 for the first jump and $25 for each additional jump. A.J. always also throws in a gift for the jumpers. It could be a tee shirt, a bottle of beer or who knows what else.

GOLF

The Vegas area has some of the finest golfing in the Southwest. There are more than 30 major golf clubs, private and public. The surrounding areas also have some good venues including one in Mesquite, about 77 miles northeast, or in Primm, 40 miles southwest.

The list below contains all of the major courses that are open to the general public, at least on a limited basis. Many of them are, however, private so it is best to call in advance for more exact information on access. If you are staying at a hotel that doesn't have its own golf course (or one that it is affiliated with), you should inquire with the concierge or guest service office about golfing opportunities since all of the major hotels can arrange for a spot for you to play somewhere.

Another way to ensure getting a spot on the links is to contact **Las Vegas Preferred Tee-Times**, *Tel. 702/893-9008 or 888/FOUR-TEE.* Another such service is **Golf Reservations of Nevada**, *Tel. 800/597-2794.* These organizations will arrange guaranteed tee times at the best courses in Las Vegas, including access to some private clubs you may not otherwise be able to get into that aren't included on the list that follows. Transportation is provided.

- **Angel Park Golf Club**, *100 S. Rampart Blvd. Tel. 702/254-4653.* 36 holes.
- **Badlands Golf Club**, *9119 Alta Drive (Summerlin). Tel. 702/562-9505.* 18 holes.
- **Bali Hai Golf Club**, *Las Vegas Blvd. South (immediately south of Mandalay Bay, on the Strip). Tel. 888/397-2499.* 18 holes. Brand new.
- **Black Mountain Golf & Country Club**, *501 Country Club Drive, Henderson. Tel. 702/565-7933.* 18 holes.
- **Boulder City Municipal Golf Course**, *1 Clubhouse Drive, Boulder City. Tel. 702/293-9236.* 18 holes. Very reasonably priced.
- **Callaway Golf Center**, *Las Vegas Blvd. South at Sunset Road. Tel. 702/896-4100.* 9 holes, but extremely convenient to Strip hotels. Lighted for night play.
- **Craig Ranch Golf Course**, *628 W. Craig Road. Tel. 702/642-9700.* 18 holes.

- **Desert Inn Country Club**, *3145 Las Vegas Blvd. South.* This course used to be part of the Desert Inn Hotel which is now closed, but the course remains open. Reservations of six months in advance are suggested. 18 holes.
- **Desert Pines Golf Club**, *3415 East Bonanza Road. Tel. 702/450-8000 or 888/397-2499.* 18 holes.
- **Desert Rose Golf Course**, *5843 Club House Drive. Tel. 702/431-4653.* 18 holes.
- **Las Vegas National Golf Club**, *1911 E. Desert Inn Road. Tel. 702/734-1796.* 18 holes.
- **Legacy Golf Club**, *130 Par Excellence Drive, Henderson. Tel. 702/897-2187.* 18 holes.
- **Los Prados Golf & Country Club**, *5150 Los Prados Circle. Tel. 702/645-5696.* 18 holes.
- **North Las Vegas Golf Course**, *324 E. Brooks Ave., North Las Vegas. Tel. 702/649-7171.* 9 holes.
- **Painted Desert Country Club**, *5555 Painted Mirage Drive. Tel. 702/645-2570.* 18 holes.
- **Reflection Bay Golf Club**, *Lake Las Vegas Resort, Henderson. Tel. 702/740-GOLF or 877/698-GOLF.* 18 holes.
- **Rhodes Ranch Golf Club**, *920 Rhodes Ranch Parkway. Tel. 702/740-1414.* 18 holes.
- **Rio Secco**, *2851 Grand Hills Drive, Henderson. Tel. 702/889-2400.* 18 holes.
- **Siena Golf Club**, *Town Center Drive (Summerlin). Tel. 702/341-9200.* 18 holes.
- **Stallion Mountain Country Club**, *5500 E. Flamingo Road. Tel. 702/436-7000.* 18 holes.
- **Tournament Players Club**, *9851 Canyon Run Drive. Tel. 702/256-2000.* 18 holes.
- **Wild Horse Golf Club**, *2100 W. Warm Springs Road, Henderson. Tel. 702/434-9000 or 800/884-1818.* 18 holes.

HIKING

Some of the best hiking in the area is in the **Red Rock Canyon National Conservation Area**. Rock climbing is also a popular activity here. The **Lake Mead National Recreation Area** also has some good hiking possibilities but many of them are quite difficult. Get information at the Alan Bible Visitor Center on US 93 south of Boulder City. Again, due to the extreme summer heat, be sure to carry plenty of drinking water, protect yourself from the sun as much as possible and try to do the most strenuous hiking in the morning. A better idea altogether is to hike during the cooler months.

A great place for easier hiking (really walking) is on the **River Mountains Trail**. Built partly as a barrier between the mountains and developed areas, the concept has been so popular that it is being extended to surround the entire River Mountains. A large section in Henderson is already open but when the 30-mile long trail system is completed it will actually be possible to walk from Las Vegas through Henderson and the Lake Mead National Recreation Area all the way to beyond Boulder City and to Hoover Dam.

HORSEBACK RIDING

Red Rock Canyon is the venue of choice in the greater Las Vegas area for those who want to stay close to town and like to ride. Horses can be rented there from **Cowboy Trail Rides**, *Tel. 702/387-2457* or at nearby **Bonnie Springs Ranch**, *Tel. 702/875-4191*. If you want to travel a little further, then visit the **Mount Charleston Riding Stables**, *Tel. 702/872-7009*. The weather is a lot cooler at the latter location.

HOT AIR BALLOONS

We have selected only those operators that have been around long enough to have established a reliable record. All of them offer a variety of standard and customized tours with features like champagne, sunrise and sunset flights, and hotel pick-up. Prices are fairly similar as well so you can just take your pick. Balloon flights explore the surrounding desert as well as the urban area.

- **Adventure Balloon Tours**, *Tel. 702/382-5325 or 800/346-6444*
- **Balloon Las Vegas Tours**, *Tel. 702/596-7582*
- **Desert Star Hot Air Balloon Tours**, *Tel. 702/240-9007*
- **D & R Balloons**, *Tel. 702/248-7609*
- **Holiday Balloon Company**, *Tel. 702/616-2291*
- **Ultimate Balloon Adventure**, *Tel. 702/869-9999*

RAFTING

Due south of Hoover Dam you can take the **Black Canyon River Raft Tour**, 3-1/2 hours of floating fun on the lower Colorado River and Lake Mojave. The trip begins at the base of mighty Hoover Dam and winds past stunning canyon lands. It's a great way to see the magnificent landscapes of this portion of the southwest. You might catch a glimpse of bighorn sheep as well as seeing natural hot springs. This is not a white water experience (of which there are none available near to Las Vegas), so it is suitable even for the previously uninitiated rafter.

The expedition depot is located at: *1297 Nevada Highway (US 93) in Boulder City. Tel. 702/293-3776 or 800/696-7238. Reservations are suggested.*

The price is $65 per person including lunch. They'll pick you up at your hotel for an extra $15.

SKIING & ICE SKATING

Even though the majority of people don't think of Las Vegas when it comes to winter sports, if you're here in the winter months you can take advantage of some great cross-country and alpine skiing. Both can be found in the Mount Charleston area in the Toiyabe National Forest. The **Lee Canyon Ski Area**, *State Highway 156; Tel. 702/872-5462 or 702/646-0008,* is located just under 50 miles from the Strip. They have double chair lifts on each of Lee Canyon's four runs. The runs are named, Highroller, Blackjack, Keno and Slot Alley! What else would you expect – this is still Vegas. Base elevation is 8,500 feet.

Ice skating has become quite popular among the locals so visitors will have no difficulty in finding a place to lace up and take to the ice. Rinks include:

- **Crystal Palace Skating Centers**, *4680 Boulder Highway, Tel. 702/458-7107; 3901 Rancho Drive, Tel. 702/645-4892; and 9295 W. Flamingo Road, Tel. 702/235-9832*
- **Las Vegas Ice Gardens**, *3896 Swenson Street. Tel. 702/731-1208*
- **Sahara Ice Palace**, *953 E. Sahara Avenue. Tel. 702/862-4262*
- **Santa Fe Station Ice Arena**, *Rancho at US 95 North (in the Santa Fe Station Hotel). Tel. 702/658-4993*

SKY DIVING

While this certainly isn't a mainstream recreational activity, it's been around in Vegas for quite a few years and seems to do okay. **A Skydive Las Vegas** provides a 20-minute lesson before taking you up in a jet to 13,000 feet where you jump out and go into a 45-second free-fall before opening your chute and taking the six minute ride back to earth. *Tel. 702/293-1860* for information on prices and transportation as well as reservations.

A little closer to earth is **Flyaway Indoor Skydiving**, *200 Convention Center Drive.* You can experience body flight in a wind tunnel after receiving instruction. *Tel. 702/731-4768 for times. The price is $35 per person.*

SPECTATOR SPORTS

PROFESSIONAL SPORTS

Auto Racing: The **Las Vegas International Motor Speedway**, *7000 Las Vegas Blvd. North, Tel. 800/644-4444*, is located in the northern part of the Valley via I-15 to Exit 54. The 1,500 acre complex opened in 1996 and has been successful in attracting a number of prestigious auto racing events, including the famous Winston Cup Series. Among the facilities are a campground and RV park and even a wedding chapel for those who want to marry and ride.

Baseball: The **Las Vegas 51s** of the Pacific Coast League (the highest level of minor league play) take to the diamond just a few blocks north of the downtown Casino Center at *Cashman Field, 850 Las Vegas Blvd. North; Tel. 702/386-7200*. The season runs from April to September and you can watch the game close-up from any seat in this attractive little stadium. If you've never been to a minor league game, check it out. Everyone has fun regardless of who wins. Prior to the 2001 season the team was known as the *Stars*. We hope the stupid alien-oriented new nickname doesn't scare away the fans.

Basketball: The basketball fans in Vegas seem to love only their college team. Minor league pro clubs come and go faster than you can say Michael Jordan. Scan the newspapers to see if there is any current pro action while you're in town.

Boxing: No city in the United States is a hotbed for boxing more than Las Vegas is. Of course, a big part of that popularity comes from people with full pockets who pay huge sums to get into the fights and then wager even bigger sums on the outcome. Some of the sports' most important matches are held in Las Vegas. Popular venues are the MGM Grand Garden Arena, the Special Events Center at Mandalay Bay and the Thomas & Mack Center on the UNLV campus.

Football: We can say with some certainty that you'll never see an NFL franchise in Las Vegas as long as there is wagering on the sport, but the new eight-team **XFL** (Xtreme Football League) isn't as conventional. The initial season is 2001 and will run from February through April so as not to compete with the NFL. The **Las Vegas Outlaws**, *Tel. 702/24-BLITZ*, play at Sam Boyd Stadium. Refreshingly, the maximum single game ticket price is only $25. Now you *really* know that it isn't the NFL!

Hockey: For past visiting hockey fans who are wondering what happened to the **Las Vegas Thunder**, alas, they are no more. However, several groups are working to bring minor league hockey back to Las Vegas so if you are here during the winter, check the newspapers. Who knows, maybe there will be a team by then.

Rodeo: Although there are several professional rodeo events in Las Vegas at various times during the year, "the" big event takes place during the early part of December when the **National Finals Rodeo** comes to town. The most important competitions are held at the Thomas & Mack Center but other venues are used as well. This is a popular event, so reservations for hotels as well as the rodeo should be made as far in advance as possible.

COLLEGE SPORTS

The **University of Nevada-Las Vegas**, commonly known by all as **UNLV**, conducts a full schedule of men's and women's intercollegiate sports. The most popular from a spectators's point of view are men's basketball and football. The **Runnin' Rebels** play their basketball at the aforementioned Thomas & Mack Center, a short ride from the Strip. The team has had its share of success, including an NCAA Championship. They aren't that good right now but are very competitive.

The football team plays at **Sam Boyd Stadium**, *7000 E. Russell Road, just off of Boulder Highway*. For many years (actually, the entire 1990's) they were a woeful excuse for a football team and wins were few and far between. They are slowly getting their act together and now have reached a level where you can go to a game and at least have a reasonable chance of winning. Tickets are reasonable and you can almost always get good seats. Basketball tickets are much harder to come by. For information and tickets for all UNLV sporting events, contact the Thomas & Mack box office, *Tel. 702/895-3900*.

MORE ABOUT UNLV

*This seems to be a good place to let you know a little about the state's largest university. Known to many people for its winning basketball teams under former flamboyant towel-chewing coach, Jerry "the Shark" Tarkanian, **UNLV** actually has a good academic program as well. The campus of this publicly supported institution is spread out over 335 acres and has about 20,000 students enrolled. In addition to the many sporting events at the Thomas & Mack, the university has a full program of cultural events, some of which you can read about in the 'Nightlife & Entertainment' chapter. The university is one of the few to offer a School of Hotel Administration, many of whose graduates help run the hotels and casinos in Las Vegas and other gambling destinations throughout the country.*

SWIMMING

Although there are quite a few municipal swimming pools for residents, it doesn't pay to even mention them here because there's scarcely a hotel or motel that doesn't have a pool for its guests. Those who like a real beach can take a drive out to the Lake Mead National Recreation Area where **Boulder Beach** can fill the bill. It's open all year but the water and air can be kind of chilly during the winter. Likewise, some hotels don't keep their pools open during the short winter season. You can count on all of them being available at least from April through October. Indoor swimming pools in hotels are quite rare in Las Vegas. If you do visit during the winter and your hotel pool is closed, then check the telephone directory for the nearest municipal pool.

TENNIS

There are no fewer than 350 tennis courts in and around the city. Many of the hotels offer tennis courts, particularly on the Strip, but priority is almost always given to guests. If tennis is an important part of your vacation plans you should consider staying at a hotel that has its own courts.

Hotel Tennis Courts
- **Alexis Park**, *375 E. Harmon Ave., Tel. 702/796-3300.* Two lighted outdoor courts.
- **Bally's**, *3645 Las Vegas Blvd. S., Tel. 702/739-4111.* Eight lighted outdoor courts.
- **Caesars Palace**, *3570 Las Vegas Blvd. S., Tel. 702/731-7786.* Three lighted outdoor courts.
- **Flamingo Las Vegas**, *3555 Las Vegas Blvd. S., Tel. 702/733-3111.* Four outdoor lighted courts.
- **Jackie Gaughan's Plaza Hotel**, *1 Main Street, Tel. 702/386-2110.* Four lighted outdoor courts.
- **Las Vegas Hilton**, *3000 Paradise Road, Tel. 702/732-5111.* Six lighted outdoor courts.
- **Monte Carlo**, *3770 Las Vegas Blvd. S., Tel. 702/730-7777.* Three lighted outdoor courts.
- **New Frontier**, *3120 Las Vegas Blvd. S., Tel. 702/794-8200.* Two lighted outdoor courts.
- **Riviera**, *2901 Las Vegas Blvd. S., Tel. 702/734-5110.* Two lighted outdoor courts.
- **Tropicana**, *3801 Las Vegas Blvd. S., Tel. 702/739-2645.* Four lighted outdoor courts.

Public & Private Tennis Courts
- **Las Vegas Racquet Club**, *3333 W. Raven. Tel. 702/362-2202*
- **Pro Tennis**, *3000 Joe W. Brown Drive. Tel. 702/732-1861*
- **Quail Ridge Estates Tennis Club**, *1 Goldfinch Avenue, Henderson. Tel. 702/456-0300*
- **Sports Club**, *Sunset Road & Eastern Avenue, Henderson. Tel. 702/260-9803*
- **Twin Lakes Racquet Club**, *3075 W. Washington Blvd. Tel. 702/647-3434*
- **UNLV**, *4505 S. Maryland Parkway. Tel. 702/895-3240*

A FINAL NOTE

The **All-American SportsPark**, *121 E. Sunset Road (corner of Las Vegas Blvd. South), was an unusual sports participation facility with something for just about everyone including a "stadium" where you could play baseball like a major leaguer in front of an authentic looking scoreboard, pool tables, rock climbing wall and a NASCAR Speedpark. It closed in early 2001 because of lack of interest but they hope to reopen again. So, if this is your type of game, then check out the current status.*

16. EXCURSIONS & DAY TRIPS

If you've come all this way to Las Vegas and never leaver the Strip, or the city for that matter, you'll be missing out on a beautiful part of the country. You don't have to travel all the way to the **Grand Canyon** to see some breathtaking sights – they're all around you, most within an hours' drive or less. The purple hues of **Mt. Charleston** in twilight, the incredible workmanship of **Hoover Dam**, the stillness of early morning in the **Valley of Fire** – these and more are all scenes that are not what leap to mind when your friends or loved one says to you: "Let's go to Vegas."

But the majesty of the southwest's mountains and canyons is an integral part of the Las Vegas scene, perhaps not as much as the neon and glitz of Casinoland, but almost. The area attractions are as exciting and interesting as you'll find anywhere. Our strong recommendation is to take a spin out to some of the sights and soak up a day or two of the great outdoors. Man-made sites are also numerous and of great interest.

Depending on your travel style, you can either rent a car and see the sights yourself, or go on one of the many tours that depart Las Vegas for area excursions. A number of the tours can be done in well under a day, while some are two days or even more. We'll show you all the possibilities in this chapter. If you do decide on the guided tour route then check back in Chapter 8 for a listing of some tour operators.

Or, just dance on down to the lobby of just about any hotel in town. There will likely either be a tour desk that can make all the arrangements for you or at least plenty of brochures on tour companies anxiously awaiting your business that you can contact yourself.

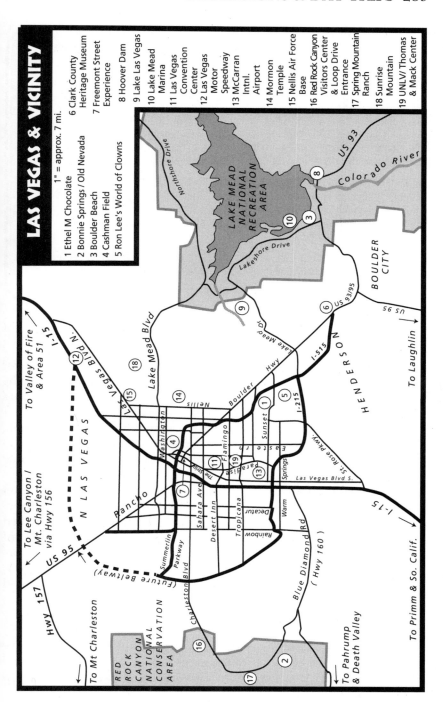

LAS VEGAS & VICINITY

1" = approx. 7 mi.

1 Ethel M Chocolate
2 Bonnie Springs / Old Nevada
3 Boulder Beach
4 Cashman Field
5 Ron Lee's World of Clowns
6 Clark County Heritage Museum
7 Freemont Street Experience
8 Hoover Dam
9 Lake Las Vegas
10 Lake Mead Marina
11 Las Vegas Convention Center
12 Las Vegas Motor Speedway
13 McCarran Intnl. Airport
14 Mormon Temple
15 Nellis Air Force Base
16 Red Rock Canyon Visitors Center & Loop Drive Entrance
17 Spring Mountain Ranch
18 Sunrise Mountain
19 UNLV/ Thomas & Mack Center

TRAVEL DISTANCES TO AREA EXCURSIONS

All distances are one-way from the center of the Strip:

Area 51	*160 miles*
Bonnie Springs Ranch	*19 miles*
Death Valley (Furnace Creek)	*129 miles*
Grand Canyon-North Rim	*307 miles*
Grand Canyon-South Rim	*290 miles*
Hoover Dam	*30 miles*
Lake Mead Marina	*38 miles*
Laughlin	*90 miles*
Mt. Charleston	*34 miles*
Primm	*40 miles*
Red Rock Canyon	*16 miles*
Spring Mountain State Park	*20 miles*
Valley of Fire State Park	*52 miles*
Zion National Park	*175 miles*

HOOVER DAM

This is by far the most popular out-of-town destination for visitors to Las Vegas and, by itself, can be done in about four hours. **Hoover Dam**, about 45 minutes away by car, is one of the great architectural triumphs of the early twentieth century. The dam, known for its first twelve years as Boulder Dam (due to its location in Boulder Canyon), provides about five billion kilowatt-hours of electricity a year to three states: Nevada, Arizona and California. Situated a few miles past Boulder City, a visit to Hoover Dam is a must-see for visitors who want to see more than three kings and a pair of tens (well, that would be a pretty nice sight too).

The dam is 726 feet high with a base 660 feet thick. It's made of seven million tons of concrete and 18 million tons of reinforced steel. Thousands of workers labored five years and 94 construction workers died before the Dam was finished in 1935. In 1955, the American Society of Civil Engineers officially declared it one of the seven engineering wonders of the world.

The mighty **Colorado River**, responsible for the creation of Grand Canyon, is diverted here and the dammed-up result is **Lake Mead** (see below).

Guided tours of the dam (highly recommended) are offered. These tours take you down to the base and through tunnels to the impressive power house where the force of the water rotates the huge turbines that generate the electric power. Tours last about 45 minutes and begin with a brief introductory film. A "hard-hat" tour takes visitors further behind the scenes for those who are more interested in the workings of the dam. You can sometimes expect to encounter big crowds and a fairly long wait for the tours, so it is advisable to get here early in the day.

In addition to the tours you can visit the modern and sleek gold glass colored visitor center (no charge) where you can view interesting exhibits on the construction of the dam. It's also an unforgettable experience to walk along the top crest of the dam to view the lake on one side and the deep gorge into which the Colorado River flows on the other side. The dam itself is located within a forbidding canyon.

You can get some good views of it on the way down to the dam via a series of switchbacks, but even better views are available if you drive across the crest to the Arizona side of the border. There are several small parking areas with overlooks that provide spectacular views. *Tel. 702/293-8321. The visitor center is open daily (except Christmas) from 8:30am until 5:30pm. Tours are offered at frequent intervals and cost $6 for adults, $5 for seniors, and $2 for children ages 2 through 12. "Hard hat" tours cost $25. Call for schedule.*

Directions

Make your way from the Strip to I-515 via either Tropicana Avenue or Flamingo Road. Alternatively, take I-15 south to I-215 east. The latter road ends just before the intersection of I-515. Head south on I-515 (which is also US 93/95). The freeway ends in the southern part of Henderson at the Railroad Pass and the old Boulder Highway loses its I-515 designation. Boulder Highway changes name to Nevada Highway, but just stay on US 93 and you'll soon reach the dam.

If you have time you can make a stop in Boulder City itself at the **Boulder City/Hoover Dam Museum**, *1228 Arizona Street*. It has a good collection of historical exhibits from the Dam's early history and also shows a movie about the dam's construction. *Tel. 702/294-1988. The museum is open daily from 10am until 5pm and the admission charge is $1 for adults and only 50 cents for children.* You can also get a map here that outlines a walking tour through the historic section of Boulder City.

LAKE MEAD NATIONAL RECREATION AREA

The **Lake Mead National Recreation Area** is the byproduct of the Hoover Dam project and a darn nice byproduct at that. In addition to providing aquatic relief from hot summers, Lake Mead, the largest man-made lake in the Western Hemisphere, supplies water to almost 30 million people throughout Nevada and the rest of the southwest. Las Vegas gets most of its water from Lake Mead by way of the **Southern Nevada Water Project**.

Lake Mead begins about 25 miles from Las Vegas and snakes its way to more than a hundred miles away. The lake has 550 miles of shoreline for you to enjoy fishing, boating (there are six marinas), rafting, swimming, and other water sports along with hiking and camping. If you're going to fish, you'll need a license. Fishermen will be pleased to learn of the variety of fish in the lake: largemouth bass, striped bass, catfish, crappie, trout, and bluegill.

If cruising along the lake in a large paddle-wheeler strikes your fancy, **Lake Mead Cruises** offers very pleasant scenic rides on *The Desert Princess*. The boat departs from a pier about a half mile north of the **Lake Mead Marina**. The 300-passenger vessel will take you out on the deep blue waters of Lake Mead, surrounded by the red sandstone cliffs. It's hard to believe that the glitter of Las Vegas is so nearby when you gaze out on the natural splendor that surrounds you on all sides. The boat turns around as it gets near the rear of Hoover Dam. In addition to scenic rides, Lake Mead Cruises also offers trips with a breakfast buffet, dinner, or dinner with dancing. The scenic cruises offer interesting commentary on the natural and human history of the area. *Tel. 702/293-6180. Excursion cruises leave at 10am, noon, 2:00 and 4pm (no late trip from November through March). The fare is $21 for adults and $10 for children. Contact Lake Mead Cruises if you want information on one of the meal cruises. Reservations are recommended.*

For the do-it-yourself boater, rental boats are also available at the Lake Mead Marina. An unusual sight at the marina are the hundreds of large-mouthed bass that congregate near the shore waiting for handouts from visitors. The water is often so thick with the fish that you can hardly see the lake! Adjacent to the marina is **Boulder Beach**, a popular spot for swimming and diving. Rafting on the Colorado River is another option if you have time. See the *Sports & Recreation* chapter for information on **Black Canyon Raft Tours**.

For the land lover we suggest an auto tour through the recreation area. There's plenty of land to see. In fact, despite the large size of Lake Mead and smaller Lake Mojave, land comprises about 87% of the national recreation area. The short tour involves taking Lakeshore Drive (State Highway 166) to Lake Mead Drive (Highway 146) and then returning to I-515. A longer tour via Northshore Road leads about 42 miles up Lake Mead and the Overton Arm to near the town of Overton at State Highway 169. This latter route is a good idea if you are going to see the Valley of Fire (see below). Regardless of whether you do either of these routes, be sure to stop on your way to or from Hoover Dam at the beautiful **Lake Mead Overlook**. It's located about a quarter mile off of US 93.

The Lake Mead National Recreation Area is open at all times and there is a $5 per auto use charge that is good for 24 hours. (The portion of US 93 that runs through the Recreation Area is, however, free.) The Alan Bible Visitor Center has *information, a desert botanical garden, and lake views. It is located on US 93 at the intersection of Lakeshore Drive. Tel. 702/293-8907. Visitor center hours are daily from 8:30am until 4:30pm except for New Year's Day, Thanksgiving and Christmas.*

Directions

From the Strip use the same directions as for getting to Hoover Dam. You reach the recreation area about five miles before getting to the dam. Use Lakeshore Drive, off of US 93, for access to other points in the recreation area including the marinas, beach, and Northshore Drive. Alternatively, exit from I-515 at Lake Mead Drive and head east. This road will enter the recreation area near the beginning of the Northshore Drive.

Many visitors who want to spend a complete day away from the Strip combine Hoover Dam, Lake Mead and the attractions in Henderson. It can be done in one full day (excluding the Colorado River raft tour and north shore excursion) and makes for a nice change of pace from the usual Vegas activities.

RED ROCK CANYON

Less than a half-hour drive west of town you'll find beautiful red sandstone and gray limestone formations and cliff outcroppings that have been carved by water and wind erosion. You'll think you're in the wilds of the great southwest rather than minutes from the hustle of the Strip. Part of the Spring Mountains, Red Rock Canyon was formerly home to the Paiute Indians. The sunlight at different times of the day changes the hues, so that the Canyon area is always a little different each time you come here.

The unique beauty and fragile environment of the area has led to its designation as the **Red Rock Canyon National Conservation Area**. Begin your trip with a stop at the **Red Rock Visitors Center** to get trail guides and maps, view the exhibits on the local plants and wildlife, and to get any other information you need on this Bureau of Land Management (BLM) administered facility that's as popular with the residents of Las Vegas as it is with visitors. The sandstone and the limestone come together at the **Keystone Thrust**, a fault or fracture where the ancient rocks collided with (and are now superimposed on top of) one another. The escarpment runs for 15 miles and is about 3,000 feet high. It is believed to be about 65 million years old.

In late afternoon, as the sun sets and just before darkness stretches over the land, you'll witness the muted colors of the desert, the subtle hues and tones of the scrub brush, the earthly pale reds of the ore embedded in the hills – all silhouetted against the many Joshua Trees and yucca bushes.

Red Rock Canyon has many nature and hiking trails, short and long, easy and strenuous. It is best to inquire at the visitor center about their difficulty if you have any questions. The easy way to see the conservation area is via the simple to drive 13-mile one-way scenic loop road., There are several good viewpoints of the red rock formations, especially in the beginning of the drive. The rocks are a favorite with rock climbers and you'll usually see dozens of people scampering over them at just about any time. If you're visiting with children take them along the short **Children's Discovery Trail**, where they'll learn about different varieties of plants and trees and see where Indians used to live beneath the natural rock overhangs.

Tel. 702/363-1921. The Conservation Area is open during daylight hours. The visitor center is open from 8:30am until 4:30pm. The admission is $5 per vehicle. If visiting during the hotter months it is best to do hiking in the morning hours. Tours are available from Las Vegas for those who don't have their own wheels. Always carry water if you're going to be out on the trails.

Directions

Head west on West Charleston Boulevard (located between the north end of the Strip and downtown) for about 16 miles and follow sign to Red Rock Canyon.

SPRING MOUNTAINS ATTRACTIONS

There are two interesting attractions that lie within the Spring Mountains in the general vicinity of Red Rock Canyon. They can be done separately, or together with the Canyon to make for a most pleasant day long trip. The **Spring Mountain Ranch State Park** and **Bonnie Springs/Old Nevada** both lie on the continuation of State Highway 159 just south of the exit from the Red Rock Canyon Scenic Loop Road.

Spring Mountain Ranch covers 500 acres and was built in 1869. It was expanded over the years and was once owned by Howard Hughes. The name comes from the several natural springs in the area that were once a source of water for the Paiute Indians. Of interest, aside from the excellent views of the mountains and portions of Red Rock Canyon, are the main ranch house which lies beneath the reddish Wilson Cliff Range and the wildlife that can often be seen by Lake Harriet. The state sponsors many events including the **Theater Under the Stars** program. *Tel. 702/875-4141. There is a $5 per vehicle park entrance fee.*

The Bonnie Springs Ranch predates Spring Mountain Ranch by about 25 years. It was a wagon-train stop along the Old Spanish Trail to California. On the premises are a petting and feeding zoo as well as opportunities for horseback riding. Adjacent to the ranch is the Old

Nevada Village, a restoration of an Old West frontier town with wooden sidewalks and saloons, ice cream parlors, a blacksmith shop, museums and souvenir shops. There's also a miniature train ride, gunfights, and even a comical hanging on the main square. These activities are, of course, delightful for children. Adults will find a real saloon decorated with dollar bills. *Tel. 702/875-4191. It is best to call for exact operating hours and prices.*

Directions

If coming from Red Rock Canyon simply turn right at the end of the loop road and you'll reach the two attractions in a few moments. If you're coming directly from Las Vegas, proceed via Charleston Boulevard (as described in the directions for Red Rock Canyon) and stay on the main road until you reach Spring Mountain Ranch and Bonnie Springs. Travelers on State Highway 159 will frequently encounter wild burros. Drive carefully, as there have been numerous accidents. You cannot stop on the main road. Pull completely off the road in order to observe them from a safe distance. Do not attempt to feed or even approach the burros as they are unpredictable.

MOUNT CHARLESTON

The **Spring Mountains National Recreation Area**, which is administered by the **Toiyabe National Forest**, is situated to the north and west of the Red Rock Canyon National Conservation Area. This huge tract of land is a good place to go for great hiking, camping, backpacking, wagon rides, horseback riding, and in the winter, skiing and sleigh riding. There is abundant wildlife (including coyotes, bighorn sheep, cougar and deer) and several dozen species of plant life, so much so that you'll wonder whether you're really still just a hop, skip and a jump away from all that blazing neon.

The mountains reach over 10,000 feet in the Spring Mountain Range which, of course, affects the weather. Be forewarned that it often gets chilly at night, although the summertime daytime highs are a much more comfortable 20 degrees cooler than in the Valley. There is also considerably more precipitation in the higher elevations than in Las Vegas – the rain (or snow) comes in from the west and falls on the mountains but often doesn't make it over them. Imposing **Mt. Charleston** rises to a height of 11,918 feet. You can reach the area in about an hour from Las Vegas. Whether you're gazing at the area's tallest peak or looking out below and beyond from up on top, the view is wonderful.

Campers can drive to a campsite and do their thing from May through September only, although you can winter camp if you walk in. There are some beautiful trails here, several of which originate behind the **Mt.**

Charleston Lodge, which is a great place to eat if you're coming up th[
way for the day.

Directions

Take US 95 north until you reach Lee Canyon Road, which is Stat
Highway 156. Turn left and proceed up the canyon and in about 1
minutes you will reach the Mt. Charleston ski area. We suggest a
interesting scenic return route rather than just reversing the abov
directions. About six miles from the ski area turn off of Route 156 ont
State Highway 158. This road winds its way along the high ground for nin
miles and offers excellent vistas. It ends at Route 157. A left turn here an
a drive of 17 miles down Kyle Canyon will return you to US 95.

This suggested route is actually three miles shorter than the way int
Mt. Charleston but does take a little longer due to the slow going on Rout
158.

VALLEY OF FIRE STATE PARK

If you like to hike or camp, hunt for old rocks, or just enjo
contemplating the nature of the Earth's geological history and the beaut
it has created, this is just the place to do it. Red sandstone juts out in a
directions, creating a picture-perfect desert landscape of rock formation
with names like the **Mouse's Tank**, **Seven Sisters** and **Elephant Roc**
Look for the bighorn sheep, burros, desert tortoise, wild horses and othe
southwestern animals that are sometimes roaming about.

Within its more than 20 square miles are formations that have bee
dated back about 150 million years. The name of the park comes from th
vivid colors that are in abundance when reflected by the sun's light. I
addition to the natural wonders, visitors can see some excellent example
of prehistoric petroglyphs. They were believed to have been carved by th
Basketmaker people who predated the Ancestral Puebloans of th
southwest. The best petroglyphs are reached by a somewhat strenuou
metal staircase that ascends **Atlatl Rock**.

Most of the important formations in the Valley of Fire are alongsid
the road or reached by relatively short and easy trails. However, for th
more adventurous, the park offers a good selection of longer and mor
difficult trails. The roads are good and consist of two routes. One is th
state highway that runs east-to-west through the park. The other ascend
a narrow gorge beginning at the visitor center and leads to som
trailheads as well as overlooks that provide sweeping vistas of th
surrounding desert and mountains. The visitor center has exhibits an
you can get more detailed information on the trails. Camping is available
Mid-day visits in the heart of summer should be avoided.

Tel. 702/397-2088. The park is open for day visits between dawn and dusk. The visitor center is open daily (except Christmas and New Year's Day) from 8:30am until 4:30pm. There is a $4 vehicle entry charge.

A nearby attraction in the town of Overton is the **Lost City Museum**. This fine facility specializes in the Ancestral Puebloan Indian culture (until recently more commonly referred to as the Anasazi) that predates the days of the Spanish explorers. *Tel. 702/397-2193. Open daily except New Year's Day, Thanksgiving and Christmas from 8:30am until 4:30pm. The admission charge is $2 for everyone 18 years of age and up.*

Directions

Take I-15 north for approximately 45 miles to Exit 75 and then follow State Highway 169 east for 19 miles into the park. The trip takes just a little over an hour. You have three options for the return trip, the first being to simply reverse the route you came by. A second choice is to exit the park on the east side and take Route 169 north through Overton to I-15 south. This allows you to visit the Lost City Museum in Overton.

Finally, you can continue from the east exit of the park for a mile to State Route 167 and then turn right. This will return you to the Las Vegas area via the Lake Mead National Recreation Area's North Shore Drive, a much slower but very pleasant scenic trip. Route 167 ends at State Highway 147 which will take you back to I-515 and access to all parts of Las Vegas.

LAUGHLIN

Many Vegas tour operators offer you a chance to do the exact same thing you'd do in Vegas – gamble – in the small town of Laughlin, some 90 miles to the south. But Laughlin isn't a smaller version of Las Vegas in one respect. It's got the Colorado River flowing through town, separating Nevada's southernmost city from Bullhead City, Arizona on the eastern bank of the river, and that means a wide variety of water fun right in front of you.

Most Vegas hotels have literature on Laughlin excursions in their lobby. You can check out the list of tour operators in the *Getting Around* chapter for phone numbers. Virtually all of them offer free transportation to and from Laughlin.

Laughlin sits just to the south of **Davis Dam** which impounds **Lake Mojave**. No tours are available which isn't so bad because the dam itself lacks the size and majesty of Hoover Dam. From a desert oasis with just 90 residents in 1983, Laughlin has come a long way. Although the building boom of the late 80's has ended there are more than 10,000 hotel rooms and nine major hotel/casinos. Many of them are Vegas off-shoots including the Golden Nugget, Flamingo and Harrah's.

THE DESERT TORTOISE

*Most people are surprised to hear that the deserts of southern Nevada are home to a **tortoise**, believing that these creatures like a watery environment. But such is not the case with this arid-loving cute little fella. It has become an endangered species as civilization encroaches upon its natural habitat. The biggest problem facing the desert tortoise is extinction due to being hit by automobiles. Of course, they're a protected species and there are a few rules that have to be followed by us humans.*

First of all, if you spot one on the road you're supposed to stop and carefully pick it up and move it to a safe location. Not only do you have to take it out of harm's way, but you are required to report its location and which direction it was headed to wildlife officials. If you want to "adopt" one for your backyard, that's alright, as long as you have an enclosure from which they cannot climb out of. After all, they might be hit by a car cruising down your street. You'll also see many low fenced-off areas in places that aren't built up. These are to make sure that the tortoises that supposedly live within the fences' confines won't get out and become traffic statistics.

So be careful: in Nevada, at least, you're probably in less trouble if you kill a person than a desert tortoise!

Just about all of the casinos in Laughlin are lined up along a mile-long stretch of Casino Drive, which parallels the Colorado River. The **River Walk** is a riverfront promenade that connects most of the hotels on the water side. It's a very pleasant place for a stroll if the weather isn't too hot or windy. You can get around nicely in Laughlin by foot via either the River Walk or Casino Drive. The furthest hotel is Harrah's and they have a shuttle bus service. However, the coolest way to travel is by river taxi. These small boats ply the river and stop at most of the bigger hotels. You can also get across the river to Bullhead City if the fancy strikes you.

The **Ramada Express** (located on the land side of Casino Drive and the only big hotel without river access) has an old-time railroad circling the property that has good views and will keep the kids amused at least for a few minutes. It's free of charge. Consult the operating schedule outside the hotel. Laughlin also has some shopping, mostly in an outlet mall located near the north end of Casino Drive.

Gambling is the main activity in Laughlin (that's why they'll bus you in from Vegas for free and throw in a free lunch) but tourists and many southern Nevadans also like the idea of outdoor fun being within easy reach (not that Las Vegas outdoor excursions are difficult to get to). Fishing, swimming, boating and various water sports are all just a few minutes away on the Colorado. Also, many budget minded visitors appreciate the extremely low hotel prices in Laughlin (starting in the $19-29 range during the week).

So, is it worth the trip? Keep in mind that the round trip takes almost four hours and that the sights in Laughlin (including the hotels) aren't anything near what you can see in Vegas. Given all that we have some serious doubts as to whether it warrants the effort to get there but the choice is yours. It's a better idea if you're staying in Vegas for a week or more and need a little time away from the Strip or if you are on a second or subsequent trip to Las Vegas and have already seen the important sights. On the other hand, if you are coming to southern Nevada *just* to gamble then, as mentioned before, Laughlin can be a very inexpensive way to do so. If you plan to go and would like more information contact the **Laughlin Visitor Center**, *155 S. Casino Drive; Tel. 702/298-3321.*

Directions

Take US 93/95 south to where they split just before reaching Boulder City. (See the directions for Hoover Dam for details on getting to Boulder City from the Strip.). Then follow US 95 south for about 1-1/4 hours to State Highway 163. Head east on that road into Laughlin. The last part of the trip descends steeply and is quite scenic.

LAUGHLIN CASINOS AT A GLANCE

Colorado Belle, Tel. 702/298-4000 or 800/458-9500
Edgewater, Tel. 702/298-2453 or 800/67-RIVER
Flamingo Laughlin, Tel. 702/298-5111 or 800/FLAMINGO
Golden Nugget, Tel. 702/298-7111 or 800/237-1739
Harrah's, Tel. 702/298-4600 or 800/447-8700
Pioneer Gambling Hall, Tel. 702/298-2442 or 800/634-3469
Ramada Express, Tel. 702/298-4200 or 800/272-6232
River Palms, Tel. 702/298-2242 or 800/835-7903
Riverside Resort, Tel. 702/298-2535 or 800/227-3849

Side Trips From Laughlin

If you drive down to Laughlin and plan on making it a full day or even an overnighter, there are a couple of interesting side trips to consider. The first is a short drive (about 45 minutes) to the Arizona town of **Oatman**. Historic for both its gold mining days and its Route 66 location, Oatman is part ghost town and part living old west history. It was established in 1906 and the gold mining operation was active for 35 years.

At its peak Oatman had 10,000 residents but fewer than 200 live here today. Visitors to Oatman can stroll the interesting main street with it town jail and original hotel. The latter is famous because Clark Gable and Carole Lombard honeymooned there. You can still see the room as i appeared during their stay. Visitors also love to feed carrots to the burro that walk up and down Main Street, all direct descendants of the origina miners' burros. A highlight is the gunfights that take place each weekend at 1pm. The area around Oatman has pleasant scenery. From Laughlir cross over the bridge to Bullhead City and drive south on State Highwa 95 for 13 miles to the signed cutoff for Oatman. It is 11 miles distant fror that point.

The second option is a longer trip to **Lake Havasu City**. This is als in Arizona but is farther down the river. While we don't suggest addin another long drive, you can take a six-hour trip via **London Bridge Je Boat Tours**. The excursion leaves at 10am from behind the Pionee Casino and arrives in Lake Havasu City around noon. It departs the latte at 2pm and returns to Laughlin at 4pm. During your two hours in Lak Havasu City you can see the transported original **London Bridge** and d some shopping in the **English Village**. A part of the jet boat ride passe through the scenic **Topock Gorge**. For information call, *Tel. 888/50. 3545 or Tel. 702/298-9737 in Laughlin.*

PRIMM

If you want to get out into the desert for a while and do some gamblin and maybe a little shopping, too, but without going as far as Laughlir then try **Primm**. It's much closer (actually on the way in or out of Las Vega if you're coming from Southern California) and just as much fun. Primm isn't really a town but a group of three casino hotels, a golf course and factory outlet mall sitting astride both directions of the Interstate higl way. It used to be known as Stateline, but that was changed in 1996 at th behest of the Primm family who founded the place. The change als avoids confusing it with the town of Stateline which is located at Lak Tahoe in northern Nevada.

The route from Las Vegas is through pleasant mountain and deser scenery. Once you leave Vegas, civilization ends fast, although there ar a couple of casinos about midway to Primm at the town of **Jean**. The thre Primm casinos are **Whiskey Pete's, Primm Valley Resort** and **Buffal Bill's**. They're connected by shuttle bus, monorail or miniature train rid but you can even walk if the weather isn't too hot. The Primm Valle Resort has the "death car" of Bonnie and Clyde as well as a John Dillinge owned vehicle on display along with other artifacts of famous gangster The new and larger facility replaces the older exhibit that was at Whiske 'ete's for many years. Buffalo Bill's has an interesting old west interior including animated characters around a hanging tree) and some wild ides – a log flume and one of the world's highest and fastest roller oasters, The Desperado. The casinos have the usual amenities found in .as Vegas. Name entertainment appears in the Arena at Buffalo Bill's. *Fee harged for amusement rides.*

The shopping mall is called the **Fashion Outlet of Las Vegas** and ontains many of the most recognizable names in fashion. The exterior ; absolutely ugly – it looks like a bunch of billboards at best. The interior, .owever, is architecturally interesting and contains many oversized .gures gazing down on shoppers. Unless you are an outlet mall specialist, /e wouldn't make the trip to Primm just for this place. However, if you're oming here for a few hours or the day to see the casinos or are just passing y, then it's a good stop.

)irections

Take I-15 south to the Primm exit (#1). It's a distance of about 40 miles rom the Strip and should take well under 45 minutes.

:HOST TOWNS & INDIAN RESERVATIONS

Most of southern Nevada's ghost towns were once thriving silver, lead •r zinc mining centers built to support the mining industry. The prosper- :y, however, was short lived. Many of these towns did not last very long t all. The main ghost town we would recommend (most of the other ghost owns have little or nothing to show for themselves) is **Goodsprings**, 35 niles southwest of Las Vegas.

The combination of a natural spring and the wanderings of one oseph Good combined to fix the town's name. Good mined the area in 861. Prospectors from Utah arrived about 25 years later and there were nore than 40 mines established. It had several thousand residents by the arly 1900's but a flu epidemic in 1918 took many lives. This was soon ollowed by the collapse of metal and mineral prices. About 100 people till call Goodsprings their home. The big tourist attraction is the old •ioneer Saloon.

)irections

Take I-15 south to Jean, turn west on State Highway 161 for seven niles to Goodsprings.

)ther Area Trips

We'll also mention now that if you intend to go up to Death Valley (see •elow), then consider the ghost town of **Rhyolite**, located near the •resent day town of Beatty and just outside the national park. It is one of

Nevada's best. A word of caution is in order for those who like to explor
these types of places. There are many abandoned mines in souther.
Nevada but all must be considered as dangerous. Several people usuall
lose their lives each year in accidents involving these mines, so **keep ou**

Although there are three Indian nations that have lived in Nevada fo
hundreds of years or even longer, there are few significant reservation
among the 25 or so that still exist. They generally are not set up for visitor
the way many in Arizona or New Mexico are. This is, depending upo:
your outlook, either good (Native Americans are not reduced to touris
attractions) or bad (opportunity for interaction and understandin
between cultures is reduced).

The largest reservation in proximity to Las Vegas is the **Moapa India**
Reservation, about an hour north of town via I-15. Other than th
fireworks stand by the side of the road there isn't much to see. The **La**
Vegas Paiute Indian Reservation is closer to the city, about a half-hour
drive north on US 95. The tribe has a golf course that is open to the publi
and is planning on building a small resort. However, there's nothing c
interest to the casual visitor. Some area tribes occasionally hold pow-wow
and perform ceremonial dances in Las Vegas and Boulder City. Check ou
current newspapers and magazines for possible activity in this regard.

AREA 51 & THE EXTRATERRESTRIAL HIGHWAY

The fascination that many people have over the secret U.S. Goverr
ment installation known as Area 51 and the belief that aliens have visite
this area have spawned a mini-tourism boom in an area to the north of La
Vegas. We don't personally recommend this trip for the average visito
because it is quite far (more than 300 miles for the round trip) and ther
isn't particularly much to see when you get there. However, we know tha
there are going to be readers who will want to take this excursion, so, thi
is for you.

Along the way as you travel on US 93 there are nice views of th
mountains and you'll pass through the **Pahranagat National Wildlif**
Refuge. Nevada Highway 375, which connects US 93 and US 6 has bee:
officially designated as the **Extrtraterrestrial Highway**. It even ha
drawings of flying saucers on the state highway sign. The center of thing
is in the small town of **Rachel**. This is where you can purchase alie:
burgers and other souvenirs. Also in Rachel is the **Area 51 Researc**
Center, a highly unofficial clearing house for learning about the suppo
edly crazy things the government is doing in nearby Area 51. It's littl
more than a gift shop although the people here are really into what they'r
doing. They'll even take groups on tours of the surrounding wildernes
and you will get to see such exciting things as the gate to the actual Are

1 base. Wow! You can also climb a nearby peak with your guides to get view of the base but you won't see anything of great interest. Area 51 is located about 30 miles via a side road off of Highway 375 that begins just west of the Hancock Summit.

Directions

From Las Vegas proceed north on I-15 to the exit for US 93 (22 miles north of the I-515/downtown interchange). Then drive north on US 93 or 85 miles to the town of Crystal Springs where State Highway 375 begins. There is no alternative option for the return trip – you have to use the exact same route in reverse.

GRAND CANYON

You're close to one of the most majestic pieces of real estate in the entire world, but it's not exactly around the corner – roughly 300 miles away. To call the Grand Canyon a Vegas area attraction is analogous to New York calling Boston a New York area attraction. Still, who can blame the city elders for wanting to claim the **Grand Canyon National Park** as their very own backyard? You can choose to visit either the North Rim or the South Rim, but not both unless you allocate several days to this excursion.

The canyon runs 277 miles in length, is a mile deep and almost 20 miles across at its widest point. It's a breathtaking, beautiful place. We're assuming here that you're mainly interested in a brief visit, so we'll limit our remarks to the very basics since huge volumes exist on the history, attractions, lodging, etc. The South Rim is the more heavily visited portion of the park although the "experts" will tell you that the relatively lightly traveled North Rim may even be more spectacular. Most visitors from Vegas don't drive to the Grand Canyon because that generally requires an overnight trip and they don't have the time to do so. There are ground tours that do it in a single day but we think that's a real knockout and doesn't even give you the time to properly appreciate what there is to see. So, how do you visit the canyon on a day-tripper? Read on.

Grand Canyon Air Tours From Las Vegas

"Flight-seeing" tours of the Grand Canyon depart from a number of places in the Las Vegas area, including McCarran Airport, the North Las Vegas Airport (most tours have relocated there in the past couple of years to relieve congestion at McCarran), and the Henderson Executive Airport. In addition to flying over either one or both Grand Canyon rims, these flights usually include a pass over Lake Mead and Hoover Dam. Flights are no longer allowed to go into the canyon for safety and environmental reasons. Therefore, you should enhance the overall experience of your flight-seeing adventure by taking a trip that includes some time on the ground at the Grand Canyon. There is an airport located there. These trips aren't cheap. Prices start at about $80 for air only and at around $120 for trips that spend some time at the canyon via a bus tour. Helicopter tours are even more expensive.

Airplane tour operators include:
· **Lake Mead Air**, *Tel. 702/293-1848*
· **Las Vegas Airlines**, *Tel. 702/647-3056 or 800/634-6851*
· **Scenic Airlines**, *Tel. 702/638-3300 or 800/634-6801*

Helicopter tour operators include:
· **Discount Helicopter Tours Adventure**, *Tel. 702/471-7155*
· **Grand Canyon Tours**, *Tel. 702/655-6060 or 800/512-0075*. This company also offers plane and bus tours.
· **Papillon Grand Canyon Helicopters**, *Tel. 702/736-7243 or 800/63. 7272*

In addition to the above operators, many of the general tour operators listed earlier in this book also offer Grand Canyon flights. Among these are **Sightseeing Tours Unlimited**, *Tel. 702/471-7155*, and **Las Vegas Tours & Travel**, *Tel. 702/739-8975*.

Directions
If you're the stubborn type and plan to make the round trip on your own (or are smarter and will do it with a stay over at the Canyon or elsewhere), the route there and back is quite simple. For the South Rim take US 93 south to I-40 at Kingman, Arizona, and then take the Interstate eastbound to State Highway 64 north into the park. For the North Rim take I-15 north to Utah Highway 9 east (north of St. George) to US 89 at Mount Carmel. Go south to the Arizona Highway 67 turnoff and follow it to the end. Combining the north and south rims by car really requires three days and is beyond the scope of this book to describe.

DEATH VALLEY
Let's begin by telling you that a trip to the highlights of **Death Valley** can be done in a single day, but you'll have to leave early and return late to make it worth the drive. You're better off making it an overnighter. Accommodations are available within Death Valley and in the town of Beatty. We strongly urge you not to go to Death Valley between late May and mid-September. Temperatures can be in the 120's and the unprepared visitor can be in for a rude surprise – even a dangerous one. Those

temperatures are just as hard on cars. The common wisdom is that the only people you see in Death Valley during the summer are German tourists. On the other hand, wintertime in Death Valley is delightful and spring and fall are definitely manageable.

Death Valley National Park is a natural wonderland with tons of beautiful scenery. The diversity of the landscape comes as a surprise to most people who figure it's just a barren wasteland. Perhaps so, but the valley is surrounded by towering mountains that soar more than 12,000 feet above the valley, and within the valley there is a bewildering variety of interesting and colorful rock formations. Besides stopping at **Badwater**, the lowest point in the United States, visitors should take a ride on **Artist's Drive**, an easy one-way loop road; and drive up to the incredible **Dante's View** where the panorama of mountains and valley is spread out before you. **Zabriskie Point** has gold colored rocks and makes you fell like you're not on this planet anymore. **Scotty's Castle** is a mansion built in the early part of the century by an eccentric millionaire. However, it is in the northern part of the park and is too far to include on a day trip. Services within Death Valley are mostly concentrated at Furnace Creek.

Directions

The quickest way to get there is to take I-15 south to Blue Diamond Road and then head west on State Highway 160. Just north of the town of Pahrump turn left on Highway 210 which crosses into California. At Death Valley Junction pick up California Highway 190 which takes you into the heart of the national park. Return the opposite way. If you're taking a two-day jaunt and want to see more of Death Valley then proceed as above as far as Pahrump and then follow Nevada Highway 372 and California 178 through Shoshone and into the southern entrance of the park.

Exit the park via Nevada Highway 267 from the Scotty's Castle area or Nevada Highway 374 via Rhyolite and Beatty to US 95. Then take US 95 south all the way back to Las Vegas.

SOUTHWESTERN UTAH

Some of the most amazing and beautiful scenery in the entire world will be found in the southwestern corner of the state of **Utah**, part of which goes by the name "Color Country." Unfortunately for Vegas visitors, it definitely requires at least two days to even begin to do it properly although it is feasible to do at least Zion National Park in one long day. It's well beyond the cope of this book to thoroughly describe the scenic attractions of this area, so we'll give you a capsule listing of the most important attractions that are reachable in a mini-trip.

Bryce Canyon National Park: Simply put, one of the most beautiful places in all the world. A fairy tale-like setting of multi-colored rock pinnacles in a natural amphitheater.

Cedar Breaks National Monument: A smaller and less spectacular version of Bryce.

Snow Canyon State Park: Colorful rock formations and outdoor recreation. Not as spectacular as the other places in southwestern Utah but it is the closest to Las Vegas.

Zion National Park: A dramatic narrow canyon flanked by massive walls and towering rock formations of different colors. Another section of the park outside the valley has splendid views into the valley as well as its own share of unusual geologic formations.

Some of the above, especially Zion, can be combined with a longer trip to the North Rim of the Grand Canyon.

Directions

Take I-15 north through the northwest corner of Arizona for several miles through a scenic canyon and into Utah. Snow Canyon can be reached by taking Utah 18 north from the town of St. George. Take Utah 9 (north of St. George) east to Zion National Park. If you're continuing to Bryce then follow Utah 9 from Zion to US 89 and then go north to Utah 14 and then east to Bryce.

Return via Utah 14 to Cedar Breaks and then rejoin I-15 at Cedar City for the return trip south to Las Vegas.

RECOMMENDED EXCURSIONS READING

*If you're interested in more detailed guide books on some of the excursions outside Nevada covered in this chapter, consider Open Road Publishing's **Arizona Guide** and **Utah Guide** – both authored by the writer of this book! The books offer much greater detail about the Grand Canyon in Arizona and Utah's parks and monuments, as well as all the pertinent travel info you can expect in Open Road travel guides.*

17. LAS VEGAS FOR KIDS

Las Vegas seems to have a Jekyll and Hyde attitude when it comes to children. At first it was an adults only sort of place. Then came the big push to attract families. Then some of the casino moguls decided that wasn't such a good idea after all. The result is that there are plenty of things for families with small children to do but you have to avoid certain places where children aren't so welcome or will be uncomfortable. That's what this chapter will try to help you out with.

In general, Las Vegas isn't appropriate for children under the age of six. Between that age and around 15 there are lots of enjoyable activities for them. Older teens present a special problem because they're old enough to want to try and sample things that they're legally not old enough to try. On the other hand, there are also many activities for youngsters in that age group. We would be leading you astray if we told you that Las Vegas is as good a place to bring children on vacation as Disneyland. It isn't. But if you have children and you're planning on coming to Vegas, there isn't any reason that you shouldn't bring them along.

LAS VEGAS WITH KIDS!

*For more details on taking the kiddies to Las Vegas, take a look at Open Road's **Las Vegas With Kids**. You'll find lots of recommendations for child-friendly hotels, babysitting services, restaurants, theme parks, rides and much more.*

CHILD CARE FACILITIES

Several major hotels have on-premise facilities and supervised activities for children. Here are some good ones on or near the Strip. The **MGM Grand** has the extensive Youth Activities Center as does the **Las Vegas Hilton**. The nearby **Orleans** and **Gold Coast** hotels also have excellent facilities, the latter being the only one to our knowledge that doesn't impose a charge. By the way, you should be aware that hotels only allow children of registered guests to be left at their child care centers. The ages of children allowed varies from place to place so you should make inquiry in advance. Another excellent option are the "Kid's Quest" facilities located at all **Station Casinos** – Palace Station is the closest to the Strip. You need not be a hotel guest to leave your child at a Kid's Quest. **Sam's Town** has recently added a major child care facility as well.

If you're staying at a hotel other than the above and need a place to drop the kids for a few hours or a whole day, it's best to inquire with the hotel concierge or front desk personnel. Every hotel will be able to recommend a reliable child care giver that you can rely on. One organization that has received official "okays" from various governmental agencies is the **A-1 Baby Sitting Service**, *Tel. 702/382-0432.*

ARCADES

There are countless arcades in the hotels along the Strip and in other locations throughout the Valley. In fact, you would be hard pressed to find a major hotel that doesn't have one of these electronic child sitters. Even some of the hotels that try not to gear themselves towards children usually will give in on this one. Children, of course, from ages six and up will have no trouble occupying themselves in almost any arcade for hours on end. That's the good part. However, we caution parents that there is often little or no supervision of the arcades. You may leave your children there but do you know that they will remain there if you go off to gamble or do something else? Our point is that, used appropriately, the arcades can be an enjoyable part of your child's visit to Las Vegas. However, they are not a substitute for parental supervision and shouldn't be treated as such.

Clark County regulations bar children under the age of 18 from being in an arcade after 10pm (midnight on weekends) unless they are accompanied by an adult.

With all that in mind, it's time to let the kids have some fun. The Strip's **GameWorks** in the Showcase center is the biggest arcade in town and has even more options than any of the hotel arcades.

AMUSEMENT & THEME PARKS

Hours and prices for amusement parks tend to vary quite a bit depending upon the season so it is always best to call in advance, especially during the winter.

ADVENTUREDOME/CIRCUS CIRCUS.
See Chapter 12 for details.

LAS VEGAS MINI GRAND PRIX & FAMILY FUN CENTER, *1401 N. Rainbow Blvd., Tel. 702/259-7000.*

A different kind of amusement park that can be loads of fun for all ages. It has kiddy karts for drivers under the age of four, go karts for the bigger kids, Gran Prix cars and super stock cars for those 16 and over. Except for the kiddy karts, you drive over an actual "race" course. By the way, the Las Vegas Mini Grand Prix hosts competition races that are open to everyone. Prizes are awarded. A game arcade and snack bar are on the premises. *Open year round.*

MOUNTASIA FAMILY FUN CENTER, *2050 Olympic Avenue, Henderson (one block north of Sunset Road and Mountain Vista), Tel. 702/898-7777.*

The usual assortment of mini-rides, slides and so forth. Best for smaller children.

SPEEDWORLD, *in the Sahara Hotel.*
See Chapter 12 for details..

SCANDIA FAMILY FUN CENTER, *2900 Sirius Avenue, Tel. 702/364-0070.*

Features miniature golf, bumper cars and boats, batting cage and a video arcade. *Children under five are allowed in for free.*

STRAT-O-FAIR, *in the Stratosphere Hotel, see Chapter 12 for details.*

WET 'N WILD, *2601 Las Vegas Blvd. S., Tel. 702/734-0088.*

Located adjacent to the Sahara Hotel, this place has swimming, floating and sliding on 26 acres of pools, lagoons and water slides. More than 1.5 million gallons of water beckon you to get wet and act wild. Try the Blue Niagara, a water slide inside a 300-foot long blue loop, a wavemaker, the Black Hole water ride and Bomb Bay. It's a nice place to cool off from the blazing summer sun. *Open April through September.*

ATTRACTIONS FOR KIDS

We won't bother going into a lot of detail repeating what has already been said in the Seeing the Sights chapter. However, to make things easier for you to plan, we'll give you a brief rundown on those previously described attractions that will be enjoyed by children.

The Strip itself, either by day or night, is a magical experience for any age. Just keep a tight rein on the little ones. (There is a curfew on the Strip that is in effect at all times. Those under the age of 18 are not allowed to be on the Strip without being accompanied by an adult after 9pm and it is enforced.) At Caesars, the **Sinking of Atlantis** as well as all the simulator rides are the focus for kids. Just about everything except the casinos at **Circus Circus** and the **Excalibur** is excellent, as is the simulator and IMAX theater at the **Luxor**. The **Secret Garden of Siegfried & Roy** and the **Tiger Habitat** at the Mirage are among the best kiddy destinations and the same can be said for the **Lion Habitat** at the MGM Grand.

Of course, the **Battle of Buccaneer Bay** at Treasure Island is just great for kids aged 3 to 103 while the various roller coasters (New York, New York, Stratosphere and the Sahara) are sure to thrill most children. The **Shark Reef** at Mandalay Bay will delight youngsters but we think older children only will enjoy **Madame Tussaud's** at the Venetian. **Paris** is mainly for adults but what kid wouldn't like the outside elevator ride to the observation desk? Two other Strip attractions where children will be at home are just about all segments of the **Showcase** complex and the **Magic & Movie Hall of Fame** at O'Sheas.

Heading off-strip, those over about eight will like **Star Trek: The Experience** at the Las Vegas Hilton, while the colorful parade of floats at the Rio's **Masquerade Village** is suitable for all ages.

The museums near downtown, the **Lied Discovery Museum** and the **Museum of Natural History**, are both entertaining as well as educational. The factory tours in Henderson are also decent ways of spending some time with the little ones.

When it comes to excursions, the best one for children is **Hoover Dam**. This is something that can and will amaze people of all ages. The natural attractions around the Las Vegas area can be enjoyed by children if they aren't too small. Nature doesn't seem to impress those under the age of around eight.

SOME HOTEL SUGGESTIONS

Where to stay in Las Vegas when you have children with you is a different question than if only grown-ups are visiting. There are some hotels that have a deserved reputation for being kid-friendly and some that seem to go out of their way to make children unwanted, although the majority lie somewhere in between those two extremes.

The most suitable hotels for children include **Circus Circus,** the **Excalibur** and the **MGM Grand**. Somewhat surprising to some people is the fact that children are certainly welcome at the **Las Vegas Hilton** and the even more upscale **Four Seasons** In fact, both have children' packages, the latter even supplying some special amenities for children upon check-in. Just about all of the off-Strip hotels (with the exception of the Rio and luxury places like the Regent) are good for kids. We remind you that all Station hotels have child care facilities.

The best places to avoid with children are most of the other upscale hotels. In this category are Bellagio, Caesars, Mandalay Bay, the Mirage, Paris, the Venetian and Treasure Island. The latter used to be one of the best for children but has done a complete turn-around in the last couple of years despite that it is the home of the pirate ship battle. Likewise, the Mirage, although it has numerous attractions for children, isn't that great for kids when it comes to staying there.

In this regard, you should also take note that both the Bellagio and Mirage hotels do not allow anyone under 18 years of age to be in the hotel unless they are registered guests. That also means you can't take a stroller inside unless you're staying there. We think that these two places have definitely gone a bit too far with the adult atmosphere.

18. WEDDING CHAPELS

Imagine exchanging vows on a 200-foot high bungee jumping plat form adjacent to Circus Circus and then, literally taking the plunge to get the marriage off to a good start. Or getting married in a helicopter, or by a singing Elvis, or in a hot tub at the back end of a stretch limo. These and almost countless other possibilities can all be reality in the wacky world of Las Vegas. Las Vegas is a place of extremes and if you want to do it, you probably can. If you have a suggestion for an unusual wedding try mentioning it to the staff of one of the more unusual wedding chapels and they might (for an extra fee, of course) do exactly what you want Believe it or not, about five percent of all weddings in the United States take place in Las Vegas! Most, however, are not quite as we have described in this paragraph.

About 100,000 couples exchange vows in Las Vegas each year Valentine's Day is always a big wedding day in Las Vegas, with more than 2,500 weddings taking place annually on February 14th. No other city can boast as many wedding chapels – about a hundred in all.

Actually, most chapels do not have Elvis performers or other such gimmicks. Many are of the standard, old-fashioned quickie marriage variety. Whether you're planning to tie the knot here, or are just curious take some time to visit one or more of these chapels. It's a fun break from all the faster-paced action in Vegas. You'll frequently see bride and groom, all dressed up for the occasion, walking through the hotels or down the Strip. Often they're at the tables or slot machines spending all of their wedding money. Wedding parties are frequently to be seen in front of some of the major hotel's best picture taking spots doing just that – snapping the official wedding photo book.

GOING TO THE CHAPEL

State law does not require a blood test for a license and there is no waiting period. If you're 18 years old, you're in, while those under 18 need a parent's or guardian's written and notarized consent. Just get a license from the **Clark County Marriage License Bureau**, *200 S. 3rd Street; Te*

702/455-3156. Remember that both you and your intended have to apply in person. At busy times, like on Valentine's Day, you'll also find quite a few spectators outside the License Bureau office because the line of lovers can often be quite amusing. *The license fee is $35. The license bureau is open from 8am until midnight, Monday through Thursday and from 8am Friday through midnight on Sunday (that is, all weekend).* If you want a Justice of the Peace and nothing fancy, walk about a block to the **Commissioner of Civil Marriages**, *309 S. 3rd Street; Tel. 702/455-3474.* They'll get you wedded in a jiffy before you know it for a mere additional $35.

Many of the better known chapels are grouped together at the northern end of Las Vegas Boulevard South, the bulk of them starting a short distance after the Stratosphere Tower and continuing for about a mile to between Charleston Boulevard and downtown. This isn't the pretty side of town and mixed in among the chapels are seedy motels, pawn shops, adult video stores and less than gourmet dining. The atmosphere, however, doesn't seem to bother anyone and the chapels do a booming business. The chapels run the gamut from simple to beautiful. If you want something on the fancier side then you might want to consider using a wedding chapel in one of the big hotels. Many of the hotels have them and they're often tied to the theme of the hotel itself.

Besides Valentine's Day, New Year's Eve and the entire month of June are the busiest times for Las Vegas weddings. Depending on what you're looking for you can spend as little as $100 for the entire package, including the license, chapel fee, minister's or judge's fee and tip. (The latter runs about $25-50.) Not a bad deal, considering the cost of weddings these days. On the other hand, you could easily spend well into four digits. In fact, the sky's the limit and the choice is yours.

Many of the best known of Las Vegas' wedding chapels are briefly reviewed here. First we'll look at the independent chapels (that is, those not part of a hotel), followed by the better hotel-based establishments.

INDEPENDENT CHAPELS

A LITTLE WHITE CHAPEL, *1301 Las Vegas Blvd. South. Tel. 702/382-5943 or 800/452-6081.*

Perhaps no other wedding chapel in Las Vegas has so many crazy ways to get married on their "menu" as this place does. Their minister will come to your place, no matter where in the area that may be. At the chapel itself you can drive (or even roller skate) through the Tunnel of Love for a drive-in ceremony. You can get married in the front seat (and, no doubt for some, have the honeymoon in the back seat). The Little White Chapel in the Sky is a colorful hot air balloon for those who want an airborne wedding. This chapel also claims the record for the most marriages performed in a helicopter. They even have a branch at the Las Vegas Motor Speedway. Among the celebrities who've tied the knot here were Demi Moore/Bruce Willis, Joan Collins (we forget which husband), and basketball great Michael Jordan.

A SPECIAL MEMORY WEDDING CHAPEL, *800 S. 4th Street. Tel. 702/384-2211 or 800/962-7798.*

Don't you like how these businesses stick an "A" in front of their name so they can get an early listing in the telephone directory? Well, competition is fierce. But this is a nice place located a block west of the part of Las Vegas Boulevard where most of the chapels are. The pretty Cape Cod style architecture is complemented by a garden with a gazebo. It is a mostly traditional sort of place except for their drive-up wedding window.

CANDLELIGHT WEDDING CHAPEL, *2855 Las Vegas Blvd. South. Tel. 702/735-4179 or 800/962-1818.*

Because of its Strip location (right across the street from the Riviera Hotel), this is one of the most frequented wedding spots in Las Vegas. The chapel provides a nice touch by offering free limousine service from your hotel. Join the ranks of Bette Middler, Whoopi Goldberg, and Michael Caine, who all were married at Candlelight.

CHAPEL OF THE BELLS, *2333 Las Vegas Blvd. South. Tel. 702/735-6803 or 800/233-2391.*

This pretty little chapel has been featured in such movies as *Honeymoon in Vegas, Indecent Proposal, Vegas Vacation* and *Mars Attacks*. A lot of famous people have also been married here. Although they'll accommodate many strange requests, it is generally a good place for a more straight forward ceremony than, say, the Little White Chapel. They have an outdoor garden that is a lovely place to tie the knot.

CHAPEL OF LOVE, *1431 Las Vegas Blvd. South. Tel. 702/387-0155 or 800/922-5683.*

This is a very nice facility with four separate chapels so you rarely have to wait for your next. The name says it all for those romantically inclined. Each chapel has a different color scheme – for instance, peach, rose or lavender. A garden chapel, a popular feature in many chapels, is also available here.

CUPID'S WEDDING CHAPEL, *827 Las Vegas Blvd. South. Tel. 702/598-4444 or 800/543-2933.*

Often photographed, Cupid's is also one of the better known establishments. It's a small place but that doesn't stop it from being a lovely establishment that is known as the "little chapel with the big heart."

GRACELAND WEDDING CHAPEL, *619 Las Vegas Blvd. South. Tel. 702/474-6655 or 800/824-5732.*

What more could a bride and groom want? Elvis belts out a tune and serves as your witness. Bon Jovi got married here and growing numbers of rockers are following his lead, making this one of the more hip wedding chapels in town. But you don't have to be a famous rock-and-roll star to get in the door here – they'll take anyone!

LITTLE CHURCH OF THE WEST, *4617 Las Vegas Blvd. South. Tel. 702/739-7971 or 800/821-2452.*

This is the most historic of Las Vegas chapels (dating back to 1942) and is now on the National Register of Historic Places. The Little Church of the West started out next to the old Last Frontier Hotel and then moved (literally – the whole building headed down the Strip) to a site on the grounds of the Hacienda. When they imploded that hotel the chapel moved once again, this time a few blocks south to its present location. Simple, no gimmick weddings. Free champagne is given to the happy couple.

VIVA LAS VEGAS WEDDING CHAPEL, *1205 Las Vegas Blvd. South. Tel. 702/384-0771 or 800/574-4450.*

The ultimate Las Vegas wedding chapel? Perhaps. They have many themed wedding options. Among the many choices from the menu are Camelot, Gothic, beach party, disco, western, Victorian, outer space and even "gangster." There are others, including more traditional options but don't overlook the Elvis/Blue Hawaiian wedding. You get the idea.

CHAPEL OF YOUR DREAMS, *946 E. Sahara. Tel. 702/734-3732 or 888/248-3732.*

Finally, we'll suggest the Chapel Of Your Dreams, even though it wasn't open as of press time. It is scheduled to begin conducting weddings during the summer of 2001. At that time it will take its place as the most elegant and elaborate of all the non-hotel wedding chapels. The design of the building and its chapels will look like a palace to many. It will also have an open air court with a pretty gazebo. Announced prices are more expensive than at most other independent chapels but this looks like it is going to be worth it for those who are seeking a classy place to be wed.

BEST HOTEL WEDDING CHAPELS

Almost all of the hotel chapels consist of two separate chapel rooms – one for small wedding parties and one for larger gatherings.

BALLY'S (Bally's Celebration Wedding Chapel), *Tel. 702/892-2222.*

The Bally's monorail has "a touch of class" written on its side and the same can be said of their chapel. No glitz, just a very pretty and formal setting for what is, after all, a serious affair.

BELLAGIO (Bellagio Wedding Chapel), *Tel. 702/693-7700.*

The Bellagio's chapels have the kind of elegance found throughout the hotel. The prices are among the highest in town (starting in excess of $1,000), but this is a first class operation. They even video the entire proceedings from behind mirrors and you receive the edited tape immediately upon leaving the chapel.

IMPERIAL PALACE (We've Only Just Begun Chapel), *Tel. 702/733-0011 or 800/346-3373.*

This was one of the first major hotels to have a chapel on the premises. The name is kind of corny but they do a real nice job.

EXCALIBUR (Canterbury Wedding Chapels), *Tel. 702/597-7278 or 800/811-4320.*

Those selecting the Canterbury have the option of either a traditional ceremony or dressing up as the lord and lady of the castle for a Medieval style ceremony. Either way, the surroundings are surprisingly luxurious and dignified for what is essentially a more frivolous-themed hotel.

FLAMINGO LAS VEGAS (Garden Chapel), *Tel. 702/733-3232.*

Located in its own little building, the pretty chapel overlooks the hotel's spacious and beautiful grounds. A trellis lined walkway faces the chapel's entrance.

MANDALAY BAY (Chapel By the Bay), *Tel. 702/632-7490 or 877/632-7701.*

The two chapels, named Sunrise and Sunset, are located in a separate building on the hotel's expansive grounds. They combine the hotel's exotic atmosphere (lots of bamboo) with more traditional styles of elegance such as elaborate chandeliers and the whole thing works quite well.

MGM GRAND (Forever Grand Chapel), *Tel. 702/891-7984 or 800/646-5530.*

There isn't any theme here but the chapel is simply beautiful and the arrangements are excellent.

MONTE CARLO (Monte Carlo Wedding Chapel), *Tel. 702/730-7575 or 800/822-8651.*

Getting married here is like the prelude to a French Riviera honeymoon.

PARIS (Paris Wedding Chapels), *Tel. 702/946-4060 or 877/650-5021.*

There is no denying that Paris and romance seem to go together and, no doubt, applies here as well. The larger *Chapelle du Paradis* looks the part of a church with its tall columns and angelic cherubs on a painted sky ceiling. The *Chapelle du Jardin* is highlighted by beautiful garden murals.

RIO HOTEL (Rio Wedding Chapel), *Tel. 702/247-7986 or 888/746-5625.*

Like most things at the Rio, this is part sophistication and part fun. An entire floor of their tallest tower is devoted to the intended couple. Not only are there three different wedding chapels and shops to purchase everything you'll need for the wedding, but there's even a Hollywood

Honeymoon Suite on the premises. It seems that newlyweds might never have to leave this floor of the hotel. Well, the Rio wouldn't really want you to do that. After all, it isn't all that uncommon in Las Vegas to see bride and groom at the gaming tables!

TREASURE ISLAND (Treasure Island Chapels), *Tel. 800/527-6393.*

The chapels are real nice but for something really special (at a substantial extra fee), how about exchanging vows in a ceremony on board the deck of the *HMS Britannia*? Don't worry, they don't fight the pirate ship when weddings are taking place.

TROPICANA (Island Wedding Chapel), *Tel. 702/798-6151 or 800/325-5839.*

The Tropicana's chapel is on the same idea as the Garden Chapel at the Flamingo and almost as nice. This one has a wood-beamed interior that is supposed to be like a Polynesian meeting hall.

THE VENETIAN, *Tel. 702/414-1280 or 877/883-6423.*

While the Venetian doesn't have a wedding chapel in the usual sense of the word, they do have a fabulous wedding package that might interest couples looking to spend $1,450. It includes a Rialto Bridge ceremony (which, according to Italian tradition, will help ensure a happy marriage), champagne, romantic gondola ride with personal serenade and much more. Other packages at lower prices are also available.

DIVORCE, LAS VEGAS STYLE

We're not trying to break up the marriage so soon after the wedding, but the flip side of the easy marriage laws in Nevada are the quickie divorce laws. With only a six week residency period required for divorce (and then six weeks more to get your final papers), a lot of people check into a hotel or extended-stay motel in order to make the qualification. In fact, after the 1931 Nevada law that liberalized wedding and divorce regulations, there was a time when more people came to Nevada to take advantage of the divorce regulations than marriages. It's how the state earned its title of the "divorce capital of the world." While the laws haven't changed and plenty of people still come to Vegas to break up, family supporters will be glad to learn that in recent years the number of divorces performed in Las Vegas is only about one-tenth of the volume of marriages. Ain't love grand?

19. ANNUAL EVENTS

The calendar of annual events keeps getting more and more filled. From the rodeo to poker tournaments to crafts shows, Las Vegas has plenty of things to do all year round. The only problem you'll have is finding the time to fit them in with everything else there is to do!

Here's the month-by-month breakdown on many of the more significant events that are held on an annual basis. Since the schedule for events is often subject to change (and the exact days usually vary), check with the folks holding the event or the **Las Vegas Convention and Visitor's Authority**, *Tel. 702/892-0711*, for exact days and times. Venues for annual events also change in many cases (which is why you won't always see the location in the list below) so, once again, it's wise to contact the LVCVA. They publish a list of events that covers two months at a time which can be found in many hotels. The visitor authority has an office at the Convention Center where you can stop by and find out what's happening. Also be sure to scan local publications and newspapers for other annual events that may be taking place while you're in town.

Although some of the events in this list are unique to Las Vegas because of their gaming nature or tie-in, one of the nicest things about some of them is that they are, by and large, for locals. However, visitors are certainly most welcome and this is one way to learn that people in Las Vegas live just like those in other parts of the country. You can get a true taste of the southern Nevada life-style and find that it, too, is a whole lot more than gambling.

JANUARY

Consumer Electronics Show, *Las Vegas Convention Center*, is a showcase for new and often unusual products that will soon be available on the open market.

FEBRUARY

Autorama Antique Car Show, *Cashman Field*.

Bridal Spectacular Show, *Cashman Field*. See the latest in bridal wear and wedding catering, then go out and tie (or re-tie) the knot at a local wedding chapel!

Great American Train Show, *Cashman Field*. A must for little train lovers.

Ladies Professional Golf Association Tournament, *Desert Inn Golf Club*. Sometimes held in March.

MARCH

Native American Arts Festival, *Clark County Heritage Museum, Henderson*. This is the largest Native American event of the year in southern Nevada.

Crafts Festival, *Cashman Field*.

St. Patrick's Day Parade and Block Party. There's a parade downtown for the major event but dozens of little celebrations dot the town as well.

Hoover Dam Square Dance, *Boulder City*.

Las Vegas 400-NASCAR Winston Cup Series, *Las Vegas Motor Speedway*.

Las Vegas Big League Weekends, *Cashman Field*, helps close out the Exhibition season of Major League Baseball. Usual dates are at the end of March as well as the first few days in April.

SUPER SUNDAY: PARTY TIME EXTRAORDINAIRE

Super Bowl Sunday generates as much excitement in Las Vegas as in the city hosting the big game, maybe even more. It's one of the busiest weekends of the year and thousands of people jam their favorite race and sports book to watch the game on big screen TV. The roars of excitement and the moans of disappointment echo throughout the casino. Even if you aren't particularly interested in the game you should try to catch a glimpse of what is going on. (Since most establishments have an admission charge for Super Bowl events it is easier to get a feel for what goes on in the way of gambling and rooting mania during earlier football playoff games.)

Dozens of hotel/casinos large and small host Super Bowl parties. Sometimes held in the race and sports book area, but more often in larger special event rooms, for a fee ranging from as low as $15 to into three digits, you get to watch the game on giant screens and the hotel throws in food and drinks and even entertainment in many cases. Cheerleaders or the Bud or Miller girls often make appearances at these parties. It's a great deal of fun and some people have even been known to watch the entire game!

APRIL

Art-A-Fair and Festival of Arts, *Canyon Gate Country Club.*

Henderson Heritage Days, *Henderson,* includes a parade down Water Street and food and craft fairs, antique auto show and more at several different venues in and around town.

World Poker Championship Series, *Binion's Horseshoe Hotel* (finishes in May) attracts some of the world's best players who compete for huge prizes. Lots of people like to watch.

Boulder City Spring Jamboree and Craft Show, *Boulder City.* Sometimes held in early May.

MAY

Helldorado Days and Rodeo, *various venues,* celebrates the old west with rodeo, parades, cooking contests, dances and general partying.

Clark County Fair and Rib Burn-off, *Sunset Park.* This isn't the "real" county fair that is held in the small town of Logandale about an hour from Las Vegas, but it still is a lot of fun.

Clark County Artists Show, *Boulder City Bicentennial Park.*

JDF Monopoly Tournament benefits the Juvenile Diabetes Foundation.

Snow Mountain Pow Wow is held by the Las Vegas Paiute Tribe on their reservation north of Las Vegas at the Kyle Canyon Turnoff of US 95.

Senior Classic Golf Tournament, *Tournament Players Club, Summerlin.*

Henderson Art Fest, *Water Street, Henderson.* In the space of a few years this has become one of the biggest exhibitions in southern Nevada. All sorts of interesting and often unusual art objects on sale by their creators. Food and entertainment, kiddy rides.

JUNE

Sand Bash Open Golf Tournament, *Canyon Gate Country Club.*

Green Valley "Concert Under the Stars" is a program of musical concerts ranging from jazz to pop and is held in various parks throughout Henderson during the entire summer.

Las Vegas International Film Festival, while the oldest such event in Las Vegas is now only the second largest of its genre. Still, film buffs will enjoy it.

JULY

Fourth of July Family Pops Concert, *Cashman Field*, featuring the Las Vegas Symphony Orchestra.

Fourth of July Damboree, *Boulder City.*

Battle of the Alamo, *Fiesta and Texas Station Hotels*. All sorts of food and fun-filled events to salute the Independence Day holiday including competition (such as a tug of war) between the staffs of these two adjacent hotels. (Both hotels are now under the same ownership but since this has become such a popular event we believe that it will be continued.)

AUGUST

Hoedown Concert Series, *Las Vegas Jaycee Park,* features bluegrass and country and western music.

CONVENTION CITY

You probably have already noticed that many of these annual events are actually conventions. Las Vegas is the world's foremost convention city. The attractions that appeal to most visitors are only part of the reason that so many conventions are held here. The biggest reason is that there isn't any other place that can match the facilities that Las Vegas possesses for holding the largest conventions. In addition to the behemoth sized Las Vegas Convention Center, there's the giant Sands Convention Center and the Cashman Field Center. And if that's not enough, throw in the majority of the Strip hotels that all have their own extensive convention facilities.

Most conventions don't have much impact on non-convention visitors but one of the important exceptions is the annual computer show called **Comdex** *that is held around the middle of November. The number of visitors to Comdex now stands at around 225,000. It obviously takes a lot of hotel space and convention space to pull off such an event and Las Vegas may be the only city that could do it so well. But that many visitors means that you, as an individual, would have trouble finding a hotel room during Comdex.*

Even if you could get a room you might not want one. Because Comdex dominates the tourism industry during its five day run, it has a negative affect on many traditional aspects of Las Vegas. Perhaps the most obvious example is that most shows are dark during Comdex because the typical Comdex attendee doesn't go for that sort of entertainment. It's been said that Comdex conventioneers arrive in town with one clean shirt on their back and $20 in their pocket and don't change either! While no other convention quite reaches the size of Comdex, there are several at different times of the year that exceed 100,000 participants. Any time that happens you begin to see an impact on show schedules and hotel rates and availability.

SEPTEMBER

Shakespeare in the Park, *Foxridge Park.* Who says Vegas lacks culture? For Bard lovers and those who like old-fashioned entertainment events.

KNR Craftswork Market, *Henderson Convention Center.*

Las Vegas Cup Unlimited Hydroplane Races, *Lake Mead*. See these jet-like boats whiz by on the lake.

Taste Of Las Vegas *Clark County Government Center*, features cooking demonstration by celebrity chefs along with live entertainment by noted bands.

OCTOBER

Jaycees State Fair, *either Cashman Field or the Convention Center*. Sometimes held in late September.

Art in the Park, *Boulder City*.

Fairshow, *North Las Vegas*. Music, food, crafts and a carnival.

Las Vegas International Golf Tournament, *Summerlin, Tournament Players Course and other courses*.

Italian Festival, *The Rio Hotel*. The Rio's large outdoor pool and beach area becomes "Little Italy" for the Columbus Day weekend as people sample delicious Italian food and take part in such esoteric events as a spaghetti eating or grape stomping contests. Absolute fun!

Harvest Festival, *Cashman Field*. This celebration of Fall sometimes is held in early November.

NOVEMBER

Comdex isn't the only special event in town this month by any means. The **CineVegas Film Festival** won't be confused with Cannes but it has become a respected event for both the motion picture industry and enthusiasts of movie-going.

THE MAGICAL FOREST - A WINTER WONDERLAND IN THE DESERT

*From late November through about the first week in January, the grounds of **Opportunity Village** (6300 W. Oakey Blvd.) become a magical land of Christmas fantasy. Imaginative holiday displays highlighted by three million lights are set up on winding pathways covered with faux snow. Even in mild Las Vegas you can feel Santa in the air, as you explore the displays that are donated to help people with learning disabilities. This has become a huge event since its inception in 1992 and, besides the main park-like display area, you can see crafts, dozens of gingerbread houses (also made of many other types of food including cake), and take a ride on a miniature train. Open nightly from 5pm through 11pm. The admission is $5 for adults and $3 for seniors and children. There is also a $2 parking fee although limited on-street parking can be found nearby.*

Antique and Classic Car Sale, *Imperial Palace Hotel.*

Wendy's Three Tour Challenge, *Reflection Bay at Lake Las Vegas, Henderson.* This is one of the nation's big golf tournaments (combining participants from the men's, ladies and senior tours). It attracts a big crowd.

HOTEL IMPLOSIONS – THE NEW VEGAS EXTRAVAGANZA!

*When Las Vegas gets ready to rid itself of an old hotel, they don't call in the wrecking ball – that wouldn't be dramatic enough for this city. They **IMPLODE** and it's become a big attraction in itself. It began years ago with the Dunes Hotel. This was a daytime implosion and it attracted so many people that it scared the city fathers so much that when it came time for the next two implosions, they were done in the middle of the night. That still didn't keep at least some people from witnessing the demise of the Landmark (seen in the zany sci-fi spoof 'Mars Attacks!') and the venerable Sands.*

So when it came time to implode the Hacienda, the moguls decided it was a good idea to have the public after all and they did it on national television on New Year's Eve in 1996. This was the "mother of all implosions" and was deliberately slowed down and enhanced with flames and other pyrotechnic displays to thrill the crowd estimated at 250,000. Then, in April of 1998 the old Aladdin came down at sunset to the cheers of happy spectators. The most recent implosion was the El Rancho, which had been closed for several years. This one went back to hiding in the night, most likely because no one was any longer interested in what had become a Strip eyesore.

While it only takes seconds to reduce a big building to a pile of dust through implosion, the process isn't as fast or simple as it looks. It takes several weeks of meticulous work to strategically place the explosives. While we don't know of any impending implosions, it's only a matter of time before some hotel developer decides that something has to give to make way for another mega-resort. And if you can be here for it, all the better.

DECEMBER

Christmas Parade of Lights, *Boulder City/Lake Mead.* Hundreds of small boats bedecked with Christmas lights set sail from the Lake Mead Marina as people watch the colorful spectacle from the shores of Boulder Beach.

The New York, New York hotel hosts the **Lady Liberty Ice Spectacular**, a free ice skating show with a Christmas theme. It is held right in front of the Statue of Liberty Replica and has attracted large and enthusiastic crowds in its first two years. All indications are that the hotel will make this an annual tradition.

National Finals Rodeo, *Thomas & Mack Center and other venues.* This is one of the largest and most prestigious rodeo events in the country. The whole city seems to take on a western theme (even the Imperial Palace's "Legends in Concert" show goes all-country during the NFR). Lot's of fun with all those cowboys visiting Vegas.

Nevada State Championship Chili Cookoff. A really hot time!

New Year's Eve Celebrations are a big thing in Las Vegas which is, after all, party city. There's a big to-do downtown under the canopy of the Fremont Street Experience but the real party is on the Strip. Hundreds of thousands of visitors and residents promenade up and down Las Vegas Boulevard in a celebration that rivals the one in Times Square in New York. The Strip is closed to vehicular traffic in what has become the world's biggest block party. The funny thing is that there often aren't any scheduled events on the Strip by the city or the hotels. It's mostly a spontaneous event although sometimes they do get together to do something extra special.

INDEX

THINGS CHANGE!

Phone numbers, prices, addresses, quality of food, etc, all change. If you come across any new information, we'd appreciate hearing from you. No item is too small! Drop us an e-mail note at: Jopenroad@aol.com, or write us at:

Las Vegas Guide
*Open Road Publishing, P.O. Box 284
Cold Spring Harbor, NY 11724*

TRAVEL & GAMBLING NOTES

TRAVEL & GAMBLING NOTES

TRAVEL & GAMBLING NOTES

TRAVEL & GAMBLING NOTES

TRAVEL & GAMBLING NOTES